lost gaels

RELATIVES FOR

JUSTICE

Relatives for Justice (RFJ) is an Irish based non-governmental organisation founded in April 1991 by leading human rights advocates who included Monsignor Raymond Murray and Clara Reilly. RFJ provide practical, social, emotional and therapeutic care to the bereaved and injured of the recent conflict in Ireland. RFJ monitor and promote human rights and document abuses, and empower victims of egregious violations to advocate for accountable justice. RFJ's support services are available to anyone bereaved or injured by the conflict, without judgement.

Relatives for Justice USA is a not-for-profit 501c3 promoting and supporting the charitable aims of RFJ.

lost gaels

Remembering the Members of the GAA Killed During the Conflict in Ireland

Peadar Thompson

for the Relatives for Justice GAA Legacy Project

MERRION PRESS

First published in 2024 by
Merrion Press
10 George's Street
Newbridge
Co. Kildare
Ireland
www.merrionpress.ie

978 1 78537 535 4 (Hardback)
978 1 78537 538 5 (eBook)

A CIP catalogue record for this book is available from the British Library.

Typeset in Adobe Garamond Pro & Helvetica Neue

Front cover image © Alain Nogues/Getty

Cover and internal design by riverdesignbooks.com.

Merrion Press is a member of Publishing Ireland.

Ar scáth a chéile a mhaireann na daoine

(People live in the shadow of one another)

Contents

Foreword

Is cúis mhór áthais dom an deis seo a bheith agam fáilte a chur roimh fhoilsiú an leabhair ríthábhachtaigh seo.

Tá éacht déanta ag 'Relatives for Justice' ainmneacha na mball uilig de chuid CLG a fuair bás le linn na dTrioblóidí a bhailiú in aon chnuasach amháin don chéad uair.

Every now and then a project of significance and importance crosses our bow and makes us sit up and take notice. It piques our curiosity, demands our attention and focuses our minds in a way that so much else of what essentially constitutes white noise in modern society does not. This body of work is one such example.

To reach for that oft-used colloquialism, 'The Troubles' touched the lives of all of those of us who lived through that period, even those who perhaps to this day don't realise it. It permeated news cycles, it impacted on relationships and emigration patterns, but more than anything, it robbed us of lives – cherished and valuable lives – of people who would have gone on to make incalculable differences to their family and community circles.

Like so much of what passes for life on this island and indeed amongst those Irish people who make lives for themselves abroad, it was, more often than not, localised. It was bitter, deeply divisive and its protracted nature meant it made a deep impression on the psyche of this country and how we were perceived elsewhere – justifiably or otherwise.

That it lasted from 1969 to 1994 – with an awful loss of life, both before and long after, is almost impossible for young people of today to process.

Of course, where you lived on the island had a major bearing on your first-hand experience and how it impacted directly on everyday life before we even consider the idea of those bereaved.

Given the privileged and undoubtedly central role that Cumann Lúthchleas Gael plays in Irish life as part of the social fabric of the island, the conflict was always going to impact on our activities and more crucially our members. Whether it was the annexation of Casement Park, Belfast, or St Oliver Plunkett Park, Crossmaglen, the delay or cancellation of fixtures and competitions, or the dread, fear and stigma of donning county or club colours or attending games in a heightened atmosphere, there were choices to be made around the playing of our games and involvement in our activities.

There was also a price to be paid on numerous occasions. The ultimate price.

More than any other single factor, it is this loss of life that resonates most from this period.

It is imperative to state that the GAA – or any other entity – does not have a monopoly or a claim of hierarchy in the sense of loss suffered by the families of those killed. However, that should not take from the importance of a project such as this, which, for the first time, captures between two covers the number of GAA members lost.

The project has been painstakingly researched and, crucially, the individual entries feature contributions from family members, those best placed to give context and background on the loved ones lost. The inclusion of our beautiful, ornate club crests alongside the entries further personalises the work and reminds us again of the concentration of the victims among our Ulster GAA members and the loss experienced by our clubs and counties in that province.

In the opening pages of *Lost Gaels* the old Irish seanfhocal or proverb 'Ar scáth a chéile a mhaireann na daoine' is included. Nothing could be more appropriate.

The Troubles represent a dark and challenging period for us to process – citizens and historians alike – and their proximity in relative terms means they continue to loom large for many. They continue to cast a long shadow across our imperfect peace and few things symbolise this better than the debate around the controversial Legacy Bill.

The least that bereaved families deserve is truth and justice.

They also deserve to be remembered.

I laud everyone involved in this project, and acknowledge the work and commitment required to bring it to fruition. The personal stories and anecdotes suggest to me that the families who contributed were proud to do so, and I certainly hope that is the case.

This offering preserves memories for those families and other club members, and serves as a useful reminder to younger members of times they were lucky to avoid.

I wish everyone connected with the publication every best wish and sincerely hope it is received the way it deserves to be.

Le gach dea-ghuí,

Iarlaith Ó Broin
Uachtarán
Cumann Lúthchleas Gael

Introduction

A Léitheoir,

Projects like this never emerge in a vacuum. Having supported and worked with families whose loved ones died as a result of the conflict, who happened to be Gaels, an exploration into the links between the Gaelic Athletic Association (GAA) and the conflict became a natural extension of the work we do around memory recording, memorialisation, truth and legacy justice.

The foremost question with this exploration was to ask how many members of the GAA died during the conflict. We were surprised that nobody had actually sat down and figured out that number, as there were other such statistics on religion, members of other organisations involved in the conflict, civilians, gender and children. The GAA remained the largest civic organisation on the island unaware of the total number of members it had lost to the conflict. This fact remained all the more surprising given the intensity of the experiences during the conflict of both the organisation itself and its membership more generally. For us, that's where it all began.

As an intern, Eoin Connolly did initial desktop research, and he was later joined by Peadar Thompson. Both lads are proud and passionate Gaels with Naomh Eoin CLG, Béal Feirste, and they brought that same passion, enthusiasm and energy to this project.

While we recognise that many members were injured in attacks and incarcerated, our research focused only on the deaths of Gaels due to the conflict.

One of the first names recorded was that of Aidan McAnespie. Aidan was killed by a British soldier after exiting the permanent border checkpoint between Monaghan and Tyrone at Aughnacloy. He was killed as he was making his way to the football field.

Aidan's case became known nationally and internationally. Much of this is due to the legacy of his late sister Eilish McAnespie McCabe, who was a founding member of Relatives for Justice (RFJ) and a tenacious advocate for justice. Many of her core values of equality, respect, tolerance, dignity, humanity

The British Army base looms over the local GAA pitch, St Oliver Plunkett Park, as members of the Crossmaglen Rangers train in May 1998. (© David Maher/Sportsfile)

and hope remain at the heart of RFJ's work today. Indeed, they reflect the values of most Gaels.

For those unfamiliar with the GAA, it was founded on 1 November 1884, in Thurles, County Tipperary. Its formation was part of the Gaelic revival aimed at preserving indigenous games, culture, language and pastimes. Set against the backdrop of colonial occupation and an attempt to suppress Irish culture, this national initiative was pivotal and visionary.

Today, the GAA is the largest sporting organisation in Ireland. Globally, it is celebrated as one of the great amateur sporting associations, with responsibility for promoting Gaelic games and Irish culture. Organised professionally on a par with most other sports, the GAA relies almost exclusively on volunteers. Its success is its ability to organise at grassroots level in every parish throughout Ireland.

The GAA is its people, and the people are the GAA. It is oftentimes described as a family, such are the bonds and friendships forged. If anything, that is in part the essence of this book: time and time again, in the darkest of times, the GAA grassroots family gathered, embraced and was there for its nearest and dearest. Therefore, it is fitting that we remember those Gaels who died due to the conflict.

Like any sport, the GAA is fiercely competitive but there is so much more to the GAA, not least in terms of its intrinsic historical and cultural value to Irish society and life in Ireland and abroad. It is uniquely Irish and an expression of Irishness in its most positive form. Wherever you find Irish people around the world you'll find a GAA club and God knows the Irish are everywhere on this planet. It is a way of life that we are all vested in and extremely proud of. It is about connection, identity, and belonging.

In the North of Ireland, during the conflict, members of the GAA were deliberately targeted by loyalist paramilitaries, with State collusion oftentimes a feature; other members were killed simply because they were Catholic. The British Army and the RUC directly targeted the GAA, and for many members harassment was a constant feature of life. This project also reveals that armed republicans not only formed a sizeable number of those members of the GAA who died due to the conflict, but were also responsible for actions that took the lives of GAA members.

During the depths of conflict, the GAA became the only place where many Northern Gaels could openly express their Irishness and identity without fear and discrimination. It is only through this prism that you begin to appreciate the added value the association had in the lives of northern Gaels.

Our focus in this book is, therefore, not on who the perpetrators were or the circumstances in which Gaels died. What matters for us is the unifying love – an grá – for the GAA that each person included in this book shared. We wanted to celebrate the role of the GAA in their lives, and the achievements and contributions those deceased Gaels made to their clubs and counties. We wanted to examine their lives through the lens of the GAA, reaching beyond just how and why they died, as told by their nearest and dearest. Hopefully, this book brings a broader dimension of their lives to what is typically known. It was crucial to us that all are remembered equally.

The RFJ GAA Legacy Project enabled the recovery and recording of historical memories. For many it broke a long silence. It allows us to bear witness. We hope it is a fitting testimony to all those Gaels who died during the darkest days of conflict.

We want to thank everyone who assisted in making this book possible.

To those who took part, we are privileged to have been invited into your lives and that you trusted us to help you tell part of this important story of your loved ones, in your own words. We are indebted and grateful to each and every one of you for sharing cherished memories where you laughed and cried tears of pain and joy.

Go raibh míle maith agaibh.

Is mise le meas,

Mark Thompson

Mark Thompson
Príomhoifigeach Feidhmiúcháin
Relatives for Justice

The Gaelic Athletic Association

Mike Cronin, Boston College

The Gaelic Athletic Association (GAA) was founded on 1 November 1884 when seven men met in the billiard room of Hayes' Commercial Hotel in Thurles, County Tipperary. In the context of the period from the 1870s through to the 1890s the creation of an organised sporting body was not unusual. The Irish Rugby Football Union had been founded in 1879, while the Irish Football Association followed a year later in 1880. The Irish Golfing Union was formed in 1891 and the Irish Hockey Union came into being in 1893. The second half of the nineteenth century was the era when modern, codified sport became a central feature of society. The GAA was established to promote and administer its games, namely Gaelic football and hurling and, until the 1920s, track and field athletics.

The GAA was not, however, a straightforward sporting body. The two driving forces in establishing the association were Michael Cusack and Maurice Davin, both accomplished sportsmen. They tied the creation of the GAA to two ideas that were otherwise absent from the dominant sporting forms of the day. First, they argued that the GAA should cater for men 'born into no other inheritance other than an everlasting round of labour'. This was important, as many of the sports that had arrived in Ireland from Britain were dominated by the upper and middle classes. The GAA would serve the working and labouring men of rural Ireland, and those outside of the metropolitan centre. Second, the GAA would resist the spread of foreign games (those British sports of soccer, rugby, hockey and cricket). This rejection of foreign games tied the GAA to the spirit of the Irish cultural revival and would mean that the association would become one of the most important expressions of Irish cultural and national identity on the island of Ireland.

A key factor in the appeal of the GAA was its organisational structure. Rather than forming teams around towns, schools or workplaces, which had been the model in soccer and rugby, the GAA organised itself around the parish and the county. This has always meant that the GAA embraced the local landscape and geography understood by all, which speaks to and embodies a sense of belonging. It has proved an enduring model and, into the twenty-first century, the GAA still rightfully contends that 'the GAA Club is the bedrock of every Irish community and provides an organised structure from which great community spirit is generated'. Wedded to the GAA's commitment to the amateurism of its games, the association has, since its foundation, overseen the emergence of a sense that it builds on local community due to the volunteer ethos that lies behind every club across the island. There are currently over 2,200 GAA clubs in Ireland, with upwards of 700,000 members. It has been estimated that 42 per cent of all community volunteering in Ireland takes place within the GAA and that this has a value to the economy of €500 million. Whether as players, members, groundkeepers, coaches, jersey washers, caterers or participants in the association's music and culture programmes, the members of the GAA (and its female equivalents in the Camogie Association and Ladies Gaelic Football Association) define what it is to be a Gael.

In the years that followed Irish independence, the GAA went from strength to strength across the island. Not only was it a way for individuals and communities to identify themselves as Irish, but the appeal of its annual competitions at county and club level grew significantly. Helped by ever-increasing levels of media coverage, following the All-Ireland competitions in football and hurling became a staple of the Irish summer. In 1961 the record was set for the biggest ever crowd in Croke Park, with 90,556 attending the football final between Down and Offaly. The following year the finals in football and hurling were shown live on television for the first time, which led to increased levels of interest in the games. Although Cavan had become the first Ulster county to win a football All-Ireland title in 1933, it was Down, in 1960, that became the first team from Northern Ireland to triumph, by beating Kerry 2–10 to 0–8. The Down victory was an historic moment. Peter Mackem wrote in 2020 that 'the crossing of the Border with the Sam Maguire cup represented a genuine passing over, a coming of age, the entry of a new age of heroes … There had been no homecoming like it in the history of the GAA in terms of crowds and excitement.'[1]

A British Army helicopter flies over Healy Park in Omagh during a Division 1a game between Tyrone and Cork. (© Ray McManus/Sportsfile)

There have been other victories for Ulster and Northern counties since 1960, but between 1968 and 1998 the GAA in the North had to play its games against the backdrop of conflict. Remarkably, given the highly localised and sectarian nature of the conflict and the strict security controls that were in place for three decades, the GAA in Ulster completed its fixture lists during every year of the Troubles. Yet, the association, its members and facilities did become targets of attack. The GAA was labelled by its detractors, in the context of a sectarian conflict, as a dominantly nationalist and Catholic organisation, which resulted in regular arson attacks on its properties, the occupation of its grounds and attacks on its membership, which resulted in injury and death.

Into the twenty-first century, the GAA has gone from strength to strength. In a world of global capital and a sporting landscape that is dominated by professionalism, it has remained true to its founding principles. It thrives at the local and community level, supporting its members through the travails of life while also, through sport, giving them a sense of camaraderie and identity. In its major club and county competitions the GAA draws thousands into stadia around the country to cheer on 'their' team. It is an organisation that operates in a similar manner to a professional sporting franchise, securing the best sponsorship and media deals, and maximising its gate receipts, so that in 2022 it generated €96 million in revenue. But with no players to pay, the GAA redistributes most of this revenue to clubs across the island to pay for pitches, floodlights, clubhouses and much more, so that the association's facilities are second to none.

The GAA's greatest strength since its foundation has been its ability to adapt to circumstances and remain relevant. It still provides a calendar of the most popular sporting events each year in Ireland and, from the local parish through to All-Ireland final day in Croke Park, offers one of the most organic and commonly shared experiences of what it means to be Irish. As Patrick Kavanagh wrote, 'no man can adequately describe Irish life who ignores the Gaelic Athletic Association'.[2] And while Kavanagh was entirely correct, his view was finessed by John McGahern, who offered the view that 'the local and the individual were more powerful than any national identity'.[3] It is the GAA that speaks to and embodies that local and individual identity, and while the association offers one representation of Ireland, its real strength still lies in the ways in which people and communities belong to, identify with and support 'their' club and county.

Endnotes

1 www.irishtimes.com/sport/gaelic-games/gaelic-football/when-down-s-1960-all-ireland-victory-brought-down-barriers-1.4367907.

2 Patrick Kavanagh, 'Gut Yer Man'.

3 John McGahern, *Memoir* (Faber and Faber, 2005).

author's reflections and notes

Peadar Thompson

The reflections below are some of my own observations on the content of this book and things that you, as the reader, might like to bear in mind as you make your way through *Lost Gaels*. For more in-depth information on the criteria for the project and how it was carried out, see the methodology at the end of the book.

A Unique Exploration of the Past

What is most significant to me, and most obvious, is that this Relatives for Justice GAA legacy project is unique in two ways. Firstly, this book goes some way to filling the gap that exists in works exploring the GAA and the conflict in the North of Ireland, chiefly by recording how many members of the association were lost to the conflict. Whilst there have been many pieces of work exploring the topic, there has been no published work seeking to record the total number of members of the GAA killed in the conflict until now.

Secondly, and of far greater importance as far as I am concerned, is what this project has been able to provide to the families involved. The book is the focal point of a broader project seeking to record the impact of the conflict on the GAA. The chief purpose was to give bereaved families and friends of lost Gaels a space where they could celebrate the lives and stories of their lost loved ones in a way that has not happened before. When meeting with the families, an almost unanimous feeling has come to light that the lasting legacies and memories of their loved ones have been wholly defined by the causes of their deaths. There could be an entirely different book written on the reasons for this, but chief among those reasons are a shameful legacy of failing to deal with the past and also a tendency in the media to focus on the sensational when examining the conflict, often forgetting that the horrific, shocking and audience-grabbing incidents leave an everlasting legacy of bereavement in their wake that requires care, thought and empathy.

In my experience, bereaved victims of the conflict have been conditioned, to an extent, to accept that the only story they have worth telling, or certainly the only one that they have felt anyone wants to listen to, is the story of their trauma. While these experiences are vitally important and must be captured, there also needs to be dedicated space for celebrating the lives lived before traumatic events took place. For most families involved in this project, this is the first time they have been able to share the everyday stories of their loved ones, the memories of growing up, of family and of sporting life. There were many occasions over the course of the interviewing process where the questions asked sparked new conversations amongst family members and where forgotten stories were rediscovered, and I hope that this process of recalling fond and dear memories of loved ones has been a somewhat cathartic experience for those involved. As Gaels, the love and passion we have for the GAA goes a long way in making up our own individual identities, and that love most often defines a lot of the ways we decide to live our lives. This book aims to bring those memories to the fore and thereby transform and broaden the lasting memory of those recorded in this book, so that he or she is no longer, solely, defined as 'victim', but as 'person' and Gael.

The Story of the GAA Reflects the Story of the Irish People

Another observation I would like to make is that, as obvious as it may seem from the outset, the GAA is a Goliath in Irish life and I agree with Patrick Kavanagh's assessment that in any depiction of Irish life it is an organisation that can't be ignored. I can think of no other institution that has a similar reach into the everyday lives of so many people. This is no more clearly demonstrated than in the entries to this book, which reflect the powerful reach the GAA has into the many different lives of Irish people, and while it can also be broadly reflective of the power of sport in bringing people together, the entries to this book show that it is the specific, community-driven characteristics of the GAA that give the association such unrivalled status in Irish society.

At an individual level, those characteristics are reflected through the accounts of local clubs rallying around the bereaved family; in the small, local tournaments and cups competed for across the country in memory of lost Gaels; and in the names of clubs affected by the conflict. At a broader level, the entries to the book reflect the shared values of passion, service and commitment to club and county espoused by Gaels across the country. These shared, ubiquitous characteristics evident in the entries will allow unaffected Gaels to immediately see themselves and their clubs in these accounts, creating a unique connection between the reader and the person and family they are reading about.

This sense of the parochial in the Irish experience also leads me to an attached, but brief, observation from my interviews – that the Catholic Church was vital in fostering and developing Gaelic games during the conflict. The role of the clergy has always been widely recognised as being crucial in the development of the GAA across Ireland from the very foundation of the association, and in a large number of the entries you will read in this book you will learn that it was the local priest who gave people their first taste of Gaelic games. Whilst the Catholic Church justly receives its share of criticism for some of the horrendous roles it has played in Irish society over the last century, during that same period there were also incredible persons of faith doing extraordinary work. Those working for the Church, in parishes across the North, were clearly dedicated to the preservation and promotion of our indigenous games, in spite of the very real threat that work presented to them.

Suffering on a Large Scale

There can be no doubt that the GAA and its membership suffered harm on a very large scale during the conflict. I make this observation as a means of giving, albeit limited, recognition to the many accounts of harm that I have heard during the interviewing process, accounts that I have not been able to record in this book and that are undeniably deserving of an entire book in and of themselves. If you are a Gael who lived in the North during the conflict, you will undoubtedly relate to the following.

In each interview I conducted, without exception, I was told anecdotes and accounts of the intimidation, harassment and violence endured over decades by people seeking to play and take part in the GAA in the North of Ireland. Whilst the entries to this book reflect these experiences, I want to draw specific

The Crossmaglen Rangers stand for the national anthem before the 2005 Armagh County Senior Football final played against Dromintee, with the omnipresent British Army base in the background. (© David Maher/Sportsfile)

attention to this subject and give some analysis to it. In conflict-related violence discourse, recent attention has been drawn to the different types of harm suffered by those who lived through conflict, and whether our definitions of what experiences constitute harm are appropriate.[1] In other words, are there events and behaviours experienced during the conflict which, upon reflection, we would now regard as incidents of harm? Experiences which, at the time, we might have known deep down were wrong, but which nonetheless went unchecked and unacknowledged.

During the interviewing process for this book, the anecdotes of experiences such as being stopped and searched because a person was carrying a hurl or wearing a GAA jersey, having team buses stopped and kitbags emptied onto roadsides, experiences of routine harassment and intimidation of Gaels, would invariably be followed by a downplaying of the impact of that harassment because 'it wasn't as bad everything else that was going on' or 'that's just the way it was'.

At the heart of the issue here is an idea that harm can become normalised and downplayed during conflict, and this often occurs when the harm forms part of a person's 'every day'.[2] These experiences are, however, harms, and that they form part of a person's habitual experience is immaterial to that fact. Moreover, none of these experiences need to be sensationalised in order to constitute a harm. What is now most apparent to me, having interviewed members of the GAA across the island, is that Gaels living through the conflict in the North came to live with the expectation of being treated differently, and often violently, because they chose to enjoy the sport they loved. The danger of not recognising and challenging this fact, and the associated everyday harms, is that we risk the perpetuation of past, wrongful behaviour towards Gaels, and the attitudes which facilitated it, into the future. It is a concern of the author that some of those same attitudes towards the GAA persist within some elements of society today and, whilst no longer mainstream, those attitudes can have deleterious effects on the association. From motivating decisions regarding the allocation of public resources right through to the recent intimidation of clubs by extremists, those actions share the same dangerous attitudes towards Gaels. They are wrong, they lead to harm and they must not be normalised or tolerated in an equal society.

Notes

The aim of my final word to you as the reader is to provide you with some thoughts to have in mind while you make your way through this book.

Firstly, you should be mindful that each entry reflects the memories, thoughts and words of the family, and sometimes friends, of someone killed as a result of the conflict in the North. The courage it took for each and every person to embark on this project cannot be overstated. It is never easy to talk about someone you love who is no longer with us, and harder again when that loved one was taken under violent circumstances. Be both cognisant of this courage and aware of the remarkable privilege it is to have access to the memories, stories and reflections of families and friends who still grieve the loss of their loved ones.

Secondly, this book reflects the breadth of experiences of the conflict, and indeed some of the Gaels you will read about were actively involved in the conflict, including as members of the IRA. I would encourage you to leave any assumptions you have about the conflict in the North of Ireland to one side before reading this book. You will read human stories in the context of political violence and these accounts are best read with a non-judgemental and empathetic eye. Some accounts might well challenge your own views or experiences of the conflict, but that, I believe, is a strength of this work.

Thirdly, please be aware that each family has had continued and absolute say over every aspect of their loved one's entry, and so each entry, although styled and shaped into uniformity by the author, will be entirely individual and may vary in its subject matter, reflections and scope. This is also reflected in the range in size of each entry, which is also indicative of how much information is still available today. The substantive content of an individual entry is exactly that – individual. Each story is told how the family wanted it to be told, and I have endeavoured to afford each family that space.

Finally, as you will be aware, each of the entries included in this book has the same ending. But I want you to look beyond that and allow the stories and memories of each person on and off the pitch to be the key takeaway. To add to the stories, where possible, a picture and a club crest have been inserted; where a club crest could not be found, a county crest was used instead. I hope that the wonderful memories shared in this book spark conversations and discussions about just how incredible the GAA can be. By doing that, and by speaking their names and telling their stories, we keep the memories of each lost Gael alive and ensure that they are no longer solely defined by the circumstances of their death, but by who they were as people and as Gaels.

Endnotes

1 See Aisling Swaine, *Conflict-Related Violence Against Women* (Cambridge University Press, 2017).

2 M. Hume, 'The Myths of Violence: Gender, Conflict, and Community in El Salvador', *Latin American Perspectives*, vol. 35, no. 5 (2008), pp. 59–76, https://doi.org/10.1177/0094582X08321957.

1970

Patrick Elliman (Pádraig Elliman)

AOIS/AGE: 62

CUMANN/CLUB: Uí Chonaill CLG, Béal Feirste/ O'Connell's GAA Club, Belfast

CONTAE/COUNTY: Aontroim/Antrim

MARAÍODH/DIED: 11 Iúil, Arm na Breataine/ 11 July, British Army

'My father was the only one in the family who played.' Patrick's son, also Patrick but known as Paddy, and Paddy's nephew Pól, describe what memories remain of Patrick's involvement in the GAA. 'All I ever got as a kid were hurls and balls as presents, but I had no interest in playing. I suppose he lived in hope! I think after all the years, the only time the hurls were ever used was when a riot kicked off and you needed something to hit the Saracen lorries with!'

Patrick Elliman was born in 1908 to parents William and Bridget. As the years have rolled on, details of his early life have faded, but we know that he grew up in the Lower Falls area of West Belfast, and Paddy believes that his father attended St Peter's Primary School on Slate Street, where he received all his formal education before searching for work. Upon leaving school aged fifteen, Patrick worked several different jobs, including mending shoes and working in a wine store, before he landed a long career working on the railways and loading wagons off the boats. We are unsure on the timeline, but Patrick eventually met and married Mary 'Marie' Langan, and the couple had four children: Leo, Gerry, Marie and Paddy. 'We lived with my mother's father. Granda Langan lived downstairs and we lived upstairs. That's the way it was back then. I remember my granda well. He was a big, tall, grey-haired man.'

When the time came, Patrick managed to get Paddy a job alongside him on the railways, and they would have often worked together over the years. Paddy's three siblings all emigrated to New Zealand when they reached adulthood, and their mother would eventually join them in the late 1960s to care for one of the siblings who had taken ill. When Marie moved, Patrick and Paddy moved in with Patrick's sister, Kathleen, at 12 Marchioness Street, also in the Lower

Falls area. By this time, Patrick's health was becoming very poor, so he would have been glad to have the care of his sister.

Patrick played hurling for the now-defunct O'Connell's GAA Club on the Falls Road. Paddy believes that because none of the rest of his family played, Patrick must have been introduced to the GAA at St Peter's school. By all accounts, it can safely be presumed that Patrick was an excellent goalkeeper, given his selection to play Senior intercounty hurling for Antrim for nine consecutive years. This would have been in the 1920s and 1930s, and Paddy remembers his father returning from matches across Ireland, so we can fairly assume that Patrick would have played his part on some of the Antrim panels who took home sixteen Ulster hurling titles over this twenty-year period. It is also certain that Patrick played a pivotal role on some of the O'Connell's panels who took home five All-County Hurling Championships over that same period. It is clear from Paddy's account that his father was bitten by the hurling bug. In the absence of any previous familial affinity with the sport, Patrick had developed a passion and love for the game, which he carried with him throughout his life, often to the annoyance of his children, who had to suffer his badgering in the hope that they might someday play too.

Patrick Elliman was shot in the head by the British Army on 3 July 1970 during the Falls Road Curfew, a period in which the British Army barricaded and imposed a curfew on the Lower Falls area where Patrick was living. 'I took my father up home at the start of the rioting and curfew, but at that time he wasn't feeling great so he must have come into the street again. He and his brother James walked to the bottom of the street, maybe for some air, and saw a rifle at the corner. My father was dressed in his slippers and a short-sleeve shirt. They shot him in the head and, remarkably, he wasn't killed instantly. The soldiers followed the trail of blood up to the house and went in after my father. They spent all night in the house, sitting on the couches and ate every bit of food we had, while my father tried to get to hospital.' Patrick died on 11 July.

A guard of honour was formed at Patrick's funeral by his GAA teammates. It was testament to the calibre of person and player he was.

1971

Seamus Simpson (Seamus Mac Shim)

AOIS/AGE: 21

CUMANN/CLUB: Coimheideach CLG, Béal Feirste/ Commedagh GAC, Belfast

CONTAE/COUNTY: Aontroim/Antrim

MARAÍODH/KILLED: 11 Lúnasa, Arm na Breataine/ 11 August, British Army

'Seamus was like any other kid, always wanting to get involved in whatever the rest of the kids on the street were doing; kick-the-tin, hide-and-go-seek, rap-the-doors.' Seamus's brother, Seannie, describes his memories of Seamus growing up. 'Our father made sure that all aspects of our lives were enriched with Irish culture, and that extended into making sure Seamus had a hurl in his hand and was out in the field when our district team was up and running.'

Seamus Simpson was born on 24 July 1950. One of eight children, he grew up in Andersonstown, West Belfast. It was a new housing development, rapidly expanding during the 1950s and 1960s to cope with the massive demand for housing caused by redevelopment of the Lower Falls area. The lack of planning meant that no schools had been established in the area and so Seamus attended school in the neighbouring Casement Park, home of Antrim GAA, which was directly across the road from the new estate.

Seamus's involvement in the GAA was with an especially talented group of players. 'Clubs in those days didn't really have Juvenile structures. So, what happened, particularly around Belfast, was that GAA teams organised, and games were played, between districts and streets. Seamus played for Commedagh Drive's first ever team.' Commedagh, named after the street that was largest with a green space in the area, was started in 1964. Seamus would play against other street and district teams, against some of his closest schoolfriends. Despite being a newly formed team, the stewardship of Antrim GAA legend Andy McCallin (senior) ensured that, in November of that year, Commedagh were eventually presented with the Volunteer Cup, becoming underage All-County Champions. Some of Seamus's teammates would go on to represent Antrim and Ulster, with one becoming Antrim's first and only dual Senior All-Star.

Seamus also loved soccer and loved going across to Scotland to watch Glasgow Celtic. Indeed, he was a Celtic fanatic, wearing his Celtic cravat everywhere.

As he grew out of the youth summer leagues and his teammates were snatched up by the established GAA clubs around Belfast, Seamus focused on other aspects of his life. After his schooling, he trained to become an engineer, working in Mackies' Engineering Works. Despite his constant reports of sectarian harassment for being Catholic in the predominantly unionist factory, Seannie recalls Seamus's spirit never being dampened. 'On Friday, coming home from work, he nearly always produced a bunch of flowers for Mum. We all got such a laugh, however, when it turned out that he wasn't buying them in a flower shop but was picking them from someone's garden.'

Seamus married Rosemary McCoey in early 1971, the same year he was killed. They had moved into their new home after their wedding, but 'they didn't even get a chance to settle into their life together'. Seamus was shot by the British Army during civil unrest in Andersonstown on Wednesday, 11 August 1971, after the introduction of internment without trial. Seamus was a Volunteer in the Provisional IRA.

Dorothy Maguire (Doireann Ní Uidhir)

AOIS/AGE: 19

CUMANN/CLUB: Cumann Camógaíocht Seán Uí Treasaigh, Béal Feirste/Seán Treacy's Camogie Club, Belfast

CONTAE/COUNTY: Aontroim/Antrim

MARAÍODH/KILLED: 23 Deireadh Fómhair, Arm na Breataine/23 October, British Army

'Dorothy was the sort of person who loved to be involved in everything.' Marie, Dorothy's friend, begins describing the young woman she grew up with. 'She was a very outgoing and

positive character and took up all that life had to offer her with enthusiasm and a great gusto!'

Dorothy Maguire was born in 1952 to Bridgit and Ned. She was the youngest of seven children and grew up in the Whiterock area of West Belfast, County Antrim, with older brothers Tommy, Ned, Michael and Martin, and older sisters Madge and Maura. Dorothy attended her local primary school, St Kevin's, before going on to St Rose's Secondary School. Upon leaving school at fifteen, she then went on to work in a shirt factory as a machinist and a stitcher.

'I met Dorothy when I was nine or so, and she was eleven. My sister and her brother Michael were married, so we shared babysitting duties and got really close. We were just normal girls at that age, going to the Falls Park and running about with other teenagers. We used to enjoy going to the chippy, putting the jukebox on and sitting in the corner with a milkshake. Dorothy also loved her fashion and always looked amazing when we would go to dances and such.' As Marie continues, she describes a young woman with a passion for life and someone whose company was always greatly appreciated. 'Dorothy was always coming out with something to make you laugh and that made her great fun to be around. Half the time she didn't even mean to be funny, which made her all that bit more endearing. She also had a great community spirit and would always be there to help out her neighbours. I remember one time she was asked to help out with the local kids in the area, so she organised a camping trip away for them. She had it all sorted and they all arrived and pitched up, but she forgot that there was a cow sharing the field they were in, and it ended up the cow chased the lot of them off! But she had a great heart.'

In terms of the GAA, Dorothy was a talented camog for the Seán Treacy's Camogie Club in West Belfast. She was first introduced to camogie by a family cousin, Mary, and began playing in her teenage years. 'You're talking over fifty years ago, but I have a great memory of her playing in MacRory Park up at the O'Donnell's club. I remember, vividly, Dorothy taking the whole length of the pitch, running with the ball and scoring a cracking goal. It wasn't her first goal and certainly wasn't her last, but it was very memorable! She was a fantastic player. Her mummy had a cabinet filled with all sorts of medals and trophies belonging to Dorothy, as well as all sorts belonging to her brothers, who were all talented boxers.'

Marie describes how camogie provided an escape for the young women on their team and how, as a team, they bonded through their shared love of Gaelic sport and competitiveness, and always found a means to play even when the conflict was beginning to break out. 'We trained once a week in the Falls Park, and there were plenty of women playing camogie in Antrim, even back then. We had a game every week, and the county set-up was very competitive. Of course, as the conflict started, that lessened and lessened, but we persevered and always had the numbers for a game. There was also a lot of poverty in those days to contend with, and I remember when we got out gym frocks for the camogie team, we would all go to this wee shop and buy a red braid to sew it all around the frocks to make the two stripes for the Treacy's colours! You always made do and Dorothy was very much a brilliant woman for bringing out the fun in those moments.'

Dorothy Maguire was nineteen years old when she was killed on 23 October 1971 by the British Army. She was killed alongside her sister, Maura, as they were driving along the Falls Road. Dorothy and Maura were part of the Women's Action Committee, and on the morning they were killed they were driving around their local area warning residents that the British Army had entered the district. As they were doing this they passed a British Army convoy, which opened fire on their car. The army claimed they were fired upon by those inside the car, but all the evidence collected from the scene is indicative of that narrative being wrong. With the windows being shattered from the outside, all that was found in the car, apart from the discharged rubber bullets and live ammunition of the convoy, was a whistle and a bullhorn. Dorothy and Maura were both members of Cumann na mBan, but were not on active service when they were killed.

'Dorothy was supposed to stay with me that night, but she wanted to stay with her sister Maura, so me and a friend, Geraldine, left them late that night. A few hours later we received the news that they had been killed. We all knew that these women were completely innocent.'

Martin McShane (Mairtín Mac Seain)

AOIS/AGE: 16

CUMANN/CLUB: CLG Fianna Oileán an Ghuail/ Coalisland Fianna GFC

CONTAE/COUNTY: Tír Eoghain/Tyrone

MARAÍODH/KILLED: 14 Nollaig, Arm na Breataine/ 14 December, British Army

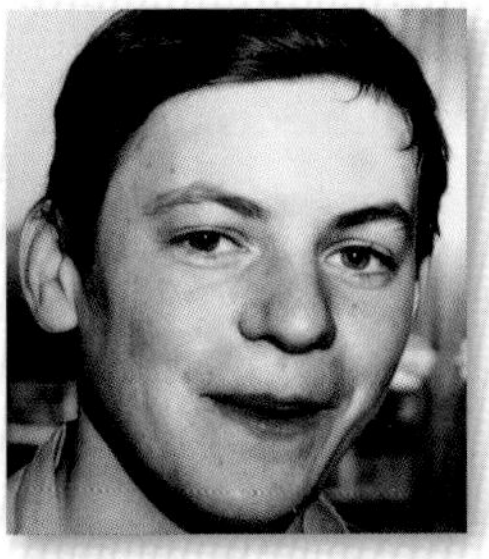

'My memories of Martin were that he was full of life; he was very active and had a great devilment about him.' Martin McShane's childhood friend, Paddy, thinks back to his youth in Coalisland. 'I suppose it's over fifty years ago now, but I remember a young lad who just loved his football and had the talent and commitment to go all the way.'

Martin McShane was born on 13 October 1955 to Seamus and Josephine. He grew up in Coalisland, County Tyrone, not a stone's throw away from the football field of what would soon become his beloved Fianna club. Martin went to the local primary school, which was where he was first introduced to the GAA by a committed teacher. 'We played in primary school, which was a bit unique at that time. Martin wasn't a big lad from memory, even though he was a bit older than me, but he was very physically strong for his age. He was fearless, even as a young lad, and the bigger the player on the opposition, the harder Martin went at him.'

Having received an early foundation in primary school, and flourishing alongside his friends and the local lads, Martin then joined Coalisland Fianna just before his teenage years. 'We wouldn't have been a championship-winning side at that age, but we loved it. Martin was unquestionably a great footballer and possessed a tremendous amount of skill for his age. I have no doubt that he would have gone on to play Senior football for the club and my lasting memory, as I progressed through the age groups, was that our club was deprived of what would have been a very important footballer. We had success in later years and Martin would have played an integral part in that had the tragedy not happened.'

Martin was the eldest child of his family. As with countless others, the specifics of memories more than fifty years old are difficult to recall due to the passing of time and all of what that passage brings with it. Martin's sister, Christina, however, speaks beautifully of her lasting memories of her older brother. 'Martin was our eldest brother and we all looked up to him. He loved and looked out for all of us; his younger brothers and me, his sister. He was loved and full of life.' In that legacy, Martin's character is encapsulated as that role model all older siblings hope to be.

Martin McShane was sixteen years old when he was shot dead on 14 December 1971 by the Royal Marines as he crossed the playing field of Coalisland Fianna. He was at the local youth club in the clubhouse, and the pitch separated his small estate from the GAA club. Of the thirty shots fired at him, Martin was struck seven times in the back.

John Bateson (Eoin Mac an Bháird)

AOIS/AGE: 19

CUMANN/CLUB: Naomh Trea CLG, Baile Mhic Uiginn/
St Trea's GAC, Ballymaguigan

CONTAE/COUNTY: Doire/Derry

MARAÍODH/KILLED: 18 Nollaig, le pléasc anabaí/
18 December, premature explosion

'The GAA was always in our house.' Jimmy and Peter Bateson begin to describe the role of the GAA in their family. 'Our da played football in his younger years for Ballymaguigan, and had a few run-outs with the Derry Senior panel, and all of us boys played too, including Johnny. Football was always in the background of our lives, no matter what else was happening, and whether you were still playing or not.'

John 'Johnny' Bateson was born on 1 October 1951 to Patrick, or 'Paddy' as everyone knew him, and Mary. He was the fourth child of ten, growing up initially in the townland of Cargin, County Antrim, with older brothers Patsy, Jimmy and Eddie, and younger siblings Finbar, Peter, Anne, Dolores, Mary and Claire. Given that he spent his early years in Cargin, Johnny's first involvement with the GAA was at Erin's Own CLG, Cargin, where he played Juvenile football as a young lad alongside his older brothers. 'He would have played the odd game for Cargin, but not much, as Juvenile structures back then wouldn't have been how they are nowadays. Most of his football would have been played for Ballymaguigan, which we all joined when we moved to the area when Johnny was sixteen or so.'

Moving just across the northern shore of Lough Neagh and into the townland in which their father grew up, it was inevitable that the Bateson boys would join St Trea's GAA club, not least because it was a Bateson who founded the club. Their father had played there for years and was a recognisable figure about the club, not only because of his playing ability but also because he always wore a flat cap, even when he was playing! It wasn't long before Johnny and his older brothers were making an impact with the club. Johnny's first flavour of Senior football came in 1969, with the Junior Championship campaign. He was part of a very young crop of players that were being blooded into the Senior panel, which included his closest friends, Martin Lee (see page 291) and Jim Sheridan (see page 15), with the club hoping that Johnny and his teammates could one day fill the gap left by the gradual depletion of a remarkably talented squad that included the famous McKeever brothers, along with his older brothers Eddie and Jimmy.

The 1969 Junior campaign saw Johnny play alongside his brother Jimmy on the forward line, and they soon found themselves in the Derry Junior Championship final against Lavey. With Johnny scoring the opening goal inside three minutes, and Jimmy also getting on the scoresheet, the Ballymaguigan men took home the title. With the Junior Championship win bringing St Trea's hopes for a return to Division 1 football one step closer, the beginning of the 1970 season brought further hope as Johnny and his teammates started the league campaign strong and news came that some old club stalwarts were to return to the team for the beginning of the 1970 Championship, including 1958 Intercounty Footballer of the Year Jim McKeever. The Lough Shore men appeared in the South Derry final that year and, despite trailing by five points towards the final whistle, Johnny and his teammates ended the game having reversed the deficit with two points in their favour.

As the 1970 Championship rolled on, St Trea's proved an even hungrier team than the previous season, reaching Celtic Park for their second Junior final in a row with relative ease. In the semi-final, Johnny was described by local match reporters as 'outstanding in the forward line', and he continued to carve out that reputation for himself in the final by scoring a goal and two points. The match report from the final at Celtic Park described the Bateson brothers, Johnny and Jimmy, as the best of the pick in the forward lines. Incredibly, Johnny's team would bring home a third trophy that season; the Marathon Graham Cup. Linking up with Martin Lee's unstoppable runs in the cup final, Johnny once again opened the scoring and ensured that St Trea's ended the 1970 season on a high. Given the success of the last two seasons, the club believed their young team was ready to enter the newly formed Intermediate levels of Derry football, and Johnny's team would justify their faith. Carrying forward the confidence of the previous season, St Trea's began the 1971 season by putting together a string of strong performances, which resulted in the club not only retaining the Marathon Graham Cup but also finishing the league campaign unbeaten. St Trea's also reached the Intermediate Championship final, but unfortunately fell short of victory. In the club reports from that season, Johnny was commended once again as a reliable provider of important scores.

A great source of Johnny's enthusiasm for playing football, according to his family, came from the great Kerry teams he grew up following. As often as they could, his mother recalls, he and his friends would be squeezing themselves into the car of whatever neighbour was headed down to Croke Park on a given summer's Sunday. 'He came back from a game one weekend, I can't remember who Kerry were playing, but he had bought a wee figure of a Kerry footballer in the green and gold kit, the same colours as Ballymaguigan. He gave it to me and said it was for good luck, and it still sits on the cabinet in my living room.'

Off the pitch, Peter and Jimmy describe their brother as a popular young man who would have gotten to know his neighbours on those long, back-breaking trips to Dublin from South Derry. But before that, life began back in Cargin, his mother's home townland. 'We were all born and reared in Cargin and lived just a few yards from the old railway line, so we like to think of ourselves as the railway children! Those early days were filled with adventure, which suited Johnny as he was full of devilment and always looking for something to do. We used to sneak into the orchards, for example, and try to grab a few apples whilst trying not to get caught, or we would get old sheets of tin and slide down the steep embankments on either side of the railway tracks. Of course, the highlight of the year in those days was the annual Toome Fair carnival, which was always great craic.'

Johnny's life was also defined by Lough Neagh, whose shores he grew up on. 'We spent our summers on the shore, either with our da fishing and poaching, or battling through the rushes with our friends to get to the water. I remember one time we made a raft for the water out of old barrels, and we thought we could sail across to the island just off the shore. Of course, we all nearly drowned! Another time, in the early '60s, the Lough froze over, and we could take our bikes out onto the ice. I think someone actually drove their car from one side to the other!' And it was across to the other side where the family would move to come 1967.

By that stage, Johnny had completed his secondary school education at St Olcan's in Randalstown and had begun serving his time as an apprentice mechanic, first in Antrim and then in Ballyronan. 'Johnny loved his motors and enjoyed being a mechanic. He had a few Minis over the years and also loved raking around on a motorbike we got for ourselves. We had to hide it from our da, though, as he would never have allowed it, and despite our best efforts, Johnny was caught on it one night by a neighbour. Safe to say, Da put it out of action after he found out; he took a sledgehammer to it! But Johnny was your typical young lad like that and enjoyed the craic and testing the boundaries. As he got older, he really enjoyed socialising, and he was great friends with Martin and Jim. They would go to all the dances together, and with his Beatles haircut and all the style of that era, the girls were always around too! He had this silver streak in his hair from birth, so his nickname was Magpie.'

As young adults, Johnny and his friends were part of a generation that witnessed the birth of the civil rights movement, and, as Peter and Jimmy explain, it became a movement that was highly influential in their lives. 'Our family wouldn't have been overly political or anything, and our da's only interest was in keeping us all safe, but we found ourselves attending marches and getting more involved in the civil rights movement as time went on. And as the marches were met with more and more brutality, you found yourself more radical without even noticing it. We were at Burntollet Bridge, for example, and then internment was introduced in the summer of '71, and it felt like everything changed overnight. You just didn't want to sit back and take it, and Johnny, and many others, wanted to do something about it.' Johnny joined the IRA aged eighteen.

John Bateson was nineteen years of age when he died on active service for the IRA, when a bomb he was handling exploded prematurely on 18 December 1971. He died alongside his childhood friends, and fellow Volunteers and teammates, Martin Lee and Jim Sheridan.

In recognition of the talent and contributions of the three St Trea's players to both their club and the standard of football in Derry, the Derry Intermediate Championship is named the St Trea's Memorial Cup in their honour. Having competed in the final of that competition's inaugural year in the summer of 1971, their teammates on the St Trea's panel bought and donated a cup for the competition in memory of their old friends.

Football remains strong as ever among the younger generations of the Bateson family. Jimmy's son, Declan, has both a club and intercounty Senior All-Ireland medal, and a number of Johnny's other nephews have played intercounty football for Derry.

Jim Sheridan (Seamus Ó Sirideáin)

AOIS/AGE: 20

CUMANN/CLUB: Naomh Trea CLG, Baile Mhic Uiginn/ St Trea's GAC, Ballymaguigan

CONTAE/COUNTY: Doire/Derry

MARAÍODH/KILLED: 18 Nollaig, le pléasc anabaí/ 18 December, premature explosion

'All the old men used to sit on the seats outside the football club, beside this big hedge. They had endless ghost stories, and they'd tell us them all as kids and have us scared for days!' Sean and Hugo Sheridan begin to recall the stories of their childhood days spent with their older brother, Jim. 'They loved to scare the life out of us, and we loved it too. It was only a ten-minute walk home from the club, but if it was late at night, boy, did you go home in a hurry after hearing one of those stories! I always remember one night, when we were a bit older, Jim arriving home in a terrible state. He was walking home on the Burn Road, which had a bridge on it that was supposed to be haunted. He said that when he crossed the bridge, he looked back and saw a black dog with red eyes glowing at him, so he ran home. It scared the absolute life out of him. We all thought of Jim as our big, tough older brother, but there he was, hysterical over something like that! We didn't let him forget about that one easily.'

Jim Sheridan was born on 13 January 1951 to Hugh and Maureen. He was the second child of eight, growing up in Ballymaguigan, County Derry, with sisters Anne, Joan, Úna and Patricia, and brothers Sean, Hugo and Fergal. 'Those days growing up were a hell of a lot different to what they are now. There's no doubt about that. There were only a handful of houses on our road, and there were no cars. It was all walking and cycling; twenty minutes from the house to the chapel! Our home was a céilí house, filled with music and singing, and the door was always open. I remember you'd get up on a Sunday morning and you wouldn't know who might be in the kitchen. We made our own fun in those days, always up to adventures and running around either in the forest or on the Lough shore. There was plenty to be at and the local farmers were always looking a hand with work, which got you a few shillings, so between that and school, we were never in the house.'

Jim attended St Trea's Primary School in Ballymaguigan before going on to St Pius X Secondary School in Magherafelt. Leaving school at sixteen, he then went to the technical college in Ballymena, where he was taught engineering. 'He found work doing fibreglass, and he was a very hard worker. Even from he was a young lad helping the local farmers, he wasn't afraid of hard graft.' Sean and Hugo describe their older brother as an easy-going and good-natured character, who enjoyed socialising with his friends, and the type of person who would go out of his way to help people. 'He enjoyed all the rascality of the day and loved winding people up, but it was always in an endearing way and there was never any badness to him. When we all started to go out to the dance halls, he was always great craic to be with. Jim also always looked sharp and well-dressed, and he was fashionable alright, with the boots always shining and he had this beautiful coat.'

As for Jim's involvement in the GAA, he was a member of St Trea's, Ballymaguigan. 'Jim was the only one of us really involved in the club. He got involved through his two friends, Johnny [see page 10] and Martin [see page 291], who became big members of the club. The three lads went everywhere together, so Jim would tag along with them to training and matches and it grew from there. He also helped with the building of the club hall. His involvement wouldn't have been as much as Johnny and Martin simply because Jim would have been a bit like ourselves, in that he hadn't a foot to kick with!' Training with his club over the years and playing the occasional game when he got the chance, Sean and Hugo explain that Jim developed a love for the ethos of the association and that he took a real interest in the cultural aspects of Gaelic games. Alongside playing the sport, Jim developed a love for the Irish language and Irish history; indeed, he attended the Gaeltacht in West Donegal, his father's home county.

Jim Sheridan was twenty years old when he was killed alongside Martin Lee and John Bateson on 18 December 1971, when a bomb they were handling exploded prematurely. All three men were on active service for the IRA.

In recognition of the talent and contributions of the three St Trea's players to both their club and the standard of football in Derry, the Derry Intermediate

Championship is named the St Trea's Memorial Cup in their honour. Having competed in the final of that competition's inaugural year in the summer of 1971, their teammates on the St Trea's panel bought and donated a cup for the competition in memory of their old friends. The club history books record, 'The last game these boys played in was the Intermediate Cup final, with Martin and Johnny, as usual, playing their hearts out.'

1972

Eamon McCormick (Éamon Mac Cormaic)

AOIS/AGE: 17
CUMANN/CLUB: CLG Ó Donnabháin Rosa, Béal Feirste/ O'Donovan Rossa GAC, Belfast
CONTAE/**COUNTY:** Aontroim/Antrim
MARAÍODH/DIED: 16 Eanáir, Arm na Breataine/ 16 January, British Army

'Growing up in Ballymurphy, the Black Mountain was our garden.' Rosemary and Brendan describe the adventures of their youth spent with their brother Eamon and the rest of the McCormick clan, exploring the vast natural playground of Belfast's Black Mountain. 'With a packed lunch and a bottle of juice, it was Eamon's favourite place to be. He particularly loved a spot up there called the hatchet field, where we would all try to catch fish in the waters with nothing but our hands and a net. Our mother's favourite thing to shout at us if she wanted some peace was, "away up that mountain and play", and we always gladly took up her offer.'

Eamon McCormick was born on 29 May 1954 to Hugh and Rose. He grew up in Ballymurphy in West Belfast with his brothers Seamus, Liam, Gerry and Brendan, and sisters Theresa, Rosemary, Kathleen and Eileen. 'We grew up in a big family, with Granny Theresa living in the three-bedroom house with us too. It might have been a tight squeeze but come winter it certainly had its benefits.' A new estate with poor planning, the initial families who moved into Ballymurphy had to walk miles for schools and shops, which meant that Eamon grew up in a community that looked after one another. 'It was a type of place that if we had any dinner left over, my mother would always get us to run it down to whichever neighbour she knew could do with some more.' Eamon's father, a docker by trade, was a well-read and committed organiser for Ballymurphy. Part of the original tenant's association, he played his part in getting the first shops, school and chapel built in the community. 'When we were children, people would always come to the house asking our father if he could help them write letters or to ask his advice on matters. He was very forward-thinking. And our mother, through her persistence at the City Council's Housing Office along with other struggling Catholic mothers, was the reason we even had a house in Ballymurphy in the first place. So, we were all surrounded by that community ethos growing up.'

Along with his brothers, Eamon attended St Aidan's Primary School. 'The teachers in the school had us playing GAA right away, and Eamon's talents were immediately apparent. He was a big, tall lad for his age and, like the rest of us, he was very athletic. He would regularly come home with medals, and he was particularly proud of one he got in his last year of primary school; he won the long-kick out of all the schools in West Belfast. He then went on to St Thomas's, where he continued to play football and hurling in school until he left at age fifteen.'

Outside of school, Eamon was just as keen a sportsman. 'He played everything. He was a great basketball player, helped because of his height, and played soccer for St Paul's Swifts. In the street we played it all, including cricket! But he had a passion for the GAA.' Eamon played for Ballymurphy in the Belfast District Leagues, set up in the absence of Juvenile structures at club level at that time. Coached and led by the famous Antrim GAA stalwart Nipper Quinn, Eamon's Ballymurphy team were unbeaten every year he played. 'They brought so much pride to our area. The boys were always the topic of conversation for the parents.' Eamon naturally progressed on to club level, where he joined O'Donovan Rossa at Minor level, and being the talented defender he was, he was also on the fringes of the Antrim football set-up.

Off the pitch, Eamon was defined by his love for Ben Sherman shirts, especially white ones. 'Every pay day, that Saturday morning, he would be straight down to Castle Street and into Fraser's department store to get his shirt.' Eamon earned his paycheck working at Curries' Timber Yard, which he joined when he was fifteen, after leaving school. However, while attending a soccer match, he was spotted by a colleague at work and subsequently identified as a target for sectarian intimidation, which ultimately led to Eamon being chased out of work for being Catholic. On the street, Eamon faced regular harassment from the British Army, admitting to his sister that one soldier in particular was always hounding him. 'He said to me, "Every corner I turn he's there. He points his gun at me and says, 'See you McCormick, I have one up the breach for you.'" It was constant.' Surrounded by an escalating conflict and dealing with his lived experience of that violence, Eamon joined Na Fianna Éireann.

Eamon McCormick was shot by a sniper of the British Army's Parachute Regiment on Halloween night 1971. On the night he was shot, Eamon and a friend were asked to sit in a house close to where there were reports of a youth disco being attacked by a loyalist mob and surrounded by the British Army. 'The woman whose house it was said to me that they were both busting for a smoke and went outside as they wouldn't smoke inside the house. One shot rang out as the pair stood at the door chatting.' Shot from the rooftop of the school where the disco was taking place, Eamon was instantly paralysed. His condition slowly deteriorated until his death on 16 January 1972. 'My mother never left his side for the eleven weeks he was in hospital. To watch him die over that entire time was unimaginable. It broke us all. And to think those exact soldiers went into Derry the week after Eamon died. Young lads then never stood a chance; they were either interned or killed.'

Despite never having the chance to make his Senior debut, Eamon's legacy is still honoured by his club, O'Donovan Rossa. Two commemorative shirts have been commissioned in his memory and the Eamon McCormick Cup stands testament to the esteem in which his short career on the pitch is still held.

John Johnston (Seán Mac Seáin)

AOIS/AGE: 19

CUMANN/CLUB: CLG Chluain Árd, Béal Feirste/ Clonard GAC, Belfast

CONTAE/COUNTY: Aontroim/Antrim

MARAÍODH/KILLED: 9 Márta, le pléasc anabaí/ 9 March, premature explosion

'John comes from a 100 per cent Clonard family.' Billy Johnston begins to describe his younger brother and his family background. 'He also comes from a very sporting

family. We all played sports to a very high standard. Our father was vice-captain of the first St Gall's team to win a Senior Football County Championship; our late brother's name, Tom Johnston, is known throughout GAA and soccer circles around Ireland and further afield; and myself and John weren't half-bad either!'

John Johnston was born in September 1952 to Josephine and Tommy. He was the couple's third boy and grew up in the Clonard area of West Belfast with older brothers Tom and Billy, and sisters Joanne, Seaneen and Roisín. John followed his brothers into St Gall's Primary School, where he got his first lessons in Gaelic football, as Billy explains. 'We all first started to play when we got to St Gall's school. It was a feeder school to the St Gall's club, of which our father was a bit of a legend, and so we automatically had to join the club when we left primary school. We weren't there long, however, before we decided to switch to the Clonard GAA club. All of our friends were joining Clonard and we wanted to go and play with them. At that time, Clonard had an excellent underage set-up, having won three Minor Championships in a row. My father hardly spoke a word to us for about a year he was that upset! But we were winning and playing with lads we hung around with, and that's where we enjoyed our football.' John then went on to St Thomas's Secondary School before finding work in Shorts Aeronautical Factory, alongside Billy.

For John, as with his brothers, sport was the preoccupation of his life. He trained in the Star Boxing Club together with his friend Paddy Maguire, who would go on to become a British champion. As a young lad, John became an Ulster champion at table tennis and competed in Ulster sprinting competitions. John also played soccer for Immaculata Football Club. Indeed, soccer was huge in the Johnston family. John's father played Irish League soccer, as did his brother Tom, who played for Crusaders and Glenavon football clubs, and his brother Billy was the captain of St Malachy's Football Club. Billy explains that his brother Tom was a renowned soccer player and coach, obtaining his coaching certificates alongside Kenny Dalglish of Liverpool Football Club and managing St Oliver Plunkett Football Club. 'In those days, however, we weren't allowed to play soccer! You'd be playing a game and next thing you would hear the clicks of a camera. The vigilantes. Before you knew it, you were requested to a meeting for breaching Rule 27, and they had photographic evidence of you playing soccer! You could get banned for a few games or weeks, so you had to be careful you weren't being watched going to games.'

Above all, however, was a love for Gaelic football. 'It was a different game back then. In some matches, the referee didn't know there was a foul until he saw the ambulance drive onto the park! I was a bit older than John so never played with him, but I have met many people who have, and they all say the same thing: What a footballer!' His talent invariably comes as little surprise to Billy and those who know of the GAA stock from which John comes. In addition to his father, his older brother Tom was not only an excellent player, but also a renowned organiser and committed Gael. Tom was an official at the infamous 1983 All-Ireland final between Dublin and Galway, alongside referee John Gough, and he also served for a time as an administrator for the Antrim Minor panels. John's brother Billy also has experience of Croke Park, playing in a 1956 Belfast v. Dublin schools' game, and he remains proud of the fact that he was part of one of the few Antrim teams to go and beat the Dubs in the capital. Billy also played on the Antrim Minor football panel.

Billy explains that his brother enjoyed other aspects of life too, outside of sports. 'He loved his music and going to the Jazz Club. He always wore the best of gear and he was seriously well-kept. He had an infectious smile and a charm which meant he always had a girl or two around him and was always one for a dance. I'm not only saying this because he was my brother, but he was a great character. John constantly had people going and he was very good-natured, although he wouldn't have tolerated anyone messing him about either. Great company.'

As Billy continues, he describes how his family, and his neighbours, experienced the beginning of the conflict, and how it shaped his brother. 'Around '68/'69, things became very difficult for people living in the Clonard area. Catholics were being burnt out of their homes and killed across Belfast. The atmosphere changed utterly and there was no hiding from it in our part of Belfast. Experiencing all of that, like most young lads at that time in the affected areas, John said, "It'll not happen again", and he decided to join the IRA at eighteen. Towards the end of his life, he was on the run, and you never knew when you'd next see him, but he was doing what he thought he had to do. Naturally, football was put on the backburner.'

John Johnston was twenty years old when he was killed whilst on active service for the IRA on 9 March 1972, when a bomb he was handling exploded prematurely. He was killed alongside fellow Volunteers Tom McCann (see page 26), Tony Lewis (see next entry) and Gerard Crossan.

Tony Lewis (Antóin Mac Lughaidh)

AOIS/AGE: 16
CUMANN/CLUB: Na Piarsaigh CLG, Béal Feirste/ Patrick Pearse's GAC, Belfast
CONTAE/COUNTY: Aontroim/Antrim
MARAÍODH/KILLED: 9 Márta, le pléasc anabaí/ 9 March, premature explosion

'Tony loved to play handball up against the gable walls.' Ray and Pauline begin describing their brother Tony. 'I remember as a kid, seeing his GAA medals about the house for the different competitions. There was always a hurl in our house.'

Tony Lewis was born on 4 April 1955 to Lily and Sam. He was their first child, and older brother to Pauline, Ray, Theresa, Gary and Colin. They all grew up in the Clonard area of West Belfast, although as the eldest child, Tony lived with his grandmother, Molly, and his aunt, Mary. 'They had him spoiled rotten. Aunt Mary didn't have children, so she and our granny would bring Tony everywhere and give him everything! He didn't move over to our house on Cupar Street until 1968 or so.' Tony attended the local St Kevin's Primary School, where he would make very good friends for life and where he received his first introduction to the GAA. He then went on to St Thomas's Secondary School and then spent a final year at St Paul's, before leaving school at fifteen to find work. 'After leaving school, he started as an apprentice joiner, but it soon ended after he came home complaining one day that he never got his lunch or a break. Mummy pulled him out after that and told him he wasn't to go back.' Tony eventually found work as an apprentice butcher and, when he wasn't working, Sam enjoyed taking him and his siblings to the point-to-point races.

Tony's life, however, soon became entirely overshadowed by the outbreak of conflict. At the age of just fourteen, loyalist mobs came into the area in which he lived and burned families out of their homes. Known as the 1969 Pogroms, Tony found himself trying to help defend his street from attack, and his young life would be irrevocably changed. 'He played a real, active role in helping defend the district in '69, having joined Na Fíanna before that. Our Aunt Mary, who looked after Tony, was in Cumann na mBan, so there was definitely strong republican politics in the family for him to take after, but he was also moulded by his own experiences. His best friend, Gerald McAuley, was shot dead in '69 by loyalists coming in to attack the area as well. They were the same age, fifteen, and Gerald had actually left his coat in our house when he was killed.'

Tony later went on to join the IRA. 'He was committed to the movement. Despite his age, he was very mature and very well respected, and from the age of fifteen, he was on the run. You'd have taken him for being a lot older than he was, even physically too, as he was a big lad. Everyone in the district knew him and he knew he could trust the people in his community to look after him. As a person, he was a very quiet sort of character, and would never have told you what that hand was doing with the other hand, so when he was taken to Holywood Barracks at fifteen, people weren't worried because they knew he wouldn't talk.'

In terms of the GAA, Tony joined Na Piarsaigh GAA club on the Antrim Road in North Belfast aged fourteen, having been introduced to the GAA by people in his primary school associated with the club. He played both hurling and football for his club and would walk to that side of the city for training and matches. At that time, Juvenile structures would have been less-than-common and therefore little more can be said of the extent of Tony's exploits on the pitch, but Ray and Pauline describe a young man who loved his sport and his Gaelic identity. Unfortunately, with the escalation of conflict, it soon became too dangerous for Tony to make his way to training and matches, and so his involvement with Na Piarsaigh eventually faded out.

Tony Lewis was killed on active service for the IRA on 9 March 1972, alongside Tom McCann (see next entry), John Johnston (see page 21) and Gerard Crossan, when a bomb they were handling exploded prematurely.

Tom McCann (Tomás Mac Cana)

AOIS/AGE: 20

CUMANN/CLUB: CLG Chluain Árd, Béal Feirste/
Clonard GAC, Belfast

CONTAE/COUNTY: Aontroim/Antrim

MARAÍODH/KILLED: 9 Márta, le pléasc anabaí/
9 March, premature explosion

'Granda Raffo, our mother's father, was a massive Gael. He hosted all the Antrim committee meetings upstairs in our house on Divis Street.' Marie and Frances, Tom McCann's sisters, begin to describe their family's connection to the GAA. 'We still have the minute books from all those meetings. And our father, Tom McCann snr, played for the Fermanagh Senior Football team, along with our uncle Kevin. So, we definitely had GAA roots in the family!'

Tom McCann was born on 20 January 1952 to Tom and Eileen. He was the third of eight children, growing up on Harrogate Street in West Belfast with his older sisters Frances and Marie, and younger siblings Bernadette, Kate, Giuseppe, Anthony and Eileen. 'We had a very happy family life. Our house never stopped, with the door always open. It was definitely a céilí house, with Mummy always singing and playing the accordion. Tom was a great singer, and he always sang "The Wild Colonial Boy" as his party piece. Mummy constantly cooked and baked too. You got three meals a day whether you wanted it or not! And it wasn't just us; anyone who called to the house got fed, including the bin men. We mightn't have had much, but we were all happy, and neighbours shared everything. Mummy was always sending a pot of something down to this house or that. As kids, we were always out in the street playing and Tom would have been out playing handball with all the other lads. Our house was up early every morning back then, as Mummy would bring us all to first Mass at Clonard Monastery. Tom would have taken after our mummy and was very religious himself, and each morning on our way back from Mass, we had to rap all of our neighbours' doors to wake them! We were never late for school, let me tell you.'

Tom attended St Paul's Primary School before going on to St Thomas's Secondary School. He then found work as a welder at Belfast's shipyard whilst also attending his local technical college. Tom's time at the shipyard was cut short, however, when he arrived home one day covered in green lead paint. He was attacked for being Catholic and his mother thought it best for his safety that Tom did not return; he then found a job in the factory next door to his home. 'He was a quiet sort of lad and very easy to get on with. Tom was a real, nice person and very highly thought of by people who knew him. I remember when we were young, I wasn't allowed out on my own, so I used to say I was away out with Tom. I would go meet up with my friends and we would meet a group of boys to go to the picture house, and Tom would be away with a girl. Then, later on, me and Tom would meet up at the butcher's shop near our house to head home together so Mummy didn't know.'

As for Tom's involvement in the GAA, his first introduction came by way of his family. His Grandfather Raffo was a lifelong active supporter and organiser for Antrim. An Italian immigrant who settled in Belfast, Tom's grandfather fell in love with the GAA and offered support to his county in any way he could, including hosting committee meetings in his home. As long as he lived, he held a season ticket for Croke Park and, for all of his efforts and commitment, the Belfast Cumann na mBunscol competition is named after him. GAA pedigree also existed on the McCann side of Tom's family, who all came originally from Belleek in County Fermanagh. 'We were brought to matches every single Sunday growing up, whether you wanted to or not! We were that small you could hardly see the pitch, but you weren't allowed to move.' Marie laughs, 'Every Sunday.'

For Tom, his first opportunity to play came at St Paul's Primary School and, like many of his peers, he then went on to his local Clonard GAA club. His brother-in-law, Larry, also played for Clonard, and describes Tom's playing days. 'Tom played football and hurling for Clonard, up in the half-forward line. He wasn't a bad wee hurler and I think he might have been in and around the Antrim squad at one stage. He definitely went to a few trials and was of that sort of level.' Larry laughs, 'Our club got the nickname "The Heap" as we had a particular reputation, however undeserved … but we had some great teams. The conflict really affected us as a club; nine of our lads were interned in '71 but we never failed to get fifteen men on the park. It didn't matter if you were going out to get beat 40–0, we were as committed as any. With the conflict breaking out and Tom being so young, he only got playing for the Seniors a short while.'

Tom McCann was twenty years old when he was killed whilst on active service for the IRA on 9 March 1972, when a bomb he was handling exploded prematurely. He was killed alongside fellow Volunteers John Johnston (see page 21), Tony Lewis (see page 24) and Gerard Crossan. Tom came from a strong republican family and joined the IRA aged sixteen.

The links to the GAA remain strong in Tom's family. His nephew and nieces all played at different stages of their lives, as do their children, with Tom's nephew, Larry, playing intercounty hurling for Antrim.

Francis Rowntree (Proinséas Ó Caorthannáin)

AOIS/AGE: 11

CUMANN/CLUB: Pádraig Sáirséil CLG, Béal Feirste/ Patrick Sarsfields GAC, Belfast

CONTAE/COUNTY: Aontroim/Antrim

MARAÍODH/DIED: 22 Aibreán, Arm na Breataine/ 22 April, British Army

'Frank loved sport of any kind; you name it and he'd play it. He was always busting to get outside and wanted to do every sport all at once. He was that type of kid.' Francis's brother Jim describes his younger brother. 'He was never without a ball under his arm. Football was his passion, and his dedication would leave no one in doubt that he was a talent in the making, had he had the chance to grow up.'

Francis Rowntree was born on 11 September 1960 to Theresa and Francis senior. He grew up in West Belfast, along with his older brothers John and Jim, older sister Mary and younger brother Michael. Frank's father was from Newry and an avid supporter of the Mourne men of County Down, and despite seldom having time to visit the stands to support his county on match day with raising his family and being busy with work as a baker, he ensured that his passion was transferred to his kids, with Frank, John and Michael all playing football. Frank played his football for Sarsfields GAA Club, getting involved in the club with the help of neighbour Sean McKearney, and for his school, St Finian's. A keen runner as well, Frank was a very active child but that had not always been the case. 'Frank had spent a lot of years in and out of hospitals. He had a rare bone disease called osteomyelitis and that took up a lot of his early life. I suppose that's why he loved being outside and playing sport so much. To make up for lost time.'

Indeed, as Frank's condition improved, he was determined to make the most of his new-found health and would not let anything stop him, even if there was a conflict going on around him. 'It was the day of the Falls Road Curfew. Burning and rioting had started to flood the streets, and everyone was running to get home. My mother was out looking for Frank, like every other mother that day, and she happened to spot Frank as she was walking up Springfield corner. He was standing across the road with his wee sports bag under his arm. My mother called him over and asked, "What on earth are you doing?" And he replied, "I'm waiting for my lift." My mother tried explaining to him that there would be no training on because of all the madness that was going on, and Frank didn't believe her. He just couldn't believe or accept that his football was cancelled that day. My mother always laughed about it. There Frank was, surrounded by chaos, with his wee bag, determined to play some football, and my mother having to persuade him to come home.'

Francis Rowntree was shot by a rubber bullet, fired from inside a fully armoured vehicle, on 19 April 1972 by the British Army. He died three days later, aged eleven years old. It took forty-five years of tireless campaigning by his family for an inquest, which found Francis's killing was unjustified. His mother, Theresa, never got to see that long-awaited day in court. The Rowntree family continue their legal action against the British Ministry of Defence in order to access the truth and justice they have so far been denied.

Terrence Toolan (Toirdealbhach Ó Tuathlain)

AOIS/AGE: 36

CUMANN/CLUB: CLG Ciceam Ard Eoin, Béal Feirste/ Ardoyne Kickhams GAC, Belfast

CONTAE/COUNTY: Aontroim/Antrim

MARAÍODH/KILLED: 14 Iúil, Arm na Breataine/ 14 July, British Army

'The GAA has always been a big part of our family.' Martin Toolan explains the role of the GAA in Toolan family life. 'It had a massive role to play in our lives growing up. It was a big family and everyone in the club looked after

one another. It was also vitally important to us in terms of our identity and learning about our culture and our language. We were proud Gaels from we were no age, and we learned an ethos that we carry with us through our lives.'

Terrence, or Terry, Toolan was born on 7 May 1936 to Catherine and Bernard. The Toolan family are originally from Roscommon, but Terry was born and raised in Ardoyne in North Belfast and was the youngest of eleven children. He attended his local primary school before going on to St Malachy's College, and upon finishing his education he trained as an electrician. He then emigrated to England to work alongside his brother Seamus in Nottinghamshire in the mid-1950s, where he also married Doreen. The pair had met back in Belfast, and Doreen decided to follow Terry over to England, along with Seamus's girlfriend. After getting married, Terry and Doreen decided to move back to Belfast to raise a family together, and it wasn't long before their first child, Bernadette, was welcomed into the world in 1958. Bernadette was soon followed by Gemma, Gerard, Paul, Mandy and, finally, Martin. 'He was a real family man and took great responsibility, along with our mum, in our upbringing. Before putting us to bed, he would play his guitar and sing each night. He also loved to tell us stories and one would always lead on to another, and he would never get any of them finished! I remember we would all go on holidays and trips across Ireland, and those memories are so special to us.'

Terry came to be a well-regarded tradesman and an electrical inspector, and someone who commanded a great deal of respect from colleagues. His friend Brendan describes Terry and begins by detailing what memories he has of Terry and the GAA. 'Terry would have been involved in Ardoyne Kickham's from the 1950s. Certainly, he was involved in the club before I joined, which was back in 1962. He was a lot older than I was, but I started training with him and the rest of the Senior team when I got to Minor level. We would have trained at the Ballysillan GAA pitches, which were run by the council. The loyalists would regularly cut down the goalposts back then and, in the end, we were left with no facilities. We had a very strong team back then, with Terry in nets, and we were jockeying for competitions. In 1969 we won the Division 1B title, but after that summer it all began to fold in on itself once the conflict erupted. Terry was centrally involved on that team. He was always involved, and I can't remember him ever missing a match. He was the type of person both off and on the pitch who gave great encouragement to young players coming through like myself. And he was a very fearless player. He wasn't very big or tall, but he'd have fought King Kong on the pitch and he was well able for it. Strong as an ox.'

As his kids explain, Terry's service and commitment to his club meant that a great deal of respect he commanded was carried through to the younger generations of his family. 'Your name was always good around the club because of the impact our da and our Uncle Lawrence had on the club.' Indeed, Terry's brother Lawrence won multiple All-Ireland handball titles for Ardoyne Kickhams and also served on the club's committee. Bernadette recalls her early memories of being around the club with her father. 'Growing up, we were taken to matches nearly every Sunday. We were always at his matches and training sessions. I even remember the loyalists attacking us all up at Ballysillan!'

Off the pitch, Brendan explains that Terry became acutely aware of the beginnings of conflict, and how he came to be involved in the republican movement. 'Terry was a very knowledgeable character. At a time when nobody was really looking at politics beyond the civil rights movement, right at the beginning of the conflict, Terry was thinking big picture. As the conflict erupted and a lot of people decided how best to react, Terry was always there cautioning people to read into things, to fully understand and grasp what it is people were signing themselves up to, and to be aware of the context of their surroundings. He had an incisive analysis of the conflict, and he knew that it was going to be a very protracted one, and he wanted to avoid a situation where young people were committing themselves to something they didn't understand. He himself was involved at the start of the conflict by helping to organise the defence of Ardoyne from loyalist attacks, before the British Army arrived in '69. He then joined the IRA as the conflict grew.'

Terrence Toolan was killed in Ardoyne on 14 July 1972 by the British Army whilst on active service for the IRA.

In the wake of their father's death, Gemma, Martin and Bernadette explain how the GAA community in Ardoyne helped their family. 'The club supported our family when our dad died, and long after. I was always grateful for them, and the support they provided our mum. They were a constant in our lives and will always be very special to us.'

As the youngest of Terry's children, Martin describes how the GAA remained a link between him and his father. 'I never knew my daddy. I was twelve weeks old when he was killed, and I never got to meet him or know his character. And speaking about our daddy never happened in the house because our mummy took it so bad after he was killed; she mourned him for forty-eight years. So I loved being around the club because that's where I heard people talking about him. When his name was mentioned, it was always in the context of the GAA, and it was like a part of him would be right there. There was always that bit of a tangible connection to him. That's why the GAA is so important to us. My dad espoused the values of the GAA and so being a Gael, I always felt that I was learning to live life with a set of values my daddy would have taught me anyway; the love for our culture and language and sport, and the respectful, competitive attitude. In Ardoyne, young people during the conflict took it for granted that they were going to have to be prepared to be next in line, if you like, in terms of armed struggle. But the GAA was there to say, "Hold on. Think. There might be another way." They weren't going to stop anyone, but they certainly acted as a voice telling people to think about what they were doing and what they were about. And that was pretty invaluable, certainly for me as a young man angry at what was happening. I was always very proud to be a Toolan and come from a GAA family. It was a pride that gave me courage on the field and gave me that necessary edge to play well. Putting the shirt on meant everything, and without my daddy's involvement in the GAA, I don't think I would have that pride which allows you to put your body on the line.'

As Martin continues, he describes a memory that led to him getting to know his father. 'The photo we always have of my da is of him with a suit and tie on, whistling in the wind. I always had this vision of my da as this straight-edge gentleman who always did right: Mr Perfect. Then my mum showed me another photo of the pair of them at the zoo. It was ripped on one side and I asked why. She said there was another man in the photo who always had a liking for her, and when I turned the photo around, written on the back was a message along the lines of, "That **** will never be in a photo with us, my love." I was shocked. I had to come to terms with the fact that my daddy was like you and me. He was human after all.'

Francis McKeown (Proinséas Mac Eoghain)

AOIS/AGE: 43

CUMANN/CLUB: Naomh Mhuire, Buiochar CLG; CLG Ó Donnabháin Rosa, Béal Feirste/St Mary's GAC, Rockcorry; O'Donovan Rossa GAC, Belfast

CONTAE/COUNTY: Aontroim/Antrim

MARAÍODH/DIED: 16 Iúil, Arm na Breataine/
16 July, British Army

'Frankie really loved his football. He loved going to matches and training, and he was always keen to turn up.' Francis McKeown's brother-in-law and O'Donovan Rossa teammate Denis recalls his playing days with Frankie. 'He never forgot his roots in the Rockcorry club back in Monaghan, and I can remember one year, Rockcorry got into the final stages of the Monaghan Championship; either the quarter- or semi-final. Frankie brought three ringers down from Belfast, including myself, to play. To get us on the park, Frankie told the officials that we were three Christian Brothers from Belfast studying in Monaghan, and we ended up being allowed to play. We showed up on matchday and went into the dressing rooms wearing the black overcoats and trousers, dressed exactly like the Brothers in those days. It worked a charm, and we ended up winning that game!'

Francis McKeown, known to everyone as Frankie, was born on 9 April 1929 to Frank and Sarah Jane. He grew up on the McKeown family farm in Monage, County Monaghan, being the eldest sibling to brothers Jack and Seamus, and sisters Eilish and Dymphna. Frankie attended his local national school in Edraguil, and his younger days would have been spent helping around the family farm, planting potatoes, sowing corn and saving the hay each summer. As he moved into his teens, Frankie would have regularly visited his Uncle Jack and Aunt Celia, who ran a corner shop on Leeson Street in West Belfast. He would have been a most welcome visitor as the couple had no children and, equally, Frankie loved to help in the running of the shop.

In September 1955 Uncle Jack passed and, with Aunt Celia no longer wanting to continue running the business, Frankie's father, Francis, bought over the shop. And so the family moved to Belfast, with Frankie's parents moving into the shop and Frankie himself moving into his Aunt Nellie's house on the Falls Road. It was also around this time that Frankie would meet Marie Boyle at one of his football matches in the Falls Park, playing for his new club, O'Donovan Rossa. Frankie's daughter, Marie, describes the moment her parents met. 'Mum's friend was going out with a fella on the Rossa team, and she convinced Mum to go along with her to one of the games. They were standing on the sideline and her and my dad caught each other's eye. Dad started making enquiries and then Mum invited him to her twenty-first birthday party, and they were dating from then!' Marie Boyle was working in the civil service at Stormont at the time, and by mid-1956 Frankie was calling to her house to take her out and to also deliver groceries to Marie's mum, Maggie. 'Mum and Dad were then married on 28 August 1957, and we soon came along. Unbelievable today, but Mum had to give up her job at the civil service as they had a rule barring married women from their employment! They lived initially in the Gransha estate and then, as more of us kids came along, we moved to Coolnasilla.' Frankie and Marie had six children in all, Francis coming first, followed by Joseph, Kevin, Marie, Terry and Gerard.

Frankie settled comfortably into his new-found family life, playing cards with friends each Saturday night and going to the dog racing in Celtic Park, and his natural business acumen was beginning to flourish. Following his wedding, Frankie acquired two new shops, in addition to the Leeson Street shop, which he had inherited from his father and was now cemented as a local institution. The first was a shop on the corner of the Springfield and Kashmir roads, and the second was in the Lenadoon estate. 'At the heart of it, our dad was a community man. He worked very hard and was a great worker, and he did it because he was proud to deliver an essential service to his community and the people around him. Regularly, he would send out parcels of food and goods to people struggling, and local people knew and loved him.' Most illustrative of his character are the actions taken by Frankie during the escalation of violence and outbreak of widespread conflict during the period of the late 1960s and early 1970s. During the pogroms of 1969, in which many of his Leeson Street customers were burnt out of their homes, Frankie was spotted putting red tape on his van in the shape of a red cross to help people evacuate the area.

The following summer of 1970 saw the imposition of the Falls Road Curfew, during which Frankie was stuck in his Leeson Street shop. Despite the shop falling victim to British Army looting of cigarettes and other goods when soldiers raided it, Frankie's chief concern was ensuring the local community had access to essentials, and that same concern was apparent when internment was introduced. Frankie, his brother Jack and father Francis created food hampers for the affected families and sent parcels of food and cigarettes to the internees. 'He never asked for a penny for any of it.'

As for his love for the GAA, the whole affair began back home in Monaghan. St Mary's, Rockcorry GFC was where Frankie first learned his trade, playing with his brothers Jack and Seamus. Family archive research places the earliest reports of Frankie's exploits on the pitch back in 1946. At seventeen years of age, Frankie McKeown is mentioned as playing a pivotal role in securing Rockcorry's appearance in the semi-final of the Junior League, with his team losing out on a place in the final by a single point against Monaghan Harps. The Rockcorry lads would have to wait until their 1954 campaign for another solid chance of success. During that season, Frankie is mentioned as having played another pivotal role in the lead-up to the knock-out stages. Playing in the forward line, Frankie's marksmanship helped bring Rockcorry into their first ever Junior League final, but, as fate would have it, Frankie himself was unable to field at the last hurdle and Rockcorry bowed out to a strong Killanny side, losing 2–3 to 4–4. The year 1958 brought another hopeful football campaign for the club, with Frankie's team matching their previous achievement by reaching the Junior League final, but, despite Frankie being fit to play and personally scoring a goal and two points, a tough Emyvale side came out as champions. Not all was lost, however, as the Rockcorry team finished that season with the Ematris Cup.

A few years previously, in 1955, when Frankie made the permanent move to Belfast, he also joined the O'Donovan Rossa GAA club in West Belfast. It was with the Rossa club that he saw major success, winning multiple county titles in 1955, 1956 and 1958. His brother Jack also joined when he moved to Belfast in 1957, and the pair were involved in the successful 1958 campaign. The brothers played for Rossa on into the 1960s, but success was fading with the emergence of the neighbouring St John's club, who won seven county titles in a row from 1959 to 1965. Frankie's love for football was a defining characteristic of his, and it was only natural that this love was passed on to his children, who all played for Rossa as children, with everyone squeezed into the car to go to matches around the county.

Francis McKeown was shot by the British Army on the morning of 15 July 1972. He was making his way towards his Lenadoon shop to make sure the community had access to essential food and goods, having just gone through an intense period of violence the week before. As he drove along Shaws Road, with his sister-in-law Anna in the car behind him, he had to stop and get out of the car to remove barbed wire from the road. A shot rang out and Frankie ran towards his van for cover. A second shot struck Frankie's head as he climbed into the cab. He died the following morning in hospital. The soldier responsible stated, unchallenged, that Frankie was carrying a machine gun. A 2017 report by the Historical Enquiries Team examined Frankie's killing and concluded that the soldier's statement was seriously mistaken and that Frankie was entirely innocent. No charges were ever brought against his killer.

In memory of their father, and as a lasting tribute to one of the club's cherished members, the McKeown clan and the O'Donovan Rossa club unveiled a plaque at the Rossa clubhouse dedicated to Frankie. On the fiftieth anniversary of his death, family, teammates and the local community came together to remember the dedicated and much-loved Gael who was Francis McKeown.

John Paddy Mullan (Eoin Ó Maoláin)

AOIS/AGE: 33

CUMANN/CLUB: Movegh; Naomh Padraig CLG, Rock; CLG Uilf Toin, Chill Dreasa/Movegh; St Patrick's GAC, Rock; Kildress Wolfe Tones GAC

CONTAE/COUNTY: Tír Eoghain/Tyrone

MARAÍODH/KILLED: 16 Deireadh Fómhair, Arm na Breataine/16 October, British Army

'John Paddy loved life.' John Paddy Mullan's nephew, Gabriel, describes his father's brother. 'He was a proud Irishman and had immersed every aspect of his life in Irish culture. He was a fluent Irish speaker and loved the GAA.'

John Paddy Mullan was born on 1 July 1939 to James and Sarah. He was the youngest of three children, growing up in the townland of Strews, County Tyrone, with his brother Frankie and sister Mary. 'They were very, very poor. It's hard to imagine how tough life would have been back then for a Catholic family in rural Ireland. I remember my dad telling me that they couldn't even afford a ball, so they used to tie up old coats or shirts and kick around the field with that.' For John Paddy, it was education that proved a means of liberating himself from the scarcity he grew up in. 'While attending his local primary school, John Paddy won a scholarship to St Patrick's Academy in Dungannon. He was very intelligent, even as a young lad. When he was at the Academy, he took up everything, becoming a fluent gaelgeoir and learning the tin whistle and fiddle. Whilst at the Academy, he also got the opportunity to go up into the Gaeltacht in West Donegal.' At fifteen years old, whilst attending the Gaeltacht in Donegal, John Paddy received the awful news that his father had died of an asthma attack.

Undoubtedly, the GAA proved an escape for John Paddy from the struggles of his young life. It was at the Academy that he got his first introduction to football, and when he was old enough, he joined his local team in Movegh. That team would fold not long after John Paddy joined, and so he then started to play football for Rock St Patrick's. 'I don't think he was one of the better footballers, but he played with great passion. He was also a big, stocky lad and could have handled himself well, so I'm sure he was useful on the field, especially as he played along the back line.' As Gabriel explains, his uncle developed a great passion for Gaelic games, and alongside playing football, he also played handball and had a love for the game of hurling. He explains that John Paddy would see out his final few seasons as a player with Kildress Wolfe Tones and that he remained a committed Gael all his life. He was a particularly keen spectator and enjoyed nothing more than the rare trips to Croke Park to watch some of the greats of the last century take to the field. 'He was a very popular character around all the clubs, and everyone knew him. When he left school, he worked for the *Dungannon Observer* covering football matches around Tyrone, writing match reports for the county.'

Outside of the GAA, John Paddy left school and found work selling insurance; he would then go on to become a lorry driver. The main occupation of his adult life, however, came to be politics, as Gabriel explains. 'John Paddy became very aware of politics whilst at the Academy. Although there would have been little politics in their house, John Paddy and my dad developed a strong sense of identity and a desire for equality. I suppose their education was a big factor in that. My dad explained it to me, in that their thinking back then was, "Why is it that our neighbour can get a job and we always struggle? Why are they allowed to vote and we're not?" In fact, some of their neighbours had multiple votes when they hadn't one between them! Even simple things like trying to organise a loan to buy farming equipment were nearly impossible because they were Catholic, and so it was inevitable that they would start agitating.'

At sixteen years old, John Paddy decided to join the IRA. Gabriel explains that he fought in the Border Campaign of the 1950s before being arrested and imprisoned for eight months in 1957. 'He read a lot of Malcolm X's writing and was a big fan of Ho Chi Minh, and my father explained to me that his decision to become involved in the republican movement was because he wanted to create the conditions so that people could live and determine a normal life for themselves; something that was denied to him.' Come the late 1960s, John Paddy also became a member of the Northern Ireland civil rights movement, and with the outbreak of widespread conflict, he remained a member of the Official IRA. Being active in the republican movement meant that most of John Paddy's adult life was spent on the run, but Gabriel explains that that fact didn't mean his days playing football were over, and that John Paddy still played the occasional game for a team across the border in Monaghan.

John Paddy Mullan was killed alongside Hugh Henry Heron (see page 291) on 16 October 1972 by the British Army. The pair were on active service for the Official IRA when they were killed near the Old Cross in Ardboe, County Tyrone.

In memory of their former player, Kildress Wolfe Tones ran a tournament for a number of years in John Paddy Mullan's name. The next generations of the Mullan family remain committed Gaels and keep John Paddy's love for the GAA alive.

Stan Carberry (Ainéislis Cairbre)

AOIS/AGE: 34

CUMANN/CLUB: Sean Uí Mhistéil CLG, Béal Féirste/ Sean O'Shea's GAC, Belfast

CONTAE/COUNTY: Aontroim/Antrim

MARAÍODH/KILLED: 13 Samhain, Arm na Breataine/ 13 November, British Army

'My father took me to my first ever championship hurling final in 1971, Tipp. v. Kilkenny. I still remember it clear as anything. Back in those days Croke Park had the wired fences, and I remember pulling myself up onto them to get a better look at the hurlers.' Stan Carberry remembers his father, Stan snr, as a hurler through-and-through. 'He was such a funny man. The craic was always to be had with my father and he was always great company to everyone who knew him. But on the hurling pitch it was a different story – you'd better not get in his way.'

Stan snr was born in Beechmount Parade in the heart of West Belfast, on 19 October 1938. He and his brother Joe grew up with hurls in their hands, playing for Mitchell's GAA Club. Despite being 'smaller than your average hurlers', the pair would forge themselves an enviable reputation on the pitch as tough and fearless competitors. Indeed, Joe would line out as goalkeeper until the age of fifty-two. Stan jnr points out that if you ever wanted to know how revered his father was on the pitch, you only had to look at those who attended his funeral. Stan remembers, even as a young kid, looking around him and recognising the faces of the stalwarts of the glory days of Antrim hurling. Playing left corner-forward, Stan snr would be an integral part of 'the great Mitchell's team of the 1960s', known all around the county as being a fearless contingent of players. Although the family is unsure if Stan played Senior hurling for Antrim, Stan jnr is certain that his father had an underage intercounty career. Stan jnr would also play for Mitchell's, in the same position as his father and under the stewardship of his father's teammates.

Stan snr married his partner, Gemma, in 1962 and the couple started a family together, bringing Donna, Stan, Joe, Betty, Pauline and Christine into this world. Stan jnr remembers his mother's stories of his parents dating, his father always bringing his mother on trips across Ireland and especially to Croke Park. Indeed, Stan brought Gemma to a plethora of All-Ireland finals. Gemma would get well used to the atmosphere of GAA crowds and found herself a constant on the sideline when Stan was playing; she was his rock of support while he was on the field as she was in all aspects of his life.

Stan snr and his brother both worked as heating engineers, but his other passion in life besides his first love of hurling was a love of cars. Stan jnr recalls that his father was always under someone's car, always eager to help neighbours with car trouble if he had any spare time. 'My father had a beautiful Jaguar, which was mad at the time considering we were living in the middle of Beechmount, but he loved it. It was in that car he brought me to Croke Park, and to all the hurling games up and down the country. I was always egging him on to open it up and drive faster, one time managing to convince him to race the train, which he would soon regret doing once my mother found out. He was my best mate.'

Stan snr's time as a player came to a gradual end as the conflict grew. Unknown to his family, he would join the Provisional IRA. Whilst on active service, he was killed in 1972 by the British Army as he tried to surrender. Stan jnr is currently suing the British Ministry of Defence over the killing.

Louis Leonard (Lughaidh Ó Lionáird)

AOIS/AGE: 26

CUMANN/CLUB: Naomh Pádraig CLG, Domhnach/ St Patrick's GAC, Donagh

CONTAE/COUNTY: Fear Manach/Fermanagh

MARAÍODH/KILLED: 15 Nollaig, Arm na Breataine/ 15 December, British Army

'When Louis and I first started going out, I knew there was something about him. Usually, if a boy was calling to the door for you, they would wait outside on you and they would be near afraid to speak to anyone. But not Louis.' Betty Leonard begins describing her late husband. 'Louis always came into my house. He would chat away with my mother and brother, usually about football, while I got ready, and they just adored him. He had that rare sort of affability and charm with people. Mum always said he was a fourth son of hers.'

Louis Leonard was born on 25 July 1946 to Desmond and Mary. He was their second child and grew up in the parish of Donagh, County Fermanagh, with older brother Hugh and younger siblings Desmond, Louise, Willy, Barry, Ciarán and Anthony. Louis's early years are described by his younger brother Ciarán. 'Louis received his entire education at the local Ballagh Primary School and left at fourteen or fifteen years old. There wasn't much economic life at that time and few prospects in terms of employment existed; there was plenty of work but no wages. We grew up on the small farm my mother and father had, which had a handful of cattle, and life back then was characterised by basic subsistence living and emigration; people were just surviving.'

An essential role, Ciarán describes, was therefore played by the GAA in Louis's local community, as it provided people with a sense of solidarity and an escape from the harsh conditions they were living through. 'The local club was the Knocks Grattons, a small, country club with no money and goalposts cut from hedges. Louis would have joined the club at an underage level, having been initially coached football at school by a committed Gael and teacher, and a Tyrone man, Pat O'Neill. Louis was part of a great generation of footballers coming through for the Knocks club. Teammates like Francie Treacy, Tom Rice and Kevin McManus had a very positive influence. This was a time when football was all the local people really had, they brought a lot of hope and optimism into people's lives and kept everyone going. The Knocks won the Fermanagh Junior Championship in 1964 and brought the club into the Intermediate Division. Louis was eventually made captain of the Senior team, and in 1968 they won the Intermediate Championship, which meant they were playing Division 1 football the next year. It was a great lift to the parish, and Louis and his generation of footballers became role models for us younger ones in the town.'

Despite the success, however, the Knocks club struggled to hold on to players. Economic and social conditions were acutely difficult for Catholics in rural Fermanagh, and come the late 1960s, clubs across the county were folding due to emigration. 'There was no employment, no houses, and no right to vote to try and change the situation!' Struggling against the coming tide, Louis organised fundraisers and carnivals to help raise funds for the club. He worked closely with Paddy Foster and others to put a plan together to amalgamate his club with the neighbouring Newtownbutler First Fermanaghs club, for whom his father had played. Not for a want of trying, however, those plans never materialised, and the Knocks Grattons club ultimately folded for a time. 'Paddy Foster, who had a huge positive influence on Louis and the whole community, was determined to develop the vision of a new club and eventually St Patrick's, Donagh, was formed in October 1971. Louis would only play one season for the club.'

As Ciarán then begins to describe his brother's life outside of the GAA, he tells of how Louis became more influential within his community. Whilst working as an apprentice butcher in Lisnaskea upon leaving school, Louis became highly active in organising a number of community projects for his local area. He also became an active organiser in the civil rights movement that was beginning to take hold across the North. 'I think Louis formed a strong sense of politics from growing up in the environment that he did. He was very level-headed, and he saw the destruction that was being caused by generations being forced to emigrate because they were being denied jobs and housing. There were no opportunities and no future. Louis and his generation coming into the '60s said, "No more! We want change and we want it now!" Louis would regularly attend civil rights marches and demonstrations, and people began to look at him as a leader. He worked with other local republicans who had a positive influence on his outlook. People like Barney Mohan, Mark Breen, Eamon Curran, Paddy Foster and Eamon Carey, all from our community, successfully campaigned for houses to be built in Donagh. Louis and his generation took strength from these developments and, at a time when everyone was emigrating, Louis took the risk of staying and, after eleven years working for the butcher's in Lisnaskea, decided to try and start his own butcher's business.'

Louis was spurred on in taking that leap into opening his own business by the support of his partner, Betty. The pair met one another at a dance in Enniskillen in the late 1960s and fate would bind them together. 'We started seeing each other after we first met, and he would call me every day. He was still working for the butcher in Lisnaskea and I was working for the local garage in Derrylin. I knew he was involved in football because he had a half day on a Thursday and used to run over the mountain every Thursday afternoon for his training. He was so proud when they won the Championship in '68, and I actually met his parents for the first time at the cup presentation for that season. It was around that time that we also got involved in the civil rights movement together, and we used to participate in the sit-down protests in the local towns and go to the marches and so forth. One thing I always remember about Louis was that he was also deeply religious. He had a special relationship with his Aunt Mary, who acted as a sort of spiritual guide for Louis, I suppose, and they adored the ground one another walked on.'

Betty continues to describe the early days of their relationship: 'I often laugh; neither of us had any money, but he was one of those guys his friends could rely on for a bit of change if we were down at the pub and they needed a drink. He was very smart with the little money he did earn, and he taught me a lot about how to save and be competent with money. He had a great foresight and a business mind to him, so when we got married in February 1972, he was confident in setting up his own butcher's shop that Easter. We were a great combination of partners with the new business as he knew the trade inside out and brought in the business, whereas I could do all the books from my time at the garage.' Betty describes how Louis was well suited to running his own shop. 'Louis was a very affable and charismatic person and was so well-got. He knew everybody and people really seemed to trust him, so people loved to come into the shop because they could chat away with him, and that was half the battle when starting out on our own. We then started to develop plans to open a number of shops across Fermanagh.' As well as their new business, Louis and Betty were also starting a new family together, and in August 1972 they welcomed their son, Tony, into the world.

Louis Leonard was shot dead on 15 December 1972 in his butcher's shop in Derrylin. Betty had left him in the shop that night to make deliveries in Lisnakea, and on her return back to Derrylin, was stopped by an RUC patrol and subjected to intense harassment. When Betty was eventually released, she arrived back at the shop to find it closed with the lights off. Assuming Louis had gone home, Betty then followed suit, only to find that Louis was not there. The next morning, Louis was reported missing. In the subsequent search for him, his brother Hugh and brother-in-law Tom Rice forced their way into his shop. Louis's body was found in one of the fridges, and it was evident that he had been shot. No one has ever claimed responsibility for Louis's death, and it was initially recorded as a random sectarian killing. However, his family believe there is more than sufficient evidence indicating that British Crown forces were responsible. In the months leading up to his death, he and his family were subjected to sustained threats by British soldiers, including threats to Louis's life. After his death, Louis was claimed as a member by the IRA.

In memory of Louis and his dedication to the GAA in his local area, St Patrick's, Donagh, has named their park after him. As Ciarán explains, 'It was never easy to play GAA back then. War, conflict and death had been brought to our communities. Trying to get to neighbouring clubs for games wasn't easy. Players and supporters would be stopped and harassed by Crown forces; they searched and abused you at every opportunity. News would come in of GAA clubs being attacked across the six counties, some person being beaten or arrested, and sometimes of someone connected to the GAA being killed. Our own club was attacked in 1973 by off-duty RUC men, resulting in one club member being wounded by a gunshot. I think Louis would be very proud of what his club has become, having emerged from those dark days. The club is now thriving, and it acts as the hub for the community. There is a great policy of inclusivity and reaching out, and Louis would love all of it. He would also be incredibly proud of the next generations of his family continuing the footballing tradition. Three of Louis's grandsons play for Derrylin, and for Fermanagh at different levels! He would also be very proud of how all of his old teammates still remember and talk fondly of him. As part of the fiftieth anniversary events, they planted a tree in his memory beside a lough close to the Knocks Grattons Hall, and a fiftieth commemorative jersey was also produced. His name and dream live on.'

Alphonsus McGeown (Alfóns Mac Giolla Eoin)

AOIS/AGE: 19

CUMANN/CLUB: CLG Roibeard Eiméid, Cluain Mhór/ Clonmore Robert Emmets GAC

CONTAE/COUNTY: Ard Mhacha/Armagh

MARAÍODH/KILLED: 20 Nollaig, le forsaí dílseach/ 20 December, loyalist forces

'Myself and Alphonsus would have gone to the football field, or Casey's field, after school.' Dominic McGeown begins to describe his memories of his older brother, Alphonsus. 'We would have met up with a few lads and spent the evening kicking about.'

Alphonsus McGeown was born on 18 October 1953 to James and Peggy, and grew up in the hamlet of Clonmore, County Armagh, bordering County Tyrone, on the small family farm with his older sisters Bernadette and Patricia, and brothers Paddy and Dominic. 'My mother and father were both from Clonmore and were involved in the club. My father played football, whilst my mother would have been in making tea and helping out. In a small, rural place like Clonmore, all you had was the school, chapel and the GAA club, so everybody has some connection with the club.' As Dominic continues, he explains that life in Alphonsus's early days moved a bit slower. 'Outside of school, there wasn't an awful lot to be at other than walking down to the football field and kicking a ball around or heading down to the Tall River or the Blackwater to do a bit of fishing. Back then, the banks would have been lined with people fishing, and the craic was always great and the rivers full of fish. On a Sunday night, after the football, all the boys would have gathered at the old railway bridge and have a bit of a yarn and a carry-on.'

In terms of Alphonsus's own involvement in the GAA, he was a member of his local club, Clonmore Robert Emmets. 'Alphonsus's involvement would have been going down to the pitch in the evenings and having a kickaround with a few lads after school. The club was more of a social outlet for him back then than anything, and he would have been more of a keen supporter than a player at most games. I suppose Alphonsus was still a young lad when he was about the club too, and then the club folded for a short while due to a lack of numbers at the age when he could have gotten more involved. When the team got back up and running, Alphonsus had left school and was very busy with work or helping my da around the farm, and so he had little time to get more involved in training or games.'

Growing up, however, their father, James, would always take any opportunity to bring his boys to football games, especially Ulster Championship ties. 'We loved going to Armagh games, but it was a very rare occurrence as it was big money! I remember getting to Clones the odd time, and if there was a car leaving Clonmore for a game, it was always piled into with as many people as possible. If we were heading to Croke Park, the car would stop along the journey at random houses to get a kettle boiled for a cup of tea. People would have thought nothing of it back then, and if you were lucky, they might bring you out a biscuit.' Indeed, James was known for having never missed an All-Ireland final.

Alphonsus attended his local primary school in Clonmore, which is where he received his first lessons in Gaelic football, before going on to St Patrick's Secondary School in Dungannon. 'From he was a young lad, Alphonsus would have always been the one to help our da with his work, growing mushrooms and the like. He was always very good around the house and outside of the house; he was a very harmless and quiet big fella. He would never have caused anyone any trouble.' Upon leaving school, Alphonsus began working for Moy Meats and then began working for a tyre company in Portadown along with one of his close friends from Clonmore. 'He was just getting to an age where he was taking the odd pint and throwing a lock of darts around the local bars. I remember he would have a wee sing after a beer in him.'

Alphonsus McGeown was nineteen years old when he was shot dead by the UVF on 20 December 1972. He and his friend had just gotten off the bus at Clonmore from work that evening and were walking along the road home when a car pulled up beside them and sprayed them with bullets. Alphonsus was killed instantly; his friend narrowly survived. Alphonsus was the first victim of what is now referred to as the 'Murder Triangle', in which the Mid-Ulster UVF killed at least 120 people. No one has ever been charged with his killing and his family continue to pursue avenues open to them to discover who was responsible for it.

In memory of Alphonsus, as well as all lost members, Clonmore Robert Emmets commissioned a remembrance plaque to adorn a pitch-side memorial at their clubhouse. The McGeown family are still deeply tied to their beloved club, with Alphonsus's nephews all playing football there. Indeed, they were part of the first Clonmore team to win an Armagh County Championship; the Junior title of 2005. Alphonsus's grandniece represents her county in camogie.

1973

Kevin Kilpatrick (Caoimhín Mac Giolla Phádraig)

AOIS/AGE: 20

CUMANN/CLUB: CLG Doire Treasc Fir an Chnoic/ Derrytresk Fir an Chnoic GAC

CONTAE/COUNTY: Tír Eoghain/Tyrone

MARAÍODH/KILLED: 13 Bealtaine, Arm na Breataine/ 13 May, British Army

'Kevin was the life and soul of the party.' Kevin Kilpatrick is described by his brother-in-law, Jim. 'He was full of devilment and loved the craic. He was an all-round good young lad.'

Kevin Kilpatrick was born to Joe and Elizabeth. He was their youngest boy and grew up in the townland of Anaghaboe, County Tyrone, with his older brothers James and John, and sisters Margaret, Angela and Siobhán. Like his siblings, Kevin attended Annaghmore Primary School before leaving to serve his time as a mechanic in Little's Garage in Coalisland. Jim explains that Kevin was very good in the house growing up and always made sure to pull his weight. 'One thing about Kevin was that he was always very good to his mum. He wouldn't have been slacking when it came to the housework, and he made sure everyone else in the house did their bit.' As he came into his teenage years, Kevin enjoyed socialising with his friends, going to the cinema in Coalisland and, eventually, when he was old enough, he started going to the local dances.

As for the GAA, Kevin came from a strong footballing family. 'His father was supposed to be a great player. He played for Tyrone from 1931 to 1934, and he has a Senior Championship medal for the Washingbay Shamrocks from back in that time. I'd say the boys inherited football from their da, and he would have encouraged them to play from an early age.' Kevin's first experiences of football would have been at school, and then he joined the underage structures of Clonoe O'Rahilly's. Kevin's senior football was played for Fir an Chnoic, Derrytresk, however, and Jim describes him as a solid player on the left half-back line. As with many Gaels, Kevin's playing career took a brief pause when he emigrated to England as a young man in search of work. However, whilst he was away, Kevin was asked to come home to help his club for the start of the 1970 season. Not able to resist the call, Kevin returned and played alongside his brother John, and he helped his club to the Tyrone Junior Football Championship final. This was hard-fought, but they eventually lost to a strong Dregish side. Kevin decided to remain in Ireland and return to work as a mechanic after that season.

Growing up in the 1960s, Kevin was influenced by the tide of political changes that gripped societies across the world, and he found himself increasingly involved in the civil rights movement. Jim explains that Kevin came from a home which had republican politics and that, as the conflict began breaking out and Kevin and other civil rights demonstrators were handled with violence, he decided to join the IRA.

Kevin Kilpatrick was twenty years old when he was shot dead by the British Army on 13 May 1973. On the night he was killed, Kevin was trying to evade capture at a UDR checkpoint that had stopped the car he was travelling in. He was shot in the back as he tried to make his escape.

Kevin's family remain involved in the Derrytresk club, with the younger generations of the Kilpatrick family keeping his love for football alive.

Francis 'Francie' McCaughey (Proinséas Mac hEachaidh)

AOIS/AGE: 33

CUMANN/CLUB: Achadh Lú Uí Néill CLG/ Aghaloo O'Neills GFC

CONTAE/COUNTY: Tír Eoghain/Tyrone

MARAÍODH/DIED: 8 Samhain, le forsaí dílseach/ 8 November, loyalist forces

'Uncle Francie was a very funny man and great company. Himself and Uncle Mick were two characters, and you are always laughing when you were with them.' Angela laughs when she remembers the time she spent with her maternal uncle, Francie. 'He used to write limericks and funny short stories and enter them into competitions using either my name or my sister Úna's. We'd have all these prizes getting sent to us from small competitions in local newspapers and the likes from across the country!'

1973

Francie McCaughey was born on 5 June 1940 to Eddie and Sarah. He grew up with his five siblings on the family farm in the townland of Glassdrummond, four miles from Aughnacloy, County Tyrone. Memories of Francie's early life have naturally faded with the passage of time, but his childhood would no doubt have centred around helping his parents at the family farm, tending to the livestock and developing a strong work ethic from an early age, which would come to define his adult life. He attended Derrylatinee Primary School and later, along with his brother Mick, built a very successful milk farming business. 'They had a very modern way of working and before Francie died, they had just got a new milking parlour, which would have been one of the few of its kind anywhere in the area. And while being hard workers, outside of work the pair of them were never far from the craic and always keen for a laugh. As kids, we used to go with them to football games in their wee old car and when they parked it up, Francie would take an old football boot and wedge it against the wheel to stop the car rolling as the handbrake was never working!'

Francie's love for football grew from an early age, and he and his brother Mick would have initially played for many years for Eglish St Patrick's, as Aghaloo O'Neills had yet to be formed. He was a reliable and tough Senior footballer for the Eglish club right up until 1969. Francie and Mick then transferred to Aghaloo O'Neills, having helped form the new club in their own parish, and the pair were eligible to play at the start of the 1970 season. As chance would have it, the very year the McCaughey brothers moved to Aghaloo O'Neills, Eglish won their first, and to this day only, Tyrone Senior Football Championship. Francie's teammates at Aghaloo describe him as a committed servant to their newly established club, both playing Senior football and later serving on the committee as vice-chairman, with responsibility for managing the club's affairs. Indeed, Francie, as vice-chairman, was instrumental in the purchasing of land that had the potential for development into playing facilities on behalf of the club. On the pitch, he earned himself a reputation as a very tough opponent, with his teammates laughing that some stories of Francie on the field of play are better left on those fields, and clarifying that, at the final whistle, he was as enjoyable and affable company as they come.

Francie McCaughey was seriously injured on 28 October 1973 when a bomb, placed by the UVF's Glenanne Gang, exploded at the door of his milking parlour. Francie and Mick were starting their day's work when Francie opened the parlour door, triggering the explosion. Mick was about to join his brother, and was standing only yards away. Francie passed away eleven days later, on 8 November.

In the following year, Aghaloo dedicated their championship campaign to Francie's memory. Mick was named captain and the club went on to win their first Tyrone Junior Football Championship. Despite the fact that Francie did not have a family of his own, today his nieces, nephews, grandnieces and grandnephews proudly follow in his footsteps through their active involvement in Aghaloo O'Neills and in other GAA clubs across Tyrone, Monaghan, New York and San Francisco.

1974

Jim Devlin (Seamus Ó Doibhilin)

AOIS/AGE: 45

CUMANN/CLUB: CLG Fianna Oileán an Ghuail/ Coalisland Fianna GFC

CONTAE/COUNTY: Tír Eoghain/Tyrone

MARAÍODH/KILLED: 7 Bealtaine, le forsaí dílseach/ 7 May, loyalist forces

'Everybody knew my da, and he knew everybody.' Eamon Devlin begins to describe his father, Jim. 'I remember us going on a day trip out in the car to somewhere in Cavan or Monaghan. We ended up calling into two or three different pubs along the way. I'd have a lemonade and Daddy might've had a beer. At each pub, I remember that everyone knew him and he them. He was very popular with people, and I remember he always talked with his hands. He got along with everyone he met.'

Jim Devlin was born on 16 June 1928 to James and Lucy, and grew up in Coalisland, County Tyrone with his older siblings Joseph, Barry, Tony, John, Sinéad and Frank, and younger brother Edward. Memories of Jim's early childhood days have faded with the natural passage of time, but Eamon describes how his father would have never been far from football growing up in Coalisland. 'I don't believe my grandfather played in football or know if there was any lineage of the GAA in the family before my father, but as with everybody else in the area, football was a massive part of school life for my da. He went to the local Primate Dixon Primary School in Coalisland and that's where he would have received his first taste of football. That then progressed as he went on to St Patrick's Secondary School in Armagh.' Indeed, Jim proved a capable footballer from a very young age, and whilst at St Patrick's he was on the first panel from the school to win a Hogan Cup in 1946. Jim's brother Edward was also on that panel, and it was remarked by Mayo footballing legend Eamon Mongey that Edward was the finest underage footballer he had ever seen. As it happened, all of the Devlin boys were talented footballers from a young age and five of them would play Senior football for Tyrone at different stages.

At the same time as he was competing at the highest schools' level in the country, Jim was also carving out a reputation as a tough and agile full-back with his club Coalisland Fianna, and it wasn't long before he was called up to represent his county at Senior level. As was wonderfully explored by Keith Duggan in *The Irish Times* (17 May 2014), Jim began his intercounty career in the 1950s, at a time when Cavan had been dominating Ulster football for the better half of two decades. A shift was to occur, however, as the back-to-back All-Ireland-winning Tyrone Minor panel of 1947 and 1948 started to break through into the Senior team. Jim and Edward Devlin were part of that change, and by the mid-1950s, with Jim at the helm of the back line, Tyrone football had established itself as one of the strongest in both Ulster and Ireland, with a breakthrough season in 1956. During that season they wrote themselves into the history books as the first Tyrone team to win an Ulster football title. Come the challenge of Galway in the semi-finals of the All-Ireland Championship that year, Jim put out a performance that is still spoken about. He marked Frank Stockwell, a player with a well-earned and fierce reputation for tormenting back lines across Ireland. Despite Tyrone narrowly losing that game, Jim held Frank scoreless. The following year, Tyrone repeated their Ulster title success. Jim also represented Ulster on multiple occasions in the Railway Cup.

As the seasons passed, Jim eventually moved into refereeing club games in Tyrone. He was known for taking little talkback and he was as respected officiating games as he was when he was battling for possession. The earliest memories Eamon has of his father and the GAA are of him as a referee. 'I have a vague memory of going to games and Daddy was the referee. He had finished playing long before I was born, around the time that Patricia was born. I think he must've picked up a knee injury as a player because I can remember he would hobble as a referee.' As Eamon continues, he is keen to point out the side of his father that he remembers. 'He was a lot more than a footballer. He lived for decades after he stopped playing. He was a father too! And a hard worker.'

Eamon goes on to describe his father's life off the pitch. 'My grandparents owned premises, which included a grocer's shop, a pub and a few attached buildings, and when my father left school, he began working in the shop, whilst his brother John ran the bar. This was the time before supermarkets, and the local women would come in the morning to put their orders through and my da would deliver their groceries that evening. Those were long hours for him and through that, everyone would have known him. He then gradually began to help John with running the pub as he was getting on in life and, with the supermarkets starting to make inroads, the grocery shop eventually closed and my da took over the bar from John. I helped out in the pub as a young lad of ten or eleven. I remember one St Patrick's Day me and my da spent the morning stocking the bar, washing the floors and all the glasses, and making sure everything was spick and span for opening. I worked the bar with him for four or five hours until 6 p.m. and Mummy came to take me home. That was one of the few times I had spent all day with my da, as he was always working very hard and long hours.'

Eamon believes his parents met at a local dance in the mid-1950s. 'Mummy came from a small townland just outside of Edendork in County Tyrone called Congo. She was the youngest of four daughters and grew up on the small family farm my grandfather had. Mummy could have talked the legs off a dead donkey; she was very outgoing and, similar to my da, everyone knew her. When they married, they lived initially on the Dungannon–Coalisland road but eventually settled in my mummy's homeplace as Granda Fox needed more care.' Jim and Gertrude, or Gertie as she was known, had welcomed their first child, Patricia, into the world in 1956, who was soon followed by her younger brothers Colm, John and Eamon. Jim and Gertie worked in the heart of the community. 'When us kids were old enough, Mummy started to work in the local library in Coalisland, and she became very well-known and liked. She helped countless people through the library and was always encouraging us to read. Mummy also became very active in the civil rights movement when it started up and took part in its very first march. I remember leaving Mass on a Sunday with her, and the short walk of fifty yards from the chapel to the car always seemed to take forever! Stopping to talk to this person or that.' Gertie and Jim, as Eamon explains, were also into their amateur dramatics. 'I remember going to the parochial hall in Coalisland to watch them in a play.

Towns and communities made their own entertainment back then, which brought everyone together. The community was a massive and defining aspect of both of their lives.' Jim and Gertie were also members of the SDLP, and spent their lives, both in and outside of work, providing service to their community.

Jim and Gertrude Devlin were shot dead by the UVF's Glenanne Gang on 7 May 1974. They were driving home with Patricia in the car, having just locked up the pub and said goodnight to Jim's brothers, John and Frank. As they came up the lane to their home, they were stopped by a figure dressed as a soldier. Gunmen then opened fire on the car. Patricia recalled the horrific details of the incident in an article in *The Irish Times* on 7 February 2021 by Gerry Moriarty. Jim and Gertrude were both killed, whilst seventeen-year-old Patricia was shot in multiple places but survived by playing dead. UVF member and British Army soldier William Thomas Leonard confessed to involvement in the killings of Jim and Gertrude some twenty months after the incident, and he also told police the names of the two gunmen involved whom he had dropped off at the Devlin house to carry out the shooting. Those individuals were not arrested or questioned because Leonard had not witnessed the shooting himself. Leonard was convicted of his involvement in 1975 and released in 1985. The killing of Jim and Gertrude Devlin is explored in Anne Cadwallader's book *Lethal Allies* and is a shocking example of collusive behaviour between the Crown forces and loyalism.

Jim Devlin's legacy in the GAA is well-recorded in the annals of Tyrone and Ulster's footballing history. In memory of one of the county's greatest talents, the Tyrone County Board commissioned the Jim Devlin Cup to be competed for at the top level by clubs across the county.

Seán McKearney (Seán Mac Cearnaigh)

AOIS/AGE: 18
CUMANN/CLUB: An Mhaigh Tír na nÓg GLC/
Tír na nÓg GAC, Moy
CONTAE/COUNTY: Tír Eoghain/Tyrone
MARAÍODH/KILLED: 13 Bealtaine, le pléasc anabaí/
13 May, premature explosion

'Seán was very funny.' Tommy and Angela begin describing their brother. 'He was a happy young lad who loved a good prank and was always quite bubbly and chatty. Very affable would probably best describe Seán; he got on with everyone, and everyone enjoyed his company. The night he was killed, before he went out, me and him were out playing football in the back garden. He was tempting me to toss the ball over the fence into the neighbour's garden and see if we could jump over and get it back before the neighbour noticed us. It was in a very jovial way, because our neighbour was an elderly man whom Seán would have helped a lot when it came to any work and tasks needed doing around his house, like lifting the vegetables he had planted. He was an easy-going personality for sure.'

Seán McKearney was born on 18 January 1956 to Maura and Kevin. He was the fourth McKearney child, growing up in the Moy, County Tyrone, with older brothers Tommy and Pádraig and older sister Margaret, and younger siblings Kevin and Angela. From the beginning, Tommy and Angela explain, football was an integral part of Seán's life, just as it was for the rest of the family. 'We've always been a family in which the GAA comes as second nature. Our father and all of his brothers played football and followed football. Even when I was a child growing up, I remember seeing my Uncle Peter playing; that was the last time The Moy contested a Senior Championship final. We would have all been taken as children to go and watch the games, and it was just a given fact that the GAA would be part of our lives.'

Before he was old enough to enter the Juvenile structures of his family club, Moy Tír na nÓg, Seán's first taste of action on the field would have come at

Moy Primary School. 'The only sport in school was football and that's where we all started out. Then, at the age of ten or eleven, you were able to start playing for the Moy club.' Tommy continues, describing early memories of himself, Pádraig and Seán playing together. 'We were only a five-minute walk to the football pitch, and summertime and Saturdays were spent on the field playing. Seán was four years younger than me, and Pádraig was two years younger, but because we hadn't a huge population in the village to draw from, we got to play on the same teams. I remember playing at u16, I was fifteen, Pádraig would have been thirteen or so, and Seán was eleven! Despite that, Seán was still the strongest and sturdiest of us all. He was well able for the football; even at that young age, he could play up a few levels with us. He was very talented.' Seán would also showcase an early prowess for football at school, and upon joining his older brothers at St Patrick's Academy in Dungannon, he immediately took his place on his year's starting fifteen. Seán's school team ranked highly through the years in the Rannafast and Ulster College's competitions, with their crowning achievement coming in 1972 when Seán and his teammates brought home the MacLarnon Cup.

Whilst football formed perhaps the defining aspect of Seán's early life, as he got into his teenage years, Angela explains how more responsibility started to come his way. 'As with all of us, as he got older, Seán started to spend his weekends helping Daddy and our uncles. Daddy had the butcher's shop, where there was always beef to be minced, sausages to be made, and all the important small jobs that come with running a shop. And if he wasn't in the shop helping, then he was with one of the uncles bringing in hay, feeding the cattle or lifting potatoes. That was how life was, and you had to do your bit to help.'

Seán eventually left St Patrick's Academy aged sixteen and went on to become a plumber at the training college in Enniskillen, where he boarded during the week. He was just over a year into his training when he died.

Seán McKearney was eighteen years old when he was killed alongside Eugene Martin (see page 292) on 13 May 1974 when a bomb they were handling exploded prematurely. He died on active service for the IRA. Seán's brothers Pádraig (see page 163) and Kevin (see page 215), and his Uncle John (see page 217), would also later die in the conflict.

Patsy Kelly (Pádraig Mac Ceallaigh)

AOIS/AGE: 35

CUMANN/CLUB: CLG Naomh Mhic Artáin, Trí Leac/ Trillick St Macartans GAC

CONTAE/COUNTY: Tír Eoghain/Tyrone

MARAÍODH/KILLED: 24 Iúil, le forsaí dílseach/ 24 July, loyalist forces

'At the heart of it, my father was a community man. He loved to help people and was always concerned with what he could do to help make the immediate lives of the people around him better.' Patrick Kelly describes his dad. 'The GAA played an integral role in my father's story, both during his life and in the legacy of his death, and the two will always be entwined.'

Patsy Kelly was born on 4 April 1939 in Trillick, in the townland of Golan, County Tyrone, a few miles from the county border with Fermanagh. He was Paddy and Rose's youngest child, growing up with sisters May, Bridie, Ethne and Annie, and brother Petey. Patsy attended his local national school in Golan, which he left aged fourteen to work, initially for a plastics factory in Enniskillen and then at the water board, a post that he held for a number of years. It was during this time that he started seeing childhood sweetheart Teresa. The pair knew one another from school but met again years later at the local dances and functions. After a few years together, Patsy and Teresa married in 1966, and shortly thereafter, having moved into the new home they had just built, their first child, Geraldine, came along. Geraldine was soon followed by Barry, Fearghal and Oonagh, and Patrick was the last. In 1974 Patsy then became co-landlord with his brother-in-law, also called Patsy Kelly, of the local pub, The Corner House. 'As a person, I suppose he found a passion for getting involved in the community. He was highly involved in the civil rights movement at a local level, and he was always seeing what he could do to help people out. That desire and sense of duty to his community eventually led to him becoming an independent councillor in Omagh District Council in 1973. There was a real sense that what really mattered to him were the bread-and-butter issues. He became involved in local politics because he cared about equality in terms of housing and employment and those fundamental everyday issues.'

The GAA was a part of Patsy's life from a young age. 'He grew up around the GAA, with Trillick St Macartans being the local club, and he would have played in the various parish leagues at that time, around Golan and the neighbouring townlands. In terms of playing ability, he wouldn't have been at the level to carry him through to Senior, but that would have never affected his passion and love for Gaelic games. The club was always in his life, him being a regular in the stands on a Sunday. When my father started managing the pub with Uncle Patsy, who was on the Senior team alongside his brother John, known as the famous Kelly Twins, he was all too delighted to be at the heart of the post-football pints, as the crowd would make their way to "the two Patsys'" bar. Those were the days when you'd have a training session or a match and go for a couple afterwards!'

Whilst the role of the GAA in Patsy's life was typical of many a Gael across Ireland, Patrick goes on to explain the extraordinary role it played in the wake of his father's death. 'My father went missing on 24 July 1974, just a fortnight or so before Trillick were due to play Ardboe in the Tyrone Championship semi-final and compete for a spot in the club's first Senior final since 1937. In those weeks before the 24th, the excitement in the village would have been palpable. When my father went missing, everything stopped. The three-week search for my father's body was then swung into effect and was driven by the local community. The GAA Hall became HQ of the search, and everything was organised from there. There were maps all laid out on the tables every morning and groups of volunteers would head out each day to search their assigned grids. There were volunteers making sandwiches and tea and making sure everybody was fuelled to go back out to search. It was a case of when something goes wrong, where did everybody congregate. It was the GAA club; everything stemmed from Trillick's Donnelly Park. It was incredible the role the GAA played at that local level, but as the search widened, the association's role became hugely important. At a county board level, the decision was taken to suspend the scheduled matches and Tyrone county board called on all of its members to mobilise and come to Trillick and help the search. People came in their droves, and soon after, Fermanagh county board made the same call of its members. GAA people from all over Ulster arrived to help with the search. Police involvement in the search was only to save face from the embarrassment of being shown up by the collective and determined volunteers from the community, of which the GAA was an integral part. Because of that role, Trillick GAA and the wider association holds a hugely important part of my family's heart; they really came to the fore and became everything you hope and believe that the GAA is.'

When the Tyrone Championship eventually resumed after Patsy Kelly's remains were found, Trillick still had to line out against Ardboe. 'When the final whistle went, I think the whole village let out this massive sigh of relief almost as Trillick won the game. My Uncle John was playing corner-back and my father's brother, Petey, came running onto the pitch and jumped on top of John and the pair fell to the ground in celebration. There is a real poignancy to that scene; that at least for those couple of seconds, it lifted the grief. It didn't change anything, and the grief would return, but football provided that brief reprieve. And it did so for the whole community, I might add.' Trillick went on to win the Tyrone Senior Football Championship in 1974 and were runners-up in the Ulster final. It was the first of five Senior Championships they would win over the next twelve years. 'The way the community reacted to the news of my father's disappearance seemed to bind people together more so than they had ever experienced. Those Trillick sides of the mid-'70s were blessed with extremely skilful players throughout the team and were destined for success regardless, but there is no doubt that a legacy of my father's killing was to have a galvanising effect on the community which had to come through that.'

Patsy Kelly was thirty-five years old when he was abducted on the night of 24 July 1974 as he locked up his bar. He was killed and weights were tied to his body, which was sunk to the bottom of Lough Eyes, some twelve miles away from Trillick. A three-week search ended when his body was discovered on the morning of 10 August by a local man who had gone out fishing. It was by complete chance that his body was discovered, the man being on the water during the short time-window where a sunken body will surface as it inflates with water, before resubmerging permanently. During the search, police had discouraged the search parties from going to Lough Eyes, stating that they had already dredged the lough. Although the UDA claimed responsibility for his killing, from the night Patsy went missing his family and the wider public more generally have considered Crown forces to be a party to his killing, attempted disappearance and the subsequent attempts at a cover-up. These suspicions were corroborated by a 2023 Police Ombudsman's report, which found evidence of collusive behaviour in the initial investigation and that Patsy's family were failed by the police. During the search for Patsy, Teresa discovered she was pregnant with their youngest child, Patrick.

'Those who did that to my father intended to disappear him and send a clear message to anyone who sought to better their community; to strike fear into Trillick and the wider area. The opposite happened. The legacy of my father's killing was the coming together of a community during a time of great loss and hurt, with the volunteers of the GAA being central to organising and helping my family. The club itself, the following year, commissioned the Patsy Kelly Memorial Cup and it is still in use by the club today in their youth tournaments. It is a huge honour to know my father is still part of the club, and that will always be a big part of his legacy.'

Ciarán Murphy (Ciarán Ó Murchadh)

AOIS/AGE: 17

CUMANN/CLUB: CLG Ciceam Ard Eoin, Béal Feirste/ Ardoyne Kickhams GAC, Belfast

CONTAE/COUNTY: Aontroim/Antrim

MARAÍODH/KILLED: 13 Deireadh Fómhair, le forsaí dílseach/13 October, loyalist forces

'Ciarán followed me into the Kickhams, as I had followed my brother before me.' Pat Murphy begins by describing his family's links to Ardoyne and the Kickhams GAA club. 'The Murphys have a long family connection with the club, and I am almost certain a distant relative of ours was one of the club's founding members.'

Ciarán Murphy was born on 19 July 1957 to Johnny and Kathleen. He was the youngest of the Murphys' six children, growing up in Strathroy Park in North Belfast with his three older sisters Kate, Ethne and Anne, and older brothers Sean and Pat. 'We [Pat and Ciarán] were the closest in age and so always very close friends.' From an early age, the Murphy boys bonded over their shared passion for football and hurling, which they inherited from their father. 'My dad always followed the club, but he couldn't kick back doors for bin men! He was more of a very engaged spectator, and he had a love for the game that he passed on to us. He would bring us to Croke Park for big games when he could, but, unfortunately, he died when we were quite young. My father had a tough life, having been interned without trial for some time. After his passing, Ciarán was like my shadow. He was ten years old or so when Dad died, and he had me tortured from then on, following me everywhere! That included following me into the Kickhams, where his initial involvement in the club was nearly like a ball boy for my team. In 1969 we won the Antrim Minor Football Championship, and in the team photo taken that day, kneeling in front of Raymond Mooney [see page 158] is our Ciarán! He grew into a fantastic asset for the club as he eventually reached an age where he could play.'

Before he began playing for the Kickhams at u16, however, Ciarán was able to sharpen his abilities on the field at school. Attending Holy Cross Primary

School, he received his initial coaching from the Christian Brothers and his school team won the Cumann na mBunscol Championship in 1968. 'He was at St Gabriel's Secondary School when he eventually started playing for Ardoyne Kickhams. By that stage, he stuck out like a sore thumb compared to his peers. At thirteen, he was over six feet tall! It would put you in mind of that movie *Elf*. And a great set of hands he had on him too, so it was inevitable that he was to be made goalkeeper for his football team. I would describe him as a steady-Eddie footballer; the type of player clubs are made of. Someone okay at underage but who, if encouraged to keep at it, will shine come Senior. I always thought our Ciarán was a better hurler than a footballer anyway. He played outfield in hurling and was quite talented for a big lad. He played up until Minor level, and as the story goes with most lads at that age, he started to enjoy the more social aspects of life too, and the GAA took a bit of a back seat.'

Outside of the GAA, Ciarán was a fantastically well-known figure in the Ardoyne area. 'He started working when he should have been in school, "beaking-off" and working under a local spark as a spool boy and projectionist at a local picture house, as well as learning to become a spark. He then got his certifications and began fitting new builds with electrical central heating. He drove a wee van for his work, and everyone knew him and his van. He would have spotted anybody from Ardoyne standing about waiting for a taxi or bus and make sure to give them a lift. He was very conscious that the conflict was on and wouldn't want people standing around alone. He'd pile everybody in and arrive into Ardoyne with sometimes six or seven people in the back of his van! Ciarán very much enjoyed looking out for people. I suppose he was very outgoing in that sense, and indeed he loved heading out socialising with his friends. He thought he was a cross between Rod Stewart and Leo Sayer, with his hair and fashion, and he loved to dance. He was very confident with himself, and, in fairness, he was very striking looking. He was just over 6ft 2in. and 14½ stone and he was always chasing a girl.' Pat laughs, 'I remember at his funeral, all these different girls arriving thinking they were the only one for him! We had a good laugh at that.'

Ciarán had a great impact on the people he met. As a natural charmer and possessing a rare affability, Pat explains that people would still come up to him to say they knew Ciarán well, even after forty years. 'I remember at my son Niall's christening, Ciarán was the godfather, and he was running around like he was the da, with a pocket full of cigars handing them out, telling people how proud he was. He did the same when he was best man at my wedding. We had some craic.'

Ciarán Murphy was seventeen years old when he was abducted and killed by the UVF on 13 October 1974. He was enjoying a night out with his friends, and when he was walking home from the bar, loyalists came upon him. They bundled him into the back of a car and eventually shot him. Aubrey Tarr was convicted of Ciarán's killing, but his family have strong evidence indicating that agents of the British State were also involved in his killing. 'Our Ciarán punched his weight as the saying goes, and if he'd been sober that night, I dare say he would still be alive and those lads who grabbed him would have got a good kicking.'

Ciarán's name is still mentioned around the Kickhams club as a player who would have been an incredible asset to their Senior set-up, and his family continue to play a pivotal role in their cherished club. Pat has managed numerous football teams over the years, and the younger generations of the Murphy clan continue to line out in the black and white of Ardoyne Kickhams.

Hugh Gerard Coney (Aodh Gearóid Ó Cuana)

AOIS/AGE: 24

CUMANN/CLUB: Ó Rathaille Chluain Eo CLG/
Clonoe O'Rahilly's GAC

CONTAE/COUNTY: Tír Eoghain/Tyrone

MARAÍODH/KILLED: 6 Samhain, Arm na Breataine/
6 November, British Army

'Gerard was a character alright. As young lads we used to go picking blackberries for the boys who would come every week to buy them off us for two shillings a stone. We'd be sent by our mother up the field to collect them, but that meant having to get past the big bull that lived in the field. One time, Gerard must have only been five or six, I was first across the field and up past the bull, but when Gerard went, he got caught out. The bull had Gerard in its sights, and he ran back over the gate terrified of the thing.' James Coney describes the cherished story of how his younger brother got his nickname. 'Everyone started laughing, singing "cowardly cowardly custard", and from then he always got the nickname "Cowardly Coney"; it's even written on his headstone, although I couldn't think of a less appropriate nickname for the young man he became.'

Hugh Gerard Coney was born to parents James and Kitty. He grew up in Annaghmore, along with his brothers Frank and James, and sisters Collette and Noelle. Gerard played football for the club whose pitch sat directly across the road from his house, Clonoe O'Rahilly's. James jnr recalls his youth being spent running around the football field, with himself and Gerard playing football from the time they could hold a ball. 'We weren't a traditional GAA family as such; our father would have gone to the county games and to Ulster finals and that, but he never played as far as I'm aware. However, all the children played. Gerard played football his whole life, and while I was maybe not as talented on the field, I was on the club committee for thirty years, helping with the structures and organisation side of things. The GAA certainly became part of our everyday lives.' Indeed, Gerard knew success from a young age, where in school he played his part in bringing home the Schools Championship in 1964, the same year the Senior team of O'Rahilly's brought home their fourth County Championship.

Whilst Gerard had an undoubted love for football, his real talent lay in billiards and snooker. From when he was a teenager, he would go every day to Gervin's Pool Hall to chalk his cue. 'He was a talented young player. When I was working in London, he came over to stay with me to compete in a British and Irish Isles Billiards Championship. He was representing the

North of Ireland, having won the domestic tournaments at only sixteen or seventeen; he lost in the quarter-final to the eventual winner.' Deciding to stay in England with his brother James, Gerard found himself a job with Wall's Ice Cream. 'He wouldn't join me on the building site as Wall's was a very handy job for him; selling ice cream was far more attractive than slaving away on some worksite. He came back home in 1969 when trouble broke out and I followed him. He was best man at my wedding the following year, shortly before being interned.'

As the conflict began to break out, Gerard decided to join the IRA. In 1971 he was arrested and imprisoned without trial under the policy of internment. With an indefinite prison sentence hanging over him, Gerard decided to become involved in a plan to escape the prison camps. On 6 November 1974, Gerard and other Volunteers of the IRA climbed through their hand-dug tunnel out into the field outside of the prison walls. As Gerard emerged from the tunnel and began running to safety, he was spotted by a British Army lookout. He was shot in the back and killed instantly. In 2024 an inquest found that Gerard was unarmed and posed no threat when he was shot dead.

Patrick Falls (Pádraig Mac Pháil)

AOIS/AGE: 49

CUMANN/CLUB: Washingbay Shamrocks; Ó Rathaille Chluain Eo CLG/Washingbay Shamrocks GAC; Clonoe O'Rahilly's GAC

CONTAE/COUNTY: Tír Eoghain/Tyrone

MARAÍODH/KILLED: 20 Samhain, le forsaí dílseach/ 20 November, loyalist forces

'Daddy loved playing football. He grew up on the shores of Lough Neagh beside the football field and on some match days the kick of the ball could be heard from Daddy's bedroom window when he was

studying for his exams.' The Falls family begin to describe the role of the GAA in their father's life.

Patrick Falls was born to Peter and Margaret on 19 March 1925 in Drumglass House, Dungannon. The fifth child in a family of eleven children, Patrick grew up in the townland of Aughamullan, County Tyrone. Patrick's parents owned and ran the local pub, shop and post office, and also tended the family farm with the help of their growing children. As a young lad, Pat and his brothers spent their days on the football field for their local club Washingbay Shamrocks. 'The sound of the game would travel along the shore and the flat bogland right into the house.' Patrick's passion for football followed him to school, where he saw top-level success in the Ulster College's competition. 'Our father left primary school and went to St Patrick's Academy, Dungannon, initially, which would have been a twenty-mile round cycle each day, before going on to St Patrick's College in Armagh to board for his final two years.' Whilst studying at St Patrick's College, Pat was part of a 1943–44 MacRory Cup-winning panel that also included Jim Devlin (see page 56). 'He was so proud of that achievement, and it was often brought up in conversation. His uncle had previously won the same competition in 1919! Alongside school football, he was also playing club football for Clonoe O'Rahilly's as Washingbay Shamrocks had folded at that time.' Pat played right half-back, and at club level he was usually tasked with marking his MacRory Cup teammate Iggy Jones.

When Pat left school, he qualified as a pharmacist in Belfast and then he sought work in England. 'While he was working in England, he came home on holiday in 1957 and met our mother, Maureen Quinn from Galbally, County Tyrone, in Belfast City Hospital. After that chance encounter with Maureen, our father returned to work in England and, following frequent correspondence with friends and enquiring about Maureen Quinn, he then returned home to Ireland and they were married in 1960.' The newlywed couple brought Aidan and Brian into the world before moving to Castlereagh, just outside Belfast. 'Our father decided to start his own pharmacy in the mainly Protestant Braniel estate in Castlereagh. However, it didn't flourish. Being a Catholic-run business in a mostly Protestant area [locals would not patronise his pharmacy for sectarian reasons], the pharmacy became a target for repeated arson attacks, so we moved to the Ormeau Road in South Belfast and he worked in the Co-op in Andersonstown. When we lived there, our daddy would walk to Corrigan Park and travel to Croke Park with his brothers to watch the football.'

With a growing family – daughters Carmel, Fiona, Colette and Brenda had followed their two sons – Pat and Maureen believed they could make a better life for themselves in England and in 1971 the family moved to Birmingham. 'We loved it there, and our parents were very happy living in Handsworth, Birmingham. They were very active, being involved in the local Irish centre and the church, where we all made a lot of lifelong friends. We had the best parents in the world; they made sure we had a very happy and full life growing up, with singing, dancing, piano and football. Our family were very settled and happy in Birmingham; Mummy particularly loved it there, while Daddy worked as a pharmacist, but he always longed to return home to Aughamullan. Our parents were characters and they were both the life and soul of every social gathering. This was reflected in how they were cherished and loved by the many friends they made there; it was just a great community feeling in Birmingham, especially with all the Irish emigration.'

Home, however, was never far from Pat's mind, especially when it came to football. 'He had this old radio he could get the football on and often he could be seen listening intently to the football matches playing in the background. He was very fond of the commentary of Michael O'Hehir, and he would also ask his brother John to send him the local newspapers every single week so he could stay abreast of the latest scores and fixtures back home. Both our parents had a great love of football. Mummy had been a great supporter of her local club in Galbally, the Galbally Pearses GAC, and as a family we were all encouraged to support our County Tyrone team, which we continue to do to this day … We think our daddy always had in his head that he was coming home eventually, and that opportunity came in the summer of 1974.'

Pat's brother, Joe, decided he was going to retire. Joe had taken over the family business in Aughamullan, and when he asked Pat if he would like to take it over so that he could retire, it seemed to Pat like a dream come true. 'We remember it being a very big decision with much deliberation for our parents.

They were happy with their lives in Birmingham and so our parents decided that Daddy would come home himself for a few weeks to test it out, with a view to go ahead if he thought he could support his family with the business he was to own. Mummy and the family had planned to follow Daddy home to Ireland shortly afterwards.'

Pat Falls was killed on 20 November 1974 by the Glenanne Gang, comprised of members of the British Army, RUC and UVF paramilitaries. He had been home for only two weeks when gunmen attacked his family pub, called Falls' Pub, in Aughamullan. Pat was working behind the bar that night and he and Maureen had decided that they could make the return to Ireland work for their family, with the paperwork due to be signed by Pat the day after he was killed. Pat's grieving and devastated family, Maureen and the children, accompanied by her late brother Paul Quinn, came home immediately from Birmingham and eventually moved into the house Pat had planned to build for his family coming home in 1974.

Pat, Maureen and their family's dream of a wonderful life back in Ireland sadly never came to fruition with the tragic loss of their much-loved and devoted husband and father, and, with that, their family business.

Maureen sadly passed away on 7 December 2020, a much-loved and devoted wife, mother and grandmother of eight.

The GAA has always been important in Pat's family. His sons, Aidan and Brian, played for Kevin Barrys GAC in the 1970s and the family band represented Derrytresk Fir An Chnoic GAC in the Scór na nÓg. The GAA tradition continues as Pat's grandchildren play a big part in their respective codes for their clubs. 'You can see our father's passion for the GAA has filtered down through the generations and that's something we as a family are very proud of.'

1975

Owen Boyle (Eoin Ó Baoighill)

AOIS/AGE: 41

CUMANN/CLUB: Achadh Lú Uí Néill CLG/ Aghaloo O'Neills GFC

CONTAE/COUNTY: Tír Eoghain/Tyrone

MARAÍODH/DIED: 22 Aibreán, le forsaí dílseach/ 22 April, loyalist forces

'Daddy would have grown up in a big céilí house, filled with music and singing.' Angela paints the background of her father's formative years. 'Daddy himself was a great singer and I often remember him in the car driving and singing as we toured the old roads everywhere. A few of his siblings lived in England and he went over for a wedding one time. It ended up that he and a few siblings went into a recording studio and recorded a song together. We still have the single record lying about somewhere! He was very good.'

Owen Boyle was born on 7 July 1933 to John and Mary. He grew up with his ten siblings just outside of the town of Aughnacloy in County Tyrone. His parents were farmers and Owen would have grown up working and helping around the family farm, instilling in him a strong work ethic, which he brought with him as he matured into adult life. Having finished his student years at Golan's Primary School, Owen went to work at a local blacksmith's, where he developed a keen interest in engineering that ultimately led to him setting up his own agricultural engineering business. 'Daddy was a seriously hard worker and would have started to see the results of that hard work pay off, where he was getting business internationally. He met my mummy, Winifred, at the dances and Mummy always laughs that he was the only one with a car at that time. We'd all love listening to the stories of Daddy taking Mummy to football games in Clones and the likes when they first met and started going out. Mummy had no interest in football, even though her brothers played, and went along just for the spin. When they arrived, Mummy would take herself for a walk around the town and tour the local graveyards and chapels while Daddy was watching the match! They married in 1960 and that's when we all came along.' First was Úna, quickly followed by Angela, Kieran, Terence, Aidan, Denis, Carmel and Noreen. His children were Owen's world and through his hard work, he was able to build his young family a new home closer to Aughnacloy town, which he mostly built himself and which the family were able to move into in 1973.

Owen's involvement in the GAA was initially limited, in that his parish had no club. 'Aughnacloy was a mostly Protestant town, so the GAA never got going while Daddy was growing up. Although, he would have been a big follower of football and would have followed Tyrone through the championship campaigns. He became directly involved in the GAA when it was proposed that a club be set up in Aughnacloy. Daddy immediately got behind the initiative and became a founder member of Aghaloo GAC, which was established in 1970. He was too old to play for the club, but he threw himself into organising games and events, and of course that meant that all of us were immediately involved too. All of us kids played camogie and football, and we all became lifelong Gaels.' Owen served in a variety of different roles for Aghaloo, including a brief stint as club treasurer, and was a volunteer his club knew they could rely on. Owen's love for the GAA fed down through the subsequent generations of his family, with the playing careers of his children and grandchildren peppered with county appearances for Tyrone, Monaghan and Limerick, as well as his family being represented in successful GAA teams abroad, including in San Francisco, Canada and in Aussie Rules in Australia. Most recently, one of Owen's grandchildren captained her university football team, TUS Midwest, to All-Ireland Colleges success. 'In a way, us all being so involved in the GAA keeps his memory and legacy alive, and that is so important to us. But at the same time, it's also quite difficult because Daddy was denied the chance to watch his grandchildren play and enjoy seeing his family's connections with the GAA deepen. He really would have loved all of it, and to see the success of all his grandchildren would have been so special for him.'

On 11 April 1975 Owen Boyle was standing in the kitchen of his new home when he was shot through his window by a UVF gunman. Angela and her siblings were in the living room when their father was struck. The eldest, Úna, was thirteen years old and the youngest, Noreen, was six months. Owen died eleven days later, on 22 April, aged forty-one. It is widely believed that UVF member and part-time British Army soldier Robin Jackson was responsible for Owen's killing.

John McGleenan (Eoin Mac Giolla Fhinein)

AOIS/AGE: 45
CUMANN/CLUB: Uí Néill CLG, An Port Mór/ O'Neill's GFC, Blackwatertown
CONTAE/COUNTY: Ard Mhacha/Armagh
MARAÍODH/KILLED: 22 Lúnasa, le fórsaí dílseach/ 22 August, loyalist forces

'I often remember summers of us all squeezing into the car, following the Armagh team up and down the province and sometimes even lucky enough to go to Clones to watch our county play in the Ulster Championship.' Sean McGleenan recalls the fond memories that come to his mind of his father's love for the GAA. 'He played until his mid-twenties, which for those days was considered old to be lining out on the football pitch. And while he maybe wasn't as able for the football in later life, he couldn't keep away from sport, always an avid spectator at club football across the county and he also got involved in "Bullets" or road bowls.'

John was born and reared in Ballytroddan, a small townland which lies on the Armagh side of the county's border with Tyrone. Born in 1929, he was one of ten children and was first involved in the GAA once clubs began reforming and reopening following the end of the Second World War. Initially, John played for The Grange, St Colmcille's, until, in 1947, his local club in Blackwatertown was able to reform after years of its pitch being used to grow flax for the war.

The reformed club did not have to wait long before seeing success. Playing wing full-forward, John helped the club to the 1954 Armagh Junior Championship, having been runners-up in 1952. That same year, John would marry his wife, Maura, and the couple would start a family together, having six kids in all: Mary, Sean, Roisín, Michael, Brian (who died at birth) and Fíona. Originally a strawberry farmer, John eventually found himself running his own pub, McGleenan's Bar, in Armagh city, which became one of the few bars in Armagh whose patrons were both Catholic and Protestant. Despite the family no longer living in the townland, John made sure his children played for his family club, An Port Mór.

Naturally, as he got older, John's GAA days as a player became fewer, but his son Sean recalls that although his boots were hung up, they were never allowed to dry. 'Back in the '70s, rural areas used to run sports days where local clubs would all come together to play each other and, in the lead-up to the big final on the Sunday, there would be a week-long football tournament. As part of that, they ran games for the older men of the clubs, and I can always remember going along to watch my father take part in those games, only to look at his feet and see he had been wearing my boots.' John also tried his hand at Bullets, where his legacy now lives on since the 2019 naming of Féile Phobail Ard Mhacha's u14 Girls Road-Bowls Cup in his honour. The first winner of the John McGleenan Cup was his youngest granddaughter.

On the day John was killed, he was doing the door of his busy pub, while his daughter Mary, who was finishing up her last year at St Mary's University College in Belfast, was working behind the bar. Two loyalist gunmen from the Glenanne Gang killed John as they forced entry into the bar, opening fire once inside and planting a bomb, which exploded as they ran to a getaway car. Patrick Hughes and Thomas Morris were also killed in the attack, while many others were injured.

John's teammate from the successful 1954 Junior Championship side, Robert McCullough, would be killed by the Glenanne Gang the following year, in 1976. In dedication to the memory of the two teammates who helped deliver the club's first championship since reforming after the Second World War, the McGleenan/McCullough Memorial Cup was held in 1978, which was contested between Armagh and Tyrone.

Sean Farmer (Seán Mac Scolóige)

AOIS/AGE: 32

CUMANN/CLUB: CLG Roibeard Eiméid, Cluain Mhór/ Clonmore Robert Emmets GFC

CONTAE/COUNTY: Ard Mhacha/Armagh

MARAÍODH/KILLED: 24 Lúnasa, le forsaí dílseach/ 24 August, loyalist forces

'The GAA is what the people of Clonmore have always had to hang on to. It means everything to a small parish like ours.' Brian Farmer, Sean's brother, explains the role of the GAA in the life of his family. 'Our house was HQ after every game. Us lads, our da and uncles, and all of our cousins. Each game would be replayed minute-by-minute. God, I remember I was playing, and I hate to admit it, but I missed two penalties in the same game. We lost by a single point. I was dreading coming home that evening for the post-mortem. I knew Sean, my da, and everyone else would be waiting. When you won, it was fantastic and everybody was full of praise, but if you lost, you just wished the ground to swallow you up on the walk home. Ma would usually lose her patience after the first couple of hours and eventually break it up and send everyone away. Football. That's what we had. It was, and is, integral to the community.'

Sean Farmer was born in 1943 to John and Lena. He was the eldest of three boys, growing up in the hamlet of Clonmore, County Armagh, with his brothers Brian and Nishi. 'We were all football mad. Our da played for Clonmore back in the '30s and '40s in midfield, but the team struggled to field in later years and the club folded for a while, so Sean's first involvement with club football was actually with the neighbouring team of Killyman, across the Blackwater and into Tyrone, which he joined in '64. Before that, he would have started playing football at the local primary school in Clonmore. In those days, the pupils would have all cycled seven miles out to Dungannon to play the CBS. Eventually, our da and a few others got the Clonmore club back up in '66, and that's where we all played our football. Da always encouraged us to. Even when we were all out in the hay field, no matter how much work was still left to do, our da would shout at us to get into the van and go to the football. He'd near push us out of the field to make sure we didn't miss a game.'

Away from the football, Sean left Clonmore Primary School at fourteen to start working with a local man who ran a laundry business. 'That's where he met Margaret. I remember when they first started going out. He had the Teddy Boy look, with the winklepickers and the hair. Sean was big into his jiving, and he would always jive about the kitchen with the broom. Ma would shout at him and call him a big eejit.' Sean was twenty-one years old when he married Margaret, and they welcomed their first child, Dessie, into the world in 1966. The young family lived initially in Sean's family home in Clonmore before they found a house in Moy village in County Tyrone. It wasn't long before Shane, Brendan, Paul and Mary-Martha all came along. The lads describe their father as very hard-working. 'He worked as a digger driver building roads and had a job on the M1 when it was being constructed. He was always away before we were up and was back late in the evening. We would have spent a short time with him before going to bed.'

'I remember our da always going out to the football. He would have followed Clonmore to every game, even after he stopped playing. I remember a game he was doing umpire for, and we were there beside him just kicking a ball, and him shouting, "Get that ball off the pitch!" Mummy was a nurse and when anyone got a serious injury, the first port of call was to go see Margaret. We were very young then, but I remember always being around the football.'

Sean Farmer was killed on 24 August 1975 by the UVF's Glenanne Gang. He was killed alongside his friend and colleague Colm McCartney (see page 292). The pair were making their way home from Croke Park, having gone to Dublin to watch the All-Ireland Football semi-final, when their car was stopped by a bogus checkpoint set up by the loyalist gang. Their bodies were found at the side of a road in Altnamackin, close to Newtownhamilton, County Armagh. The circumstances of Sean and Colm's deaths have been closely examined by Desmond Fahy in his book *Death on a Country Road*, and also visually retold in the award-winning documentary *Unquiet Graves*. The conclusion that their deaths were a result of collusion between British Crown forces and the UVF has been inescapable for all those who have examined the incident, including the Historical Enquiries Team. Sean's killing was the second time tragedy had struck his family that year, as his daughter, Mary-Martha, died just two months previously from illness.

'When we were at the football, we missed having our father at the games. You would see the other das on the sidelines shouting and encouraging, and it's sad that we never really got that. Although there were definitely lads, I'm sure, during those games who wished their das weren't there, as they did more shouting than encouraging! But football was always a connection to our da. We all played our whole lives and are still involved. Although we played for The Moy because we lived across the road from that club, we also maintained our connection with Clonmore and played for them too from u14 to Minor when Clonmore were getting their youth teams set up. I remember pulling on the green and gold jersey of Clonmore for the first time. You stood six inches taller. There was just so much pride in being that next generation of the Farmers to play.' Brendan interrupts Dessie, joking, 'And then you would remember there was a number 18 on the back!'

The GAA continues to play an important role in the lives of the Farmer family. Not only do all of Sean's sons continue their involvement with their clubs, including as far afield as the Easts GAA club in Brisbane, where Shane played for almost a decade, but so too do his grandchildren. Sean's brother, Nishi, was a talented footballer, playing for Armagh Minors in the late 1960s, whilst his other brother, Brian, emigrated to Canada in 1975 and became a massive organiser for the GAA abroad, serving as the president of the Canada GAA Board for twenty-one years.

Brian explains how the GAA has been, and will remain, a strong link to his brother. 'The day he was killed, Derry were playing Dublin in the Championship semi-final in Croke Park, and Sean had also gone to see the Tyrone Minors play in the game before. Over the years I have been to a great number of All-Ireland Football finals, and when the Artane Boys Band parade around the pitch and "Amhrán na bhFiann" plays, I can't help but think back to Sean and Colm. I imagine them in Croke Park that day, just soaking up the whole build-up to the game, and that's when the tears form and a tingle goes right down my spine. I take that moment before the game throws in to say a prayer for Sean and Colm.'

Denis Mullen (Donncha Ó Maoláin)

AOIS/AGE: 36

CUMANN/CLUB: CLG Uí Raithilligh, Tailte an Cholaiste/ Collegeland O'Rahillys GAC

CONTAE/COUNTY: Ard Mhacha/Armagh

MARAÍODH/KILLED: 1 Meán Fómhair, le forsaí dílseach/ 1 September, loyalist forces

'My father lived for the GAA.' Denise Mullen begins to describe her father's passion for Gaelic games. 'I can remember us driving along the Armagh Road in his burgundy Austin 1100 and passing a football field on the right-hand side of the road, where there was a game being played. He pulled the car in and we jumped out and watched the match. He probably didn't even know who was playing, but the love of the game pulled him in. He didn't smoke or drink; instead, football and hurling were his things.'

Denis Mullen, or Dinny as he was known, was born on 31 December 1938 to Ellen and Christopher. He was originally from Dún Laoghaire in County Dublin, where he grew up with his sisters, Anne and Geraldine, and his brother, Joe, until the age of nine, when his parents separated. The separation process resulted in the three younger children going into care, until their maternal grandmother, Mary, took Denis and Geraldine into her care. Mary brought her grandchildren to live with her in Collegeland in County Armagh, and that is where Denis spent the rest of his childhood and early adult life. Settling into a new life in Collegeland, Denis was helped not only by joining the local primary school, St Peter's, but also by joining his local GAA club, Collegeland O'Rahillys. Whilst early memories of Denis's involvement in the club have faded, Denise explains that her father developed a passion and love for his club and the GAA from a very early age, which could perhaps even have begun in Dublin, and carried it with him through his life. As he progressed through the age groups of the club and reached Senior level, Denis was part of the 1956 Armagh Junior Championship-winning side for Collegeland.

'He had a very tough upbringing and that shaped the man he became. There is no doubt that the GAA provided an escape for him. A few years ago, a gentleman called with me and presented me with a photo of my father in the Collegeland team, along with some background information on the photo. He explained that whilst my father was living with his grandmother and her adult family, they were a poor family, and certainly didn't show kindness, respect or care to my father. He pointed out that my father actually played with two different jerseys tied together. In the photo, the rest of the team can be seen in full kits and my father has two tops stretched across him, and, in a way, it was very sore for me to learn that. But if you look at his face in the photo, you can see the smile from ear to ear and see just how proud he is to be playing for his club. And that, I think, shows you the type of man he was.'

Denis's playing days came to an end when he made the decision to emigrate to Birmingham in search of work. He eventually landed a job as a bus conductor, having initially worked in the hospital there, but, as Denise explains, he remained unsettled in Birmingham. 'He had met my mother a number of years before he emigrated to England, and when he moved away, they kept in touch for a while by writing letters to each other. It sort of fizzled out until one day he landed at my mother's front door, and the rest is history. They were married within a few months and my mother went over to Birmingham with him. They lived there for about four years, and my mother always recalls how football was still a massive part of their lives. When there was a championship game on, especially Armagh, groups of their other Irish friends in Birmingham would come to the house to listen to the game. Everyone would arrive early and my mother would be up making tea and sandwiches. It was an all-day affair, and there could have been twenty of them squeezed into the living room for the game.' Indeed, Olive is herself a passionate follower of the GAA, and Denise explains that she comes from strong footballing stock, having had two of her brothers play for Tyrone in the 1950s, and with two of her nephews playing for the Tyrone Senior footballers in the 1980s.

Denis and Olive decided to return to Ireland to start a family, moving initially back to The Moy, County Tyrone, where they welcomed their first child, Denise, into the world in 1971, followed by her younger brother, Edward, three years later. Starting their new life together, Denis found work as an ambulance controller for South Tyrone, and as Denise describes, he was only too eager to return to the GAA. 'Daddy went straight back to the Collegeland club when he got home. Although he was no longer playing, he never missed a match and was always there to lend himself wherever he could. Daddy also had a great love for hurling; he was engrossed by it, and he would go to Croke Park as often as he could to go see semi-finals and finals. He bought a ten-year ticket for the hurling, and I often wonder did that love for it come from his time in Dublin, as there would have been little hurling in our part of Tyrone and Armagh.'

As Denise continues to talk about her father, she describes a kind, caring and loving father who adored every minute of being a parent. 'I think because of his very difficult childhood, he was very conscious of trying to make the best life for his own family. He adored his family and only ever wanted the best for us. I remember a neighbour telling me that my father would often be seen pushing the pram around the village, which he remarked that most men in the early '70s wouldn't be caught dead doing. But it always stuck with me that things like that would have never bothered him because he was so very family orientated. He was a big, gentle giant.' Denis's placid nature also complemented his passion for his community. Both Denis and Olive were civil rights activists and both were very active members of the newly formed SDLP, and they threw themselves into helping their neighbours.

'He was very involved in the community and very passionate about helping people. He would have helped people in getting jobs and housing, and he and Mother worked as a team to help so many local people who were being denied a basic living. So many people have told me over the years that they wouldn't have their homes or got their first decent-paid job without my parents' input.

He was a real people's person and people took to him, and he would happily give up his time to help anyone struggling. His personality and warm heart warranted him being the face of sorting issues in the community, while behind the scenes it was my mother, Olive, who was completing housing and job application forms and advising my father on the course of action required. They made a strong team!'

Denis Mullen was thirty-six years old when, on the night of 1 September 1975, he was shot dead in his own home. Denis was called on to open the front door, and upon doing so, Garfield Beattie, a leading member of the UVF and a member of the British Army, shot him with a machine gun taken from a British Army base. Another gunman fired thirteen shots at Olive as she fled out a rear window and across a field. Upon hearing the noise, four-year-old Denise came out of her bedroom and discovered her father lying dead on the doorstep of their home. The group sent to kill Denis and Olive that night consisted of three members of the British Army and one member of the RUC. All were members of the UVF's Glenanne Gang. Beattie served sixteen years for Denis's killing, and one of the guns used in the attack was used four weeks earlier in the Miami Showband Massacre.

Denise remains connected to the Collegeland O'Rahilly's club, and the Mullen family keep Denis's passion for the GAA alive. 'I remember on the thirtieth anniversary of the Junior Championship win, the whole team was being honoured by the club. It was a very emotional night, not only for us as a family, but also for Daddy's teammates, as my eleven-year-old brother, Eddie, went up to receive two plaques on behalf of his father's sportsmanship and team playing. The club meant everything to him, and I, too, am proud to be a member.' Denise herself followed in her parents' footsteps, not only in instilling a love for the GAA within her own children, but also in becoming active within her community, serving as a councillor in Mid Ulster for ten years. She is also a passionate and vocal campaigner for victims and survivors of the conflict across Ireland.

1976

Brian Reavey (Brían Ó Riabhaigh)

AOIS/AGE: 21

CUMANN/CLUB: Naomh Cillian CLG, Crois Bán/ St Killian's GAC, Whitecross

CONTAE/COUNTY: Ard Mhacha/Armagh

MARAÍODH/KILLED: 4 Eanáir, le forsaí dílseach/ 4 January, loyalist forces

'We were out training in the field one night, preparing for the start of the '69 Championship. Brian was only u16 at the time, but he was out with us.' Eugene begins describing a fond memory of his talented younger brother. 'So, I'm out in the field, and I'm standing with my hands up, waiting for the highball to come down. The next thing, young Brian is up over my shoulder, his backside in line with me head! And as quick as that, he was away with the ball. I said to myself, "God! Where'd that fella come from?" At that time, everybody played football static, but not Brian. He was part of a new generation of footballers forging a modern way of play, receiving a new type of coaching at school. I'm telling you; he could have gone up into the clouds to catch a ball!'

Brian Reavey was born on 9 March 1953 to Jimmy and Sadie. He was the eighth child in a family of twelve children. He grew up in the village of Whitecross, County Armagh with his brothers Seamus, Frank, Eugene, Oliver, John Martin, Anthony and Paul, and sisters Kathleen, Eileen, Úna and Colleen. From a young age, it was obvious that Brian was a natural athlete. 'He was a great sportsman. Any competition outside, whether it was sprinting the 100 yards or running the five-mile, or whether it was the high jump or the long jump, Brian won them all through school. I remember one time St Killian's put on a twenty-mile run as a fundraiser for the club. At that stage, all of us would have been fit and able, but Brian was still home and dry an hour and a half before everybody else!'

Just like the generations of Reavey men before him, Brian played his football for St Killian's, Whitecross. As Eugene describes the days of Brian's youth, the conditions for moulding a great footballer become obvious. 'We

Reaveys maybe weren't the biggest men on the football field, Brian particularly so, but we could make a good player look very ordinary! Brian would have grown up playing out in the field with us older lads and he'd have gotten no preferential treatment, and that would have toughened him up.' Brian quickly learned his trade from his older, more experienced brothers. 'He was a half-back, and by the age of sixteen, he was playing for Armagh Minors and Senior football for the club! The year of that '69 Championship was when he started breaking into the Senior squad, with my father as the joint manager. He was the link between the defenders and the forwards before there was ever any word of that sort of role. We ended that season as Armagh Junior Football champions.'

However, Brian's early promotion to Senior football was not without its risk. His youth and smaller physical size exposed him to a new level of physical demand, for which no amount of toughening up from playing with his older brothers could have prepared him. 'When Brian started playing Senior, he'd be playing against big, rough fellas from around Armagh, and they would always leave the big arm out and hit him. Brian would usually come flying up to the big defenders, show them the ball, then he'd be away on by them; but not all the time, and when they got a hold of him, oh, it was rough! There was one time he was brought to hospital and the doctor, having viewed the X-ray, asked me if Brian was hit with a sledgehammer. He didn't believe me when I said it was a loose fist at the football.'

As he progressed and got used to the increased physical demand, Brian then made the Armagh u21 squad, aged eighteen, and established himself as a full Senior footballer for Whitecross, but he was to become, in a certain sense, a victim of his own success, in that his opposition's inability to deal with the threat he posed on the pitch oftentimes resulted in him being on the receiving end of reckless and callous challenges. 'When he was eighteen, we were playing a local, rival team, and Brian had been running riot the whole game. And I mean running riot. I was in corner-back, Seamus was No. 5, Oliver was No. 7, and Brian was No. 10. They couldn't deal with his speed, so a fella went in on him and broke his leg.' Brian put himself through a whole rehabilitation process and bounced back from his injury in a relatively short recovery period, but when he returned to football and went back out to play, he found himself lining out against the same opposition. 'He went back out to play, when he recovered, against the same team, and the same incident happened again. We nearly killed the fella responsible. And poor Brian, that challenge put a stop to his county football. The recovery of the second break took a long time, but when he came back to play club football, thankfully, he was as good as he ever was!'

Off the pitch, Brian was like any other young lad his age. He attended his local primary school in Whitecross before heading to St Paul's, Bessbrook. It was at St Paul's that Brian was exposed to the modern way of coaching, which gave him an edge at club level. On leaving school, he went on to become a talented joiner, which was of surprise to no one in the Reavey house, as Brian had always shown a keen talent for mending and making things with his hands. 'He was very intelligent and had great hands on him for helping around the house. He was always making small projects when he was growing such as making craft art.' In his late teens, Brian met a young girl called Alice and the pair started seeing one another, heading out to the local dances and enjoying their young lives together.

Brian Reavey was twenty-two years old when he was killed on 4 January 1976 by the Glenanne Gang. He had only arrived at the house fifteen to twenty minutes before the gunmen, having dropped Alice in to work at Daisy Hill Hospital that evening. He came in and was sitting on the arm of the sofa, watching the TV with his brothers John Martin and Anthony, when gunmen followed him into the family home and opened fire. Brian and John Martin (see page 90) were killed where they sat. Anthony (see page 93) later died on 30 January.

On the day Brian was to be married, Alice and his family visited the graves of John Martin, Brian and Anthony. They were met by British soldiers. 'There were soldiers in the graveyard, who became very hostile and nasty towards Alice and my family. There was also a group of young girls going to confession in the chapel nearby. The next thing, a soldier, lying on his stomach with a heavy machine gun mounted on a tripod, fired a shot. It struck one of the young girls. That young girl was Majella O'Hare, and she died on her way to hospital.

Alice had tried to save her but was beaten back by the soldiers as she tried her best to administer care to the young girl.'

The crowd in attendance at his funeral was testament to the calibre of person Brian was. 'There were football men from across the country at that funeral. Every club in Armagh was represented that day. People would come up and introduce themselves, and when asked how they knew the lads, it was invariably through football. Each person would laugh that their memory of Brian was running around a pitch for sixty minutes, trying to catch him, but they never could!' St Killian's honoured the memory of Brian, John Martin and Anthony on the twenty-fifth anniversary of their deaths by hosting an event in their honour. Amongst the star-studded crowd in attendance was then-GAA President Seán McCague. The Reavey family presented their club with a plaque and a match was played between Donegal and an Armagh select panel, which included Eamon Reavey, a nephew of the Reavey brothers and then captain of the Whitecross team. Brian is depicted alongside John Martin and Anthony in a recent film, *Reavey Brothers*, directed by their nephew John Reavey. Eugene Reavey has recently published a book detailing the story of his brothers. It is a compendium of his family's ongoing quest for truth and justice and serves as essential reading for the direct experience of bereaved victims of the conflict in the North of Ireland.

John Martin Reavey (Eoin Mairtín Ó Riabhaigh)

AOIS/AGE: 25

CUMANN/CLUB: Naomh Cillian CLG, Crois Bán/ St Killian's GAC, Whitecross

CONTAE/COUNTY: Ard Mhacha/Armagh

MARAÍODH/KILLED: 4 Eanáir, le forsaí dílseach/ 4 January, loyalist forces

'The Reaveys have been in Whitecross for over 125 years.' Eugene begins his brother's story by carefully placing his upbringing into the context of his family's fascinating and deep connection to their parish and love for football. 'Since 1958, the Reaveys have been on the Senior football panel for St Killian's.'

John Martin Reavey was born on 23 May 1951 to Jimmy and Sadie. He was the fifth child of twelve, growing up in the town of Whitecross, County Armagh, with his seven brothers – Seamus, Frank, Eugene, Oliver, Brian, Anthony and Paul – and his four sisters: Kathleen, Eileen, Úna and Colleen. Typical of a rural upbringing at the time, Eugene explains how John Martin and his siblings knew hard work from an early age. 'My father was a scutcher in the flax mill. It was a dirty old job, where the men would be soaked through each morning as they climbed into the damns of water to turn the flax while it retted. My father would be lucky to get anything more than the cost of his seed and maybe his labour, so as young lads we were out working, either helping with thc flax by tying it into bundles ready for the rotting process, or out gathering spuds for the local farmers. Picking blackberries come the time of year was also a great way to get a bit of money in your pocket! And of course, whatever money we earned went straight to our mother.'

1976

As a young boy, John Martin attended his local primary school in Ballymoyer and got his secondary education at Bessbrook Technical College, and, as Eugene describes, he went on to serve his time as a bricklayer. 'As Catholics back then, our options were limited. We couldn't become accountants, or engineers, or join pretty much any profession. Those were closed shops for us and almost exclusively Protestant, so we mostly went to the trades. After leaving school at fifteen or so, John Martin started serving his time on the building sites. He absolutely loved his work, and he'd come home every night to share all of the jokes, slagging and stories from work at the dinner table. He became very talented at his work, and he worked very hard, so managed to have a bit of change on him. I remember John Martin being the first of us all to buy a car, buying it from a neighbour for £4. We all pushed it home from over the road at Kingsmills, and he eventually got it going. But back then there was no such thing as checking miles or anything like that, and we had to push the thing everywhere the whole time he had it!' As a character, John was known for his good and caring nature. 'John Martin was always a lovely man. He was very good to my mother and father, always there to take them to Newry in his car when they needed to go places, and always trying to help. He was great company.'

As for his footballing career, John Martin, as with all the Reavey men, played for St Killian's, Whitecross. Before joining the Juvenile structures of the club, his days would have been spent in the field with his brothers, wrestling over a ball and learning the basic skills of the game. When his time came to don the green and white jersey of St Killian's, he joined his older brothers Seamus, Frank and Eugene. 'Whilst his ability on the pitch wasn't at the standard of maybe Brian or Anthony, John Martin was committed to his club. He only played underage football for the club, as work started to take up more and more of his time as he travelled to and from jobs, making it harder to get to training sessions, and so his playing days ended sooner than the rest of us. But he never missed a football match, as, although he hadn't the time to train, he always made sure he was there on the match day to shout from the sidelines! He was a permanent figure in the crowd, usually in his good suit.' Eugene laughs, remembering how, on occasion, John Martin's match-day attire may not have been the best choice. 'Many's a man at the football would be wearing his good suit on a Sunday and have it ripped off him, as there'd often be a row started on the pitch which would have spilt into the crowd! But that's the way with football and that's how everybody dressed.'

John Martin Reavey was twenty-five years old when he was shot dead on 4 January 1976 by the UVF's Glenanne Gang. He was sitting in his living room watching *Celebrity Squares* on the TV with Brian (see page 87) and Anthony (see page 93) when masked gunmen entered the house and opened fire.

The Reavey brothers' love for the GAA has been a defining aspect of their legacy. The St Killian's club have always remembered the three brothers, having held different events in their memory. On the twenty-fifth anniversary of their deaths, Whitecross held an event to remember them. The Reavey family presented the Whitecross club with a plaque and a memorial match was played. The club also held a Gala Ball on the fortieth anniversary, in which there were talks by and discussions with Mícheál Ó Muircheartaigh, Joe Brolly, Marty Morrissey and Joe Kernan. The Reavey family's love for football continues to be a source of great connection between the younger generations of the Reavey clan and John Martin, Brian and Anthony. John Reavey's film about his uncles opened to great acclaim at the beginning of 2022.

Anthony Reavey (Antoine Ó Riabhaigh)

AOIS/AGE: 17
CUMANN/CLUB: Naomh Cillian CLG, Crois Bán/
St Killian's GAC, Whitecross
CONTAE/COUNTY: Ard Mhacha/Armagh
MARAÍODH/DIED: 30 Eanáir, le forsaí dílseach/
30 January, loyalist forces

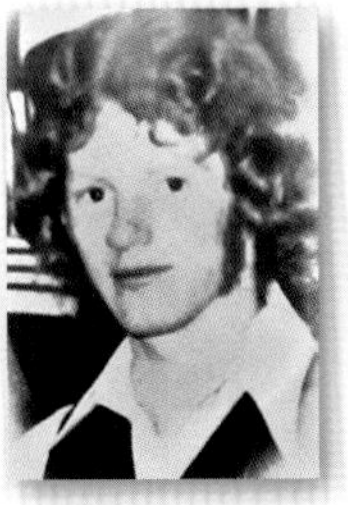

'Young, tall and a big head of ginger hair on him!' Eugene Reavey describes Anthony, the youngest of the three brothers he lost. 'He would have been the tallest in the family, and I always felt he grew up very quickly.'

Anthony Reavey was born on 31 March 1958 to parents Jimmy and Sadie in the parish of Loughgilly. He was the ninth child of twelve and grew up in the village of Whitecross, County Armagh. Just like his siblings before him, Anthony attended his local primary school, before going on to join his older brother Brian at St Paul's, Bessbrook. 'He was very workman-like from he was no age, always wanting to help out and start earning his way. When he was young, Anthony started rearing turkeys each Christmas, which I was able to help him with as I worked in the chicken trade. I used to show him how to pluck the birds and clean them out. Those niche wee jobs helped him gather a few pounds as he grew up and, eventually, he built up enough money to buy himself a car when he was fifteen or so!'

Upon leaving school, Anthony joined his brothers Seamus and Frank as a labourer and proved himself a very hard and valuable worker. He then secured himself an apprenticeship to begin serving his time as an electrician, which would have meant that all the trades would have been represented between all the Reavey brothers. Through his teenage years, Anthony developed a small notion of writing poetry from time to time about the world around him and the things he cared about and observed in that world. 'Anthony wrote a lot of poetry. He used to write these poems and my mother would send them across to her sister in England. He wrote about his dogs and pigs and the other animals he cared for. I don't know where he took that from, but he'd take the odd inkling every now and again and write something!'

Above all things, however, as with his older brothers, was a love for Gaelic football. Anthony played for St Killian's, Whitecross, and played all through school with St Paul's, Bessbrook, where he was on the receiving end of cutting-edge coaching and won an Ulster College's Championship. Having grown up battling against his older brothers out in the field, Anthony became a fearless and tough footballer, and a promising young talent at his club. 'He was a big fella but needed to do a bit of widening out. I remember one night, Anthony's team were playing in the Minor Championship and a bad row started, with people jumping the wire to get onto the pitch. I can still see Anthony and this older man boxing! Anthony was taking lumps out of this guy twice his size, and I thought to myself, "God! I didn't know our Anthony could box." The next thing was, Anthony was called up to our Senior team!'

Anthony had proven himself capable of handling the tougher elements of the football played in those days; he could go toe-to-toe with bigger, tougher opponents, and so, despite being only sixteen years old, he was promoted onto the Whitecross Senior football panel alongside his older brothers, and quickly earned himself a starting place in midfield. 'He was playing in the middle of the park for us, and that would not have been easy for a young lad, playing against all of those rural Armagh teams, who each had a reputation for being rough opponents! But he held his own despite his youth.'

Anthony Reavey was seventeen years old when he was shot by the UVF's Glenanne Gang on 4 January 1976. He was sitting in his living room watching

TV with his older brothers Brian (see page 87) and John Martin (see page 90) when gunmen entered his home and shot him where he sat. John Martin and Brian were killed instantly, but Anthony survived the attack by getting into a bedroom and diving under a bed. The gunmen sprayed the bed with bullets and left after sweeping the house for others. Anthony then crawled out of the house and onto the road, eventually getting himself to a neighbour's house.

He was taken to hospital, but his ordeal was not over. Whilst receiving treatment, staff had to hide Anthony in the gynaecology ward when suspected loyalist gunmen arrived, having heard that he had survived the attack. Surviving this suspected second attempt on his life, Anthony was eventually released from hospital after twelve days to recover at home, having undergone serious treatment, and he was making good progress and walking with crutches. Eugene then describes how Anthony decided to spend a night at his girlfriend's house. The following morning, Anthony was left in the house by himself as he was unable to walk up the steep hill leading to the chapel to attend Sunday Mass. Upon returning to the house, the family found Anthony unconscious. In circumstances that the Reavey family have never been comfortable with, Anthony then spent the next while in hospital, but he succumbed to his injuries on 30 January. Eugene details compelling evidence in his book, *The Killing of the Reavey Brothers*, that suggests Anthony may have died as a result of foul play.

Matthew Campbell (Maitiú Mac Cathmhaoil)

AOIS/AGE: 22

CUMANN/CLUB: CLG Naomh Mhuire, An Bhoireann/ St Mary's GAC, Burren

CONTAE/COUNTY: An Dún/Down

MARAÍODH/DIED: 27 Aibreán, le forsaí dílseach/ 27 April, loyalist forces

'Growing up in Burren as a young lad, you couldn't help but want to get involved in the football.' The Campbell family begin to describe the role of the GAA in their lives from an early age. 'Before we were old enough to join the club, many's a Sunday a crowd of boys would have come up to our house to play football or we would head to some other house to play. Any field would do, as long as there was a ball. We would have happily walked for miles to play for a few hours then walked home again. In those days there was nothing else, but there was nothing else needed!'

Matthew Campbell, or Mattie as he was known, was born on 1 August 1953 to May and Pat. He was the fourth of five children, growing up on the family farm in the village of Burren, County Down, with his brothers, Patrick, Mícheál and Gerard (Gerry), and his sister, Maeve. Mattie attended Carrick Primary School in the village before heading to St Joseph's Secondary School in Newry. As his siblings explain, Mattie was born into a rural life characterised by strong community bonds. 'In a rural community like ours, you always had your part to play in helping out on the farm. Whether it be milking cows or turning hay, there was no dodging work and lying on the couch, you had to muck in! And that's just the way it was. Neighbours helped one another, especially with doing jobs like the hay, and there was a real sense of togetherness about it all. We shared what little we had, and everyone who called to our house left with a bag of spuds and vegetables and whatever Mum was baking that day, and that included the postman, who was also Mattie's godfather.'

That sense of collective effort and community was instilled into Mattie from a young age, and as his family explain, Mattie was always willing to play his part. 'Nothing was ever too much trouble for Mattie. Even when he was very young, he was always happy to give his time and help where it was needed. No matter what, Mattie seemed to always be there.' Upon leaving school at fifteen years old, Mattie brought that same work ethic to his chosen professional career as a plasterer. Completing his training in Newry and beginning work with a local plasterer, Mattie, incredibly, had his time as an apprentice served by the age of seventeen.

Perhaps the defining aspect of Mattie's life, as his family continue to recall their memories of him, was his passion for the Burren community and its people. Growing up in an environment in which neighbours relied on one another shaped Mattie's outlook on life, and he threw himself into community work from a very young age. 'Mattie loved where he lived and the people in it. He was very much a community person and had great friends in the village. He did work for the community that no other young lad his age would have been doing. He got stuck in with the local youth club, taking all the professional courses in his own time to ensure he was doing everything the proper way; he helped organise the local darts league; he was part of the village's first soccer team, Millburn FC; and, of course, he was part of the football club.'

Indeed, given that Mattie so clearly exuded the foundational community values of the GAA, coupled with family connections to Gaelic games, his involvement with his local club, St Mary's, Burren, was an inevitability. 'Our father played football in his younger days and loved to go to games, so there was football in the family. And then, of course, growing up in Burren, football was everywhere, so it's always just been taken for granted that the GAA is part of your life. We loved going to the football, and missed a game only if there was work needing doing on the farm.' Brendan, Mattie's brother-in-law, laughs when recalling a rare occasion that the lads had to give the football a miss. 'I remember one night, we were at hay and there was a match on that evening. May, God bless her, came up to the field with cups of tea and sandwiches for us all, and we sat on the hedges to have a quick rest. Someone started to talk about the football that night, and Pat quickly intervened to say that there'll be no football until all the hay is in. And someone from the club could come up to the field looking us, but it'd make no difference. Hay came first and that was that! End of story. It could rain the next day and we couldn't leave Pat to do it himself.'

Mattie's first involvement with his local club came at the Juvenile level at u15, which was the earliest opportunity he had to play for Burren. He then progressed through the age groups, playing Minor football and then onto the Senior Reserve football team, as Gerry explains. 'Mattie mostly played seconds when he reached Senior level, playing the odd game for the Seniors if they were stuck for men. He played along the back line and though we were two years apart, I got to play along the back line of the Reserve team with him for a while.' Whilst giving his time to play for his club, Mattie also got involved in coaching as he got older, managing different youth teams coming through for Burren. 'He always had his car packed with young lads, bringing them to games and training. At twenty-two years old, there weren't many his age giving up their time like he was. He was so well-thought-of in the club because of his commitment to it.'

As they continue, Mattie's family describe his character. 'Mattie was very soft-spoken and a deep thinker. He was a very calm and easy-going sort of person and that definitely made him great around the likes of the youth club. He was always so kind and a naturally very caring character.' Gerry laughs, 'He was the opposite of me anyway! I remember we were playing a reserve game one day and there was a boy on the field who hit him badly. Mattie wasn't reacting to him and, eventually, he had to come off injured by your man and I was sent on to replace him. It wasn't long before that lad had to come off injured too! But that shows you the character he was. You couldn't annoy him and I can never remember him getting angry.' Brendan remembers Mattie also being a great source of advice and counsel for the people around him, and someone who seemed well beyond his years. 'He was good-humoured and one thing that I always remember is that you couldn't get the newspapers off him either! He'd read them front to back, and always knew what was going on around him.'

Matthew Campbell was twenty-two years old when he was killed by an explosion planted by the UVF at the Ulster Bar in Warrenpoint on 24 April 1976. On the evening of the explosion, he had just dropped home a few players of the Burren u14 football team he was managing and had made his way to the bar to watch *Match of the Day*. Shortly after Mattie arrived at the bar, loyalist bombers detonated the explosive device, leaving over twenty people in hospital, before going on to detonate a second no-warning bomb in Hilltown. Mattie was taken to hospital, where, on 27 April, he succumbed to his injuries.

'No one ever came to our door to explain to us what happened to Mattie, and when we asked about the case, we were told that the investigating officer died in a traffic collision a few weeks after Mattie was killed, and that's where it was left. We were just left to accept it and move on.' A subsequent Historical Enquiries Team report into Mattie's death concluded that both explosions that evening were planned and carried out by a single person who is now deceased. Considering the logistical and practical difficulties of planting, detonating and fleeing the scene of two separate explosions in such built-up areas, Mattie's family have been left with many reasons to question the findings of that report.

'The bomb went off on the Saturday and Mattie died on the Tuesday. There was a game that Tuesday night and word came down to the team that Mattie had died, and the game was then called off. That was a big thing for us as a family, and it showed us what people thought of Mattie. He had the biggest funeral Burren has ever seen.' Mattie's loss shocked the Burren community, which had remained largely untouched, in a direct sense, by the conflict until his killing. For his family, particularly his brother Gerry, the GAA provided a coping mechanism and escape. 'They never had to do anything. It was just important for me to know that training was going to be there for me if I wanted to go, and I could go for a few hours in the week and just focus on football. I am very grateful to have had that outlet.' What also becomes clear from speaking to the Campbell family is that Mattie's passion and love for his community and the GAA remain strong in the younger generations of his family. Gerry managed various Burren teams of all ages and codes for over twenty-five years. Mattie's nephew, Colm, manages the Down u14 Ladies Football team, and Mattie's nieces Shauna and Geraldine both played and managed teams. Indeed, Geraldine won an Intercounty All-Ireland Junior Football Championship with the Antrim Ladies, picking up Player of the Match in the final in Croke Park. Mattie's family are also still involved with Millburn FC.

Máire Drumm (Máire Ní Droma)

AOIS/AGE: 57

CUMANN/CLUB: CLG Gael Uladh, Béal Feirste/ Gael Uladh GAC, Belfast

CONTAE/COUNTY: Aontroim/Antrim

MARAÍODH/KILLED: 28 Deireadh Fómhair, le forsaí dílseach/28 October, loyalist forces

'I was eight years old the first time I was ever in Croke Park was in 1956. My mum took me down to see Antrim play Cork in the All-Ireland Camogie final.' Seamus begins to describe the memories he has of the GAA and his mother. 'Antrim won that day, and I remember we travelled down and back with the team on the train. Those were the heydays of Antrim camogie, and my mum was right in the middle of it all.'

Máire Drumm, née McAteer, was born on 22 October 1919 to Jim and Margaret. She was the eldest of their four children and grew up in the townland of Killean, South Armagh, with her sister, Theresa, and her two brothers, Tommy and Seán. As Seamus explains, whilst Killean would now be described as a border town, at the time of his mother's birth it was simply a townland in rural Ireland. Partition was then enforced while his mother was a toddler, and Seamus tells an anecdote of a neighbour of his mother's waking one morning to learn that his field was to be split equally between the two newly created states. Máire attended her local primary school in Killean before going on to Our Lady's Grammar School in Newry, where a lifelong love of camogie and the GAA began. Aged sixteen, Máire emigrated to Liverpool with her sister, Theresa, in search of work. After a brief period in England, she came back to Ireland and remained for a short while in Dublin before eventually settling in Belfast in 1939, where she found more consistent work.

'My mum then started to play camogie for Gael Uladh in Belfast. It was a great club, with an ethos that made it more than just a camogie club. It was connected to Conradh na Gaeilge and was very much a cultural organisation promoting Irish language, dancing, music and sport. It would have hosted a lot of céilís and the like for local people and my mum would have been involved in organising a lot of that.' Whilst Máire gave her all for her teammates and club on the pitch, her talents truly lay in the organising and promotion of Gaelic games. Her passion and commitment saw her appointed as the Antrim secretary for camogie, then as the Ulster chairperson; she was promoted once more to be national vice-chair of camogie. Máire also served, for many years as the secretary for her Gael Uladh club, and during her stewardship, in which she was also a player, the club won the 1946 South Antrim Junior and Senior leagues. 'Prominent GAA figures around the country knew her because she was a fanatic about promoting the GAA. My mum helped raise money for the building of Casement Park, and I clearly remember her bringing me to the official opening. She was absolutely delighted with it and happy to have played her part in getting it finished.' As Seamus continues, he describes numerous other projects and initiatives his mother organised and committed herself to for the promotion and preservation of the GAA, and it becomes abundantly clear that Máire was an invaluable asset to the GAA at a time when its survival, particularly in the North and acutely with the women's game, was far from guaranteed.

Outside of the GAA, Máire's name is widely known for her endless dedication to another cause, Irish politics. 'Granda Jim had a big political influence on her. He was an amazing character with a great history. He attended big rallies and talks by Connolly and Larkin at the time of the workers' strikes. There was also a direct family connection to the Tan War, so republicanism was always there. Then when my mum moved to Liverpool, she joined the Gaelic League, and then she later joined Sinn Féin when she lived in Dublin.' As Seamus explains, republican politics came to determine much of Máire's life as a young woman, and when she moved to Belfast, it is what led to her meeting Seamus's father, Jimmy. 'My mum joined the Green Cross, which provided help to republican prisoners and their families. It was common for members of the Green Cross to visit republicans in jail back then, and it was on one of these visits that my parents met. My da had been interned in 1938 and he wrote to my mum and they began to see one another, despite him still being in jail! They got engaged while he was still interned and they were married in July 1946, after he was released. At their wedding, all of the camogs formed a guard of honour with their hurls for them to run through as they left the chapel.'

Starting a new life together, Máire and Jimmy soon welcomed their first son, Seamus, into the world, closely followed by twins Margaret and Seán, Catherine and, finally, Máire Óg. Inevitably, all Máire's children grew up with hurls in their hands and were all members of Gael Uladh. 'We weren't allowed to watch or play soccer! It was only ever GAA in our house. She always made sure we read loads of books too, and it wasn't until we were well into our teenage years that we got a TV. My mum was a very, very generous and caring person. Anyone who knew her would tell you the same. She spent all of her time helping people and came into her own in '69 when huge amounts of people were really left with nothing.' Seamus explains that his parents opened up their home to refugees burned out of their homes around Belfast, giving up their own beds and creating a rota for other families to use their bath to wash, whilst his sisters cooked big pots of food for those who needed it. Seamus laughs that his brother, Seán, would complain that he didn't mind the other kids getting a bath or using the toilet, but his patience would end when they got to pick the TV programmes! 'Nowadays it takes twenty meetings for anything to get done, but back then, she used to just do. If someone needed something, she didn't wait around. The Falls Curfew is the classic example I always think of. Thousands of families on the Falls Road were cut off from the rest of the city by barricades and barbed-wire fences set up by the British Army. My mum, along with a few other women, decided they would break it. She led over 3,000 women on a march down the Falls Road with food parcels for the trapped families. They pushed through the soldiers and broke the curfew.'

Seamus describes other memories he has, including the close relationship Máire had with evicted Traveller families after she successfully took up their cause when they were on the receiving end of discriminatory practices from the local bishop, which resulted in them being evicted from the land they were living on. 'All the caravans ended up getting moved to the field beside our house in Belfast, and my mum took charge of it all and helped the families. A lot of them, still to the day she died, were very close to her. She was very caring to them and, eventually, they got their own houses built and could move on, but our door was always open to them, and to anyone else who was in need.'

A lot of Máire's community work was complemented by her work as a member of Sinn Féin. She and Jimmy were very active members of the party and were both elected to its Ard Comhairle, with Máire holding the position of vice-president at one stage. For her political activism, Seamus describes how his mother was under the constant watch of the security services and laughs that when the Traveller families could move on from the field opposite their home, the British Army erected a barracks in the field, with a watch tower looking directly into their living-room window. 'They built a sentry post right outside our front door, and if they saw someone they didn't recognise come into our house, you could guarantee our front door would be kicked through because they wanted to know who it was!'

Máire's life and political activism are explored meticulously in Gerry Adams's book *Máire Drumm. A Visionary: A Rebel Heart*, and whilst the events of her life are too numerous to expand on in this entry, a particular anecdote included in that book merits retelling here. In February 1971 Stormont Prime Minister James Chichester-Clark outlawed the carrying of hurling sticks as one of a number of measures introduced following an incident in Belfast in which an RUC officer was struck on the head with a hurl. Attached to this measure was a mandatory prison sentence of six months for anyone caught breaking this rule. In protest, Máire and other women attempted to march to the courts in Belfast carrying their hurls. Máire also led protests against the occupation of Casement Park by the British Army in September 1972. For her activism, Seamus explains that Máire spent brief periods in both Armagh Women's Prison and Mountjoy Prison, under the various offences associated with her making political speeches.

Máire Drumm was fifty-seven years old when she was killed in her hospital bed on 28 October 1976 by a loyalist gunman. She was in hospital for an eye operation when two gunmen from the Red Hand Commando entered the Mater Hospital in Belfast and shot her. The security guard of the hospital was convicted for his role in Máire's death.

'She had one of the biggest funerals Belfast has ever seen. There was something like 50,000 mourners there. People still remark on the impact my mum had on their lives and continues to have. We lived in an open house, where everyone was welcome, and you'd give your bed up to anyone needing it. She gave everything to her community and, for that, she was idolised by its people.'

Máire's family continue to have a deep connection with the GAA, with her children, grandchildren and great-grandchildren continuing to play the sport she loved.

1977

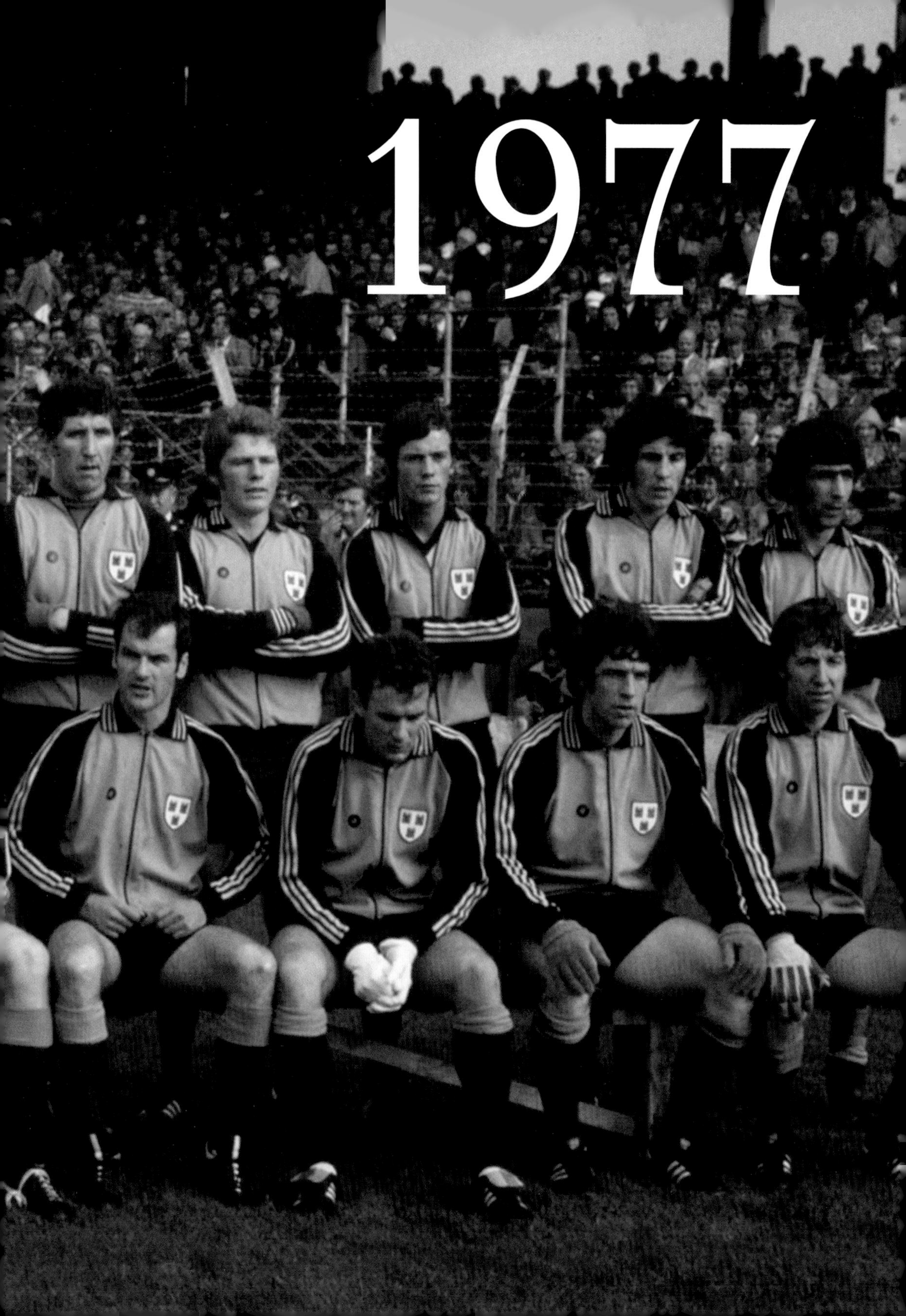

Mick McHugh (Mícheál Mac Aodh)

AOIS/AGE: 34

CUMANN/CLUB: CLG Naomh Dabhóg Achadh Uí Araín/ Aghyaran St Davog's GFC

CONTAE/COUNTY: Tír Eoghain/Tyrone

MARAÍODH/KILLED: 21 Eanáir, Arm na Breataine agus forsaí dílseach/21 January, British Army and loyalist forces

'To know Mick is to know how happy he was to live and work on the land he grew up in and knew.' Mary McHugh, along with her two daughters, Roisín and Deirdre, begins to describe her husband. 'His love for his family and his farming; his animals and his football. To know Mick is to know he loved Aghyaran.'

Mick McHugh was born on 25 January 1942 in Aghyaran, County Tyrone, to Alice and Tommy. He was the eldest of six children, all boys: Mick, George, Tom, Willie-John, Patsy and Gerry. Mick's family are known in the town as the Shoemaker McHughs, so prescribed owing to the need to use family trades to identify the various McHughs in the area from one another. Mick grew up working on his family farm, dedicating his energy to the land. In 1963 he met Mary Rush from Castlederg at a dance on an Easter Sunday night; they both loved the Showband dances. After completing her teacher training in Newcastle upon Tyne, England, Mary got a teaching job in Laught, a few miles from Corgary in Donegal. Mick was engaged in forestry, while also working on his small farm and caring for his elderly uncles. The couple settled into their new life together, marrying in 1968 and bringing three daughters into the world: Michaela, Roisín and Deirdre. Michaela was only four years old when she was tragically killed in a road accident on 18 May 1973.

Driven by his deep sense of truth and justice, Mick would have been the person in the community to approach the authorities where tensions existed. He always stood up when people were being stopped, searched and harassed while trying to go about their day, heading to work or attending Mass. Although his leadership meant that Mick was singled out by the authorities for special treatment, including routine harassment and intimidation on his way to work, he never let it get to him or let it stop him. He continued to be a source of advice for his family and his community. Indeed, such was the high esteem in which his community held him, and testament to Mick's work ethic, that they elected him to the county council.

Mick's involvement in the GAA reflected his deep-rooted commitment to bettering his community. A founder member of the most westerly club in the six counties, St Davog's GFC, Mick used his digger to drain the football pitch. To those who knew him, it was unsurprising that Mick was undeterred by a complete lack of funding to establish the club. Growing up, Mick and his brothers would play football in their fields with a blown-up bladder of the most recently slaughtered pig. As children, the boys secretly put all their savings together to buy a pair of football boots to share between themselves, the younger boys stuffing the toes to make them fit. Mick's love for football was unwavering and little stood in his way, even if he and all his brothers had to ride on the same bike together to training or games. Indeed, he was known to play anywhere he was needed: goals, full-forward, midfield. Earning various write-ups in the local papers, Mick's ability on the pitch played a key role in delivering early success for the club.

In 1962 St Davog's were crowned West Tyrone Junior League winners, and in 1965 Mick was part of St Davog's West Tyrone Intermediate title-winning team, himself being hailed by the *Ulster Herald* as a 'local hero when he saved a fierce shot by S. Gillespie'. Mick was also a keen boxer and was known to sweep up at the club's sports days. After a long day of working in the forestry and then on the farm, he would turn up to the sports day and toss the sheaf further than anyone. He was also a renowned anchor in tug-of-war. He loved sports of any kind and had no inhibitions about playing basketball and other sports at the State school. Mick's memory is celebrated every year at St Davog's by way of the Mick McHugh Memorial Trophy, previously a sporting event, now a very competitive quiz.

Mick McHugh was killed on 21 January 1977 by the UDA/UFF in collusion with the SAS and other British forces. Before he was killed, he was sent a death threat, supposedly written by loyalists but which leading human rights campaigner Fr Denis Faul believed to be written by a State agent. As a leader in his community, Mick was routinely and falsely accused of being a member of a paramilitary group by State forces, and so searches on his property became not only routine operations but also artificially created an outward image that Mick was somehow involved in wrongdoing. This put a target on his back, and Mick noticed certain individuals following him to and from work. On the day of his killing, he had just left Mary and his two young daughters to drive to work in his yellow Forestry lorry. When Mary heard machine-gun fire, she ran out to find her husband had been killed. Ten years later, in 1987, William Bredin was sentenced to life for Mick's killing. His guilty plea, on the evidence of an informant, means that few details are publicly known about Mick's killing. Bredin was released as part of the Good Friday Agreement. The McHugh family continues to campaign for justice and the truth about the circumstances of Mick's death.

The younger generations of Mick's family continue to keep his love for the GAA and community alive through their involvement in many sporting activities. They believe that, 'To live in the hearts of those we leave behind is not to die.'

Joe Campbell (Seosamh Ó Cathmhaoil)

AOIS/AGE: 49

CUMANN/CLUB: Ruairí Óg CLG, Bun Abhann Dalla/ Ruairí Óg GAC, Cushendall

CONTAE/COUNTY: Aontroim/Antrim

MARAÍODH/KILLED: 25 Feabhra, le forsaí dílseach/ 25 February, loyalist forces

'While my brother Tommy was a teacher in St Mary's, Limavady, he received a written account from a friend who was associated with an older man in the Bogside who was a big Gael.' Joe Campbell details a story of the role of the

GAA in his father's life, and how his shared identity as a Gael allowed a transcending of the social and political division normally represented by his employer, the RUC, and the GAA community. 'The letter detailed an encounter the man had with my father while going to Mass close to the RUC station my dad was training at in Derry. At the time, this person was the secretary of the local GAA club, which always struggled in those days for numbers. He approached my father, knowing he was a trainee officer, and asked where he was from. Upon learning he was from Scotstown, he asked if my dad played football and if he would tog out for the club: my dad didn't give it a second thought. I believe he played three or four matches for them while he was posted in Derry, which is something we as a family are very proud of. While it leaves us with a lot of questions, what it does tell us is that it is clear my dad wasn't a politically motivated man. In playing football, he was doing something that came perfectly natural to him and that, at that micro-level, there are some things more important than Rule 21 and the associated politics of it – there was a club struggling for numbers and a Gael willing to line out on the pitch.'

Joe Campbell was born on 26 October 1928 to George and Wilhelmina in Rathmullan, County Donegal. Joe was one of four children, growing up with brothers George, a.k.a 'Sonny', and Cyril, and with his sister, Amy. Their father was a sergeant in An Gárda Síochána, and with the redesignation of posts within that line of work, the family eventually found themselves moving to the footballing stronghold of Scotstown in County Monaghan. Playing football was everything to the boys and, indeed, Joe's older brother went on to play for Monaghan Senior footballers. Joe attended St McCartan's College, where he and his brothers had Ulster Colleges' success as young footballers, and from where he then had to decide what to do for work. 'One day in the '50s, my father and uncle decided that they were going to follow in their father's footsteps and join the gardaí. They cycled into Monaghan Garda Station, but at that time there was an embargo on recruitment, so they went back out to Scotstown to have a think and some lunch. They then cycled out the other road from the town and into Enniskillen, where they joined the RUC. I have no doubt they didn't join for any ideological or political reasons, but that the career offered a steady, reliable job. Yes, with hindsight you would like to look back at that decision and think "if only" or "what if?", but I was nineteen when my father was murdered so we didn't get that opportunity to sit down and have that father-to-son conversation about how life evolved.'

Initially, Joe was stationed in Derry, where he met Rosemary in 1954. They were married and had their first child, Tommy, by 1956. They would bring seven more children into this world: Joe, Peter, Mandy, Paula, Rosemary, Sarah and Phillip. 'After Derry, my parents moved to Moneymore, where myself and three other siblings were born. My dad's connections to the GAA are vague for those following years after Derry until we moved to Crossmaglen. I don't know about the particulars of his GAA life in the town; however, when the locals discovered that we were being relocated to another posting after a few years in Crossmaglen, a local politician got a petition moving to have us stay: it received some 1,600 signatures!' But, despite the town's efforts, the family was relocated to Cushendall, in the Glens of Antrim.

'Heaven on earth. In Cushendall, we were largely sheltered from a lot of the conflict, with the exception of very isolated incidents. It was like we lived in a different country. I suppose that's why the political view of what my dad's uniform represented didn't really click with me until after his murder. I remember playing in an u16's Féis final in Waterfoot and my dad was standing behind the fence on the sideline cheering me on in his full uniform. Only later did I realise how sad that was, because that perfectly natural sight of a dad supporting his son on the hurling field could be viewed entirely differently. That his uniform would be the defining characteristic of that scene, even though his uniform went in no way to define him as a person. However, I am very conscious of what his uniform did represent to so many other people who were subjected to violence by others wearing that same uniform.'

Joe ensured his family was steeped in the GAA, with all his children lining out on the camogie and hurling fields for Ruairí Óg's. Indeed, his son Peter represented the family in both codes on the Antrim Minor panels and, off the pitch, Tommy and Paula were crowned Ballad Group Ulster Scór champions. 'My dad absolutely loved being involved in it all. Sadly, he was only forty-nine when he was killed and therefore robbed of so many opportunities to enjoy his culture and the involvement of his family in the GAA.' However, Joe's passion was passed to his children, who each espouse the values of the GAA, and generationally, Joe's legacy lives on through his grandchildren, who have all played: Joe's grandson Eoghan is captain of the Antrim Senior Hurling panel.

Joe Campbell was killed by the UVF as he locked up the police station on the night of 25 February 1977. It is widely believed that he was killed because he discovered the blind eye the RUC had been turning to loyalist gunrunning. Whilst an RUC Special Branch officer was acquitted of his killing, Joe's family believe the accounts of ex-RUC whistle-blowers, who claim he was set up by his colleagues.

'My father was a GAA man through and through. He never missed an Ulster football final for as long I can recall, and he made sure we all grew up with hurls in our hands and footballs at our feet. He refused to be defined by a uniform, and I don't need to qualify or put anything to his legacy as those anecdotes from those who knew him in the Bogside and Crossmaglen speak to that legacy for themselves.'

William Strathern (Liam Srath-Éirne)

AOIS/AGE: 39

CUMANN/CLUB: Bhuilf Tóin CLG, Baile Eachaidh/ Wolfe Tones GAC, Bellaghy

CONTAE/COUNTY: Doire/Derry

MARAÍODH/KILLED: 19 Aibreán, le fórsaí dílseach/ 19 April, loyalist forces

'Anytime we meet someone who played with our dad, they are always so excited and happy to see us. They are always so complimentary about him.' Kevin and Paddy Strathern explain the pedestal their father is put upon by legends of Irish football. Kevin recalls, 'I went to an

1977

event in Magee University in honour of a great Derry side of the past. There I met Phil Stewart. I introduced myself and his eyes lit up immediately, so visibly excited to meet a son of Willie Strathern. He told me that my father was a very successful and fine footballer and had played on the '58 team right up until the semi-final of the All-Ireland Championship, when Phil came in to replace my young dad. He was standing beside his jersey from the '58 final, which he pointed to and joked that my dad's sweat was in that jersey, which is probably true given that jerseys were strictly held for positions rather than for players back then. But he also said more seriously that it was a great pity for Derry that my dad wasn't playing that day.'

William Strathern was born in 1937 to Anne and Frank, and grew up in Killyberry, just outside of Bellaghy, County Derry. One of five children, William was the son of a farmer and would initially become a joiner by trade. He played his football for Bellaghy Wolfe Tones, a club whose name is now known across Ireland thanks to the dominance of big Willie Strathern's team. A hugely successful underage contingent, winning three consecutive Minor Championships, the team was also bound for Senior success. No one could have predicted, however, that William's team would not only bring home Bellaghy's first Senior County Championship in 1956 but would also repeat the achievement eight times over the next ten years, now known as Bellaghy's 'Decade of Dominance'. Lining out in midfield, William's passion and dedication to his football not only earned him a consistent spot on the Derry panel and the 1963 Derry Player of the Year, but also the accolade of being the toughest player Derry icon Jim McKeever had ever played with or against.

William's love for football knew no limits. 'It was his life,' explain Kevin and Paddy. 'My father was badly injured in a tragic accident, in which his brother Johnny had died. The death of Johnny put the house into strict mourning for a year, which included no football, and which my grandmother carefully monitored. Not long after being released from hospital, my dad was at the club watching a football match. Having lost a finger, part of his ear and still wrapped in bandages, he stood on the sideline beside a friend, watching Bellaghy being beaten in a game. Half-time came, and my father had disappeared. With the teams back out for the second half, my dad was finally spotted, lining-out on the field. He couldn't stand idly by watching Bellaghy being beaten, although he soon had to come off as he was not fit to play. After the game my father made sure that not a single word of this was ever to be whispered for fear of my granny finding out. Nothing could keep him away.'

William married Kathleen Young in 1964, and despite major efforts from the newly married couple to buy a house in Bellaghy, it wasn't to be. Instead, an opportunity arose to buy a house and grocery shop business in Ahoghill, and they took it. The young couple had seven children in all and lived happily among their newfound neighbours. Indeed, William was active in the community and could always be relied upon to help erect the Christmas decorations in the town every year. A very trusting man, he always saw the good in people and, as one family anecdote details, never gave a second thought to lending his car to a stranger whose car had broken down outside of the shop whilst on their way to a soccer match. He was especially trusting of anyone who played sport because 'they wouldn't have time to be bad'. 'My father espoused the values of our Gaelic games.'

However, Kevin describes the isolation the family felt as one of the few local families who were identifiable as the 'only Catholics in the village'. For two weeks every year in July, the customers stopped coming and the wooden boards would be put up around the windows. Indeed, Kevin doesn't recall Gaelic football ever being mentioned or played around the house when he was growing up. 'I suppose he was trying to protect us from being identified as Catholic and being picked on, but we had never even seen a game of football. It was only ever soccer.'

William Strathern was killed in the early hours of 19 April 1977, having been woken by a voice on the street calling for the shop to be opened to get medicine for a sick child. Because of his reliably good-natured selflessness, William went down and opened the front door. He was shot dead where he stood. John Weir and Billy McCaughey, police officers who were also members of the UVF's Glenanne Gang, were convicted of his killing, but two other prominent members of the gang escaped without trial.

Jim Conway (Seamus Mac Conmhaí)

AOIS/AGE: 49

CUMANN/CLUB: Clan na Gael CLG, An Lorgain/ Clan na Gael GAC, Lurgan

CONTAE/COUNTY: Ard Mhacha/Armagh

MARAÍODH/DIED: 15 Bealtaine, Arm na Breataine/ 15 May, British Army

'My da was a great Gael and a tough player.' Jim Conway begins to describe his father. 'I remember talking to an older man and him telling me that he'd played against my da, and that his ribs are still sore! He was a handy footballer by all accounts; not particularly special, but a reliable and committed player.'

Jim Conway was born in 1929 to John and Elizabeth in the townland of Derrytrasna, County Armagh, but grew up with his six siblings in Silverwood, Lurgan. Jim's son explains that his father had a tough start to life, with his father passing when he was just three years old. As a result, his mother was left to raise Jim and his siblings on the little money she made rearing a handful of pigs for slaughter for the local butchers' shops. Aged fifteen, Jim left his local primary school in Silverwood to help his mother with the pig business, but a wave of blue ear infected the animals and wiped their entire stock out. Consequently, Jim sought work as a labourer on local building sites, a job he continued to do for most of his life before going to work in a paper factory local to Lurgan. As a provider for his family from a young age, Jim took on a guardian role for his sister's son, John. Sadly, Jim's sister, Mary-Jane, had passed away as a young woman, so Jim stepped in to help raise John. 'My da raised John like a son, and he was like an older brother to me. He wouldn't have thought twice about that decision. My da always looked after his family.'

In terms of the GAA, Jim and his siblings were all members of the Clan na Gael club in Lurgan. Indeed, his brother, Dan, was one of the first groundsmen for the club. However, Jim's first introduction to the GAA was in primary school, where he developed a keen love for football that he carried with him throughout his life. 'We were young when my parents died, so a lot of those early memories are lost to time but the GAA always had a big presence in my da's life. I was told one time about a match he was playing. He was in nets, and a row started in the goalmouth, with everyone piling in. By the time everybody was dragged out, my da was lying at the bottom of it!' Jim laughs, 'Football was a different sport back then.'

As he progressed through the years with his club, another local GAA club was set up in the Shankhill estate in Lurgan called Barry Óg's. 'I found out that my da had transferred from the Clans to Barry Óg's for a short while. I don't think he was getting his full place in the team and I suppose wanted more time on the field. Whilst playing for the Barry Óg's team, I think that's when he met my mum. She was a through-and-through Shankhill woman and that's where they trained and played their matches, and so they must have met when my da was playing football.' It wasn't long before Jim and Teresa Magee, known to everyone as Tessie, were married in 1955 and began their new life together. They soon welcomed their first child, Jane, into the world, who was closely followed by Maura, Bernadette, James jnr and Caroline, Gary, Sean and Lisa. 'My da encouraged all of us to play, and we all got involved in the club. In fact, John, my da's nephew, went on to captain the great Clan team that reached the All-Ireland final in '74. The GAA played an important role in our lives growing up.'

Jim then describes his father's life away from the pitch. 'As a labourer, my da financially had very little. But he would have given anyone who needed it the coat off his back. I always think of him as a nobleman in that sense, and everyone knew him for his generous and humble spirit. He always insisted on working and was proud that he never took any benefits for himself or his family, even though there were eight of us. All he had to get himself to work was a wee scooter, and I remember one morning looking out the bedroom window to watch him leave for work. The roads were covered in frost and the bike skidded slightly, and I could see his shoes coming up as he got his balance. There were big holes in the bottom of them. That's how poor we really were, but he made sure that all of his kids were looked after.

'One thing I always remember about him was his love for animals and the outdoors. You see he was a countryman at heart, and he loved to keep dogs and pigeons. I remember him taking us out on walks in the countryside and he would show us all the different birds. He knew their calls and would call them down and tell us about each of them. He could tell you about all the different plants and trees too. He was very gentle and patient in that way.' In his spare time, Jim also enjoyed spending time with his close friend Fred, the caretaker of the local Protestant graveyard in the Shankhill estate. Jim would help Fred with the upkeep of the graveyard, and the pair would regularly spend time walking through its history.

One morning in 1972, Jim's life, and the lives of his family, would be irrevocably changed. 'My da hadn't been feeling well, so he took the day off work. By the afternoon he was feeling better and decided to walk up the town and get some paint for the house, just to make sure the day wasn't wasted. While he was away, the British soldiers came into the estate. There was a character on the estate with Down's Syndrome called Dan. Everyone knew and loved Dan, and each morning, Dan's wee job was to go to the shop for a bottle of milk. This particular day, the soldiers started harassing Dan, as well as a pregnant woman who tried to stop them. My da was making his way back home with the paint when he came across this scene. My da ran over to help, and Dan and the woman got free, but all the attention was then turned to my da. They hit him on the head with the butt of their rifle and I'm sure a couple of punches were thrown, and they all struggled, before chasing my da home. As he got to the door of a neighbour, he was hit with two rubber bullets in the back. With my mum and sister in the house, the soldiers smashed their way into the house and followed my da in, beating him relentlessly and splitting his head open with the butts of their guns. They then dragged him unconscious into the street and continued to beat him.'

As Jim continues to explain the horrific experience of his father's treatment at the hands of British soldiers, he recalls that his father's brother-in-law, Billy, came upon the scene and tried to intervene. 'Billy was an ex-serviceman for the British Army and a highly respected one. When he pleaded with the soldiers to stop, they shot him with rubber bullets too.' Eventually, Jim was brought, unconscious, to a police holding cell, from which he was taken the following day to appear before a magistrate, who convicted him of riotous behaviour.

Despite many civilian witnesses testifying to Jim's character, including Fred, his Protestant best friend, the magistrate chose to believe the testimony of the soldiers. 'He partially recovered from the attack, but he was never the same. When he came home to us, the stitches right around his head looked like someone had taken a tin opener to him.'

This story is mentioned here because on 15 May 1977, aged forty-two, Jim Conway dropped dead on the football field of Clan na Gael. He was playing an older men's match when a blood clot, caused by the beating he received, travelled to his heart. Despite the best efforts of the local dentist, Antoin, in administering CPR Jim died. His death was a direct result of the injuries he sustained during the attack described by his son.

One of the British soldiers responsible for Jim's death was Corporal Jimmy Johnson. Johnson would leave the British Army in 1973 and killed two people in England over the course of a decade; he is currently the longest-serving prisoner in HMP Frankland. He wrote a book about his experiences in Ireland and describes the assault on Jim in grim detail. In that book, alongside other events, Johnson attributes his attack on Jim as having been a root cause of his PTSD, which he claims is to blame for the killings he committed. Jim jnr says, 'He has tried to, in a sense, blame my dad for what he did to those people in England. My dad was a victim of a decision to release a uniformed psychopath onto our streets. Johnson served in Aden, where they tortured, murdered and terrorised the locals, before he was sent to Ireland to do the same. In 1972 he viciously and violently beat my father. He then left the British Army and went on to murder people in England. He is held up as a leading voice for veterans' rights and a figure of public sympathy, whilst my father's story goes unspoken.'

In the wake of Jim's death, the local GAA community rallied behind his family to provide them with support. 'When he died, the club gathered up a bit of money and gave it to us to help see us through. I also remember a neighbour coming to the house and telling my mum and sister about what my da had done for her when he was alive. She described how my da used to work Sundays and give her the money he made for that day to help her and her kids through the week. Now, our family had nothing, and still he was toiling away not only for us but to help another struggling family too. And what's more, my da never told anyone that he was doing that. He kept that woman's privacy. He was just an incredibly kind person.'

1980

Seamus Quaid (Seamus Mhic Uaid)

AOIS/AGE: 42

CUMANN/CLUB: CLG An Fheothanach–Caisleán Uí Mhathúna; Faythe Harriers CLG/Feohanagh–Castlemahon GAC; Faythe Harriers GAC

CONTAE/COUNTY: Luimneach/Limerick

MARAÍODH/KILLED: 13 Deireadh Fómhair, le Óglaigh na hÉireann/13 October, IRA

'Seamus loved to whistle. It is something that has almost completely died out now, but he was a great whistler.' Dónal Quaid describes his older brother, Seamus. 'I can remember when he was on his way home from the farm he worked at, he would cut across the local farmland as a shortcut, and you could hear him whistling in the distance as he got closer. And you knew then that Seamus was on his way home, whistling all the way.'

Seamus Quaid was born on 13 November 1937 to William and Bridget. His father was a native of Castlemahon, County Limerick, and his mother was from Duagh, County Kerry. Seamus was the eldest of nine children, growing up with his younger sisters, Mary, Síle, Peg and Angela, and younger brothers, Dónal, Dave, Billy and Thomas. 'My parents both worked in the same farmer's house, the McCarthy family, in Castlemahon. When they were married and Seamus was first born, they lived in Castlemahon, and in 1943 that's where he initially started school; then the family moved to the neighbouring parish of Cloncagh in '47 and Seamus moved to the local school in Ahalin. As more of us came along, my parents then got a house built back in Castlemahon, and we moved back there in 1951. However, Seamus continued his education in Ahalin until he finished aged fourteen or fifteen. He then went to work for a local farmer. Times were tough at that time, and he wouldn't have been getting much money for what was hard work. He then got a job at Nash's Mineral Waters for a while before our cousins, Jack and Jim Quaid, got him some labouring work along with them for a man in Milford, Cork.'

As Dónal continues, he explains that whilst Seamus never shied away from any kind of work, his heart was set on a particular path. 'Seamus always wanted to join the Guards. He always spoke about it, even as a young teenager. He knew what he had to do to get there, so he contacted his old teacher in Ahalin, Micheál de Búrca, and the two of them came to an arrangement where Seamus would receive lessons in Irish and some other subjects. Every day for about a year, Seamus travelled from Castlemahon to Ahalin to join de Búrca's classroom, and the hard work proved successful. He applied to join the Guards in 1957, aged twenty, and was accepted into the training college in Phoenix Park, Dublin, that year. He graduated from his training the following year in '58 and was posted to Wexford town.'

In terms of Seamus's involvement in the GAA, it is hard to overstate his prowess on the field of play. His name is etched into the annals of hurling history, having lifted the Liam MacCarthy Cup in Croke Park, but before his crowning sporting achievement, a young Seamus Quaid first lifted a hurl back in Castlemahon. 'There was no hurling in Castlemahon when my father was younger, only a bit of football. It wasn't until the arrival of a new parish priest to the area did something get up and running for the youngsters. Our cousins, Jack and Jim, who were a bit older than Seamus, were part of that first Juvenile team, and then Seamus got his chance to join the Feohanagh–Castlemahon club at u16 level. He was the leading light on that team from the start and progressed right through to the Senior team.' Before long, Seamus was joined on the Senior team by his younger brothers, and the Quaid family established their hurling pedigree at their club, winning the Limerick Junior Hurling Championship in 1954. 'On the great Feohanagh team of that era, there was our cousins Jack and Jim Quaid, and their brother Tom, and then there was Seamus, myself, Dave and Thomas. Seven Quaids on the same panel!' Seamus's famous twin cousins, Jack and Jim, were on the Limerick Senior hurling panel, and Dónal explains that while Seamus was of the same ability on the field, he, initially, didn't get the chance to line out for his own county, having been unsuccessful at a trial for the Limerick Minors. 'He was maybe 5ft 9in. or 5ft 10in. but very, very fast and very fit. Seamus did a lot of training and was very meticulous about the way he lived. He never smoked nor drank, and life back then for him was all about hurling. There was a bit of football here and there, but it was almost all hurling for him.'

With Seamus then being stationed in Wexford town upon completing his training with An Garda Síochána in 1958, he took the decision to join the famous Faythe Harriers hurling club. 'It would have been a very difficult decision for him, but travelling to Limerick for training and games just wasn't doable back then.' The club had just been promoted to Division 1 when Seamus arrived, having won the 1956 Intermediate Championship, and Seamus would help the club to their first Senior County Championship in 1960. In that season, he excelled on the field and his talents drew the attention of the selectors of the Wexford Senior hurling panel, and he was persuaded to throw in his allegiances with the county set-up. It proved an excellent decision. Seamus lined-out for Wexford at right half-forward, wearing number 12. Reaching the Leinster Championship final, he was the star of the game as Wexford overpowered Kilkenny.

Next up was the All-Ireland series, and Seamus played a vital role in his team reaching Croke Park for the final and a chance to lift the Liam MacCarthy Cup. 'My father and I were at that game. I will always remember it. We left Castlemahon at 6 a.m. to drive with a neighbour to Kilmallock to take the train to Dublin. Seamus met us at the station in Dublin and took us around the city that morning. He was trying to relax, of course, for the final that afternoon. He played very well that day, marking the famous Mick Burns of Tipperary, but he suffered an injury to his hand and had to come off.' The game finished on a scoreline of 2–15 to 0–11 in favour of Wexford, and Seamus became an All-Ireland Hurling champion.

Dónal goes on to describe how Seamus eventually came back to play hurling with his home club in 1964, making the journey from Wexford town to Limerick each week for training and matches. This also allowed Seamus to finally don the green and white of the Treaty County, when, on his return to the Feohanagh–Castlemahon club, he was called up to the Limerick Senior hurling panel; an unquestionable source of pride for him.

Outside of hurling, Seamus loved to be in the company of family and friends. 'He loved dancing. When we were living in Cloncagh we made lots of friends and Seamus always seemed to be very popular. Every summer, he'd spend his nights dancing with his friends. A car would come to collect him and they'd all go for a dance at the ballroom in Ballybunion. He was also a very nice singer and loved to sing a song for us all. I have also never met anyone like him who was so meticulous about his appearance! He had great, dark brown hair and always kept it well, and would be very conscious of how he presented himself. It would have all translated well for his job as a Guard. He was a very straight and honest person, and whilst he could be strict at times, the people in Wexford would tell you that he was very well-liked and would have looked out for people. He wouldn't have been a stickler for little things here and there and would have always been very helpful.'

In 1959, having just landed in Wexford town, Seamus met Olive O'Neill. Dónal laughs that his brother's decision to join the Wexford hurling panel was made easier by the fact that Seamus had met a Wexford girl, but there is an incredible truth to it. Within a few years of starting to see one another, Seamus and Olive were married, and Seamus had truly settled into his life in Wexford. The couple soon welcomed Mary, Caroline, Eamon and Angela into the world.

Seamus Quaid was forty-two years old when he was shot dead by a member of the IRA, Peter Rogers, on 13 October 1980. Seamus and a colleague were tracking Rogers following a report of an armed robbery in Kilkenny carried out by the IRA, when they came across his vegetable van parked in Cleariestown. Seamus and his colleague knew Rogers and approached the van to search it. As they did so, Rogers pulled a gun on them and a gun battle ensued. Seamus was shot by Rogers and died at the scene. Peter Rogers was convicted of Seamus's killing and sentenced to hanging, which was later commuted to life imprisonment.

'While Seamus was hurling, our father never missed a match. He went to all of his games. After Seamus was killed in 1980, he never went to another game. Seamus's death had an unimaginable impact on my parents and they both died soon after Seamus, in 1984.'

The Quaid family remain deeply connected to the GAA to this day and have perhaps one of the most recognisable names in Limerick hurling. Seamus's famous twin cousins were the first of the family to line out for their county, winning a Munster Championship and All-Ireland Junior Championship in

1955, and Jack Quaid's son, Tommy, starred for Limerick in goals when they were the runners-up for the Liam MacCarthy Cup in 1980. Tommy's cousin, Joe Quaid, was also a star goalkeeper for Limerick, winning two Munster Championship titles, two National Leagues, and being twice named on the All-Stars list. Tommy's son, Nickie, is the current goalkeeper for the Limerick Senior hurling team and became the second Quaid to lift the Liam MacCarthy, after Seamus. In recognition of the contribution Seamus made to his club and county, the Feohanagh–Castlemahon playing field is named Pairc Seamus Mhic Uaid.

1981

John Dempsey (Eoin Ó Díomasaigh)

AOIS/AGE: 16
CUMANN/CLUB: Gort na Móna CLG/Gort na Móna GAC
CONTAE/COUNTY: Aontroim/Antrim
MARAÍODH/KILLED: 8 Iúil, Arm na Breataine/
8 July, British Army

'John was a very social kid. He would always be playing in the streets around his home in Turf Lodge or on his way down the Monagh Bypass to St Teresa's youth club.' John's sisters, Angela, Dianna and Martina, describe their brother. 'He was really passionate about his music. He loved The Clash, Stiff Little Fingers and Siouxsie and the Banshees and the like. So much so, in fact, that he dressed up as Adam Ant for a disco at his youth club!'

John Dempsey was born on 15 December 1964 to Jimmy and Teresa. He was the third of five children, growing up in Turf Lodge, West Belfast, with older sisters Angela and Dianna, and younger siblings Martina and Stephen. 'We had a very happy childhood growing up in Turf Lodge, even though it was tough times throughout the Troubles.' John went to Holy Trinity Primary School and then to Gort na Móna Secondary School, where he was first introduced to the GAA by Brother Maroney. Being the active kid he was, John joined both the hurling and football teams and would play on both teams for the next five years. Seeing the enthusiasm of John and his classmates for the sport, and recognising it as a means of providing a focus for the local youth outside of the escalating violence around them, Brother Maroney established Gort na Móna CLG in the community. John jumped at the opportunity to join, deepening his love for Gaelic games, and he would represent his club from u12s right through to u16s. 'He was always at the club. Playing matches, meeting up with his friends and teammates, or socialising at St Teresa's disco.'

Away from the club, John was never far from the GAA, as childhood friend Dominic Marley recalls. 'We grew up in the '70s together. He was known as Johnny to his friends and, as with most boys our age at the time, Johnny was always playing in the streets around his home or in the Falls Park. We would regularly go to the Coolers to swim and spend our days playing football and hurling. If, like many kids, you didn't have a hurl, you would borrow one. It didn't matter if it was too big or too small, just so long as you could strike a ball with it. Johnny could always be seen with a football or hurling stick and sliotar.'

In the winter of 1974 John was selected, along with his sister Angela, to travel to America to sing in Carnegie Hall on 18 December. Whilst a wondrous trip for him, John was always thinking of home. 'He sent a letter home while he was in America. He was given ten dollars for his trip and in his letter he wrote that he had seven left and that he was going to use the remainder of his money to buy a radio to keep his daddy company in his cell in Long Kesh.' Jimmy, like so many other Catholics, had been interned without trial. Indeed, the reality of the conflict through which John was growing up was almost inescapable, with the Ballymurphy and Springhill Massacres happening on his doorstep. As a result, John gained a strong sense of politics from an early age and decided to join Na Fianna Éireann, the youth wing of the IRA.

John Dempsey was shot dead when he was sixteen years old by the British Army on 8 July 1981. Within hours of hunger striker Joe McDonnell's death, John and other members of Na Fianna were headed inside the Falls Road Bus Depot, intending to set one of the buses alight in protest at his death. Spotting British soldiers already there, John and his friends fled. A shot rang out and John was struck by the bullet. He later died in hospital.

Forty years later, some of John's friends are still members of Gort na Móna and have fond memories of their teammate. In John's memory, Gort na Móna has held the annual John Dempsey Memorial Cup to give younger children an opportunity to participate in the GAA. This recognition of John's contribution to his club and sport is a source of great pride and honour for his family, and it has kept John's memory alive not only for his friends but for his nieces and nephews, who were robbed of the chance to meet their Uncle John.

Kevin Lynch (Chaoimhín Uí Loinsigh)

AOIS/AGE: 25

CUMANN/CLUB: CLG Cumann Iomanaíochta, Dún Geimhin/Kevin Lynch GAC, Dungiven

CONTAE/COUNTY: Doire/Derry

MARAÍODH/KILLED: 1 Lúnasa, ar stailc ocrais/ 1 August, on hunger strike

'Kevin loved to do a bit of fishing. Growing up, we would all spend countless hours sitting by the River Roe talking and laughing, waiting for the prize of a salmon or some white trout.' Ollie Lynch describes the days of adventure growing up in Dungiven with his younger brother Kevin and his other siblings, developing a deep connection with the land around them. 'When we were very young, we would always enjoy going down to the burren that was beside our house to see what fish we could catch. We would get into the deep holes and catch the fish with our hands! If you knew what you were doing, you could often come away with some trout. We caught a fair few in our time and they'd always be eaten. Nothing went to waste.'

Kevin Lynch was born on 25 May 1956 to Bridie and Paddy in Park, County Derry. He was the youngest of eight children, growing up with Míchael, Patrick, Jean, Francis, Mary, Bridie and Ollie. Whilst his older siblings grew up in Park, the family moved into the new estate being built in Dungiven town when Kevin was still an infant. 'It was pure luxury for us when my father managed to get one of the new houses on the Garvagh Road in Dungiven. It was a nice, brand-new house that brought a big change from our one before, which had no electricity or running water! Loads of families were moving into the area, so there was great excitement about the town.' Kevin's father, Paddy, worked as a stonemason, and a potato digger in Scotland before that, but having settled into the new home, an opportunity arose to take charge of a local pub. 'The pub went up for auction and my father put in the highest bid for it, finding himself a new career as a publican, and a successful one at that. Our pub would host all the dances and the like, with busloads arriving from all over the county to take advantage of our big dance hall. My father was able to renovate it a few times over the years, putting in a state-of-the-art darts hall with air-conditioning before anyone knew what air-conditioning was, and a modern lounge area. We would host big competitions and had a large capacity, so, naturally, we all had our jobs. Everybody had to do their bit to help run the pub, Kevin included when he was old enough! My father always said, "Don't serve a man who doesn't know what he wants, serve the man with money in his hands." He knew what he was doing all right! So those great memories of everyone helping with the running of the pub formed a key backdrop to Kevin's formative years.'

As a young lad, Kevin attended St Canice's Primary School before moving on to St Patrick's Secondary School, both in Dungiven. Ollie recalls this period of their lives as a period of adventure and exploration, spending their days fishing and roaming the lands around them. 'A great memory of this time is when my father bought a big car, an Austin 16. He would throw us all in the back of it and take us on trips to Donegal, and when we arrived, he would line us all up and say, "Right! Three good deep breaths of fresh air!" And we would all gulp the fresh Donegal air. I still laugh thinking about it. It was part of what made up a great childhood.'

The other, defining, aspect of Kevin's youth, was his absolute love for the GAA. His older brothers all played for Banagher, which they had joined before the move to Dungiven, but with the new influx of people into the town in the late 1950s, a Kilkenny man decided to establish the Dungiven Hurling Club, which Kevin joined. 'That was the start of the hurling in Dungiven, and Kevin took to it immediately. His coach would take the boys training and on trips around Ireland to play in games and tournaments.' It didn't take long for the Dungiven boys to see success, winning the right to represent their county at the very first Féile na Gael in 1971. 'It was in Mullinahone, County Tipperary. Kevin had his appendix out about a fortnight before the tournament, and my mother said he could go down with the team but on the condition that he is not to play. Of course, when all was said and done, Kevin was named as one of the stars of the tournament, helping Dungiven bring home the Michael Cusack Trophy for the Division 3 All-Ireland title, beating St Mary's of Ardee, County Louth, on a score line of 7–4 to 0–0! In the following years, Kevin's performance at the Féile was remembered and saw him included in an *Irish Independent* article naming a team of the greatest hurlers to play at the tournament.'

It comes as no surprise, then, to learn that the following year, 1972, saw Kevin named as captain of the Derry u16 county hurling panel; the same year in which he led his county to All-Ireland victory at Croke Park. And it wasn't just hurling that Kevin played. He was also a gifted footballer for St Canice's GFC in Dungiven. 'He was fiercely competitive and when he went up for a ball, he made sure he caught it. He was a big lad and all muscle, carrying very little fat and training five or six days in the week, which meant he could always take a shoulder in his stride. But it also meant at the age of fifteen or sixteen, he started to get a lot of harassment from the British Army and police. He was a big, big lad for his years and maybe looked a bit older, but he got fierce harassment from a very young age.'

On the back of this abuse from authorities, Kevin made the decision to join his brothers Patrick and Míchael in Bedford, England, aged sixteen, to work as a bricklayer. 'He settled well over in England, and I remember coming over to join the lads for a while and when I arrived, Kevin had me training with a team he joined in Luton that very Tuesday! We played for St Dymphna's over in England, and at the age of sixteen, Kevin was starting in the middle of the park. Those games were some craic, and nobody held back. You hit hard and you got hit hard, and after the game everybody would shake hands and go for a beer and have the craic. Whilst based in Bedford, Kevin would be back and forth to Ireland to see family and play hurling. The Dungiven lads would call him to say, "Look, we need you to come back for a game", and that's how it was. All told, Kevin was in England for three to four years before he walked in one day and said he was heading home. He had earned himself a good bit of money and wanted to move back.'

Kevin continued his trade when he returned home to Dungiven, and enjoyed being back with his family, but Ollie explains how the escalation of the conflict came to affect his younger brother and how he was unable to escape the abuse which caused him to leave home in the first place. 'When he was back home, himself and a few lads were going to a dance, and on the way home he got a real bad beating by the police. They threatened to shoot the lads and it wasn't until another car arrived on the scene and the brave couple inside refused to leave unless the boys were safe, did the police let them go. It was around this time that Kevin decided to join the Irish National Liberation Army. A few months later, in December, the house was raided, and Kevin was dragged into the street by his hair in front of my mother and father. He was then taken to Castlereagh Interrogation Centre, and he told me afterwards the horrific treatment he suffered there. He detailed a terrifying situation that you couldn't imagine and after days of constant torture, his only escape from the abuse was to sign a statement. He then found himself in Crumlin Road Gaol.'

Ollie goes on to describe how Kevin's incarceration did not mean an end to his sporting life. 'There were a few very talented footballers in with Kevin at the time, and what they used to do was collect a load of old socks and make a football out of them. There was a Tyrone footballer inside at the same time and when he got out, I met him. He said to me that he had never met anyone with a pair of hands on him like Kevin. He told me, "I thought I was a good footballer, but when Kevin went for a high ball, no one stood a chance. He would go up for the ball, and just as he was passing you, he'd give a wee nudge to throw you off your stride, and next thing, he was away with the ball!" So, he was well-regarded inside.'

Kevin was then transferred to the H-Blocks of Long Kesh Prison, which Ollie describes. 'When he was sent down the blocks, he had to run the gauntlet of batons and boots and one thing and another, stripped naked and dragged and beaten and eventually thrown into his cell. After he got to know who he was sharing the cell with and trying to settle down, he was told the first thing anyone must do is sing a song. Of course, Kevin wasn't in any form to be singing that night, but he had no choice, so he sang "Finvola, Gem of the Roe". It's a song about Dungiven and a young chieftain's daughter, and a beautiful story of Irish folklore. Anyway, he sang the song for all in the wing to hear, but he wasn't the best of singers and so he got fierce slagging by the lads! But a few years later, he had to sing again. This time it was because he had just earned his Fáinne, which he was delighted with, and they said to him that they wanted him to sing a song. He sang "Finvola, Gem of the Roe", once again, but this time *as Gaeilge*.' Kevin had taught himself the language of his land and sang passionately, transporting all those listening back to the place he grew up and the town of Dungiven. Ollie describes how the block fell silent after Kevin was finished singing. 'There was nobody slagging him that day.'

Kevin Lynch died on 1 August 1981, after seventy-one days on hunger strike, aged twenty-five. He was the ninth of twelve to die on hunger strike during the conflict. His decision to join the strike followed his earlier decision to join the blanket protest, in opposition to, and in direct conflict with, the decision of the British government to remove the political status of prisoners, and in protest at the conditions of the prisons and the treatment of prisoners within them.

While on the blanket protest, and then on hunger strike, Ollie explains how Kevin came to be on the receiving end of criticism surrounding the GAA. 'As the strike went on, the GAA, as in Croke Park, were dismissing the growing demand within its membership to speak out, and the prisoners inside became disillusioned with any prospect of the organisation speaking out in support of their demands. But Kevin was absolute in his support for the GAA and would have passionately defended the GAA in debates and discussions within the prison. He stuck by them no matter what. Unfortunately, despite being their biggest advocate, and having himself taken a cup out of Croke Park, the GAA refused the request to hold a minute's silence following his death on hunger strike. They let him down.'

You need only drive through Dungiven town to assess the legacy left by Kevin Lynch. His beloved hurling club is now named in his honour, with a mural of sixteen-year-old Kevin lifting the All-Ireland u16 hurling trophy for Derry in the centre of the town. There are now three Irish-language median schools in Dungiven, which locals will attribute as being a testament to the impression left on his townland by Kevin's passion for restoring pride in his national culture and language. The street Kevin grew up on in Dungiven is also now named after him. It backs onto the River Roe, creating a permanent connection between Kevin's legacy and the ancient waterway that defined so much of his life, just in the same fashion that the Roe's connection to Finvola allowed Kevin to bridge her memory and story across millennia to those with whom he shared a prison cell.

Kieran Doherty (Ciarán Ó Dochartaigh)

AOIS/AGE: 25
CUMANN/CLUB: Naomh Treasa CLG, Béal Feirste/
St Teresa's GAC, Belfast
CONTAE/COUNTY: Aontroim/Antrim
MARAÍODH/KILLED: 2 Lúnasa, ar stailc ocrais/
2 August, on hunger strike

'The GAA was always present.' Michael Doherty, Kieran's brother, begins to describe the earliest memories of the GAA in his family's life. 'Our father played GAA as a young lad and in his elder years helped with the raising of funds to help build Casement Park. I remember him taking us as young lads to all the big matches, especially the Ulster Championship games at Casement. We would be sat on the grass embankments surrounding the pitch, amongst the crowd some 40–50,000 strong, usually watching the great Down teams of the era!'

Kieran Doherty was born on 16 October 1955 to Alfie and Margaret. He was their third child, growing up in Andersonstown, West Belfast, with older brothers Michael and Terence, and younger siblings Róisín, Mairead and Brendan. As Michael describes their childhood, it becomes clear that sport came to define Kieran's early life. 'As kids, the big steep field at Commedagh Drive was the hub of everything. It was a green space in the middle of the estate, and, at night, hundreds of kids would gather to play and socialise. You couldn't get onto it at times with the number of young people out playing! Three matches of hurling, football and soccer, all on at the one time, with stray balls being chased in every direction. The field was on a slant too, and because of that, we developed our own unique skills and abilities. That's where Kieran began playing GAA, and with the number of kids in the area, some of the parents decided to set up a team to represent the street in the District Leagues of that time, which were set up in the absence of Juvenile structures at the club level. Kieran's Commedagh team ended up being a particularly talented bunch and were very successful, winning the Féile na nGael.' Indeed, the reading of the scoreboard in that 1971 victory for the

Division 2 Hurling Canon Fogarty Trophy was Commedagh 8–6 to 1–1 for Cappawhite of Tipperary.

Following his older brothers, Kieran attended St Teresa's Primary School, where he competed in the various Cumann na mBunscol tournaments, before going on to the Christian Brothers Secondary School on the Glen Road, where he represented his school on the field of play in each of his schooling years. Antrim stalwart Brian White was a school teammate of Kieran's and described him as one of the best midfielders he had ever seen line out on a football pitch, so it is of no surprise that it wasn't just on the hurling field that Kieran saw early success. He was called up to join St Teresa's GAC to play Minor football aged fourteen. 'Our Kieran ended up at 6ft 2in. and was very well built, even from a young age, so he was able to get playing for the club. I remember him playing on my Minor team during the '69 Championship. I was young at sixteen, playing u18/Minor level, and Kieran was getting a run-out in some of the games at fourteen! When he was on the pitch, we would work the ball together up the pitch and you could see, even then, the talent he was growing into. We won the County Minor Football Championship that year. And repeated the achievement in '70 and '71.' Michael laughs, 'I remember Kieran getting into a bit of bother back then with the club. The men who ran the Commedagh team were also St John's men, and they convinced our Kieran to play a few games for their club. When the Brothers found out he was donning the blue and white of St John's, they had words with him and safe to say he was back to St Teresa's very quickly!'

Alongside the GAA, the Doherty boys were also very keen cyclists, particularly Michael, Terence and Kieran, and the lads regularly entered races across the country. 'I was really into my cycling and raced at a high, competitive level. If I was competing in a big race, Kieran would have entered into the Junior race. He enjoyed his cycling a lot and was well able for it.'

Michael goes on to describe the young man Kieran was growing into off the pitch. 'He was a very reserved sort of character. Quiet and unassuming and would never be the type to speak out of turn. But also, a very popular character and the people in the area loved him. He never boasted about anything but had a real quiet confidence about him that made him very mature. One thing that also always sticks out about Kieran was how well-dressed he was. His Wrangler jeans were always well-pressed, his boots always shined, and he was never without his lovely jacket and Ben Sherman shirt.' But despite the outward descriptions of a normal teenager seeking his path in life, the reality is that Kieran and his brothers were born into a generation that would witness the violent repression of civil rights activism and the subsequent outbreak of armed conflict.

As he became politically aware, Kieran joined Na Fianna Éireann in 1971, before going on to join the IRA the following year. This put an end to his GAA career as he committed himself to the republican movement. In 1973 Kieran and Michael were interned in Long Kesh, with Terence having been interned the previous year. 'I was in Cage 5 and Kieran was in Cage 4. There was a fifty-yard gap between our cages so I could shout across to him. Whilst there, the lads in our cage got caught trying to escape, so we weren't allowed food parcels for a week. Kieran, being in the opposite cage, put some stuff, sausages and the like, into a plastic bag with a bit of weight and tried throwing it across to me.' Michael laughs, 'The bag hit the electric wires that surrounded the cages and knocked the lights out! That meant trouble for me because the boys couldn't make their tea that night.'

Although Michael and Kieran found themselves a long way from their beloved St Teresa's club, football found a way into their lives, as Michael goes on to describe. 'Once a fortnight, we were allowed out of the cages and onto the gravel pitch to play football. I organised it for my cage, and we would get two teams picked to play. The matches were extremely competitive and if you fell on the gravel, you'd be hours in the medical centre picking stones out of your knees. There was the odd inter-cage match, but they tended to sometimes get a bit out of hand and the screws put an end to them. We had some decent footballers in those matches, including Hugh Coney [see page 68] who was in my cage. He was some player; an incredibly talented footballer.'

Both Kieran and Michael were eventually released, with Kieran getting out in November 1975, but he was re-arrested the following August. 'He was caught during an operation and sentenced to eighteen years. It was totally different from the cages and the prisoners now faced horrendous conditions.

Kieran immediately joined the blanket protest. His physical size meant that he could put up a good fight against the wardens who would drag and beat him for strip searches.' Whilst Michael leaves out most of the details of Kieran's experience on the blanket protest, he does describe his brother's unflinching spirit and resolve, and the moments of solace he was able to find in the depths of darkness. 'He became a fluent Irish speaker whilst inside, and that was something he was very proud of. He also couldn't keep his competitive side at bay, teaching himself chess, and he won a few tournaments between the prisoners!'

However, the reality of Kieran's conditions could not be kept at bay. 'In 1978, Kieran was hospitalised by the wardens, so when the first hunger strike started in 1980, Kieran put himself forward and joined it for the last four days before it was called off.' Following the reneging of the deal struck between the prisoners and British government for better conditions, Bobby Sands began a second hunger strike in 1981. Kieran Doherty replaced Raymond McCreesh (see page 294) on 22 May 1981. In a letter to his family, Kieran wrote, 'Even if I fall into a coma, do not take me off the Hunger Strike, unless the five demands are met … The British and Thatcher will not break me or my comrades …' During his time on hunger strike, Kieran was elected TD in Cavan–Monaghan. 'When Kieran took bad, we were allowed in with him, and my father and I did nights. Kieran was the last cell on the left-hand side, and Kevin Lynch [see page 128] was last on the right.'

Kieran Doherty died on 2 August 1981, after seventy-two days on hunger strike. He was one of the twelve hunger strikers who would die over the course of the conflict, including fellow clubmate Joe McDonnell (see page 294). St Teresa's GAA club run an annual tournament to commemorate the legacy of both Kieran Doherty and Joe McDonnell as beloved and committed members of their club. For over twenty years, teams have competed for the Kieran Doherty Shield and Joe McDonnell Cup. The club grounds are also named after Kieran and Joe.

'Kieran would tag along with me, Terence and our friends during the summers of our childhood. I remember us all cycling to Newcastle one time to camp out. We lit a fire and I let Kieran have two bottles of Guinness, his first-ever drink, and then he sang a song for us around the fire. We camped there for about three days then all cycled home. He was a giant of a man, but at the end of it all, he was, and always will be, my wee brother.'

Larry Kennedy (Lorcán Ó Cinnéide)

AOIS/AGE: 36

CUMANN/CLUB: CLG Ciceam Ard Eoin, Béal Feirste/ Ardoyne Kickhams GAC, Belfast

CONTAE/COUNTY: Aontroim/Antrim

MARAÍODH/KILLED: 8 Deireadh Fómhair, le forsaí dílseach/8 October, loyalist forces

'Although he wasn't from here, Larry took to Ardoyne and its people. And the people of Ardoyne took to Larry.' Jackie Donnelly begins to describe the life of his friend, Larry Kennedy. 'Community was at the heart of everything he did, and for that, he was loved by the people of Ardoyne.'

Larry Kennedy was born in 1945. Jackie describes what little information is known about Larry's early life. 'Larry came from a small, rural area in Tyrone. He was an only child, and he was raised by his mother. He first came to Belfast as a young lad in the early '60s and I remember when people asked him why he came to Belfast, he would always say, "Ah, I just decided to get on a bus!" He had a very independent spirit, you see, and Larry was a very social type of character, so I suppose he knew he wasn't suited for the more isolated, rural setting he was born into. When he got to Belfast, he struck up a brief friendship with the Keenan family in Ardoyne, but he wasn't in Belfast long before he went over to England, where he stayed for two years in search of more adventure. He then came back to Belfast in his late teens and landed on the Keenans' doorstep, who took Larry in as one of their own!'

Electing to stay in Belfast, something had brought Larry back to Ardoyne, which Jackie notes as being the people he had met. He found an extension of his family in the Keenans and a sense of belonging in the Ardoyne community, which he now called home. As Jackie continues to describe Larry, it is clear that he was someone eager to immerse himself in the sense of communal cohesiveness that so evidently captivated him. 'Although I can't remember Larry having any discernible job as such, he was very active in the community and helped run various community projects. He was a founder member of the Shamrock Social Club, which became the social hub of Ardoyne, and he was always the first to volunteer for any projects in the area. When loyalists attacked the area and burnt down a lot of the bars, buildings and homes in Ardoyne in '69, Larry was one of the key figures in the rebuild.'

Towards the end of 1973 Larry, like so many other young men in Ardoyne and other nationalist areas, was interned without trial. 'Larry was never a member of any political organisation or anything like that, but I suppose it didn't matter come internment. He came into my cage in Long Kesh and that's where we first met. My first impression was that there was no doubting that he was a country boy! But he had something different to him as well, in that inside the cages he was very content to sit and read and study, while the rest of us mucked around. Much to his detriment of course, as we all had him tortured! He was a very jovial character and very difficult to wind up, despite our best efforts, and great company to be in. He was the type of guy who could sit down and talk to a complete stranger as if he'd known them for a lifetime. He took a big interest in sociology whilst inside and with the non-stop studying, we gave him the nickname "The Brain".'

When Larry was eventually released from internment in 1974, he entered Queen's University Belfast, where he graduated with a degree in sociology. Putting his education into work aimed at the betterment of the community, Larry was persuaded into representative work. 'While Larry never joined any political organisation, he was very sympathetic to the republican movement, and particularly the anti-H-Block cause. He agreed to run in the local council elections in 1980/81, on the condition that he could run as an independent under the Anti-H-Block Committee. Ardoyne voted him in in droves and really rallied around him, and he was a brilliant councillor. Larry was very plain speaking, never saying anything he didn't mean to say, and he took up every issue that mattered to the people, in spite of all the intimidation and harassment that regularly came at him.'

In terms of Larry's involvement with the GAA, Jackie believes that he won an underage hurling medal with Tyrone and that he was involved in his local GAA club in Tyrone. Naturally, when Larry came to Ardoyne, he joined Ardoyne Kickhams GAA club. Owing to his deep involvement with the community, the Kickhams became an integral part of Larry's life. 'Even though he played hurling as a kid, Larry played football for Ardoyne and got the nickname "Specs" because he always wore his glasses on the field. He also loved handball and was a very big promoter of it in the club.' From Jackie's description of his friend, it is evident that he was a committed Gael who espoused the community-centred values of the association and displayed a clear belief in working and contributing towards something bigger than oneself.

Larry Kennedy was thirty-six years old when he was shot dead on 8 October 1981 by the UFF. He was leaving a community fundraising event in the Shamrock Social Club when gunmen approached and opened fire. No one has ever been convicted of his killing.

'It was a very brave decision to run as a councillor back then. It put Larry into a spotlight that he wouldn't have wanted, but he was committed to bettering life in Ardoyne and was willing to put his head above the parapet to do so. He was loved by Ardoyne, and his funeral, which was one of the biggest I can remember in the area, was a testament to the life he lived.'

1983

Brian Campbell (Brian Mac Cathmhaoíl)

AOIS/AGE: 19

CUMANN/CLUB: Ó Rathaille Chluain Eo CLG/ O'Rahilly's GAC, Clonoe

CONTAE/COUNTY: Tír Eoghain/Tyrone

MARAÍODH/KILLED: 4 Nollaig, Arm na Breataine/ 4 December, British Army

'Brian was like any other young lad growing up, playing football at every opportunity.' Brian's sister Mary describes the young man she knew as her brother. 'The football field was where Brian and all his friends would always meet up. They mightn't have had a pair of football boots between them, nor a kit bag, but nothing got in their way.'

Brian Campbell was born on 24 March 1964 to Brendan and Kathleen. The fifth of eight children, he grew up in the parish of Clonoe, County Tyrone. He joined Clonoe O'Rahilly's GAC from the time he could hold a ball, playing through the different age groups. 'Through the years, Brian loved nothing more than a derby game. He loved playing the other local clubs around the parish but particularly loved playing against Fianna Coalisland. I suppose that's because he really enjoyed mixing and playing with friends he knew and all the locals; he was a very sociable and good-natured young lad. Whenever there was a club bus going somewhere, he would be on it.' Indeed, Brian was no stranger to the open road, spending the weekends of his youth either on the club bus heading to days out organised by his club, or squeezed into the back of the family car heading to Croke Park. 'Back then there was no need for tickets, so my father would pack us all into the car and we, as a family, would all head to Croke Park for the finals of the Championship. Every year we'd do it together and as a result the GAA really was a part of us.' It was therefore not surprising that when O'Rahilly's organised a trip to the USA in March 1983, Brian had no hesitation in making the long journey. 'He made great memories out there, and was even offered a good job, but he decided to come home. Sometimes you can't help in thinking how things would have been different if he had stayed.'

Aside from football, Brian's other main passion in life was cars. 'He went to St Patrick's Primary School in Annaghmore, then to St Joseph's, Coalisland, and Dungannon Technical College. There was only one place he was going to end up; the family garage.' Brian, just like his father, uncle and older brothers, trained as a mechanic in his family garage. By the time he was thirteen, he had his own stock car. Somehow, he also managed to balance the commitments of football and garage work with an interest in boxing, enjoying lacing his gloves for Clonoe Boxing Club.

As he grew older, Brian came to know the sharp end of the conflict. Fellow O'Rahilly's member and neighbour Hugh Gerard Coney (see page 68) had been killed and Brian's brother Seamus was sentenced to fourteen years in prison, which led to direct harassment from the RUC and British Army of Brian and the rest of his family. 'Brian was constantly having to deal with routine searches and arrests without charge. When Seamus escaped Long Kesh in 1983, Brian was arrested and held without charge at Gough Barracks, where he was told that they would even up the score for Seamus's escape. We logged that threat along with the many other death threats we received, not realising that this one would come to fruition a number of weeks later.'

Brian Campbell was killed alongside Colm McGirr (see page 143) on 4 December 1983, aged nineteen. They were killed without warning. The killing of Brian and Colm is considered a stark example of the shoot-to-kill policy of the British government at that time. In dedication to the memory of both Brian and Colm, two memorial cups are annually competed for by local teams from East Tyrone. The Colm McGirr and Brian Campbell Cup has been contested for by the Senior teams of local clubs from 1984 until the present day, and there is also a cup competed for by local pub football teams in Clonoe and the surrounding areas. There is also a cup dedicated to the memory of Brian's father, Brendan, set up after his passing in 1987.

Brian's family remain deeply involved in the Clonoe O'Rahilly's club. Brian's brothers and sisters are lifelong members and volunteers for their club, and the family garage, now run by Brian's brother Peter, has been a club sponsor since 1999. Brian's nephews, nieces and great-nephews and great-nieces now play for Clonoe.

Colm McGirr (Colm Mac an Gheairr)

AOIS/AGE: 23

CUMANN/CLUB: CLG Fianna Oileán an Ghuil/ Coalisland Fianna GFC

CONTAE/COUNTY: Tír Eoghain/Tyrone

MARAÍODH/KILLED: 4 Nollaig, Arm na Breataine/ 4 December, British Army

'We grew up fifty to eighty yards from the football field. It was more than just our GAA park; it was our playground. Every evening we were home from school, the bags would be thrown into the hall, and everyone would be straight out onto the field. That's where we learned our trade.' Colm's brother, Brian, and good friend and cousin, Paul Hampsey, explain how football defined their childhood. 'There were no play parks in those days like there are now. It was bags for goalposts, and you had three or four matches being played at the one time in the field.'

Colm McGirr was born on 22 September 1960 to Paddy and Alice. He was the youngest of twelve children, with three older sisters and eight older brothers, and grew up in the town of Coalisland, County Tyrone. With Granny living with them too, Colm was one of fifteen inside the three-bedroom house. He played his football for Coalisland Fianna, growing up on the adjacent estate from the clubhouse, and although 'he mightn't have been the most skilful footballer, he was a very enthusiastic player along the half-back line'. Despite Colm's age group seeing limited success, his enthusiasm and talents furthered his club in many other ways outside of the trophy cabinet. A natural organiser, Colm was always the first to offer a hand where the events and functions of the club needed organising. Amongst his community, he had earned himself a reputation for reliability despite his young age. 'Everyone knew they could turn to him if they needed a hand. He was killed so young. God only knows in what ways he would have flourished at the club had he the opportunity.' Indeed, even from a young age, Colm always had a job to do around the club and could usually be found as a young lad on any given Sunday chasing stray balls behind the goals. 'Because we lived right beside the club, it became our lives. Every Sunday was spent at the park.'

As Brian continues, he explains that the football field was their escape as young lads. Not only did they lose an older brother at seventeen to a tragic and fatal car accident, but they also had to learn to live with a conflict that came quickly and brutally into their young lives. Colm witnessed three of his closest neighbours being killed during his short lifetime: sixteen-year-old Martin McShane (see page 9), who lived two doors down; Denis Quinn, who lived next door; and Tony Doris (see page 208), who lived across the street. In response to the escalating situation, the football club opened their facilities to be used as a youth club to keep the local young people safe, and Colm was always to be found there. He enjoyed the dances, ceilís and fleadhs and, being the naturally social person everyone knew him to be, he was always in the middle of them. However, the realities of conflict were never far away, and indeed inescapable for Colm, as from the age of ten, with one of his brothers imprisoned and another on the run, his house was routinely raided by the RUC and British Army, and, additionally, his estate was constantly locked down by soldiers and military vehicles. As Brian describes the life of his younger brother, it is clear that trying to live an ordinary life was made impossible for Colm.

As the conflict intensified, and with Coalisland and Colm's estate being particular focal points, Colm began to take an interest in politics and got involved in the republican movement around the age of sixteen. This decision meant that the later stages of Colm's life were dedicated to the republican movement and, therefore, his involvement with his club stopped.

Colm McGirr was killed alongside Brian Campbell (see page 141) on 4 December 1983, aged twenty-three, whilst on active service for the IRA. They were killed without warning. The annual Colm McGirr and Brian Campbell Cup is contested by the Senior teams of local clubs every year in their memory, with Colm's cousin Paul captaining Fianna to victory in the cup's first year.

1984

Declan Martin (Deaglán Ó Mairtín)

AOIS/AGE: 18
CUMANN/CLUB: CLG Cúchullain, Dún Láthaí/ Cuchullains GAC, Dunloy
CONTAE/COUNTY: Aontroim/Antrim
MARAÍODH/KILLED: 21 Feabhra, Arm na Breataine/ 21 February, British Army

'We used to have this big CB radio pole out the back of the house. It must have been 30 feet high and it soon became Declan's preferred method of getting in and out of the house; climbing onto the roof and getting in through the skylight, especially when he didn't want anyone knowing he'd been out.' The Martin clan laugh when remembering their eldest sibling. 'That was typical of his nature; very adventurous and daring and little fear. It's also where he got his nickname "Monkey".'

Declan Martin was born on 13 July 1965 to Anna and Seamus. He was their firstborn and grew up in the hurling stronghold of Dunloy in the Glens of County Antrim, with younger brothers Seamus, Dónal, Sean, Turlough and Cahir, and younger sisters Brídín and Fidelma. Declan came from strong hurling stock, with his father Seamus being one of ten boys who all played hurling for Dunloy Cuchullains. 'They were very tough men back then, and their games were nothing short of blood-battles. Hurling was in the family and indeed Declan's godfather, Uncle Dan, played Senior hurling for Antrim. So, you could say it was only a natural progression that Declan was to play as well. In addition to that family connection, we grew up right beside the field and the GAA was part of our life, culture and identity as young Irish people. In our rural area, the GAA was all we really had, and that included the club being the centre of the community; for dancing and music, as well as sports. If you weren't involved in the GAA, you'd have had nothing!'

For Declan, his Dunloy career started when he could first join, which back then was at u12s. Before that, however, Declan and his siblings would spend their days playing hurling and football up in the mountains behind their home, in eager preparation for the day they came of age to play for the club. Donning Cuchullains' green and yellow jersey as the first of the next generation of Martin servants to play on Pearse Park, Declan would keenly and often successfully line out through the age groups until he reached Senior level. 'He was a talented hurler and as brave a player as you'd ever meet. He loved the GAA and Gaelic culture, as we all still do!' And those roots have continued to flourish for Declan's family. 'The year our father died, 2004, Dunloy reached the All-Ireland final, and the Loup, from Derry, were in the semi-final but lost to Corofin. If the Loup had reached the final, our father would have had one godson captain in the football final and another captain in the hurling!'

Off the pitch, Declan attended St Joseph's Primary School in Dunloy, before going on to Our Lady of Lourdes Secondary School in Ballymoney. 'Declan left school at the end of his third year and went straight into the family plumbing business, as all the boys would eventually do. That was the inevitable course for Declan, having been in his father's van working and helping from he was eleven years old, if not younger. In fact, when Declan turned eighteen, he had almost his time served! That was practically unheard of, but he was incredibly capable and intelligent and very enthusiastic about his work, and that also carried over into his social life. He got on well with everybody and was quite popular. He was very involved in the local youth club, and when the organiser of that youth club, Father Meeney, started to get older in age, Declan managed to raise the most money as part of a local fundraiser to help make home adaptations for him. He wouldn't have thought twice about putting himself forward to help in the community.' As Anna recalls the fond memories of her son, Declan's siblings are keen to remember that Declan would also have not thought twice about taking any opportunity to have the craic with his family and friends. 'When we were kids, there was this old, abandoned house up the road that everyone was afraid of, and I can remember on occasion Declan climbing up into it. He would sit at this broken window with a light, waiting on us or a group of lads to pass by, and then would jump out to scare the life out of us all. It got to the stage where you kind of knew to expect it, but he still managed to get us all running and screaming with fear!'

'Life back then wasn't easy, however.' The Martins describe the context of Declan's upbringing. 'Growing up, we were well used to getting stopped and searched by the police and British Army. We were a majority nationalist village, surrounded on all sides by staunchly loyalist areas, and we grew up very much aware of that fact and that anyone from Dunloy was always to be treated with suspicion by our neighbours and the Crown forces. Even thinking back to our daily routine as kids trying to go to school. We went to secondary school in Ballymoney, and at the bus stop every morning there would be four buses to bring kids to the different schools. Our bus was always the last to leave in the morning, and it was the first to arrive to take us home. Everyone was already in school by the time we landed in, and then we were forced to leave early. Then the bus itself would be stopped and searched twice every day, once by the police and then again by the British Army. And of course, being the Catholic bus, it would get pelted by stones at different stages along the journey.' In 1978, when Declan was entering his teenage years, a local boy, John Boyle (see page 294), was shot dead by the SAS in the local graveyard, aged only sixteen. 'That was what we were growing up with and Declan knew that none of it was right. He saw so much deprivation and experienced first-hand the harassment and violence of the State, and it affected him.'

Declan Martin was killed on 21 February 1984 by the SAS, alongside Henry Hogan. Declan was a Volunteer for the IRA and on active service when he was killed. Neither Declan's closest friends nor his family knew of his involvement in the IRA, which began when he joined aged seventeen. Local witnesses made public their testimony of seeing Declan being fired upon as he lay on the ground injured.

Harry Muldoon (Éibhear Ó Maoldúin)

AOIS/AGE: 45

CUMANN/CLUB: CLG Ciceam Ard Eoin, Béal Feirste/ Ardoyne Kickhams GAC, Belfast

CONTAE/COUNTY: Aontroim/Antrim

MARAÍODH/KILLED: 31 Deireadh Fómhair, le forsaí dílseach/31 October, loyalist forces

'Harry Muldoon was devoted to his mother.' Angela describes the father she lost. 'From a very young age he was keen to be out working as he liked to bring home money for my granny. He found all sorts of ways of getting money to her and always made sure she was looked after.'

Harry Muldoon was born on 14 October 1939 to Mary-Ellen and Patrick. He was the third of seven children, growing up in Brookfield Street, North Belfast, with older brothers Tommy and John, and younger siblings Lena, Mary, Kathleen and Pat. 'My father wasn't always well in his early life and suffered different phases of sickness as a child, which meant that he came out of school with little education, aged eleven or twelve years old. But once that stage of his life was behind him, he was out working. He was determined to help his family in any way he could, particularly his mother, and that had him doing all kinds of work! One of his ideas was to start running local picture shows, which usually attracted a decent crowd because he collected all the ends of buns from the local bakery before the show and gave them out to those who came. He was also, apparently, great at playing the coin toss. He had the nerve to be the last kid to run away when the police came, which meant that he could lift all the money left lying on the ground! As a young lad, my daddy could also be spotted walking around with his cart, filled with bundles of sticks and my aunt Lena sitting on top of them, selling them door to door. All of it was to bring home money for his mother.'

Harry's various initiatives came to define his character as a young man and soon led him to a life on the boats. 'He was delivering shoes one day down at Belfast docks, another one of his jobs, when he noticed that someone hadn't turned up for a job on the ship that was docked. My daddy asked one of the ship workers, "If he doesn't come, can I go with you?" The next thing was, he asked somebody to bring his bike back to Brown's Shoe Shop and to tell his mother that he is away on the boats. And just like that, aged fourteen, he was gone! That was the beginning of a long career and he loved it.'

As always, however, Harry would make sure to send money home each month to his mother, and it was always a special occasion when he returned home from time to time. 'There is a photo of when he first returned from the boats. He had bought himself a beautiful overcoat and bought my granny a china tea set. Of course, the china set was put into the cabinet and never allowed to be used! Unfortunately, it was lost to fire when they were burnt out of the house in '69.' On one particular visit home, having a few years at sea under his belt, Harry met his future wife, Mary Ann Flynn. 'He was out one night in the Plaza, and that's where he met my mummy. She was previously engaged but they fell for one another almost instantly. They got married in October 1961, and then I was born in '63. My mother worked as a stitcher, and her and my dad were very hard workers. My dad came off the boats when I was born and worked in Bass Ireland and a few other jobs before becoming a black taxi driver, and he and my mummy managed to buy our first home in 1965 in Ardoyne, North Belfast.'

Angela's younger sister, Tracey, was then born in 1973 and the family moved again, to another area of North Belfast. 'My mummy was always very proud of her home, and her and my daddy loved to host guests. They would regularly have people to the house and enjoyed their home life. Sadly, in 1973 my mummy took ill, and she eventually passed away in 1978, aged thirty-eight, having battled with breast cancer for a number of years.' Having lost his wife, Harry's world was turned upside down, but his love and devotion to his daughters, aged only five and fourteen when they lost their mother, kept him going. In describing her father, Angela paints of picture of a man defined by his generosity and selflessness, driven by a great sense of duty to both his family and neighbours. 'Even today, people still come up to me and tell me about my daddy. How he helped their family when they were in need; how he never hesitated to reach into his own pockets to help a friend who was stuck. There are so many stories of how Harry Muldoon helped people; how he was there for people. Even after he died, a week or so after, two bags of coal arrived at my granny's house, paid for and all. It was an order made by my daddy for my granny.'

In terms of the involvement of the GAA in Harry's life, he was, by all accounts, a talented handballer for Ardoyne Kickhams. With the nature of Harry's work at sea, his playing days would have been when he was visiting home and then when he made the permanent return once he was married. Angela is unsure when her father began playing for the Kickhams but remembers the club and the GAA being a pillar of his social life. 'Every other Sunday he went to watch the hurling and football. He had a lot of good friends at the club, and everybody knew him and had a good word to say about him. Those Sundays were my dad's escape; where the chaos of life could be put on hold. He particularly loved his trips down to Croke Park and would always return with a teddy bear in the colours of whichever counties were playing. Boxing was another passion of my daddy's, his own father being a boxer, and social time that wasn't spent in the Kickhams was spent in The Star Social Club, also in Ardoyne.'

Harry Muldoon was killed on 31 October 1984 by the UVF, aged forty-five. He was at home with his two daughters when gunmen broke into the house and shot him dead in his daughter Angela's bedroom. Eleven-year-old Tracey was hiding in her bedroom next door. Denis McClean was convicted of Harry's killing. A decision not to charge a second suspect, despite evidence placing that person at the Muldoon home, including having on his person gloves containing fragments of glass matching the glass fragments collected from the murder scene, has given the Muldoon family strong suspicions of collusive activity in Harry's killing.

Harry's love for the GAA continues to be reflected in the younger generations of his family. His granddaughter Nicole played camogie for Ardoyne Kickhams and his grandson Ryan briefly played Gaelic football. Harry's granddaughter Aoibheann plays handball for her county, while his nephew Damien Muldoon is also a great handballer, both continuing the line of strong Muldoon handballers. Just recently Aoibheann finished runner-up at the County Antrim 3 Wall girls u15 competition. 'He would be so proud of his family now and would have loved to go watch them play. In our own ways, we keep his legacy alive and his passion for the GAA lives on in our family.'

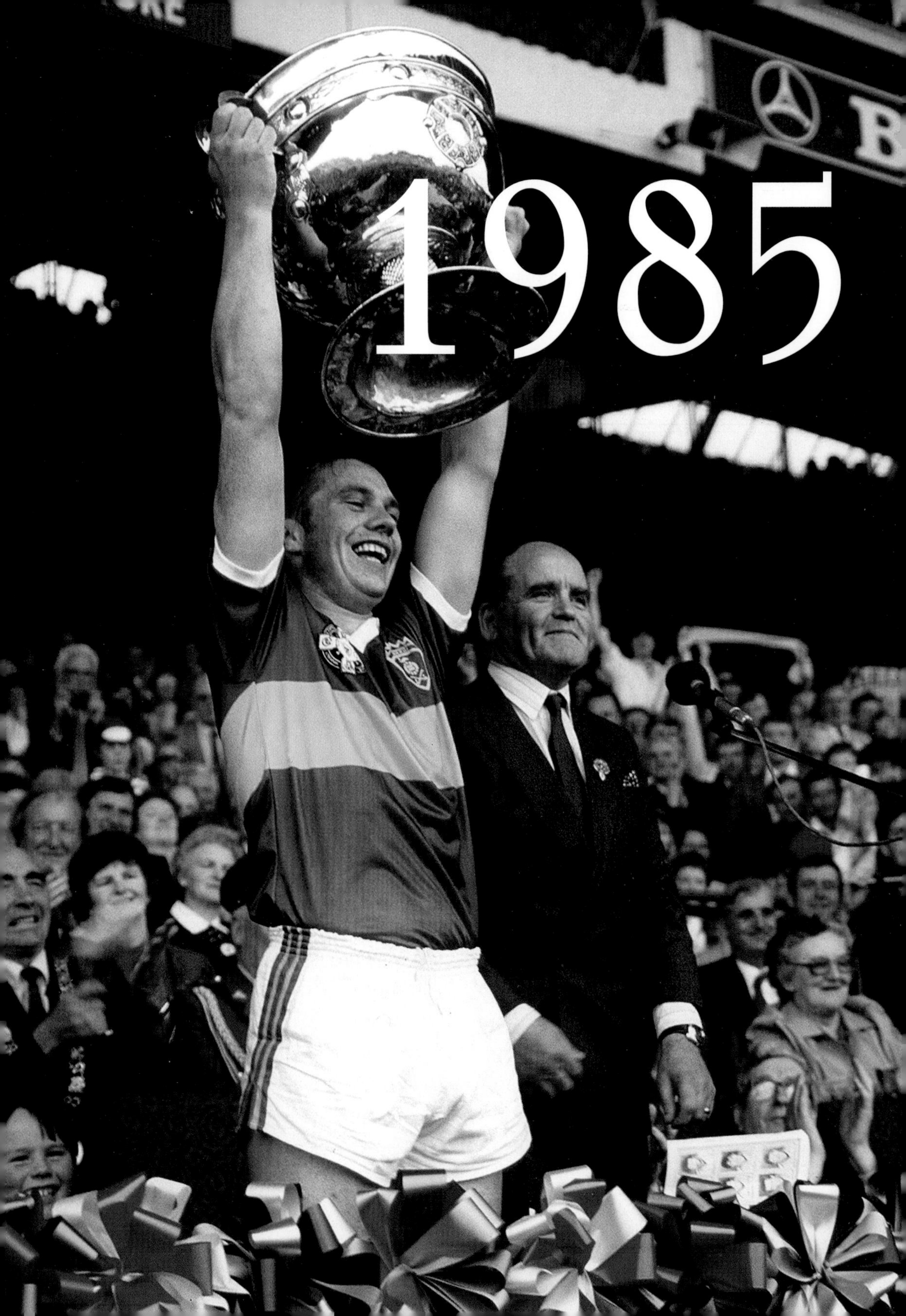

1985

Kieran Murray (Ciarán Ó Muireadhaigh)

AOIS/AGE: 22

CUMANN/CLUB: Na Pluinceidí CLG, Cabhan a Chaorthainn/Pomeroy Plunketts GAC

CONTAE/COUNTY: Tír Eoghain/Tyrone

MARAÍODH/KILLED: 23 Lúnasa, le Óglaigh na hÉireann/ 23 August, IRA

'Kieran was very much a home bird. He was very content with the life he was living.' Kieran's family describe the young man they lost. 'He was a happy, outgoing child and a very peaceable youngster. He would have always walked away from a bad situation.'

Kieran Murray was born on 7 July 1963 to Dan and Nora in the townland of Bracky, Omagh in County Tyrone. Kieran was the youngest in a family of seven children, growing up with Thomas, Noreen, James, Francie, Martin and Charlie. In 1964, when Kieran was just an infant, the family moved to Pomeroy, County Tyrone, and that is where Kieran would come to spend his childhood. 'He was a very sociable young lad and had a large circle of friends from a young age. That would have been because of his peaceable nature; he would have never been involved in any fights.' Kieran was especially close to his brothers Martin and Charlie, 'the three wee boys' as they were known, as there was a bit of an age gap between them and their older siblings. The lads attended St Mary's Primary School in Pomeroy and then went on to Dean Maguire College in Carrickmore, which Kieran left aged sixteen. 'He had a keen interest in motor mechanics and farming and was very talented with his hands in practical lessons in school. He would regularly bring home woodwork and metalwork projects. When he left school, he would have had regular work repairing cars, doing joinery jobs and labouring at farm work.' As he matured, Kieran's social life flourished. 'He loved going to the dances and that with his friends. It was of no surprise at his funeral when the priest described him as someone who brought joy and pleasure to all who knew him.' Kieran also became involved in local politics, volunteering his time to participate in electioneering for Sinn Féin, and he found his own way of contributing to the republican movement by canvassing, collecting money and helping with elections.

Kieran played football for Pomeroy Plunketts GAC. Details of his days on the field are limited, but his family remember the Gael he was and how GAA was omnipresent in his life. Pomeroy Plunketts formed a guard of honour at his funeral and placed his football shirt on his coffin.

Kieran Murray was killed on 23 August 1985 by the IRA. He was twenty-two years old when he was shot dead whilst travelling to a dance in Cookstown, Tyrone, with his close friend Pat Molloy. Pat was driving the car when the IRA fired at them. After Kieran's killing, the IRA issued an apology to his family and a public statement to the effect that they had mistaken the car Kieran was in for another car belonging to their intended target. No one has ever been charged for Kieran's killing.

1986

Francis Bradley (Proinsias Ó Brolacháin)

AOIS/AGE: 20
CUMANN/CLUB: Naomh Trea CLG, Baile Mhic Uiginn/ St Trea's GAC, Ballymaguigan
CONTAE/COUNTY: Doire/Derry
MARAÍODH/KILLED: 18 Feabhra, Arm na Breataine/ 18 February, British Army

'Francis was a very fun-loving and affable character.' Brian Bradley describes his brother. 'He was very popular with everyone in the community and the sort of person who made friends easily because of his kind and caring nature.'

Francis Bradley was born on 25 March 1965 to Eddie and Rosemary. He was the eldest of four children, growing up on the family farm in Derrygarve Park, between the parishes of Ballymaguigan and Newbridge in County Derry, with his sister Roisín and two brothers, Edward and Brian. 'Growing up, there wasn't a lot of money about, but everyone seemed to be in the same position and there was always a great community spirit between neighbours.' Francis, or Bambi as he was sometimes called because of his small build, went to the local St Trea's Primary School in Ballymaguigan before going on to St Pius X High School in Magherafelt. Brian explains that the early days of Francis's life would have been filled with helping his father out on the farm, as well as helping his grandparents, Eddie and Sarah, with their farm too. 'His grandparents were very fond of him to the point they almost treated him like their very own son. He had a special bond with them and would often help them, as they reached old age, around the house, as well as on their farm.' This time spent on the farm led to Francis developing a great interest in farming and animals. Brian explains that his older brother had a passion for animals, which was complemented by a natural instinct he had in caring for them. 'He reared his own cattle and looked after animals on both the farmyard as well as around the house for years. He had dogs, ducks, ferrets, lambs, and he bred turkeys for friends and family in the run-up to Christmas! He could always be seen driving along the laneways in his blue Ford tractor as a young cub, and everyone knew him.'

Upon leaving school at sixteen, Francis found work making windows at McElhone's Joiners Shop in Newbridge, which allowed him to finally save up to get himself a car. Brian explains that Francis, like most young men his age, was busting to get out on the road. 'He passed his driving test when he was seventeen and went through a few cars after that, but he was famously renowned for driving his very distinguished yellow Ford Escort. Nearly everyone known to him had a sail in it at one time or another. That wee car covered some ground as Francis and his friends went out on drives. They would often recall that Francis was always full of devilment and rascality in search of a good laugh, and he loved the harmless banter and fun of that age.' Francis also enjoyed going to the local swimming pool and snooker club with his close friends and was a member of the Newbridge Snooker Club. 'Despite his great interest in snooker, we often ridiculed him for not having won any trophies for it!' When he got older, Francis met Eilish Kennedy and the pair began a serious relationship to the extent that they were gearing towards settling down and starting a family together like a lot of their friends were doing.

In terms of the GAA, Brian doesn't recall specific details other than the fact that his brother was a committed Gael from a very young age. Francis received his first introduction to football at primary school and played in both primary and secondary school. He also joined the Juvenile ranks of his local GAA club, St Trea's in Ballymaguigan, and played every year right through to Senior level. 'He was well-known in Ballymaguigan and Newbridge because of the football. He loved to play and, despite his size, he was a very strong young man. He showed little to no fear on the field when he was attacking the goal, and always kept a calm head in possession of the ball.' Growing up, the GAA club meant more to Francis than just football. Like many communities in Ireland, it was the social hub for his young life, where he could go to the discos and dances, and meet his friends. Brian describes his brother as a great Gael.

Francis Bradley was twenty years old when he was killed on 18 February 1986 by the British Army. He was walking to a barn with a friend to play cards when soldiers, lying in wait, shot him dead. A second inquest into his death, yet to be completed at the time of writing, found that Francis was shot eight times, with wounds indicating that he was shot while he was on his knees and then while he was lying on his back. The soldiers responsible for killing Francis believed him to be a member of the IRA, and an RUC officer claimed to have found a rifle lying by Francis's side at the scene of his death. In the months leading up to his death, Francis and his family were subjected to intense harassment by Crown forces. 'I was thirteen years old at the time, and the RUC would often come into our home in the middle of the night, wrecking the house. They wanted Francis to be an informant and offered him thousands of pounds. Thankfully Francis didn't, but that's when he was told he would be killed.' Indeed, one of the hearings into Francis's death heard evidence of an occasion where he was arrested and taken to Gough Barracks in Armagh, where he was told that he would not see his twenty-first birthday. The soldier responsible for killing Francis is also the soldier responsible for the killings of Dessie Grew (see page 197) and Martin McCaughey (see page 296). The IRA later claimed Francis Bradley as one of their members.

Raymond Mooney (Réamonn Ó Maonaigh)

AOIS/AGE: 33

CUMANN/CLUB: CLG Ciceam Ard Eoin, Béal Feirste/ Ardoyne Kickhams GAC, Belfast

CONTAE/COUNTY: Aontroim/Antrim

MARAÍODH/KILLED: 16 Meán Fómhair, le forsaí dílseach/ 16 September, loyalist forces

'One of the things which always stood out to me about my dad was his involvement in his community. Whether it was involvement with the church or the GAA, all of the different aspects of his life have all felt very linked through his passion for organising for the wider community.' Chris Mooney pieces together the stories and memories he has heard over the years to paint a picture of his father. 'I always remember this tin in our house growing up. It was full of medals, hundreds of them, mostly Irish dancing and céilí medals, all belonging to my father. I was fascinated by them as a kid, and the memory of going through each of them has always stayed with me.'

Raymond Mooney was born on 2 April 1953 to Tommy and Catherine. He was born and raised in the Ardoyne district of North Belfast, a fact that remained a source of great pride in his life. Raymond was the second of four children, growing up with older brother Gabriel and younger brothers Patrick and Martin. With the passing of time, details of Raymond's early life have naturally faded, but from an early age we can be certain of the influence and presence of faith and the GAA in forming foundational elements of his identity. 'My dad served the altar at Holy Cross from a young boy and did so until his death, and his involvement in the GAA was very much the same as with the church. I am unsure where he attended primary school, but he went on to St Gabriel's Secondary School, from which he landed, by all accounts, a great job for Northern Ireland Electricity.'

As a young man, Raymond personified service to his community, as his friend Brian explains. 'I was a couple of years younger than Raymond. He was our prefect when I started serving the altar, and even from then you could tell how reliable a character he was. You knew he would be there every morning, no matter how early the start, driven by a deep commitment to his faith. He was also heavily involved in running community-based projects, and I think he might have played a role in setting up the local credit union. And Raymond was always a central figure in these initiatives too, never on the periphery. He was a real servant, and as I got older, I came to know Raymond more personally as he approached me to help run some of the community initiatives with him. I remember on one occasion him asking if I wanted to help him run a few céilí nights. I agreed, and went along thinking it would be a fun, easy mess about. But on arriving, I soon discovered how serious Raymond was about it. He rarely did half-measures. I said, "Raymond, what is going on here?" pointing to the kilts and stuff he had out. He replied, "Sure if we're doing it for fun, why not go for a few competitions as well!" He loved it all, and ended up winning a few prestigious events, including an Ulster Championship or two. He was a genuinely good guy.'

It was around this time that Raymond was introduced to Briege. 'My mum lived only a few streets from my dad in Ardoyne. So, naturally, they met in Bundoran!' Chris laughs while recalling the story of his parents' meeting, which seems to reveal exactly the person his father was. 'My dad and granda met first, actually! They were all on holiday at the same time, and my dad and granda bumped into each other while both were searching for somewhere to watch the GAA. After chatting briefly, my dad then asked if my granda knew of anywhere he could get to Mass. My granda asked why a young lad of his age would want to go to Mass, so my dad explained how he served the altar at Holy Cross and was an ecclesiastic minister, etc. My granda's eyes lit up and he immediately introduced my dad to his daughter, my mum! My mum's brother always laughs that the arrival of my dad into my granda's life was like the arrival of this golden child, passionate about his GAA and faith, and so it wasn't long before Mum and Dad were married.' The newlyweds had four children, the first coming along in March 1981, and Chris, the second youngest, in February 1984. 'My dad was devoted to us and his family. Anyone who knew him would always tell you the same thing; that he was a gentleman, passionate about his faith and his culture and, above all, his family.'

In terms of the GAA, Raymond played both hurling and football for Ardoyne Kickhams. From an early age, he became a committed member of the club and had tasted success coming up through the age groups. The crowning achievement came in 1969, when Raymond played his part in bringing home the u16 South Antrim Football Championship, which is still remembered in the club. 'My dad's nickname around the club was "Stitch-y" because he was always picking up injuries.' Perhaps this was because, on the hurling pitch, as Brian points out, 'Raymond usually elected not to wear a helmet when he was playing, which, for a keeper, meant that he was getting injured most games!' Raymond is still remembered by the older generations in the Kickhams club, and Chris describes how important the club has been in establishing a personal connection between him and his father. 'My father was killed when I was very young, and in the aftermath of everything, for all different reasons, I never really got to know who he was. But I remember starting to play for the Kickhams, and the first few times going into the club I saw pictures of my dad on the walls. He stuck out to me like a sore thumb, and I recognised him right away. I knew it was him, but I never really spoke to anyone about it. In my own wee way, I had this picture in my head of my dad and thought to myself that maybe he once stood exactly where I am right now. It was comforting to me in that sense and football became that link between me and my dad, and when my team got to u16, we managed to repeat the achievement of my dad's team! That achievement remains another important link for me with him.'

Raymond Mooney was thirty-three years old when he was killed on 16 September 1986 by the UVF. He had just finished chairing a prayer group in the grounds of Holy Cross Chapel in Ardoyne that evening, and was locking up the hall with another parishioner when three gunmen approached them. The woman with Raymond was forced to watch as the gunmen shot and killed him within the walls of the chapel. The Protestant Action Force, a pseudonym for the UVF, claimed Raymond's killing was a retaliation on the Catholic community for the IRA's killing of a prominent loyalist, who was buried on the day Raymond was killed, despite Raymond having no connection whatsoever to republicanism. There has been a recent discovery of significant evidence of collusion between loyalist forces and the RUC in Raymond's killing. No one has ever been arrested in connection to his killing.

In tribute to Raymond's memory, and in recognition of his service to his parish and community, a prayer room in the Houben Centre, located on the grounds of Holy Cross in Ardoyne, has been named after him.

1987

Pádraig McKearney (Pádraig Mac Cearnaigh)

AOIS/AGE: 32
CUMANN/CLUB: An Mhaigh Tír na nÓg GLC/ Tír na nÓg GAC, Moy
CONTAE/COUNTY: Tír Eoghain/Tyrone
MARAÍODH/KILLED: 8 Bealtaine, Arm na Breataine/ 8 May, British Army

'Pádraig was a reserved character.' Angela and Tommy start to recall the memories they have of their brother. 'He was born prematurely with a twin, who sadly died at birth, so it was a difficult start to life for him, almost seventy years ago in rural Ireland. But he succeeded and thrived, despite the odds.'

Pádraig McKearney was born on 18 December 1954 to Maura and Kevin. He was the third child in a family of six children, growing up in the village of The Moy, County Tyrone with older siblings Tommy and Margaret, and younger siblings Seán, Kevin and Angela. As with all the McKearney boys, Pádraig's youth was spent on the football field, which was just a stone's throw away from the family home. As Angela explains, the GAA meant everything to the rural community in which Pádraig grew up. 'Not only were our father and uncles fanatical about football, but the village was also. In those days, I suppose it was the only entertainment people had, and the passion was always there for it. Our father and mother ran a butcher's shop in the village, and football was always the talking point in the shop. The local people would come in and the talk would always be how much better we were to this team or that, and all the tactics of the weekend's game were mulled over.'

What Angela and Tommy describe is a ubiquitous passion for football that all Gaels experience, where little else matters in those moments of conversation. It is that passion that infected Pádraig, which Tommy explains. 'Where perhaps Seán and I had a bit of a natural talent for football, Pádraig was there out of pure enthusiasm. He might not have been the most skilful of players, but he could always be relied upon, especially if an argument broke out on the pitch!'

Certainly, for a small, rural club like The Moy in those days, it was passion and enthusiasm that were its lifelines. Before each game, Pádraig and the lads would have to go out to sweep manure off the pitch because a local farmer had use of the field. Tommy laughs that the mouth of the goal was a particular hotspot as the cattle used the posts to scratch themselves. While an unpleasant task in itself, Pádraig understood that this type of job formed the necessary preparatory work for football to be played.

Away from football, Pádraig attended Collegeland and The Moy primary schools before heading to St Patrick's Academy in Dungannon. 'He went to school and I suppose he enjoyed it as much as any young man does; in other words, he didn't like it! And like the rest of us, if he wasn't in school or at the football, he would help our father in the shop or our uncles on their farms with any tasks needing to be done. I remember as we were getting older, our father would get us to help him in the shop, so we would always try to sneak by him on a Saturday morning. If he spotted you, that was you working for the day!'

Tommy and Angela explain that alongside a strong footballing tradition, their family also had a strong history of republicanism, and that politics came to be another defining aspect of Pádraig's life. 'Both of our grandfathers were involved in the republican movement. Our paternal grandfather played his part in the 1916 Rising, forming part of the group of Volunteers who were sent to Coalisland, and our maternal grandfather was highly active in the Tan War and subsequent Civil War. So, growing up and spending time with our grandparents, particularly our maternal grandfather, was certainly influential in our outlook on the politics of our country. He would recount stories of the Tan War and also of the people he knew who went to Spain as part of the International Brigade. He passed on his contextual method of viewing the world, and so it was inevitable that we would grow up with a strong sense of politics, especially when combined with the circumstances in which we found ourselves growing up.' Tommy continues, 'We lived in an area where the civil rights movement began. I remember our teachers marching in the streets, and committees being set up by local members of the GAA to collect funds to send to Belfast as relief for the families being burnt out of their homes. That people were being met with batons, and then to lift the newspaper to read "Man shot dead in Armagh" by the B Specials; the atmosphere had escalated terribly.'

At sixteen, Pádraig took the decision to join the IRA. In August 1972 he was arrested for involvement in an explosion at the post office in The Moy. He was then rearrested in late 1973 and was on remand when his brother Seán (see page 60) died in May 1974. Pádraig was then released in 1977 but would be arrested again in August 1980 and sentenced to fifteen years. He would only serve three and a half years before escaping in 1983 and going on the run.

Pádraig McKearney was killed whilst on active service for the IRA on 8 May 1987. He was one of eight IRA Volunteers to be killed in an ambush designed by the British Army's SAS. Known as the Loughgall Ambush, the circumstances of the deaths of the Volunteers have long been the subject of international attention and investigation, and the ambush is considered a key example of the British government's shoot-to-kill policy. It was the biggest loss of life for the IRA in a single incident during the conflict.

1988

Aidan McAnespie (Aidan Mac An Easpaig)

AOIS/AGE: 23

CUMANN/CLUB: Achadh Lú Uí Néill GLC/
Aghaloo O'Neills GFC

CONTAE/COUNTY: Tír Eoghain/Tyrone

MARAÍODH/KILLED: 21 Feabhra, Arm na Breataine/
21 February, British Army

'Aidan was a quiet lad in his own way, you know?' Vincent McAnespie remembers his younger brother. 'He would have gone to his work every day and enjoyed filling his downtime either at the football or around scramblers and motorbikes. Just a typical lad his age.'

Aidan McAnespie was born on 22 June 1964 to John and Liz. He was the youngest in a family of eight, growing up in the border town of Aughnacloy in County Tyrone with older brothers Vincent, Gerry and Sean, and his two older sisters, Margaret and Eilish. He attended St Mary's Primary School in Aughnacloy before going on to St Ciaran's Secondary School in Ballygawley. 'Like us all, Aidan would have been first introduced to the GAA through the local priest at school, who was setting up the Juvenile football, and then the town finally set up a local club, Aghaloo GAC. Aidan was about eight years old when the club was founded and our father was one of its founding members so, as kids, we were never away from the field. In the beginning, it was just a cattle field and before every game, the cattle would be pushed off and a group of lads would be sent out with old bags and shovels to clean the field.'

As Aidan moved up through the Juvenile structures, Aghaloo was finding its feet as a new club, and the focus was, therefore, on maximising enjoyment and learning. 'We never had the numbers for a competitive, winning side, but everyone was happy to be there and taking part. We would have all played for the club growing up and done our bit to keep it going; I can recall a time when my father jumped into goals with his work boots on for Sean's team so as to not forfeit the game! Aidan would have been of a similar mind when he became a Senior footballer. He never liked to see the club stuck and would have continued to line out for them, despite his knees giving him a good bit of bother. As he got older, Aidan also started getting into refereeing and had begun Juvenile refereeing with the hope of strengthening the club.'

After finishing school at sixteen, Aidan got a job just across the border at a poultry products factory in County Monaghan. 'Everything was grand in the early years. He would get a lift to and from the factory with the people he worked with, and that meant that crossing the border checkpoint was a lot less hassle as they were all in a group. Growing up in Aughnacloy, you had to quickly learn the best tactics for avoiding harassment by the British soldiers or police.' Vincent explains the backdrop of Aidan's childhood and how, as he got older and began navigating adulthood, the reality of life in Aughnacloy for anyone not of a unionist persuasion became quickly and violently apparent.

'It was a real garrison town, being home to a UDR, RUC and British Army barracks and, also, the checkpoint to cross into Monaghan. Our family would have been subjected to a lot of harassment by all of them as we were identifiably republican. I remember, for example, during the time of the hunger strikes, solidarity and support were our family's main priorities and that meant football for all of us took a back seat while we attended rallies and such. The Crown forces liked to make their disapproval clear, I suppose, which we were used to over the years, but they singled out Aidan as he got older. They knew he was the youngest in the family and he had to cross the checkpoint at least twice a day to get to and from work. When he turned seventeen, he got himself a motorbike which, for himself, gave him some much-needed independence, but it kicked off a period of intense harassment at the checkpoint as he was then crossing it by himself, and he was still only a young lad. On one morning when he was crossing the checkpoint to get to work, he was stopped, and the bike was taken off him to be searched. When he was eventually let through and got into work, he opened his lunchbox to find all his food soaked in urine. It reached a stage where Aidan would regularly tell us that the soldiers told him they would kill him one day. I was living across the border in Monaghan at the time and asked Aidan about moving in with me, but he didn't want to leave Mum and Dad on their own. He was the last child in the house and was always making sure our parents were taken care of. To try to ease the harassment, Aidan eventually got a car, and our mother would usually travel to work with him as the soldiers, generally, weren't so bad in the presence of an older woman. That intense level of harassment just became a fact of life for Aidan, but he could never get used to it. No one could.'

Aidan McAnespie was killed on 21 February 1988 by the British Army as he crossed the Aughnacloy border checkpoint into County Monaghan. Aidan had been attending a funeral across the border in Monaghan that day and had left a bit early to get a fire lit to warm the house for his parents coming home. He then began to make his way to Aghaloo's pitch, where he was to play in the Jim Devlin Cup against Killeeshil. Although the pitch was in Tyrone, it sat on the border and getting there necessitated going back through the border checkpoint. Aidan was already through the checkpoint, with his back to it, when he was shot by a mounted machine gun operated by a soldier sitting within the checkpoint sentry box. The soldier responsible, David Holden, was found guilty of manslaughter in November 2022.

Aidan McAnespie's name is known throughout Ireland and beyond. His sister Eilish was one of the foremost voices for bereaved victims of the conflict and led a monumental campaign seeking justice for the killing of her brother. Eilish and the McAnespie family were some of the founding members of Relatives for Justice and for over twenty years, Eilish led her family's fight, which was then taken on by her father and siblings when she sadly passed in 2008. Neither Eilish nor John got to see their family's day in court, but without their relentless campaign, Aidan's killer might never have been brought to justice.

Aidan's name and legacy has been honoured in the founding and naming of the Aidan McAnespie GAC in Boston, USA; an act the McAnespie family are hugely honoured by. The Boston club is now regarded as one of the elite North American GAA clubs, having had past All-Ireland football winners line out for it at different stages and having successfully brought home a few USGAA Championships. The club's jersey is also one of the highest-selling pieces of GAA merchandise. At the time of writing, the McAnespie family had received news that Tyrone GAA will be erecting a monument dedicated to Aidan's memory at their GAA Centre of Excellence.

The McAnespie family remain deeply involved in the GAA. Vincent continues to manage and coach club teams, and Aidan's nieces and nephews carry on his passion for football, with many of them playing at the top intercounty level for Monaghan Senior men's and ladies' football panels.

Sean Savage (Seán Sábhaois)

AOIS/AGE: 23
CUMANN/CLUB: Naomh Gall CLG, Béal Feirste/ St Gall's GAC, Belfast
CONTAE/COUNTY: Aontroim/Antrim
MARAÍODH/KILLED: 6 Márta, Arm na Breataine/ 6 March, British Army

'Sean Savage was not your typical guy around the corner.' Jude, Sean's brother-in-law, begins to describe the young life of Sean Savage. 'He was a quiet lad who very much kept himself to himself, but he was also a very deep-thinking and thoughtful character.'

Sean Savage was born on 26 January 1965 to Elizabeth, known to everyone as Lily, and John. He was one of four children, growing up in the Lower Falls Road area of West Belfast with sisters Anne and Mary, and his brother, Robert, where their father, for decades, was a well-known and respected bar manager. The family was devoutly Catholic, and so Sean attended St Finian's Primary School in Clonard, where he received his first introduction to the GAA by the Christian Brothers who ran the school. 'They would have been the greatest influence on Sean in getting involved with the GAA, and the school itself would have been known as a feeder school for the St Gall's GAA club. In terms of the extent of his playing career, little memory still exists. What we can say is that he had a passion for Gaelic culture from a very young age and Sean would have played both hurling and football for St Gall's. The influence of the Christian Brothers would have continued when he reached La Salle Brothers' Secondary School, where I imagine he also competed in the college competitions.'

As is natural with the passing of time, memories of Sean's days on the field of play have faded, but as Jude goes on to describe his character, it is clear that Sean was someone who cared deeply for the values and roots of the association. 'Sean was totally in touch with his cultural roots. He had a passion for the Irish language and its revival and, indeed, was part of a sub-culture that existed in Belfast at the time seeking to promote the language. He was a very keen cyclist and would regularly cycle to West Donegal to get the boat from Magheroarty to Tory Island, and just immerse himself in the daily life of the Irish language. He also had strong politics, certainly inheriting republican values from his uncle, Billy McKee, who was, for decades, at the centre of the republican movement, but you got the sense that Sean clearly understood his own beliefs and he spent a lot of time thinking about his own position. He would share his politics through his art, which he made a lot of. It would usually depict his republican and internationalist view of the world, and also reflect that he came from a family steeped in Catholicism. As a person, his mind was always with something else or in some other place, and looking back, I now think he was acutely intelligent. In a normal society, you could imagine Sean as someone who would have gone into social, progressive campaign work. The quiet researcher who does all the real work. Or, in fact, a priest, with his tendency to seek solitude and space to think.' Jude pauses and laughs, 'One thing about Sean is that he never supported a soccer team, which made him a good man in my eyes!'

Sean Savage was killed by the SAS on 6 March 1988, while on active service for the IRA in Gibraltar, alongside fellow Volunteers Mairéad Farrell and Daniel McCann. The circumstances and nature of their deaths, and the fact that they were unarmed when shot, led to international condemnation. Sean, Mairéad and Daniel are now collectively known as the Gibraltar Three and their killings are one of the most prominent examples of the shoot-to-kill policy employed by the British government.

John Murray (Eoin Ó Muirigh)

AOIS/AGE: 27

CUMANN/CLUB: CLG Ó Donnabháin Rosa, Béal Feirste/ O'Donovan Rossa GAC, Belfast

CONTAE/COUNTY: Aontroim/Antrim

MARAÍODH/KILLED: 16 Márta, le forsaí dílseach/ 16 March, loyalist forces

'Of course, when somebody dies, they always say, "God, weren't they very popular!" But in John's case, it was very true.' Mary describes her younger brother. 'Our John really loved his life and his family. He was so vibrant and had a very romantic view of everything around him.'

John Murray was born on 30 January 1961 to Alice and Jackie. 'He was third in line in our house. There was me, Geraldine and then John, then Peter, Patricia, Roisín and Alice.' John and his siblings grew up, at first, in the New Lodge area of North Belfast, before the Murray family moved to South Belfast when John's father was offered a new job which came with accommodation. 'We are all so close as siblings and we had a great life growing up with each other. Our parents instilled in us a love for Gaelic culture and all things Irish, and it was always stories, jokes and singing in our house. And indeed, John was a fluent Gaelgeoir. My parents were also devout Catholics, as was the norm for a lot of their generation, and so John attended St Patrick's Primary School, before heading on to the Christian Brothers' School when we moved to the south of the city. It was at the Christian Brothers' where John would have been first introduced to the GAA, and he really took to it. In no time there were hurls lying all about the house and the talk was always about football and hurling. A local club, Holy Rosary, was then formed, which John and Peter joined as soon as they could, and under committed local Gaels, John's love for the GAA was fostered and deepened.' When the time came for John to move on to secondary school, and after doing well in his 11-plus exams, he was admitted to St Mary's Christian Brothers' School in West Belfast. At the school, John's passion for the GAA was cherished and he played an important part on both the hurling and football teams of the traditionally very strong St Mary's.

It was not always easy, however, for John to follow his passion for Gaelic games. Making his way from the south of the city to West Belfast each day for school during the conflict would have been a daunting journey. And making that journey with his hurl would not have made it any easier. 'There was one day Mummy and Daddy got a call from the police to say that John had been arrested. Mummy was so concerned and asked why, explaining that he was only fifteen years of age, to which the officer replied, "He was arrested for carrying an offensive weapon." Mummy knew then that they meant his hurling stick. My parents raced down to get him, and of course, my mother being my mother, gave the police officers the whole lecture on the history of the hurl!'

Mary describes how her brother grew up in an environment which tried to make criminal his love for the GAA, and in which expression of that love came with added attention during the conflict. At club level, John's beloved Holy Rosary had to fold due to the escalation of the conflict. Drawing unwanted attention and based in a relatively isolated nationalist enclave in South Belfast, Holy Rosary's struggles became insurmountable, despite the best efforts of local Gaels. 'I suppose the positive to come out of that difficult time, however, was the foresight of the local men who oversaw Holy Rosary, who came to my parents to say that they saw potential in John and Peter. They said that they would bring the boys over to the Rossa club in West Belfast, along with a couple of the boys from Holy Rosary who were still keen on playing. So that's when John and Peter would have started playing for Rossa.' It was to be a significant gain for the O'Donovan Rossa club. In John, they found their 1979 Minor football team captain and a player who would often successfully line out alongside his brother Peter, right up to the last.

Outside of the GAA, John would eventually find a successful career as a heating engineer. 'He left St Mary's at sixteen and my parents were asking him what he wanted to do, and he just gave the typical teenager response of "I dunno." Well, Mummy wasted no time. There was a worksite just across from our house, and Mummy walked onto it and managed to talk John into a job interview for him to become a heating engineer. That was his career choice made for him there and then; and he loved it!' John then met Catherine, the Irish dancing teacher. 'He was smitten. I do not exaggerate when I say he loved her beyond words. Catherine was a brilliant singer, the voice of an angel, and our John would sit and she would teach him to sing, with little success, but it didn't matter to him and he would sing away. I remember he used to write mountains of love letters to her, and, of course, there would have been no room in our house for secrets with the amount of us all piled in, so if one of us found a letter, it was getting read aloud. There was a popular song at the time called "Love Letters in the Sand", and we used to laugh that our house was "Love Letters in the Drawer"! It just gives you a sense of what type of guy he was. And, inevitably, he and Catherine were married in 1985 when John was twenty-four, and along came babies Niall and Aisling, whom John also loved no-end. With his family, friends and the Rossa club, he was as content as can be.'

John Murray was killed by loyalist gunman Michael Stone whilst attending the funerals of Sean Savage (see page 170), Daniel McCann and Mairéad Farrell, the Gibraltar Three, on 16 February 1988. He was one of three victims of the attack, which left a further fifty people injured as Stone threw hand grenades and shot indiscriminately at the mourners. John, seeking to protect those around him, was shot dead as he charged at the gunman and chased him down alongside others. Niall was three years old and Aisling was only ten months.

In the wake of John's killing, the O'Donovan Rossa club have been committed to keeping his memory alive. 'On the tenth anniversary of John being named captain, one year after his death, Peter was named captain of the Senior footballers and the team dedicated their championship campaign in John's memory. As underdogs, they won the Antrim Senior Football Championship! Afterwards, in the following days, Mummy was tending John's grave and she found a medal had been placed on it. The team had a medal pressed for John, and one of his teammates came and placed it to rest with him. The Rossa family have always been so supportive, and they never forgot John. That has been so important to us. They were so kind to Mummy and always made sure she was taken care of.'

Seamus Morris (Seamus Ó Muirghis)

AOIS/AGE: 18
CUMANN/CLUB: CLG Ciceam Ard Eoin, Béal Feirste/ Ardoyne Kickhams GAC, Belfast
CONTAE/COUNTY: Aontroim/Antrim
MARAÍODH/KILLED: 8 Lúnasa, le forsaí dílseach/ 8 August, loyalist forces

'Seamus's contribution to his community was one of commitment and achievement on the Gaelic fields of Antrim, representing his family and parish with dignity, courage and skill.' These are the words read aloud each year on the anniversary of Seamus Morris's death. His home district of Ardoyne in North Belfast is fiercely proud of Seamus and continues to keep his memory alive as a Gael who exemplified the core values of the GAA. 'Seamus will always be a beacon of light in our memories in Ard Eoin GAC. Days like today bring good memories; memories that are treasured by everyone who was lucky to have known Seamus Óg Morris.'

Seamus Morris was born on 14 January 1970 to Madeline and Seamus snr. He was the eldest sibling to brothers Conor and Kieran and sisters Lisa and Roisín. Seamus grew up in Ardoyne, North Belfast, where he went to Holy Cross Primary School and was first introduced to Gaelic games by local teacher and GAA man Tom Dore. Recognising the talent of Seamus and his brother Conor, Dore directed the boys to join Ardoyne Kickhams GAC. Madeline brought the boys along that very Sunday, where the talent that had just fallen into their lap was quickly apparent to the coaching staff. A family friend recalled, 'There was to be no restraining the boys as they excelled in demonstrating their many abilities on the field of play. Seamus quickly became proficient in honing his skills and was justifiably player of the year in all age groups from u10 to Minor. He was an outstanding footballer and many of his teammates remember him as the spine of the club's underage teams from 1978 to 1988. This must also be remembered in the context of Seamus's surroundings, where it was not easy for youth to steer clear of trouble. His dedication to Gaelic games shows the leadership qualities he developed and the example he set for his family and friends.' Seamus always wore the number 13 shirt, although he played in midfield on the football and hurling teams. Whilst he enjoyed training, Seamus revelled in the competitiveness of match battles. He was considered a hot prospect for his club and was on the radar of the Senior panel from a young age.

Off the pitch, Seamus was remarkably bright. Finishing his primary school exams, he was admitted into the prestigious St Malachy's College, Belfast: no easy feat for a working-class boy. Naturally, Seamus proved a star on the football field for the college, winning the u14 Belfast Championship in 1985. 'He was a vibrant, kind of funny and charming young lad with huge potential to do great things. On the day of his funeral, the postman delivered a letter from the civil service offering him a job. He had big dreams of travelling and he wanted to go to America.'

Seamus Morris was eighteen years old when he was killed on 8 August 1988 by the loyalist Protestant Action Force. He was standing at the corner of Etna Drive with his younger brother Conor talking to a friend, on their way to play a game of snooker. The pair stopped before crossing the road to allow a car to pass, which contained the gunmen who opened fire as they drove slowly past. Seamus was killed where he stood. The gunmen also shot and killed Peter Dolan moments later as they crashed into his lorry while attempting to the flee the scene. No one has ever been prosecuted for the killings.

Gerard Harte (Gearóid Ó hAirt)

AOIS/AGE: 29

CUMANN/CLUB: Naomh Treasa CLG, Loch Mhic Ruairí/ St Teresa's GAC, Loughmacrory

CONTAE/COUNTY: Tír Eoghain/Tyrone

MARAÍODH/KILLED: 30 Lúnasa, Arm na Breataine/ 30 August, British Army

'Gerard was always a leader, and you could see as he progressed through life, he always wanted to follow his own path.' Seán Harte describes his younger brother. 'Playing football and games in the fields growing up will always be cherished memories, and back then, even as a small boy, Gerard was competitive as hell. I was much older than he was, but it mattered not to him when it came to getting stuck in!'

Gerard Harte was born on 7 April 1959 to Winnie and John. He was their third child, growing up in the village of Loughmacrory, County Tyrone, with older siblings Seán and Kathleen, and younger siblings Theresa, Ignatius and Martin. 'Like any other working-class family in Loughmacrory, we had very little. We kept a garden of vegetables and a lot of pigs, which my mother would have worked when my father was working out of the house – initially working as an insurance salesman, then as a delivery man for my aunt's grocers. So those early days of Gerard's life were mostly filled with going to primary school at St Teresa's in Loughmacrory, Mass on Sunday, and back home.'

1
9
8
8

After leaving St Teresa's Primary School, Gerard then went on to join his older brother at what is now the Dean Maguire College in Carrickmore. 'He was very astute and sharp, and he had the rare quality of being a great listener. Mixed with his clear sense of independence, Gerard had already begun forging a career path for himself from an early age. I always remember when he was going to school, he would get off the bus in Loughmacrory and go into a local man's house. The man was a teacher, as well as an architect, and between Gerard as keen a learner and the man a great teacher, Gerard became an architect. He would have only been fifteen years old or so when he was first taken under that guidance, but he went on to become a very good architect and was responsible for the designing of several houses in the local area, including his own!'

Seán recalls a treasured memory from 1976, when Gerard and their parents were able to fly out to visit him in Canada for his wedding, and it wasn't long before Seán made the return journey for Gerard's marriage to Róisín. The daughter of local music star John Mitchell, Seán recalls Gerard and Róisín's house always being full of music and life, with the couple bringing their son, Colm, into the world.

In terms of the GAA, Seán explains that he and his siblings were somewhat late to the game. 'We, as youngsters, never got to the football initially. The first game I ever saw was in O'Neill Park in Dungannon, and it was by complete chance. We were visiting an aunt just outside Dungannon, but it turned out she wasn't in, so we came back into the town and saw this big crowd all walking in the same direction. Upon learning it was for a football game, we begged our father, who wasn't a GAA man, to let us go. We won him over and got to see our first ever Senior Football Championship match between Carrickmore and Clonoe in the Tyrone Championship semi-final! That was in 1966 and our next opportunity with football was to actually play when we got to the Dean School in Carrickmore. St Teresa's GAA club in Loughmacrory was then founded in 1972, when Gerard was thirteen or so, and we all joined as soon as we could. On the football field, Gerard was a wiry corner-back, pulling and annoying the sharpshooters of the opposition.' As with the rest of his family, Gerard became a stalwart of the new club and was represented through the age groups right up to Senior, and then gradually moved onto Senior Reserve. Indeed, the year before his killing, Gerard won Reserve Footballer of the Year.

Gerard's real talents, however, lay in coaching and organising. His old schoolteacher, friend and fellow stalwart of St Teresa's, Seamus Mullan, explains. 'Gerard was a great organiser and managed a load of our underage teams. The lads he coached were very fond of him and, in fact, it was his u16 team which brought home our first underage county title in 1982. His younger brother Martin was a leading player on that team! Gerard was a very generous man and put his heart and soul into everything he did. He was very community orientated in that way and would have no hesitations in giving up his time for his neighbours. He helped in the local youth club for a while and I also remember him being interested in stage work and, with me included, Gerard had actually managed to get a crowd of actors together and a choir. They entered competitions throughout Tyrone and won several accolades, with Gerard as the lead star of the show. That was great craic and we ended up putting a couple of shows together for the community in the following years. He was a good lad.'

On 30 August 1988 Gerard Harte was killed whilst on active service for the IRA by the SAS. He was killed alongside his brother Martin (see next entry) and Brian Mullin. The undercover operation which led to their assassination became known as the Drumnakilly Ambush.

Martin Harte (Máirtín Ó hAirt)

AOIS/AGE: 21
CUMANN/CLUB: Naomh Treasa CLG, Loch Mhic Ruairí/ St Teresa's GAC, Loughmacrory
CONTAE/COUNTY: Tír Eoghain/Tyrone
MARAÍODH/KILLED: 30 Lúnasa, Arm na Breataine/ 30 August, British Army

'Martin was the best athlete in the house, no doubt about it. He was an exceptionally strong boy and a really hard footballer. He could play anywhere down the middle spine of the field, be it full-back, midfield, or full-forward.' Seán recalls his memories of his youngest brother. 'He was a very solid and reliable character.'

Martin Harte was the youngest of the Harte family, born on 3 October 1966 to Winnie and John. With five older siblings, life for Martin growing up in Loughmacrory, County Tyrone, was defined with helping his mother manage the small family farm of vegetables and pigs, and attending his local primary school, St Teresa's, just as all his siblings had before him. 'For ourselves as the older siblings growing up and going to school in Loughmacrory, it was all about handball. The football club wasn't founded until 1972, so we were always playing handball instead! It was a slightly different experience for Martin, him being the youngest. The club would have been very present in his life right from the get-go, and whilst our father had no interest in the GAA, our Uncle Micky was steeped in it and would have been the familial influence on our passion for Gaelic games. He was a great player for both Carrickmore and Tyrone, and Martin grew up in that GAA environment, with all of his older siblings playing: the lads for St Teresa's and big sister Kathleen for Carrickmore.'

As the Loughmacrory club historian and ex-teacher Seamus Mullan recalls, Martin grew into a talented footballer. 'He wasn't all that tall, but he had the guts of a great footballer and really shone on the pitch for us.' As he matured through the age groups, Martin came under the stewardship of his older brother Gerard, who was taking the Loughmacrory underage teams. In 1982, with Gerard as coach and Martin on the field, St Teresa's u16 team took home the club's first County Championship. It was around this time, too, that their older brother Seán was visiting home from Canada, and all the lads got to play together at a Senior Reserve game. 'I happened to be home on holidays, and it was arranged that I could line out for the club and get stuck in with the rest of the lads. It was great craic and a very fond memory of the one game all four of us as brothers got to play together.' It the following years, Martin broke onto the Senior panel with ease, and in the same season, before their deaths, Gerard was named Reserve Player of the Year and Martin was named Senior Player of the Year. Seamus believes that Martin would have been named captain for the following season.

Off the pitch, Martin attended the Dean Maguire College in Carrickmore, then left to join his brother Ignatius in carpentry. Still learning his trade and making a life for himself, Martin got married to Bríd Mullin, and soon after they had a son, Declan. 'As a character, Martin would have had a keen sense of politics and social justice, like the rest of us I suppose. He would have heard the stories of our involvement in the early days of the civil rights movement and of us being beaten off the streets during our marches. As with Gerard, he was a great listener and no doubt the context of his upbringing in Loughmacrory would have shaped his identity. The Crown forces would have taken exception to the lads playing football and would have used their usual tactics in making life difficult from they were young boys, and Martin's experiences of that would be no different in terms of the constant, violent harassment and intimidation. In that need for change, Martin and Gerard took the decision to join the IRA.'

Martin Harte was twenty-one years old when he was killed on 30 August 1988 by the SAS. He was on active service for the IRA with his brother Gerard (see page 176) and Brian Mullin. The undercover operation which led to their assassination became known as the Drumnakilly Ambush.

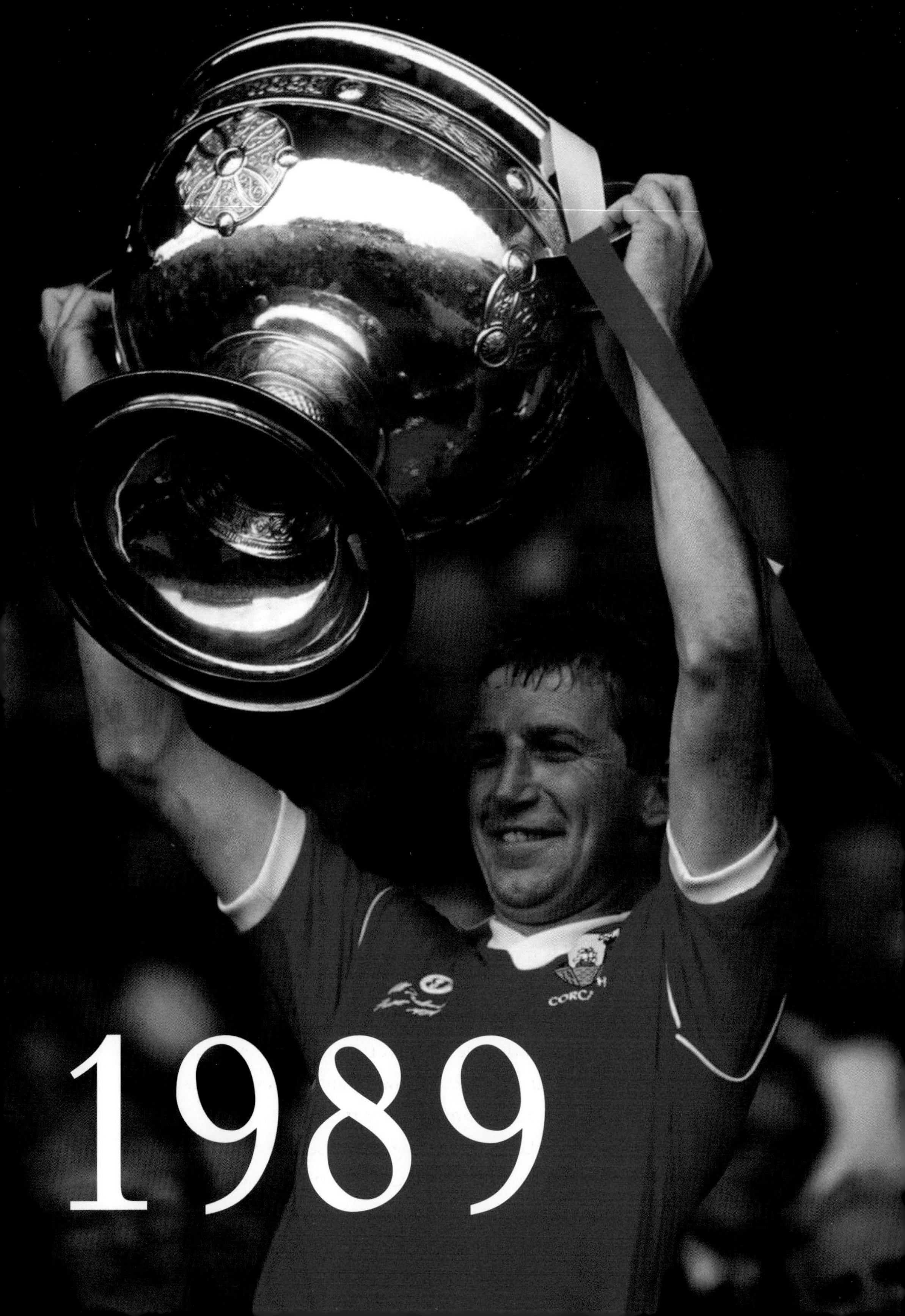

1989

James Joseph Connolly (Seamus Seosamh Uí Chonghaile)

AOIS/AGE: 20

CUMANN/CLUB: Naomh Eoghan, Caisleán na Deirge/ St Eugene's GAC, Castlederg

CONTAE/COUNTY: Tír Eoghain/Tyrone

MARAÍODH/KILLED: 6 Feabhra, le pléasc anabaí/ 6 February, premature explosion

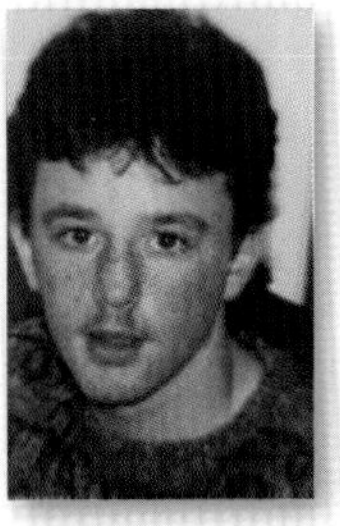

'Josie was a very popular lad. He was well-got and everyone knew him for his sport, particularly his boxing.' Kevin, Barry and Áine begin to describe the life of their eldest brother, James, known to everyone as 'Josie'. 'He wouldn't have smoked nor drank but would have still been known about the pubs as he loved getting out and having the craic.'

James 'Josie' Connolly was born on 19 August 1968 to Joey and Anna. He was their first child, and his life started in Glasgow, Scotland, where his Irish parents had emigrated seeking work. Josie was soon joined by his first brother, Charlie, in 1970, and the young family stayed in Scotland until 1975, when the decision was made to move back home to Aghyaran, County Tyrone. Josie's second brother, Kevin, was born in that same year, and while the family initially struggled with the lack of housing, they finally settled into a new home built in the village of Castlederg, Tyrone. Josie attended St Patrick's Primary School in Castlederg and that is where he got his first taste of the GAA, which fed naturally into the decision to join his local GAA club, St Eugene's GFC. 'All the coaches and people who ran the club were our neighbours and they made sure the new kids moving into the estate were getting involved in the club. Josie and Charlie both started playing at u12 level and because they were only just over a year apart, they got to play on the same team together every other year. At that time, Castlederg hadn't even got their own pitch, but with the big influx of young families, like our own, moving into the new estate, I suppose it would have been an exciting time for the club.'

Before long, Josie and Charlie were receiving their first taste of success on the football field. With Josie in corner-back and Charlie up in corner-forward, St

Eugene's u14 team won both the Tyrone Division 1 League and Championship. Kevin remembers watching his brothers play the final in Healy Park, Omagh, and it wouldn't be the last time he witnessed his two older brothers competing at the highest level, trying to bring home silverware for their club. 'They were a wild successful team! I remember in 1987 they reached the Minor Championship final in Pomeroy. Unfortunately, they came up against The Shamrocks, who were an amalgamation of Galbally, Eglish and Killeeshil, who proved to be too strong for Castlederg. Josie and Charlie were the two corner-backs that day. Charlie played Minor the following season, this time at centre half-back, and Castlederg reached the final again. They played Carrickmore, who had a good seven or eight County Minors on their team compared to none for Charlie's team. Despite that, Castlederg won, and they also won the league that season, and in doing so became the first team in Tyrone to do the double at Minor level!'

As he reached Senior level, Josie's involvement with the club lessened as his focus turned to boxing. He had a particular talent for being in the ring, winning a plethora of Ulster titles and contesting at a national amateur level, representing Derg Valley Boxing Club across Ireland in various amateur competitions. But this didn't put an end to his footballing career and he managed to continue fielding for Castlederg Senior Reserves. He also ran cross-country at a competitive level.

Away from sports, Josie attended his local St Eugene's High School before going on to Omagh Training Centre to become a bricklayer. 'He had a talent for bricklaying too. He got all of his qualifications handily and was actually made Apprentice of the Year in 1987 by the training centre.' Josie also developed a strong sense of politics, and his family explain how his character shaped his view of the conflict into which he was born. 'Josie was a very fair-minded sort of character, and the type not to walk by someone getting hassled. In Castlederg, that could get you into a lot of bother. We grew up in a very sectarian town, and most nights there would be cars full of drunk UDR soldiers driving around looking for people on their own. On top of that, walking to the football field was guaranteed to get you stopped and harassed, if not chased. Josie could never accept that. If someone was getting chased or hassled, he would go looking for those doing the chasing. For a lad of 5ft 5in., he wasn't to be messed with! My mother used to recall one night Charlie being attacked by a group of four drunk UDR men outside our house. They had spotted him walking home alone after a night out and chased him up to the door, where they started beating him. Our father was on a walking stick at the time with a bad back so could only call on them to stop, but when Josie woke up, he ran out and leapt onto the soldiers. He took them to the ground, and it was soon over. So, it was with that context and his natural view of the world that Josie's politics came about. From the '81 hunger strikes on, he became very aware of the political situation and made his own judgements as to the role he wanted to play.'

Unknown to those closest to him, Josie made the decision to join the IRA at seventeen years of age. He was twenty years old when he was killed while on active service for the IRA on 6 February 1989, when a bomb he was handling exploded prematurely.

Josie's love for the GAA carries on through the younger generations of his family, with his brother Barry still lining out for the Reserves, laughing that his Senior days are behind him, and Josie's nieces and nephews playing in the Juvenile structures. For the twentieth anniversary of Josie's death, a game was organised between Castlederg and neighbouring club Aghyaran, with the winner supposed to take home the Josie Connolly Cup. 'The match was abandoned! Not for fighting or anything like that, but because the boys were dropping like flies. It was as cold a winter's night, the ground frozen, and all the players were over forty! Pulled muscles and twisted ankles forced enough men off the pitch that we could no longer play on.'

It was decided to include in Josie's entry to this book the following section dedicated to the memory of his brother Charlie. Whilst Charlie was not killed by conflict-related violence, the circumstances of his death were created as a direct result of such violence directed towards him. In spending time with Kevin, Barry and Áine, both Josie and Charlie are always mentioned in the same breath, and it is only right that Charlie is included alongside his older brother.

'Charlie was born on 5 January 1970. He and Josie were a year apart and lived initially in Scotland, too, before our parents decided to bring the family home and moved into Castlederg. Charlie followed Josie into St Patrick's Primary School and then into St Eugene's High School. Charlie then went on to train as a joiner. I suppose the difference between them was that Charlie was a bit more outgoing, but they both enjoyed socialising and having the craic. Even though they joined the GAA club together for Juvenile football and played right the way through to Senior level, Charlie was always more about the football, whereas Josie maybe took more to the boxing. Charlie was a main player on his Minor team that won the Division 1 county double in 1988, and in the same year, he won Senior Player of the Year for the club. In that season he was only eighteen years old and had only really broken into the Senior team! He was a flying machine on the football field, and he did a bit of sprinting and athletics off the pitch, which no doubt helped him with football. Charlie also boxed with Josie and won an Ulster title, but it was more to keep his fitness for football.'

With being named Senior Player of the Year at the club's dinner dance in January 1989, and Castlederg being promoted into Division 2 Senior Football, Kevin, Barry and Áine explain how Charlie was relishing the beginning of a new season where the lads he won the Minor double with were all bursting through. Within one month, that would all change. With the death of Josie in February, Charlie found himself not only mourning his best friend and brother but also on the receiving end of serious abuse. 'After Josie was killed, Charlie got serious harassment. It didn't matter where he was, police and soldiers would single him out. He used to work in Omagh, and they would come into the work site and abuse him, knowing that singling him out on the mixed work sites in front of everyone would make for a dangerous situation. They were trying to make him a target. Charlie never got finishing his time on the sites before being forced to emigrate. The torture was constant, and he could no longer stay at home.' Charlie moved to San Francisco in the USA six months after Josie was killed, before the '89 season could get underway. Whilst in San Francisco, he found some light amongst the dark days he was living through in the form of the Ulster Gaelic Club. This no doubt proved an invaluable link with home for Charlie and it wasn't long before he was lining out for his newfound club at centre half-back. As any Gael who finds themselves living abroad can attest to, the local GAA club becomes an important refuge for the scattered Irish, and the Ulster Gaelic Club was no different for Charlie.

Charlie Connolly was killed in a road traffic accident on 1 December 1990. His family describe how his death came about as a result of a period of the most intense harassment from both the British Army and RUC, which forced him to emigrate to the USA. Charlie was denied the right to grieve the loss of his brother at home with his family; a right which, if enjoyed, could have prevented the creation of the circumstances which led to his death.

In the aftermath of Charlie's death, the Ulster Gaelic Club raised funds to arrange for the return of his remains to his family back in Tyrone. He arrived home along with the centre half-back jersey of his second club, which also established a memorial tournament in Charlie's honour. For the twentieth anniversary of Castlederg's Minor double in 1988, Charlie's family were presented with a replica shirt of their club's iconic young team.

John Davey (Eoin Ó Dáibhidh)

AOIS/AGE: 61
CUMANN/CLUB: Rogha Éireann Leamhaigh CLG/ Erin's Own GAC, Lavey
CONTAE/COUNTY: Doire/Derry
MARAÍODH/KILLED: 14 Feabhra, le forsaí dílseach/ 14 February, loyalist forces

'He had a great love for the Irish language, music, dance and of course, the GAA.' Pauline Davey describes her father, John. 'He lived to promote all aspects of Gaelic culture in the community and was always looking to develop that sense of identity and pride; an ethos if you will.'

John Davey was born on 1 May 1927 to parents James and Annie. He was the eldest of seven, growing up in the village of Dunloy, County Antrim, with brothers James, Hugh and Robert, and sisters Annie, Rosaleen and Mary. With the passage of time, memories of John's childhood have naturally faded, but Pauline tells us what she can. 'My dad was born in Dunloy, and you could say that he was always a Dunloy man at heart, and certainly always an Antrim man! He would have received a primary school education from the local school in the village and then, as he got older, he took an opportunity to go to Australia with his brother Robert. It wasn't long before he came home, however, and he found work as a digger driver. I always remember him saying that he drove a D-8; whatever type of digger that was, I don't know, but he was proud of that fact!'

At a dance in Ballymena in the 1950s, John would meet Mary, a nurse from Bellaghy, and the pair were married in 1960, before they had their first child, Eugene, in 1961, followed by Pauline and Maria in 1963 and 1965. As a young family, they initially lived just outside of Dunloy, before both John and Mary were offered work in County Derry. 'My mum was offered a post in Magherafelt, and my dad was offered work with F.P. McCann, so they decided to move to nearby Lavey. My mum must have been able to see past the local rivalry between Lavey and Bellaghy,' Pauline jokes. The Davey family settled well into life in Lavey, and their new home provided plenty of space for John to not only raise his family, but his animals too. 'Alongside working as a digger driver, my dad also liked to do a bit of farming and we always had animals in the fields around the house. I liked to call it the funny farm because we had everything! Goats, ducks, cows, hens, etc. He had a great love for animals and enjoyed caring for them. At times of the year when the birds were nesting, we were told not to enter certain buildings in case we disturbed them. He made sure it was out of bounds and the birds protected, and once the chicks hatched, he would have brought us out and quietly showed us what was happening. He was always very caring like that, and had great wit, which made him a calming presence and someone people enjoyed being around. That, in turn, meant that it was very hard to get a quiet moment in our house, with people coming day and night, seeking my dad's company, help or advice. We were also a céilí house, so the tea pot was never off!'

John was also a committed republican and organiser in his community, which began with early involvement in the civil rights movement of the late 1960s. 'My dad had a very strong sense of social justice in him and so, instinctively, became very involved in equality issues. He was a natural orator and spoke at many rallies, and then began campaigning and working for Sinn Féin. He always made sure he was there to help everyone in the community and no matter who they were, he was there, willing to help.' He was elected to Magherafelt Council in 1985 and became known as a strong advocate for equality and language rights. 'He would have regularly spoken Irish in the chamber and sought to promote the language, and he was also highly involved in implementing the anti-discriminatory MacBride Principles.' For his campaigning, John was the target of endless harassment, abuse and violence, beginning in 1971 with internment. He and five-year-old Maria were detained; she was later found alone in the barracks in Maghera, while her father found himself in prison.

John was eventually released after three years, having never been charged with a crime; he would continue to suffer numerous arrests over his lifetime. Whilst in the council chamber, Pauline describes how her father was regularly assaulted, both verbally and physically, for standing up for his beliefs, and on one occasion, upon being elected deputy chair of the council, he was struck on the head with a chair by another councillor. Most grave was the use of parliamentary privilege by a unionist politician sitting in Westminster to claim that John was 'an active terrorist'. This led to a failed loyalist attempt on John's life in 1987. 'None of this stopped him, not even the first attempt at killing him. He got up the next morning and went to where he needed to be and got done what needed to be done. He was such a strong character, which meant we were never afraid, despite all the threats and the raids to the house.'

'In terms of his involvement in the GAA, my dad never actually played. His strengths were as an organiser and promoter of the games and wider culture in the community. I remember when we came to live in Lavey, Erin's Own GAA club had just begun building their new GAA grounds right beside our house. You looked out of our window and the pitch was there. My father was out with the workmen each day, helping to construct the new club, driving the digger. Unfortunately, he was denied the chance to attend the grand opening of the final result because he was interned, but he was still very proud of his contribution.' Over the years, John organised fundraisers for the club, including putting on céilís in which Eugene, Pauline and Maria all took part, and a plethora of initiatives aimed at keeping the lights on. 'He loved the community of it all.

Getting together and sharing tea and sandwiches with GAA people from all over, talking football.'

For John, the most important thing was securing the involvement of young people and fostering within them a love of the GAA, and he rightly recognised the need for the community to have dedicated spaces for the local youth to enjoy. Following the erection of the new clubhouse, John played a pivotal role in saving the old GAA hall from ruin. 'He raised money to buy it and turn it into the community hall. That building is now an amazing hub for the people of Lavey.' John was also involved in Gael Linn and ran Irish-language classes for his neighbours. 'My dad enjoyed every minute of working for his community. He was getting a great sense of love from it all and got as much from it as he gave to it. Everything felt alright in the community because he was at the helm.'

John Davey was killed on 14 February 1989. His body was found in his car, which was stopped on the laneway leading to his home. John's killing was claimed by the UVF, but British military personnel are widely believed to be responsible, with many noting that his car was found parked with the handbrake engaged. Given previous attempts on his life, John's family believe that he would have only stopped his car for an official military or police checkpoint.

'Lavey is now a very strong and vibrant community, and my dad helped it get there by keeping it going through the darkest days. Back before it was popular to be involved in the GAA and Irish culture, and, in fact, back when it was seriously dangerous, the GAA was an essential escape for my dad from everything that was going on around him and it formed the backdrop of our lives.'

Gerard Casey (Gearóid Ó Cathasaigh)

AOIS/AGE: 29
CUMANN/CLUB: Naomh Mhuire CLG, Ros Earcáin/ St Mary's GAC, Rasharkin
CONTAE/COUNTY: Aontroim/Antrim
MARAÍODH/KILLED: 4 Aibreán, le forsaí dílseach/ 4 April, loyalist forces

'We met at school when we were twelve,' Una, Gerard's widow explains. 'We were only kids when our wee crush started and started seeing each other until just before we turned sixteen; when we both left school. I went on to work at Gallaghers tobacco factory in Ballymena, and Gerard went to work with his dad and brother as a joiner. We met again when we were eighteen, and decided we wanted to get married.'

Gerard Casey was born to Kathleen and Hugh. He was their fourth child, growing up in Rasharkin, County Antrim, with siblings Anne, Liam, Dessie, Bernie, Ciaran and Veronica. He went to Our Lady of Lourdes School, where he played for the football team and also met his future wife, Una. Following school, Gerard went to learn the family trade of joinery, being taken under the wing of his father and brother. 'Gerard was a very good worker and could have put his hand to anything.'

On meeting again, Gerard and Una rekindled their relationship and were set on forging a new life together. 'Having known each other from we were children, we wanted to start a family, and decided to build a home for our new family on a field up beside Gerard's parents' house. He was never done doing work to the house, always perfecting wee jobs here and there. We had four children: Paul, Kevin, Tara and Geraldine. He loved them dearly. A favourite thing of Gerard's was to bring the kids into the garage to teach them how to play pool. His children have only small memories of their dad because they were so young, so they love to listen to me telling them the stories about Gerard. He also had a keen sense of politics because of the conditions of conflict he lived under. The Caseys had a very hard life, and when we built our new home, we were constantly raided and each time we got in the car we were stopped and forced to get out to be searched. It was terrible conditions to live under, and I think that's why Gerard decided to join the IRA.'

Gerard played football for St Mary's GAC in Rasharkin. Although his family are unsure of the level of his involvement, there is no doubt that he loved his club and the GAA. 'Between work and family, Gerard would always find time to enjoy going to watch a football match at the club or watch the county play. If he could, he would bring one of the kids with him as well.' His love for the GAA was passed down to his children, with Gerard's son Kevin becoming a fine footballer before his playing days were sadly ended by the onset of Guillain-Barré Syndrome.

Gerard Casey was shot dead by the UDA as he lay in bed beside Una on 4 April 1989. Their house had been raided by the RUC five months prior to his killing, during which his legally held firearm was confiscated and detailed drawings of the inside of his house were made. After being arrested and released, Gerard made public the statements of his interrogators, who assured him that he would soon be in a coffin or a cell. After years of campaigning, Gerard's family finally have the truth about his killing: he was killed as a direct result of collusion between the RUC and UDA. His eldest child, Paul, was eight years old when his father was killed, and Geraldine was three months old. Gerard was a member of the Provisional IRA.

Liam Ryan (Liam Ó Riain)

AOIS/AGE: 39

CUMANN/CLUB: CLG Setanta, Báile na Móna/ Moortown Setanta GAC

CONTAE/COUNTY: Tír Eoghain/Tyrone

MARAÍODH/KILLED: 30 Samhain, le forsaí dílseach/ 30 November, loyalist forces

'Liam would have been a big lad growing up. Being big and broad meant he was a tough opponent on the hurling field and, like the rest of us, he was a bit of a hatchet man. We had a bit of a reputation for having no reservations in getting stuck into any team we played.' Lifelong friend and fellow Moortown Setanta teammate Pearce McAleer describes Liam Ryan. 'He was a great hurler.'

Liam Ryan was born to William and Sally. William, or 'Willie', was a native of Tyrone and worked as a fisherman. Liam's mother, Sally, née McGinley, came from Donegal and was a fluent Gaeilgeoir. The family grew up in the Tír na nÓg area of Annaghmore in County Tyrone, with Liam being the third of twelve children. The others were Mary, Joseph, Brigid, Margaret, Christopher, Donal, Eugene, Joseph, Anthony, Elisabeth and Nancy. Liam's older brother, Joseph, died tragically in infancy as a result of health problems, which Liam also suffered from. Liam's siblings say that this led to a particularly strong bond between Liam and Sally. The family were struck by tragedy again in 1972 when Liam's brother Donal was killed in a car accident on his return from the All-Ireland football final in Croke Park aged just eighteen.

The Ryans have fond memories of growing up, where everyone had their chores to carry out; Liam would have helped Willie run the lines for work on the boat. Each autumn, the siblings would have all gone blackberry picking, competing with one another to pick the most after school. Liam then started going to dances when he turned sixteen, his sister Brigid explains: 'He loved dressing up. Loved his style, and his hair always had to be perfection. His personality was magic, and he could talk to anyone. Plenty of girls were all mad about him!'

Liam was first introduced to the GAA by his primary school principal, Master Thomas Magner. Pearce recalled, 'We had never been exposed to hurling before Master Magner came in. He tried first introducing it to the school, but it fell through after a few years. It wasn't until we were playing cricket at the school, having tried lots of other sports, that we realised that if we played hurling instead, everyone would get more than one turn hitting the ball. So that's where it grew from.' Liam and his schoolmates took to hurling instantly, although none came from hurling stock. 'At first, we played with cudgels cut from hedges, as if we were all trying to be Cú Chulainn himself because most of us couldn't afford hurls. We then upgraded to making our own hurls by gluing pieces of plywood together.'

It was from the boys playing at school that the Moortown Setanta Hurling Club grew. Also taken by Master Magner, Liam and his teammates would soon find themselves in the back of buses and cars travelling across Ireland to line out against any team who would play them. 'Despite not even having proper hurls at the start, we were a very talented bunch. Master Magner had us well drilled and we saw good success. We might have come across a bit rough but there was no denying our talent.'

Indeed, Liam and a good number of his Setanta teammates soon found themselves lining out for their county. When Moortown Setanta won the Mid-Ulster Minor League in 1965, with Liam being mentioned as one of the driving forces in defence so critical to their success, it was no surprise that the County Minor team the following year was littered with the Moortown men. In 1966 the Tyrone Minors reached the Ulster final but lost to Antrim. The following year they reached the final again but fell to Down, who went on to win the 'special' All-Ireland for weaker hurling counties. There is no doubting that Liam's talents, and indeed those of the other Moortown Setanta boys, were the fruits of Master Magner's efforts. 'Each year he would bring a handful of lads down to Gormanston College for the hurling camp. Liam went in 1965 for the week-long course. The coaches included Kilkenny's Tommy Maher and Dublin and Meath's Dessie Ferguson.'

Liam would stop hurling when life took him to America, having completed his electrician training at Cookstown Training College. Having spent a long time between the Bronx in New York and Ireland, Liam became a US citizen in 1984 before returning to Ireland. Whilst in America he became a republican activist and ended up receiving a suspended sentence there for procuring weapons. On his return to Tyrone, he bought the Battery Bar and became a publican. Not long afterwards, he met Geraldine. The couple were married in 1989 and soon afterwards baby Declan came into their world.

Declan was only ten weeks old when his father was killed on 30 November

1989 by the UVF, alongside Michael Devlin. Liam was working in his bar, which was hosting a darts competition that Michael, a local farmer, was taking part in, when gunmen forced their way in and opened fire. Liam and Michael put themselves between the gunmen and the rest of the bar, no doubt saving the lives of other patrons and staff, including Liam's sister Elisabeth, and wife, Geraldine, who were both working in the bar that night. Those suspected of Liam's and Michael's killings were also members of the British Army.

1990

Dessie Grew (Deasún Mac Giolla Rua)

AOIS/AGE: 37

CUMANN/CLUB: CLG Naomh Colmcille, An Ghráinseach/ St Colmcille's GAC, Grange

CONTAE/COUNTY: Ard Mhacha/Armagh

MARAÍODH/KILLED: 8 Deireadh Fómhair, Arm na Breataine/8 October, British Army

'Dessie was the most intelligent person you could ever meet.' Marese begins to describe her brother Dessie Grew. 'It's hard to explain just how extraordinary he was. He was fluent in all sorts of languages … Irish, French, Arabic … He could have done anything he set his mind to.'

Dessie Grew was born on 14 September 1953 to Pat and Kathleen. He was the second of their eleven children and grew up on the family homestead in Grange, County Armagh. Marese describes the area the family still live in as an idyllic place to grow up in as children. They lived in what they saw as a giant, natural playground of fields, rivers and hills for them to explore. The Grew family was very close-knit, with their grandmother living next door, and from an early age, Dessie and his siblings were all involved in helping with the harvest and selling the locally grown fruit and vegetables. Dessie's father, Pat, was known in the area for running an apple-peeling business, and Dessie would help his father with his work, as well as help out with keeping the cattle and maintaining their cabbage patch. Dessie and his brothers would travel all over the counties in the North with their father, helping him to sell their produce at all the local markets.

'The boys' summers would have been spent doing the hay, picking berries and out hunting with the Kinnego Hunt Club. And even from those early days, Dessie would have been thought of by his friends and brothers as a leader. He would have been known as being very intelligent and quite articulate, and he had a natural ability to take charge and organise people.' Dessie attended the local primary school in Knockaconey before going on to join his older brother, Seamus, at Armagh CBS in 1965. Whilst excelling in his year group for most subjects, Dessie developed a love for languages, particularly the Irish language, and in 1969 he went to the Gaeltacht in Donegal to fully immerse himself in his native language, quickly becoming fluent.

In that same summer, Marese explains that Dessie, along with his brother Seamus, decided to join the civil rights movement, having both developed a strong sense of politics from their experiences of growing up in rural Armagh. Whilst their parents were apolitical, Dessie and Seamus were influenced by global movements at that time, including those in France and the USA, and by socialist writings coming out of Cuba, China and the Soviet Union. Aged sixteen, Dessie joined and became active in People's Democracy, participating in local marches and protests, and in 1970 he decided to join the PIRA. Concerned for Dessie, and in an attempt to shield him from the escalating conflict, his parents sent him to live with his aunts in Birmingham, England, in September 1970. Marese explains, however, that Dessie's passion for politics and social justice could not be quelled and when he wasn't working as a clerk for National Rail, he would spend every Saturday in the Bull Ring at Speaker's Corner in Birmingham speaking to crowds about the political situation back home.

Dessie then briefly moved to London with a friend before coming home upon learning about the introduction of internment in the summer of 1971. His life from then on was one of committing himself to the republican movement, and he spent various periods of his adult life either in prison in both the North and South of Ireland, or on the run. On 12 December 1982, while Dessie was in Portlaoise Prison, Seamus was killed while on active service for the IRA (see page 295). Dessie was released in 1988 and he returned to active service for the IRA. Marese explains that he tried to spend as much time with his family as he could after his release, spending his Christmas with her and her family. He enjoyed singing, and his party piece was 'Óró sé do bheatha bhaile', which he taught to all of his nieces and nephews.

In terms of the GAA, Dessie, along with all of the Grew boys, played for St Colmcille's GFC, Grange. Whilst Marese is unsure of the achievements of his teams, she explains that Dessie joined the club at the earliest opportunity within its Juvenile ranks. He also played at school and is said to have been an excellent footballer, just like his older brother. As he committed himself to the republican movement, Dessie's playing days would have taken a sharp decline, although he did play football in Long Kesh Prison when matches were organised between inmates. An ex-prisoner who served time in jail with Dessie describes his ability as a footballer. 'Dessie's prowess on the GAA field was what I valued most in prison. He helped secure victory for our team over Jim Lynagh's! Our team won the prestigious leather medal in the final, but for Dessie there was more enjoyment in the fact that our team, made up of Armagh boys, had defeated the Tyrone team.' When Dessie was on the run in Monaghan, he also managed to get playing football for Tyholland, as did Seamus. They were both described by their Monaghan teammates as excellent footballers, and they helped the club reach the Junior Championship final in 1974. The game went to a replay and, unfortunately, Tyholland were defeated, despite the best efforts of the Grew brothers.

Dessie Grew was thirty-four years old when he was killed by the SAS while on active service for the IRA on 8 October 1990. He was killed alongside fellow Volunteer Martin McCaughey (see page 296) and their killing is considered a clear example of the British government's shoot-to-kill policy deployed at that time. In 2017 the European Court of Human Rights found that Dessie and Martin's Article 2 Right to Life had been violated through the failure of the authorities to properly investigate their killings. A detailed account of Dessie's life is available in the publication *'Dessie': Scholar – Socialist – Revolutionary.*

1991

Malcolm Nugent (Maolcholuim Mag Uinseanáin)

AOIS/AGE: 20

CUMANN/CLUB: Piarsaigh An Ghallbhaile CLG/ Galbally Pearses GAC

CONTAE/COUNTY: Tír Eoghain/Tyrone

MARAÍODH/KILLED: 3 Márta, le forsaí dílseach/ 3 March, loyalist forces

'We are a very close-knit family.' Siobhán Nugent, Malcolm's sister, describes the days of Malcolm's youth spent playing with his siblings and cousins. 'There were only a few fields separating ourselves and our cousins, and any free time they could get, the lads were in those fields wrestling and chasing after a football. Jumpers as goalposts and all the drama that comes with a game of football. The winning, the losing and all of the fallouts and making up. I don't think they had a pair of boots between them, but they couldn't care less nor be any happier!'

Malcolm Nugent was born on 10 November 1970 to Brendan and Susan. He was the third oldest in the family, growing up in the parish of Altaglushan, County Tyrone, with older brothers Francis and Mark and younger brother Brian, and his two younger sisters, Siobhán and Caitríona. 'Our father worked as a lorry driver and our mother stayed at home to raise us. Life was pretty normal growing up and we all have happy memories of childhood. Malcolm, like the rest of us, went to primary school in Cabragh and then went on to St Ciaran's Secondary School in Ballygawley. Sadly, my mum took sick in 1980 and died of cancer aged only thirty-four, when Malcolm was ten years old. Whilst it was a lot for our dad to take on, we have always been a close-knit family and our aunts, uncles and cousins would have been around all the time to help look after us.'

Undoubtedly, the strong bonds with their wider family provided Malcolm and his siblings with great comfort during this difficult time in their lives. He was particularly close to his cousin Peter, and Siobhán laughs that the pair were always to be seen running about together. Upon leaving St Ciaran's, Malcolm joined a local engineering works in Cappagh and began training as a fitter. As he got older, he started to enjoy heading out socialising and meeting friends. Malcolm had a particular interest in, and talent for, pool, and he successfully represented his local Boyle's Bar team in the Clogher Valley League. 'He was a quiet lad and the type of guy you would have to spend a lot of time with before you got to know him, but once you did, he was always great craic. Everyone would describe him as very loyal and he was very popular with those who knew him.'

Malcolm played his football for Galbally Pearses. 'He joined the club at underage level along with his brothers and cousins, and I remember they would all have gone down to the club together carrying their plastic bags. No fancy kit bags and gear like nowadays! The football was a massive part of their younger lives, and he would have played in all of the local tournaments and blitzes.'

As Malcolm progressed into adulthood, football, and indeed most aspects of Malcolm's life, fell to the periphery as the reality of the conflict came to the fore. 'It was impossible to escape the harassment and intimidation growing up where we did. Whether it was going to and from the football or just trying to go about your day. It was constant. And then when Malcolm was sixteen or so, Loughgall happened. He would have known of some of the lads who were killed, and that event really shook the local community. Malcolm then decided to commit himself to the republican movement. He was a very mentally strong young man and fluent in his politics, and he had a great sense of what he was about and why he was doing what he was doing.'

Malcolm Nugent was killed on 3 March 1991 by British Army soldiers who were also members of the UVF. He was sitting alongside his friends Dwayne O'Donnell (see page 203) and John Quinn (see page 205) in their car, pulling up to Boyle's Bar, where he played his pool, in Cappagh, Tyrone. Gunmen killed all three friends along with Boyle's Bar regular Thomas Armstrong. There is strong evidence of collusion in the Cappagh Killings, which has been noted by a plethora of investigative bodies, including a UN Special Rapporteur.

Galbally Pearses remember Malcolm, and each of the members they have lost to the conflict, with immense pride. 'The club doesn't forget the lads and they have been a huge source of strength for us as families. They are present at every commemoration and anniversary.' Malcolm's nephew Sean continues the strong family connection with the Galbally Pearses club, lining out for the Senior football panel. In the 2022–23 season, Sean's team reached the All-Ireland Intermediate final, winning the Tyrone and Ulster titles on route to Croke Park.

Dwayne O'Donnell (Dubhán Ó Domhnaill)

AOIS/AGE: 17
CUMANN/CLUB: Piarsaigh An Ghallbhaile CLG/ Galbally Pearses GAC
CONTAE/COUNTY: Tír Eoghain/Tyrone
MARAÍODH/KILLED: 3 Márta, le forsaí dílseach/ 3 March, loyalist forces

'All of us are involved in the GAA.' Séana, Dwayne's sister, begins to describe the role of the GAA in her family's life. 'From a young age, we were involved with the local club and playing football.'

Dwayne O'Donnell was born on 27 July 1973 to Briege and Brian. He was the eldest of five children, growing up initially in Donaghmore, and then Galbally, County Tyrone, with his three brothers Barry, Mark and Fergal, and his sister, Séana. Dwayne's cousin and close friend Gary describes his earliest memories of him and Dwayne playing for their local club, Galbally Pearses, and spending the summers of their childhood playing football. 'Every summer, the teams in Galbally were split into the four provinces to play games and blitzes, with Dwayne always playing in defence. Back then, the club only had one set of jerseys for the underage teams, and they were the old long-sleeved ones. I remember playing u12 and wearing the u14 kits; they were massive on us!' After a few years, when he reached u14 level, Dwayne stopped playing football, but Séana explains that he maintained a love and passion for the ethos and cultural side of the GAA, and a love for his club.

Away from the GAA, Dwayne attended his local St Joseph's Primary School, where he quickly made lifelong friends, and then went on to St Patrick's Secondary School in Dungannon. Whilst at school, Dwayne showed a real interest in Irish history, and Séana explains that he was known for being an attentive pupil. Upon leaving school aged fifteen, Dwayne decided to pursue a career in engineering at a local firm in Cappagh called Masterskreen and was enjoying his time there until he suffered a serious work-related accident in April 1990, which resulted in a broken pelvis and leg. Despite a consultant telling Dwayne he would not likely return to work, his determination saw him back at the engineering works by January. According to Séana, what sped up his recovery was that Dwayne missed the craic with his friends!

To all who knew him, Dwayne was known as a likeable young person who went about his life with a happy-go-lucky attitude, which made him a very affable character. However, his young life was peppered with incidents of harassment and intimidation. Going to football games as a young boy with his friends, or to the youth club to socialise, Dwayne and his friends were often stopped and harassed by British Army soldiers or the RUC. When he was just fourteen years old, he was arrested and brought to Gough Barracks, where he faced intense interrogation and was charged with collecting information that could be useful for terrorism. From that incident, the instances of harassment and intimidation only got worse for Dwayne, as he was singled out and his home became a target for routine raids. As a result of his experiences, Séana explains, her brother joined the republican movement.

Dwayne O'Donnell was seventeen years old when he was killed on 3 March 1991 by British Army soldiers who were also members of the UVF. Dwayne was in a car, pulling up to Boyle's Bar in Cappagh, County Tyrone, along with Malcolm Nugent (see page 201), John Quinn (see page 205) and Malachy Rafferty, when gunmen approached and opened fire into the car. Dwayne died en route to the hospital. Another man, Thomas Armstrong, was also killed. He was drinking in the bar and was shot when the gunmen decided to open fire on the building as well.

Dwayne's family continue to have a deep involvement in the GAA. His brother Fergal captained Galbally football teams at every age group up to Senior level, and Séana played for many years with Galbally Oonagh Celts GAA and also for Galbally Gaelic 4 Mothers & Others. All of Dwayne's nephews and nieces continue to represent their local club. His eldest nephew, Caoimhin, achieved many awards during his time with Pearses, and now plays for St Brendan's GAC in Manchester and for Lancashire GAC. Caoimhin's brother, Conall, was part of the Tyrone Minor panel who won the 2022 Ulster Championship. Dwayne's club remember him, and indeed all of their lost members, every year through tournaments and memorial events.

John Quinn (Eoin Ó Coinn)

AOIS/AGE: 22
CUMANN/CLUB: Piarsaigh An Ghallbhaile CLG/ Galbally Pearses GAC
CONTAE/COUNTY: Tír Eoghain/Tyrone
MARAÍODH/KILLED: 3 Márta, le forsaí dílseach/ 3 March, loyalist forces

'Our John's football career with Galbally Pearses may have been short, but he packed a lot into the years when he proudly wore the club jersey with distinction.' Póilin begins to describe her brother. 'His place is assured in history in Galbally as he was part of the first u14 side that ever represented the club.'

John Quinn was born on 13 June 1968 to Pat and Peggy. The second-youngest of six children, he grew up in Cranogue, County Tyrone, with brothers Gerard and Damien, and sisters Martina, Póilin and Moira. As his family explain, John's early years were strongly characterised by his love for football. 'Patrick McGeary and Danny Kerr were the managers who began football at that age group in the club in 1979. Little did they know they planted the seeds for what was to follow in later decades. In only their second year, Galbally reached the East Tyrone u14 final, having beaten Moy, Eglish and Donaghmore, and whilst they were well-beaten by a strong Dungannon side in the final, it was only the beginning of things to come.'

Indeed, Póilin describes how John and his teammates were back the following year stronger than ever. Getting through the preliminary games, a 1-point win in the quarter-final against a favoured Coalisland side set up a semi-final meeting with Ardboe. 'The Pearses eventually prevailed in that match, played at Brackville, and Dungannon awaited in the final again!' Unfortunately for John and his team, Dungannon once again proved too strong, but the young men of Galbally Pearses could take solace from the fight they put up. 'Galbally played in white jerseys in the final, and John and his teammates in defence more than held their own against a much-vaunted Clarke's attack, who had been racking up big scores in the build-up to the final.'

In 1982 and 1983 John progressed to u16s, and his family describe him as a young, committed footballer. 'His dedication to the team both in training and on match days was second to none. John was a mainstay in defence, and while he was a tight marker, one of his biggest attributes was his ability to kick the ball long off the ground from frees. This was something you had to do back in those days, and not every player had the technique.' A fit and naturally fast player, John was always on the team sheet, lining out at number 5. 'He had the blessing and curse of being light and should he get knocked down, he jumped up again almost before he hit the ground!' In 1983 John was part of the u16 championship-winning side, although he missed the final through injury. That same year, his team were narrowly edged out by Coalisland from completing the league and championship double. 'In those five years from beginning at u14, John accumulated four medals as part of a group of lads who helped put Galbally on the football map within the county.'

As is the case with many Gaels, as John became a young adult, his involvement with his club lessened, although he always made a point of lining out each year at Senior level for the Martin Hurson Tournament, held in memory of the hunger striker who died on 13 July 1981. 'He always enjoyed that tournament and was very proud to take part in it as, although he was only young when Martin Hurson was laid to rest, John attended his funeral.'

Off the pitch, John attended St Joseph's Primary School in Galbally, before going on to St Patrick's Secondary School in Dungannon. 'John took his responsibilities seriously and had a love for his community and his people. He had a great *grá* for Irish traditional music, and would play with his sisters, whistling along and playing the drums.' He joined a local engineering firm upon leaving school and came to be regarded as a steady and conscientious worker.

The reality of growing up in conflict, however, was never lost on him. 'John was acutely aware from an early age that the things he cherished were threatened daily by State oppression and discrimination. It was no surprise to those who knew him that he would eventually rise to an inner call to confront and resist the British forces of occupation.' Turning down the prospect of a different life in Australia, John decided to join the republican movement. Upon reflection, he would say that his decision was not a reaction but a response to a situation of war. 'A strong sense of loss and grief is felt to this day by his family and friends. There is a rawness of a wound that has not healed ... many questions remain unanswered.'

John Quinn was twenty-two years old when he was killed on 3 March 1991 by UVF gunmen, who were also active soldiers in the British Army. He was killed alongside Malcolm Nugent (see page 201), Dwayne O'Donnell (see page 203), and Thomas Armstrong. John, Malcolm, Dwayne and their friend Malachy, had just pulled up to Boyle's Bar in the small village of Cappagh, when gunmen approached and opened fire. John was killed instantly. The circumstances surrounding his killing have led to many questions that remain unanswered, and there is strong evidence indicating collusion between loyalist paramilitaries and British Crown forces. The incident has become known as the Cappagh Killings.

The memory of John remains engraved on his family and his club. Galbally Pearses continue to be present in providing moral support to his bereaved family in their quest for truth and accountability for his killing. 'He didn't live to see his county of Tyrone lift Sam Maguire for the first time in 2003, or the following times, but he is a part of the history of his club Na Piarsaigh. He is a part of a legacy which the club carries forward. It is important to understand how so many young men from this club died, or how so many young men and women were imprisoned. How their consciences brought them to play their part in the struggle against the forces of occupation.'

Tony Doris (Antóin Ó Durasa)

AOIS/AGE: 22

CUMANN/CLUB: CLG Fianna Oileán an Ghuail/ Coalisland Fianna GAC

CONTAE/COUNTY: Tír Eoghain/Tyrone

MARAÍODH/KILLED: 3 Meitheamh, Arm na Breataine/ 3 June, British Army

'We grew up in Meenagh Park, and our house looked right onto the football field of Coalisland Fianna. We were that close.' Marty Doris describes how the GAA played a defining role in the young life of his brother, Tony. 'There'd be a club game on every Sunday, with training on in the background, and sometimes the odd county game. As kids, we would be the constant spectators, sitting on the roof of the clubhouse and cheering the team on. Of course, the most exciting aspect for us back then was when the game was over, as a big scramble ensued as we searched for any change that might have been dropped by the men in the stands!'

Tony Doris was born on 4 January 1969 to Pat and Mary Catherine, known to everyone as Kate. He was the second youngest in a family of five children, growing up in Coalisland, County Tyrone, with his older brother Marty and sisters Anne, Joan and Donna. 'Dad was a labourer and Mum was a nurse. Coalisland was a great place to grow up and we had many happy days as kids. For everyone who called Meenagh Park home, the club was a very important part of your life. Fifty-four houses were built and almost every house in the estate had, at one stage or another, someone playing for the Fianna. And so there was always a large group of kids to play and with whom to get up to mischief, both on and off the field!'

Marty explains that while proximity to Coalisland Fianna's MacRory Park helped bring the GAA into his and Tony's life, the omnipresence of football was a non-negotiable aspect of Doris family life. 'The Doris family are a big GAA family. John Doris, our eldest uncle, was a big figure in the GAA in both Coalisland and Clonoe, and he played for Tyrone in the '50s. Our dad, Pat, played for Coalisland, and the rest of our uncles played for either Coalisland, Clonoe or Brackaville; the three clubs in the area. So, there is a very proud footballing tradition in the family, and you had very little choice in playing!' Tony began playing for Coalisland Fianna when he joined at u12 level and he played right through to Minors, with some Senior Reserve experience also under his belt. 'He was a big lad, massive! When he was fourteen, he shot up and was all of a sudden this big, tall, strong young lad. He took after the Dorises, who are all tall men. At seventeen, he was 6ft 4in., and he could move quickly! He was a very good player for the club and generally played in either midfield or at full-forward, depending on where they needed his size. I have no doubt that if he stayed on, he'd have made an excellent Senior footballer. He was not only athletic, but he had a bit of swagger and skill on the ball not usually seen for some bigger players.'

Off the pitch, Tony attended the Primate Dixon Memorial Primary School in Brackaville before heading on to St Joseph's High School in Coalisland. He found work as a labourer upon leaving school and eventually got his HGV licence, which put him on track to fulfil his ambition of becoming a lorry driver. 'Tony was a gentle giant, and he naturally commanded a lot of respect both on and off the pitch. I think it was because he had a presence to him, and an affability which made him a much-loved young lad, even from a very young age.'

In describing his brother, Marty tells a story from his childhood that captures the enchanting qualities of Tony's character. 'As young lads, we used to go exploring around the local fields. Tony would tag along, despite being a lot younger than us. We were following along this old railway line, which was on a wall with maybe a fifteen-metre drop on the other side. Tony got over the edge of the wall and started hanging by his hands, and we were all shouting "What are you doing?", and he calmly turns and says, "The edge of the world." Of course, a friend ran over and grabbed him before he lost his footing, but I often think about that story and those words when I think of Tony. He had an undeniable charm, which served him well, as he also had a wicked sense of humour! My wife, Catherine, always laughs at a memory of Tony back in his teens. She, Tony and Mum were sitting in our small living room, with Mum in the armchair overlooking the open fire. Mum was glued to the TV, and Tony stood up, winked at Catherine and threw an empty lighter into the fire before heading towards the door. All of a sudden there was a huge bang and Mum was covered in soot and ash. She leapt up and chased Tony out of the room!'

As he grew into his late teens, Tony met Brigid and the pair were with one another for two years before welcoming their daughter, Róisín, into the world on St Patrick's Day 1991. Tony's life was also, however, terribly overshadowed by the extremes of the conflict, as Marty explains. 'Tony was born as the Troubles broke out, and so he grew up witnessing rioting and the locking-down of our estate on a near weekly basis. Our estate was essentially under siege for the duration of the conflict, constantly surrounded by the British Army and RUC. Our neighbours were regularly beaten and imprisoned, and even killed, starting with sixteen-year-old Martin McShane (see page 9), who was shot dead near the football field. He also witnessed an older resident of Meenagh Park being brutally beaten. I got to experience a bit of life before the conflict, but it was all Tony knew, and we would spend our nights talking about it in bed. The defining moment for Tony was when he was around twelve years old. He was at a protest in Coalisland following the death of Bobby Sands. The RUC picked him out, given his size, and he was struck by their batons. As he got older, Tony found it more difficult to ignore the reality and injustice of the society we were living in. He joined the republican movement aged seventeen, and he was totally committed to it. Football and work took a back seat as he put 100 per cent into the republican movement.'

Tony Doris was on active service for the IRA when he was killed alongside fellow volunteers Lawrence McNally (see page 211) and Michael 'Pete' Ryan on 3 June 1991 by the SAS, in what became known as the Coagh Ambush.

'Growing up, the football field was our escape from it all. The GAA was such an incredible source of good for our community in Coalisland and in our young lives. It has been remarkable to witness the excellent transformation of the club over the years and the growth of the game. It was so important to us during those dark days and remains just as important today.' There is little doubt that Tony would have taken immense pride at the growing of his beloved Fianna club, just as he would be immeasurably proud to learn that he is now also a grandfather, with Róisín bringing a daughter of her own, Lile, into their growing family. His daughter and granddaughter are proud supporters of Derrylaughan GAA club.

Lawrence McNally (Lorcán Mac Con Uladh)

AOIS/AGE: 39
CUMANN/CLUB: CLG Setanta, Báile na Móna/ Moortown Setanta GAC
CONTAE/COUNTY: Tír Eoghain/Tyrone
MARAÍODH/KILLED: 3 Meitheamh, Arm na Breataine/ 3 June, British Army

'Lawrence was the same as any other lad: happy-go-lucky, full of devilment, and the laughter was something else when he was up to something bad.' Henry describes his younger brother. 'He was a good footballer and a gifted hurler. I can remember one time we were playing Ballygawley; he was right corner-back and Mickey Harte was in at full-forward. He warned Mickey not to come past his line and, of course, Mickey crossed the line and scored a goal. But not without it costing him two teeth. Lawrence felt very bad about that for a long time as he was very close to Mickey's brother, Barney. But that was the nature of the battles we had on the field back then.'

Lawrence McNally was the ninth child of seventeen, including four older half-siblings, to Terry and Sarah. He was born and raised in Moortown, Ardboe in County Tyrone. 'Daddy had no interest in the GAA and had only time for farming, but our mother's side were big GAA people from Moortown. She grew up in a family of ten children and her brothers would regularly field a family seven-a-side football team to play other local teams! Football was no doubt in our blood, but the GAA started off with myself and Lawrence when we went to school. Lawrence was only a year younger than me, and it was Master Magner who first introduced us to hurling, at St Peter's School in Moortown, when we were around twelve or thirteen.' Indeed, Lawrence and Henry were part of the same class as Liam Ryan (see page 192). 'We'd no hurls so what we had to do was go and cut sticks off the hedges which had a shape sort of like a hurl, with a wee hoop on it. It's mad now thinking back to it, but not one of us back then would have had any money to pay for a proper hurl. We played with those sticks for a long time until Magner decided we could make our own hurls by sticking bits of ash he managed to get his hands on together. We played all over: Antrim, Tyrone, Derry, Armagh – anywhere we could get a game. There were some serious clashes back then, especially in Tyrone when we played the likes of Carrickmore, Omagh and Killyclogher.' Lawrence cemented himself as a regular on the half-back line and his strength made him a formidable opponent. 'Eventually, when we got to Minor age, we were able to play football and Lawrence would have played right up until the Troubles started in and around '67 or '68. It all changed then.'

Henry describes how the escalation of violence affected himself and Lawrence, and the relationship they had with the GAA, as they grew up in the context of conflict. 'Life was very tough growing up. We were very poor: we would go to school in our bare feet, as many of our neighbours would have at that time. There were seventeen of us in a house with one bedroom and a tin roof. No bathrooms or kitchens like nowadays. Six of us would be in one bed with coats for blankets and for curtains. If we weren't in school, most of our time as kids would be out on the Moss working at the turf and cutting sticks. Then came the late '50s and the B Specials. I can still picture them clear as day if I close my eyes, with their uniform and rifles. They really started torturing us all, beating our parents and accusing them of helping hide IRA men. It wasn't enough that it was freezing cold with water coming in through the roof, but that at any time of night the police might come in and raid the place just for the sake of it. Myself and Lawrence were only seven or eight years old at this time. So, in that context, you can only imagine what it was like to have the GAA come into your life. It was a total godsend for us all. We finally had something to look forward to. We were poor, starving and constantly harassed on the road, but we had the GAA to hold on to! When we went on trips down South, it was like heaven. You didn't want to come home and crossing that border … it was like walking into a fire. You know? The freedom you felt to then have to come back into the Dungeon. The GAA was just a massive escape for Lawrence and me from the harshness of life, but even that became dangerous as we got older. Going to and from matches on the bus or in cars was hell, with constant harassment by the UDR, and you never knew who was waiting on you, especially at night. We had to know the areas not to go through and which roads to side-step. It was like the only life that you had, that of a Gael, you weren't allowed to live either. I suppose that contextualises Lawrence's decision to join the IRA when we turned seventeen, which put the GAA to one side.'

Lawrence was arrested in April 1971 and was sentenced to seven years, of which he served five and was released in 1976. 'He got out in 1976 and started playing Senior football with me for a year until he went back on the run. What I remember is that he hadn't lost any skill or fitness because the boys inside would have trained non-stop and there were some talented footballers in with him. After being arrested and acquitted again in 1980, he decided to go to America, where he and his partner Dymphna had their daughter, Ciara. He then came back to Ireland in 1987 and built his new family a home in Tyholland in County Monaghan.' Lawrence was home just over a year when loyalist gunmen killed his younger brother Phelim in his other brother Francie's house. Phelim had been on his way home from the hospital after visiting his wife and newborn, and had called in to see his brother when loyalist gunmen attacked. 'It wasn't long before Lawrence became active again, with the killing of Phelim and then Liam Ryan the following year.'

Lawrence McNally was killed on active service for the IRA on 3 June 1991, alongside Michael 'Pete' Ryan and Tony Doris, in what is known as the Coagh Ambush. The SAS carried out the ambush, which saw the bodies of all three men burned beyond recognition.

1992

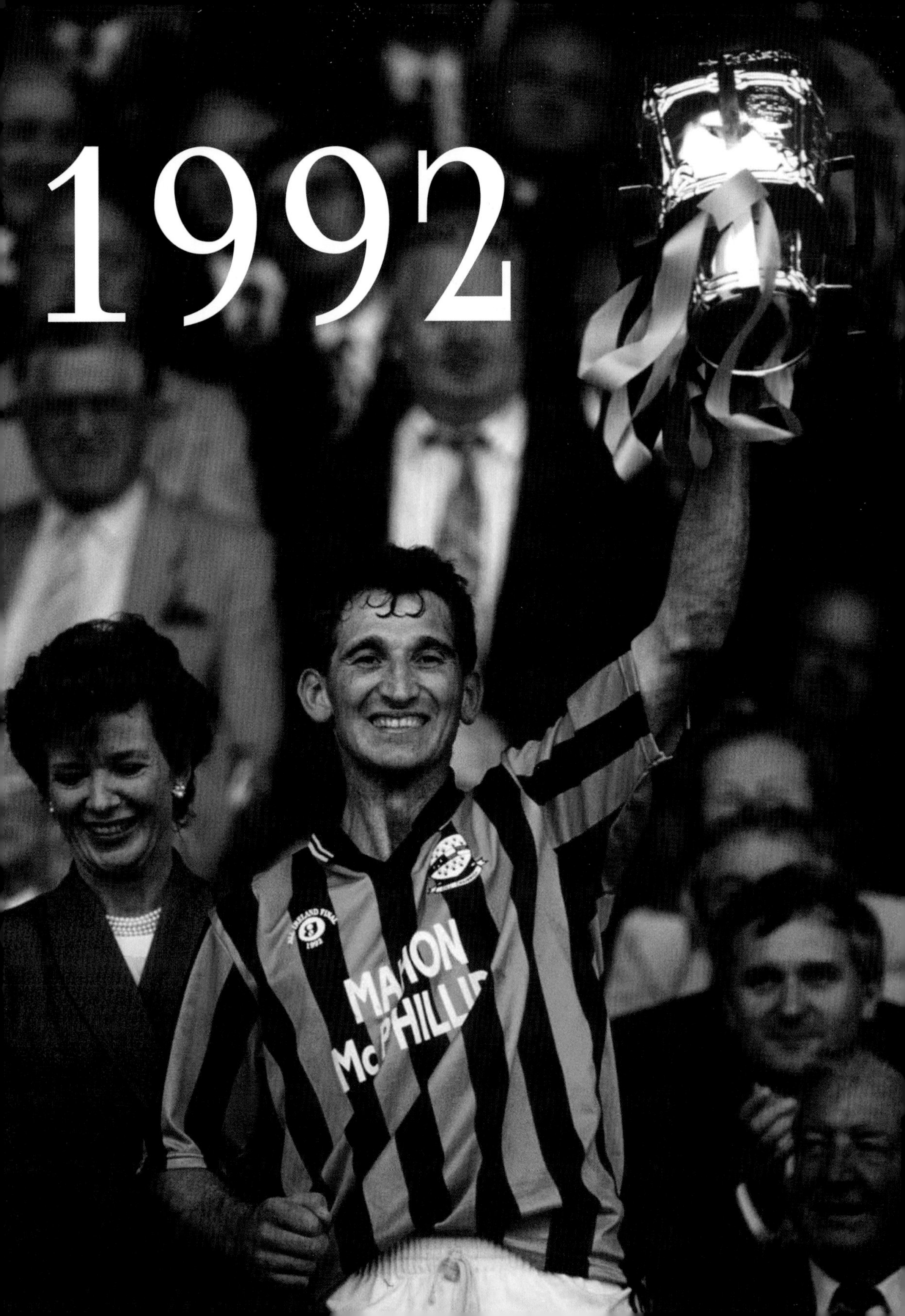

An Mhaigh G.A.C. Tír na nÓg

Kevin McKearney (Caoimhín Mac Cearnaigh)

AOIS/AGE: 32

CUMANN/CLUB: An Mhaigh Tír na nÓg GLC/ Tír na nÓg GAC, Moy

CONTAE/COUNTY: Tír Eoghain/Tyrone

MARAÍODH/KILLED: 3 Eanáir, le forsaí dílseach/ 3 January, loyalist forces

'Kevin was a very reflective sort of person.' Angela begins to describe her older brother. 'You could always talk to him and he would always listen. To most people, he might have come across as having been a bit of a quiet person, but he was the type who never felt the need to talk for talking's sake.'

Kevin McKearney was born on 26 October 1959 to Maura and Kevin snr. He was the fifth child of six for the McKearney family and grew up in the village of The Moy, County Tyrone, with his brothers Tommy, Pádraig and Seán, and sisters Margaret and Angela. Being a good bit younger than his brothers, Kevin's initial involvement with football would have been walking the short distance from the family home to the field to watch his older brothers play. Indeed, his older brothers, father and uncles all played for Moy Tír na nÓg, and Kevin would have been waiting eagerly for his chance to lace the boots.

He first started with the club's Juvenile structures and was as keen a footballer as any of his brothers, learning from the McKearneys who came before him and carving out his own name at the club. Angela remembers that in Kevin's early days at the club, he and his cousin Raymond began a bit of a competition with one another. 'Raymond was the same age as Kevin and played for our local rivals, Dungannon. The pair of them would always tally each other's wins, losses and scores. That was big business when you were that age!' Before Kevin even got going, however, tragedy struck Kevin and his family – his brother Seán (see page 60) died as a result of a premature explosion. 'The football stopped for Kevin after that. I think he was u12 when Seán died, and he just never played again. Circumstances took over and, for his own reasons, he felt he wasn't able to play football anymore.' Angela and her brother, Tommy, go on to describe how the role of the GAA in Kevin's life evolved from player to spectator, and it becomes clear that that evolution did not mean a dilution of their brother's passion or enthusiasm for football. 'He continued to be a lifelong member of the club and was always to be seen on the sidelines supporting the teams through the years; football and the club remained in his life long after he stopped playing.'

Outside of the GAA, Kevin attended Moy Primary School and, like his older brothers, went on to St Patrick's Academy in Dungannon. Upon leaving school at sixteen, he initially found work in an abattoir before joining his father in the family butcher's shop when he was twenty-one. As Tommy and Angela describe Kevin's life, what becomes evident is that he was someone who was endlessly dedicated to his family and defined by his role in caring for those in his life. The particular circumstances of the impact of the conflict on Kevin's family came to place a lot of responsibility onto him from an early age. All of Kevin's older siblings were active republicans, which meant that they could not be in the family home. His eldest sister, Margaret, remained on the run; his brother Tommy was imprisoned and would later join the 1980 hunger strike; and his other brothers, Seán and Pádraig, both died on active service for the IRA. 'This meant that myself [Angela] and Kevin were the only two left in the house. Kevin took responsibility to care for the family shop and look after the family. Daddy took ill in the mid-'70s and Kevin then took on a lot of the work; and gladly did so, without complaint. He worked all day in the butcher's shop and came to be known by everyone. In a country area like The Moy, the butcher's shop was the stopping-off point for people to tell you their stories and complaints. It was more than a shop; it was a social hub for the village. Kevin would have listened to all of it and gladly lent people his advice on their troubles.'

As time went on, Kevin met Bernadette and they were soon married. In 1981 the couple welcomed Seána into the world, who was closely followed by Cathal, then Paul, and finally Pádraigín in 1988. Naturally, all of Kevin and Bernadette's kids joined Tír na nÓg. With the new task of raising a young family, Kevin began plans to expand the family business. 'He learnt a lot from the locals who would come into the shop, especially when people would talk business. He started to create plans to modernise the shop and the small farm he had got for himself. He was seeing where he could bring in modern advancements to help expand and was also very aware of the power that could come by joining the trade unions. For someone working in a butcher's shop, he had quite the foresight!'

Kevin McKearney was thirty-two years old when he was shot dead by the UVF on 3 January 1992. He was working behind the counter in the butcher's shop with his Uncle John (see next entry) when a gunman walked in a shot them both. Kevin was killed instantly. John died on 4 April. Nine months after the attack, the same UVF gang killed Bernadette's parents, Charles and Teresa Fox. A recent inquest and a past investigation by the Historical Enquiries Team have linked these deaths, and the family believe there to be strong evidence of collusion in both instances between loyalist gunmen and Crown forces.

John McKearney (Eoin Mac Cearnaigh)

AOIS/AGE: 68

CUMANN/CLUB: An Mhaigh Tír na nÓg GLC/ Tír na nÓg GAC, Moy

CONTAE/COUNTY: Tír Eoghain/Tyrone

MARAÍODH/DIED: 4 Aibreán, le forsaí dílseach/ 4 April, loyalist forces

'I remember my father saying that John was an excellent footballer.' Angela and Tommy McKearney begin to describe their uncle. 'At over 6 feet tall, he was by far the biggest McKearney; he had a great build and stature for midfield, especially at a time when the average man was probably 5ft 7in.'

John McKearney was born on 21 April 1923 to Tom and Ellen. He grew up in the village of The Moy, County Tyrone, with his older siblings Mary, Pat, Hugh and Eileen, and younger siblings Kevin, Peter, Angela and Tom. 'Our grandfather, John's father, opened a blacksmith's forge in the village and earned a decent living for that time. Interestingly, our grandfather was in Coalisland for the 1916 Rising and learned of the birth of Pat, John's brother, on his return home.' In terms of his education, John attended his local national school and his father ensured that he, like all of his siblings, learned a trade upon leaving. 'John trained as a motor mechanic, and he stuck with it for a while, but he was a natural contrarian and had to part ways with his training when he fell out with the owner of the premises! After leaving that, he came to help run the small farm our grandfather had. In many ways, John became a bit of a jack-of-all-trades in that he helped people out with all sorts of tasks and was always about the place.'

John would mostly come to help Angela and Tommy's father, Kevin, with the running of the family butcher's shop, where his knowledge of livestock helped keep the business reputable amongst the local people, as Tommy explains. 'Before the '50s, when my Uncle Pat and father first opened the butcher's shop, the slaughtering of cattle would generally happen out the back of the butcher's shop itself, and one of the most important aspects of a butcher's trade was ensuring that people knew you were slaughtering good-quality cattle. That's where John would be invaluable. He had a good eye for choosing good cattle at the local farms and markets and always steered my father in the right direction.' As Tommy continues, selecting good beef was one thing, letting people know you had good beef was another. 'John would help walk the cattle down into the village square, to be brought through to the back of the shop. But before that, he would "accidentally" tip the cow on the backside and have it run around the square for a bit. As people came out to help capture the animal, they would get to see the size and strength of the beast, and before long people would start talking and say to each other how the McKearney's have great and fine beef! Free advertising.'

As Angela and Tommy describe their uncle, it becomes clear that behind the exterior of the contrarian, John was someone who cared deeply for his family, and his younger brother Kevin in particular. 'He always saw himself as a sort of guardian for our father in the sense that he was his older brother and physically a lot bigger. He also would make sure he was in the shop should his help be needed, especially when it came to physically demanding work like mincing beef, which had to be done by hand back then! He took umbrage over all sorts of things and could drive our father mad at times, but he was a very good-hearted person.'

As for the football, John played for Moy Tír na nÓg, along with all of his brothers. In recalling life on the pitch almost eighty years ago, memories and stories have naturally faded, but it is clear that John was particularly talented. 'I remember our father saying that John was either asked to play for the county or did play and something happened that made him stop. Regardless of the detail, we do know that he was certainly at that top level of talent and ability.' As with all of the McKearney family, the GAA played an important part in John's life. As far as his family can recall, he never missed an Ulster football final, and he was always there to help his local club with any jobs needing doing. He lived his whole life in The Moy village and dedicated it to his family and his club.

John McKearney was shot on 3 January 1993 by the UVF. He was working behind the counter in the family butcher's shop with his nephew Kevin (see page 215) when a gunman walked in and shot both of them. Kevin was killed instantly. John died on 4 April due to his injuries. John's family believe there to be strong evidence of collusion in his and Kevin's killing, and recent investigations have linked the incident to the killing of Charles and Teresa Fox, Kevin's parents-in-law, which occurred nine months after John was shot and which was carried out by the same loyalist gang.

Joseph Mac Manus (Seosamh Mac Mághnais)

AOIS/AGE: 21

CUMANN/CLUB: Naomh Mhuire CLG, An Mhachaire Bhuí; Cúil Irra–Leathros CLG/St Mary's GAC, Maugheraboy; Coolera–Strandhill GAC

CONTAE/COUNTY: Sligeach/Sligo

MARAÍODH/KILLED: 5 Feabhra, Arm na Breataine/
5 February, British Army

'Happy' is the word which comes to the minds of Helen and Seán Mac Manus when remembering their son Joseph. 'He was a happy young lad, who loved his football, his music, and the girls.' A short life filled with achievements on and off the pitch, he never had the chance to fulfil his many ambitions. 'He had a love for rock music which led him to buying a guitar, and although a master of the air-guitar, he never had the chance to master the actual guitar. He just really enjoyed life. Always the life and soul of any room he was in.'

Joseph was born in Harlesden, London, on 23 May 1970, the city where his parents met and married. In 1976 the family returned to Ireland, settling in the Maugheraboy area of Sligo town so that Joseph and his brother Chris could be educated in Ireland. Traditionally a more soccer-oriented town, St Mary's GAA club had just formed in Sligo town the very year Joseph and his family moved there. Joseph's involvement in the club was inevitable when you consider the two big influences on his early life – his dad and his schooling. His father, Seán, is a native of the rural west of County Cavan and was reared on stories of Cavan's successes in the 1940s and 1950s. Seán admits that his keen interests in the GAA would have rubbed off on both of his sons, but particularly on his eldest, Joseph. Seán and Helen describe that 'going to St John's Marist Brothers National School was also a big influence on Joseph's GAA life'. With the exclusive focus of GAA at school, Joseph came under the stewardship of Brother Bonaventure, who ensured Joseph's involvement in various underage footballing leagues, including the Marist Cup, from primary right through to secondary school.

Indeed, Joseph would be a key part of a very successful underage group for St Mary's. Despite being a relatively new club, Joseph's team would deliver all-county league and championship titles at u16 and Minor levels in the mid-1980s. Notwithstanding that he was playing ages above his own and still developing as a young man, his teammates attest to his opponents coming up against a hard, challenging defender in Joseph Mac Manus. The same can be said for his presence on the soccer pitch, which became more prevalent as Joseph moved into his late teens, finding that there was a more social aspect to the sport in Sligo town. But while Joseph certainly enjoyed soccer, he was never far from his first love of the Gaelic games, going on to join Coolera–Strandhill GAA for at least one season.

While known to all who knew him as a laid-back, happy-go-lucky guy, Joseph was also very political. His friends were unaware of his commitment to the republican movement when, on 5 February 1992, he was killed by a member of the British Army whilst on active service as a Volunteer of the IRA.

Jack Duffin (Seán Ó Duibhchinn)

AOIS/AGE: 66
CUMANN/CLUB: Uí Chonaill CLG, Béal Feirste/ O'Connell GAC, Belfast
CONTAE/COUNTY: Aontroim/Antrim
MARAÍODH/KILLED: 5 Feabhra, le forsaí dílseach/ 5 February, loyalist forces

'No matter what pitch I went to with him, no matter what county in Ireland, everyone knew him.' Thomas, Jack Duffin's son, describes his father. 'Within some GAA circles, he was treated like royalty to a certain extent. I suppose that was because people were aware of where he came from and his unending commitment to keeping grassroots GAA alive.'

Jack Duffin was born on 24 August 1925 in Glasslough, County Monaghan. One of four children, the family moved to Walmer Street on the Ormeau Road in South Belfast when Jack was very young. He married Helen Toal in 1948, and the couple lived together at Jack's family home until they secured a house of their own in Balfour Avenue, also on the Ormeau Road. The young couple started a family, having three children: Martin, Patrick and Thomas. Jack came from a strong GAA family, his grandfather a former intercounty player for Monaghan. However, 'growing up on the Ormeau Road in the south of the city, the presence of Gaelic games was virtually nil. And so, it wasn't until he started working in O'Neill's stoneyard on the Falls Road, at the age of fifteen, did he find the opportunity to finally get involved. His colleagues in work got him to join their club, O'Connell's, around 1941/42.' A dual player, Jack would join a team littered with some of Antrim GAA's most decorated and celebrated players, including Kevin Armstrong. A formidable presence in the O'Connell's full-back line, Jack would help his team to multiple Antrim hurling championships in the 1940s and 1950s. 'He was a staunch GAA man and never let anything diminish his passion for Gaelic games. He walked proudly each weekend to matches and training from the Ormeau Road to the Falls Road with his hurl in his hand, undeterred by the potential unwanted attention it might bring from elements of society who might use his hurl to justify targeting him. Later, he would do the same with myself and my underage teammates as we made our way to and from training and matches.'

Jack's playing career ended in 1962 after he underwent a big procedure in hospital, but he continued to play an instrumental role in his club's successes. Attired in his suit, he was always to be found patrolling the sidelines of GAA fields across the country. He became a stalwart of O'Connell's GAA club, keeping the club running for as long as he possibly could, but with the escalation of the conflict, no public funding and no facilities or ground, the club fizzled out in the late 1960s. Keen to keep the legacy of the club alive, Jack became its president in the late 1980s, hosting social events dedicated to club achievements and individual stars.

Fundamentally, Jack was a proud GAA man, proud of his identity and of his culture. Indeed, he was committed to sowing the roots of Irish culture into his community: he ran céilí lessons in his local Parochial Hall and, when asked, he helped establish a local underage GAA team, Holy Rosary. When his efforts were met with resistance by those suspicious of Irish culture, ultimately ending in the collapsing of the underage team, Jack ensured that his sons and the local children could still play their national sports. 'Every Saturday morning, my dad, like the Pied Piper, walked us down the Ormeau Road with our hurls in our hands into town, put us into taxis and sent us up to Rossa House for training at our new club. He would come up himself later, have a pint in the clubhouse and we would all be dropped home by the club mini-bus.' Some of those kids would go on to play at the highest levels, in no small part thanks to the efforts of Jack.

Jack Duffin was killed by the UDA in collusion with British State forces, in his local bookmaker's shop on the Ormeau Road on 5 February 1992, along with Christy Doherty, James Kennedy (see next entry), Peter Magee (see page 226) and William McManus. Jack was killed in what is now known as the Sean Graham Bookmaker's massacre, the subject of a 2022 Police Ombudsman report that found extensive evidence of collusion.

James Kennedy (Seamus Mac Cinnéidigh)

AOIS/AGE: 15

CUMANN/CLUB: Naomh Maoileachlainn CLG, Béal Feirste/ St Malachy's GAC, Belfast

CONTAE/COUNTY: Aontroim/Antrim

MARAÍODH/KILLED: 5 Feabhra, le forsaí dílseach/ 5 February, loyalist forces

'The thing about our James was that he was a character; everybody knew who he was, and he had mates from everywhere. He was a very funny young lad with a heart of gold and a rare charm to him, which made it very difficult for

people not to like him.' Bosco and David Kennedy remember their brother James. 'He could have honestly been anything in life because people really loved him and the craic he brought. The gift of the gab, as they say.'

James Kennedy was born on 20 June 1976 to John and Kathleen. He was the second of five boys, growing up with older brother John-Bosco and younger brothers David, Michael and Paul. The family lived in the Markets area of South Belfast, where the boys collectively became known to their neighbours as 'the Kennedy five-a-side' for their insatiable appetite for playing football and soccer, especially in the street. 'Five boys and we all played soccer and football. There wasn't a window in the house that wasn't smashed with us playing on the driveway or on the street. We were all very sporty and spent the morning, noon and night of every day with a ball at our feet or in our hands. James, to be fair to him, was the best out of us all; in soccer and football. My father always loved recalling a story of one summer evening, with the coaches calling to the door to see if James could come to play a match for the club that night. It was a Saturday and James had already played a match that morning and a second that afternoon! My da laughed that James hid behind the door, pleading silently with my father to convince the coaches he wasn't in as he was busted and couldn't face a third game on the same day. That tells you all you need to know about his talent on the pitch and how in-demand he was from everybody.'

Those coaches at James's door that night had a committed PE teacher from James's primary school, St Colman's, to thank for their talented player. 'We were all introduced to the GAA in the school; it was strictly hurling and football in school and, through that connection, we all became involved in St Malachy's GAA club from an early age.' James would establish himself as a very talented attacking player, lining out among the forwards every weekend in the black and amber of his club, with the eyes of the older players in the club watching him in the hope that James would soon mature into a top talent for the club.

Outside of GAA, James was as equally talented on the soccer pitch. 'He played soccer for Rosario up the Ormeau Road, which was unheard of back then for a lad from the Markets. They wouldn't have normally taken a Markets man, but they wanted James. At secondary school, St Augustine's, he was a supreme talent and the school's star player the year the college reached the School's Cup final. We still have the video of it, where you can see the massive, big banner on the terraces reading "James Mush Kennedy" – Mush being his nickname. For the school to have even reached the final was an incredible achievement, being a tiny school with a cohort of about thirty-five boys to choose from. They were playing Boys Model, and, with five minutes to go, were 2–0 up thanks to James's two brilliant goals. Boys Model managed to bring the final to a draw, and eventually won the replay, but James really stood out on that pitch. We had a good life growing up and never wanted for anything. Every one of us had our own bike and we were part of a great community. We would have all gone to the youth club every night after school to meet up with all the other kids and play table tennis, snooker and arcade games. That's where James was a natural hit with the girls, whom he had running here, there and everywhere after him!'

James Kennedy was killed on 5 February 1992 by the UDA as he stood in Sean Graham's bookmakers on the Ormeau Road. He was one of five people killed by loyalist gunmen now proven to have been working in collusion with the State. 'James, like the rest of the lads, enjoyed getting into the bookies for wee 10p, 50p and £1 bets, the winnings of which would always be shared excitedly with Mum. That's what he was doing that day.' James's mother, Kathleen, would die within two years of James's killing. 'I wouldn't have been one to say or believe someone could die of a broken heart, but our mother wasn't a smoker nor a drinker. After James was killed, we watched Mum die slowly in front of us.'

Peter Magee (Peadar Mac Aoidh)

AOIS/AGE: 18

CUMANN/CLUB: Naomh Maoileachlainn CLG, Béal Feirste/ St Malachy's GAC, Belfast

CONTAE/COUNTY: Aontroim/Antrim

MARAÍODH/KILLED: 5 Feabhra, le forsaí dílseach/ 5 February, loyalist forces

'It's very difficult to talk about Peter without talking about Martin. They were identical twins and did everything in life together.' Peter's brother-in-law Mark and teammate Billy describe Peter and Martin Magee. 'They were inseparable. The only time in life they weren't together was when Peter took an interest in greyhounds, and he would head away each Tuesday night with his great friend and mentor, Tyrone native Seamus Toal, to different racecourses around the country. The twins were together every other time in life; going to and from school, playing on the same sports teams, and messing about on the streets. Everyone on the road knew they came as a pair.'

Peter and Martin Magee were born on 22 November 1973 to Clara and Patsy. They grew up as the last of Clara and Patsy's seven children and came a bit later than their older siblings Tommy, Rosena, Clara, Maria and Patrick. As such, the twins were their parents' blue-eyed boys, and Mark describes the family home as being adorned with pictures of Peter and Martin. The boys went to St Colman's Primary School in the Market area of South Belfast, neighbouring the area of the Ormeau Road where they grew up. It was at school that Peter and Martin were first introduced to the GAA, and it soon became apparent that the twins had serious potential, drawing the attention of the Juvenile coaches of their local club St Malachy's GAC. 'They joined St Malachy's at a young age and that was the pair of them hooked. They both played football, and Peter would have also enjoyed playing hurling when he could, but there wouldn't have been much hurling to play.'

A few years older than the twins, Billy describes the up-and-coming Magee brothers. 'They were both brilliant footballers and Peter was a flying machine. He was like a whippet on the pitch and there wasn't a pick on him. They both lived for football and never missed a match. Peter's name was always first on the team sheet through all the age groups, and Martin's was second.' Although sometimes, as Mark explains, the boys took a bit of convincing to get them to the training pitch on the cold nights or in the early mornings. 'When the manager came round to collect them for training and they didn't want to go, they would hide in the house. But usually if one didn't want to go, the other did, and the manager knew that if one came outside, the other was hiding inside. He'd be straight into the house and more or less trail the pair of them out to go and play. Once they got going, however, they were always glad for it and always gave their all on the pitch.'

The twins' ability on the field also drew the attention of another club. 'What usually happened at our club was, if you were any good, Bredagh came looking you. Now, it was taboo to play for them as far as most people from our area are concerned, but Peter and Martin ended up playing for them for a bit. They were underage still, probably under-14s, and suffice it to say it wouldn't have gone down well. They were back playing for St Malachy's before long and with their ability, I'd say they were quickly forgiven.' Billy and Mark continue. 'It wasn't the attention from Bredagh which had us worried, however, but the attention of others. Players of St Malachy's trained under a constant death threat from loyalists. We trained at Cherryvale pitches on the Ravenhill Road, surrounded by loyalists, and it came to the point where the British Army had to stand and watch us train to deter any attack! There was also the constant harassment by the police and British Army when we travelled to matches in other parts of the city. Each time we came back into the district, the minibus was stopped, everyone was taken off, and our bags emptied and searched. Every single game. So Bredagh was a minor worry for our club on the grand scale of it all!'

As the boys got older, they started to get a taste of Senior football – both were playing Senior Reserve – and in 1991 the twins had a great hand in St Malachy's bringing home the South Antrim Junior Championship. 'We had a great team then and it was looking really good for us with the young ones coming through. Myself [Billy] and Peter played on the half-forward line. I was on the left and Peter was on the right. Peter was actually breaking onto the Senior panel and was set to be given u18 Player of the Year at the annual dinner for that '91 season.'

Outside of the GAA, Peter and Martin went from St Colman's Primary School to St Augustine's Secondary School. They were always to be seen running around the streets of the Ormeau Road area, involving themselves in the antics young lads love to have. 'They were two wee characters. As Belfast as they come. They never stopped making you laugh and no matter who was in front of them, they were willing entertainers. They always had to be where the action was, and they were mad for it. They'd be sitting eating their dinner and if they heard a siren go by, everything was dropped and out they'd run to see what was happening. It reached a stage where they were on first-name terms with the firemen! They could even tell by the siren if it was the police, fire service or an ambulance. They were very streetwise too, and always testing if they could pull a fast one. At the top of their street was an old derelict house, and as teenagers, we went in and took it over. It was a great spot to get in out of the rain and play cards for a bit of money. I always laugh, their da Patsy had a bit of a knack for knowing when the twins were in front in a game of cards, maybe a few quid up, and they'd be called in for their dinner. It was like a smoke signal was sent to the house. The pair of them were just so content in each other's company and it didn't matter what was going on around them, they would always find the craic.'

One week before he was to be named St Malachy's u18 Player of the Year, eighteen-year-old Peter Magee was shot dead by the UDA on 5 February 1992. He was killed alongside fellow St Malachy's youngster James Kennedy (see page 223), Jack Duffin (see page 221), Christy Doherty and William McManus. He had just entered Sean Graham's bookmakers on the Ormeau Road when gunmen immediately followed him in and opened fire indiscriminately. Mark was in the bookmakers too and suffered multiple gunshot wounds, while Billy's father, William McManus, was killed trying to charge the gunmen. The day after Peter was killed, Martin took his first drink of alcohol, which was the beginning of a fifteen-year battle with alcoholism that ultimately led to his death. 'It's hard when you talk about Peter, as he's the person directly killed by loyalists, but indirectly, they also killed Martin.' A recent Police Ombudsman's report found that the gunmen involved were assisted through collusion by the Crown forces. 'We had so much hope for the club with the youth in our Senior team coming through, and Peter was one of our very talented youngsters. Then the bookies happened. It devastated us as a club and community, and it took us years to rebuild.'

Kevin Barry O'Donnell (Caoimhín Barra Ó Domhnaill)

AOIS/AGE: 21

CUMANN/CLUB: CLG Fianna Oileán an Ghuil/ Coalisland Fianna GAC

CONTAE/COUNTY: Tír Eoghain/Tyrone

MARAÍODH/KILLED: 16 Feabhra, Arm na Breataine/ 16 February, British Army

'In 2003 when Tyrone won their first All-Ireland Senior football final, we put the county colours on Barry's grave; to us, it was very important to have included him in this joyous occasion as following Tyrone was such a big part of his and indeed all of our lives. In fact, we brought home some of the grass off the field in Croke Park that day to place on his grave.'

Barry's family explain how foundational the GAA was to their identity and lives. 'From we were children of no age, we spent every Sunday with our dad following our club Na Fianna, or our county team Tyrone.'

Kevin Barry O'Donnell was born on 24 March 1970 to Jim and Celine. He, and his six siblings – Róisín, Feargal, Caoimhe, Deirdre, Niall and Séamus – grew up in Coalisland, County Tyrone. With the GAA field close to his home, Barry was playing football for his local club, Na Fianna Coalisland, from when he was a young lad.

On the pitch, Barry was part of a successful team at the club, playing along the back line, and every other year got to play on the same team as his older brother Feargal. Barry also played football for his school, St Patrick's Academy,

Dungannon, and for Loughry College, where he went to study agriculture and poultry. 'He stopped playing for Fianna at under-16 level, but he continued to play for the college. His love for the GAA never faded thereafter; he was always to be seen coming and going to matches.' Undoubtedly, Barry's love for the GAA was strengthened and complemented by his passion for the Irish language, with him and his siblings growing up learning their native language and attending courses in the Gaeltacht areas of Donegal every summer.

A very curious mind, Barry was never without a book in his hand. 'He was always reading, a fondness that Daddy instilled by bringing us to the library every Saturday morning.' More than anything, Barry had a passion for nature, particularly for birds, which led him to further study at agricultural college. 'He always had wee ducks, hens and quails at the house, which explains why he studied poultry.' His inclination for looking after nature was typical of Barry's personality. 'He was a very kind and thoughtful person. He would always take time to ensure that everyone got their fair share.' One of the proudest moments in his life was when his son, Ruairí, was born, just one month before he was killed.

Barry's life, however, was not without struggle. At the age of nineteen, Barry spent ten months on remand in Brixton prison, before he was deported home. 'It was a hard experience, as he was isolated as an Irish prisoner over in an English prison. Although he was very determined to not let it affect him.' When he got home, Barry faced routine harassment and death threats from the RUC, UDR and British Army. It was a hard time for many people in our community. 'I believe that having the GAA in his life, being able to attend matches and follow his county team, provided an escape that he and so many of us needed during those hard times.'

Kevin Barry O'Donnell was killed on 16 February 1992 by the British Army while on active service for the IRA. He was killed alongside Peter Clancy, Patrick Vincent and Sean O'Farrell, in the grounds of Clonoe chapel.

Hugh McKibben (Aodh Mac Giobúin)

AOIS/AGE: 21

CUMANN/CLUB: Cumann Mícheál Uí Dhuibhir, Béal Feirste/Michael Dwyers GAC, Belfast

CONTAE/COUNTY: Aontroim/Antrim

MARAÍODH/KILLED: 27 Lúnasa, le IPLO/27 August, IPLO

'He was a quiet lad; no harm in him.' Catherine Madden describes her son Hugh. 'When he was killed, no one understood or believed it. How did my Hugh, of all people, get mixed up in all that?'

Hugh McKibben was born on 10 January 1971. He was Catherine's first son and was soon joined by younger brother Paul and sister Sharon. He grew up just off the Grosvenor Road in West Belfast, attending St Peter's Primary School and then St Paul's Secondary School. From a young age, Hugh showed a keen interest in sports. 'He was always out in the street with his hurl, banging the ball off the wall. He could fairly whack the sliotar; indeed, he won the Poc Fada at the local leisure centre when he was a young lad. Along with hurling, he played football for the Dwyers team on the Grosvenor Road and soccer for the Hibernians' Seconds team. Hugh also boxed for a short while too.'

Outside of sports, Hugh's passion was for 'Mod' culture. 'He had great taste in music. He particularly loved all the '60s stuff and was obsessed with The Who. Hugh had his side of his bedroom covered in posters of The Who and The Blues Brothers. His scooter was bought soon after leaving school and that was him. It was a brilliant sight when all his friends called to the door for him; the street was lined with scooters, everyone wearing their long green coats. And off they went into the town, where all the Mods would meet up at City Hall. He was friends with people from all over Belfast as the Mods were from everywhere, Catholic and Protestant.'

Hugh became a true disciple of Mod culture, wearing the iconic roundel on the back of his jacket, and his style didn't go unnoticed. 'He came home one day after being out with them, to say he had been approached by people from a modelling firm and was asked would he come to their studio for a photoshoot. Of course, when I asked him if he had gone, he said, "No I did not! Are you mad?" He wouldn't listen when I told him he could make something out of his good looks. I remember our Hugh attracted everybody; he was tall and had his blond hair and good looks. In fact, he was always tortured by ones on the road who were jealous of the attention he got. Not that he was ever fussed!'

Hugh fathered two children: Sarah and Peter. Sarah came first, on 1 May 1989, and although it didn't work out with Sarah's mother, he remained a committed father. Hugh then met Susan, who moved in with Hugh and his family and the couple were together for a number of years until Hugh's killing. They had a son together, Peter, who had yet to reach his first birthday when his father was killed.

Hugh McKibben was killed on 27 August 1992 as a result of an internal feud in the Irish People's Liberation Organisation (IPLO). He was on the Dwyers' team bus after having played a football match at Lámh Dhearg, when gunmen boarded the coach and shot him in his seat. 'It was the last thing anyone expected, Hugh getting involved. I saw a change in him after a number of Catholics were killed in random attacks, and I think because there was no real response, he felt he needed to do something. He was, also, always reading the book on the Shankill Butchers, who murdered relatives of our neighbours. I don't know how he ended up joining the IPLO, but we all got worried seeing the company he started keeping. Undesirables. The day he was killed, I remember thinking, *thank God he's away playing a match and not with that other crowd I saw him with*. Silly me, I guess.'

1993

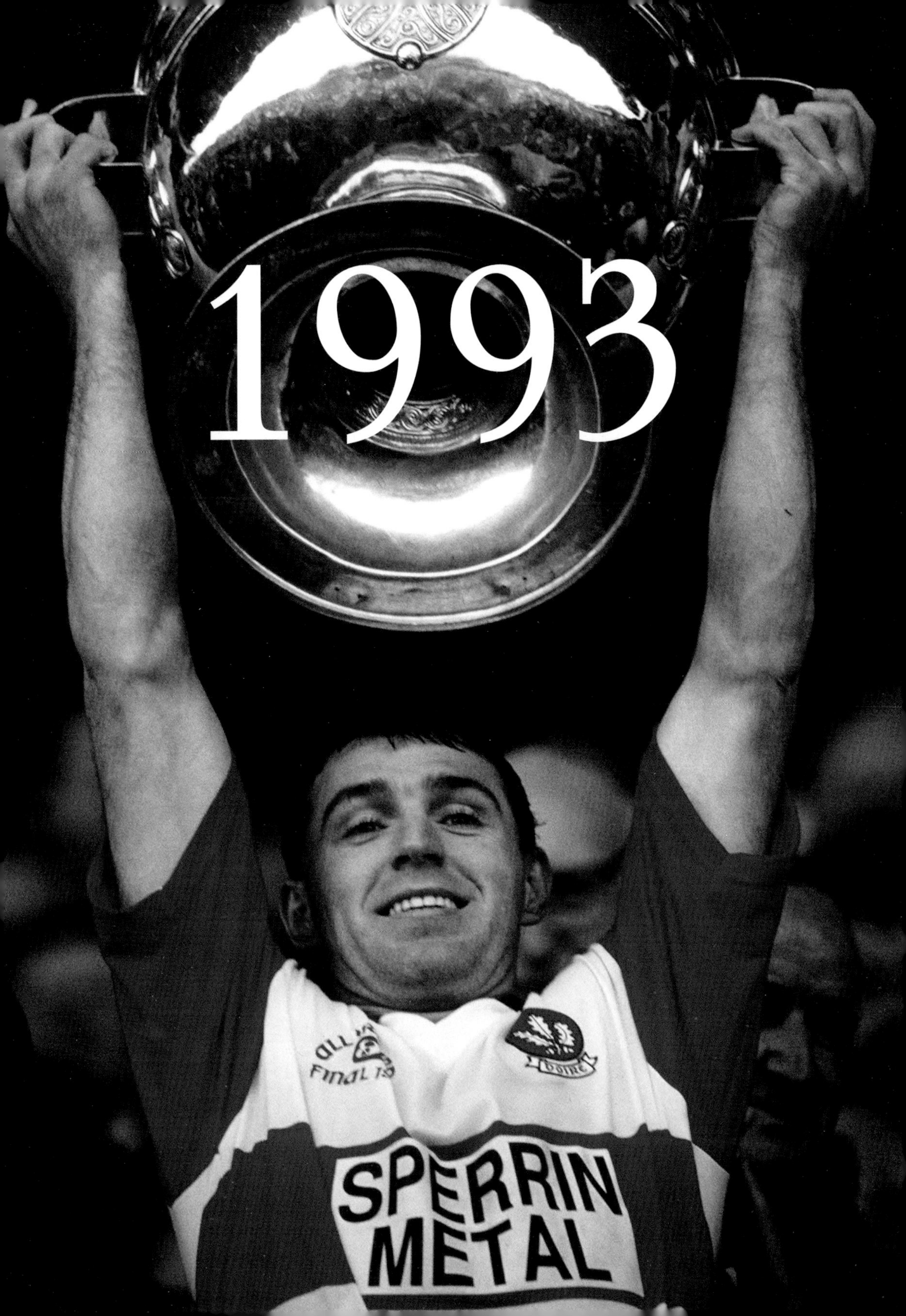

Patrick Shields (Pádraig Ó Siadhail)

AOIS/AGE: 50

CUMANN/CLUB: CLG Fianna Oileán an Ghuail/ Coalisland Fianna GAC

CONTAE/COUNTY: Tír Eoghain/Tyrone

MARAÍODH/KILLED: 3 Eanáir, le forsaí dílseach/ 3 January, loyalist forces

'The Tyrone team never got very far without him. Whether it was America in the '70s, Canada in the '90s, or even to Clones each summer, Daddy had to be there, and they had to have him there.' Maggie, Patrick's daughter, describes the pivotal backroom role her father played for the Tyrone Senior football panel. 'He was the backbone of the backroom staff. Long before it got all high-tech, Daddy would be making sure the lads were best prepared for any occasion. Whether that meant packing his own car with players to get to matches, on the sidelines with water, or in the changing room with his special mixture of rubbing oils he got from a local chemist he was friendly with. For all his service, to know he is still held in very high regard all these years later by the best of Tyrone football is very important to us.'

Patrick Shields was born on 17 March 1942 in Coalisland, County Tyrone. One of twelve to parents Maggie and Francie, he grew up immersed in football, playing for Coalisland Fianna. Patrick went to Primate Dixon School in Coalisland before going out to work, which would see him earn his way as a bread delivery man, caretaker of the local St Patrick's Academy and as a lorry driver amongst other work. In 1962 Patrick met Bríd at a local ballroom in Dungannon, where the pair kindled a romance that would find them married two years later. Starting a family together, the couple had four children. Settling into their new life, Bríd managed to balance her time as a mother with her duties in running the family shop, post office and snooker hall, whilst Patrick did the same alongside full-time work and his steadfast commitment to the footballers.

'He loved sports of any kind – if it was on the TV, he would be watching it. He played football for Coalisland Fianna in his younger years but got involved in the backroom of the county panel from at least the start of the '70s, if not before. He played a bit of bowls and golf, but he was utterly committed to Tyrone football. If he wasn't spending his Sundays with the county panel, he was out on the pitches around Tyrone refereeing club games. As kids, we rarely had the chance to join him at the county games because the car would be full of players! Often thinking of missed opportunities, my dad would have loved the decade of the noughties. He saw Tyrone reach the All-Ireland final once in 1986, but they were beaten by Kerry that year. He would have been right in the middle of the first lifting of Sam [Maguire Cup] in '03. The morning after that day in '03, one of Daddy's best friends came to the door with every newspaper he could buy that had even the slightest mention of Tyrone's success, and him and Mummy sat and replayed every second of the match together. In fact, the house never stopped that day, with friends of Daddy's, the royalty of Tyrone GAA, coming to share the celebrations with Mummy. Frank McGuigan arrived a few days later with Sam to the house to show Mummy.'

Patrick Shields was fifty when he was killed alongside his son Diarmuid by the UVF on 3 January 1993. Patrick was in bed when gunmen entered their home through the family shop, killing him and Diarmuid, aged twenty, and shooting and injuring his other son.

'Diarmuid was my big brother. Born on 6 March 1972, we were the closest in age, and when the two eldest left for uni, me and Diarmuid got really close. He was very understated and a quiet lad, but incredibly bright and intelligent. He was bumped through years in school and even taught himself how to read. This makes him sound like some sort of super child, but he was terribly smart. He taught me how to play chess and cards.' Maggie talks about the life stolen from her family and the robbed opportunities her brother Diarmuid would have loved. 'He really could have been anything. He had no real interest in football but was passionate about the Irish language, history and music. He would have absolutely relished the iPod and digital music age. And don't get me started about how Diarmuid would have reacted to the beginning of the internet. His interest in books and knowledge was never academically motivated, but out of pure interest for subjects. When he died, he was doing research for the Irish World Heritage Centre.' Shortly after his killing, Diarmuid's girlfriend died by suicide.

A charity football game was held in honour of Patrick and Diarmuid in the aftermath of their deaths. Played between Patrick's Tyrone footballers and the football team of Diarmuid's Queens University Belfast, the proceeds raised were donated as assistance to their family. Patrick and Diarmuid's legacy lives on through the generations of their family. Patrick's love for football has filtered down to his grandchildren, who match, if not exceed, their grandfather's passion for Tyrone GAA.

Thomas Molloy (Tomás Ó Maolmhuaidh)

AOIS/AGE: 32

CUMANN/CLUB: CLG Roibeard Eiméid, Cluain Mhór/ Clonmore Robert Emmets GFC

CONTAE/COUNTY: Ard Mhacha/Armagh

MARAÍODH/KILLED: 11 Feabhra, le forsaí dílseach/ 11 February, loyalist forces

'Thomas was a character.' Margaret and Eileen begin to describe their brother, Thomas Molloy. 'He was a creator of havoc and full of devilment. There was never a dull moment in his company and always great craic!'

Thomas Molloy was born on 29 August 1960 to John and Nancy. He was a middle child of a family of four boys and four girls, growing up in Tullyroan on the edge of the hamlet of Clonmore, County Armagh, with his brothers Martin, Sean and Malachy, and his sisters Mary, Margaret, Eileen and Kathleen. Margaret and Eileen describe their family's connection to the GAA, and the beginning of Thomas's involvement with his local club, Clonmore Robert Emmets. 'In a wee, rural community like ours, the GAA club is the hub of all social activity. Every evening, the club is buzzing with something going on, and so the GAA was always a massive part of our lives growing up. It was also such a big part of our lives because our father was a massive Gael. From the day he was born until the day he died, he was a committed GAA man. In fact, Daddy used to cycle from Ballymacnab to Croke Park for All-Ireland final day in his younger life! That of course meant that all the boys followed their father into the football from they were no age. Martin was first to join the Clonmore club, then Sean, then Thomas, and finally, Malachy. We're a family of six-footers, so the lads had a big presence on the football field. Martin was a great footballer, just like his dad, and Sean made the Armagh Minor panel in 1977, with whom he won an Ulster Championship, so there was definitely a bit of talent in the family.'

As his sisters explain, Thomas inherited his father's love and passion for football and their club from a very early age, and was a keen underage footballer, carving out a position for himself as the goalkeeper. 'Thomas, Sean and Malachy would cycle down the road and check out the pitch from the roadside and join the other young boys, who may already be there, or they would be first there with the ball and others soon joined when they heard the ball kicking. An old building, "Clarkes Shop", was the clubrooms then and it was also on the side of the road, so it was a meeting place for the youth. Every evening and weekend was spent on the field in front of our house or football field with his neighbours and brothers, chasing footballs and wrestling with one another.'

Margaret and Eileen describe how that time in Thomas's life was somewhat idyllic, in that the GAA club provided his childhood with a sense of shelter from the reality of growing up in the so-called Murder Triangle during some of the darkest days of the conflict. As he got older, Thomas's playing days came to an end and he made the transition to devoted supporter. 'He continued to play Junior football and never missed a Senior match, whether he was playing or not. Thomas always made a point of being there for his team; to support them in any way he could, including jumping into goals on a very rare occasion if they were short a player.' As his sisters continue, they describe Thomas growing into a selfless and committed member of his club, giving up most, if not all, of his free time to the club; whether that be in driving lads to games in his orange Ford Escort car; bringing boots and equipment to training and matches; serving on the various club committees; or lending a hand to repairs and maintenance work about the grounds. 'Of course, after every game the team would head into Monaghan or Keady for a drink and Thomas would be in the middle of them all recounting every detail of the game. He was Clonmore's very own Mícheál Ó Muircheartaigh, and as far as he was concerned, he knew the details of the game best, as the players only played in the game, but he watched it!'

As for life outside of the GAA, Thomas attended his local primary school in Clonmore before heading to secondary school in Dungannon. 'Thomas was a beautiful child. I can remember being so jealous of his blond, curly hair. He was so handsome! Unfortunately, an incident occurred in his childhood when we were all walking home from school, in which one of his friends died in a road accident. The incident scarred Thomas badly and from that day he was always very anxious about taking care of his younger brother Malachy. He feared something happening to him and always acted as a sort of guardian to his brothers.'

Upon leaving school, Thomas went on to train as a bricklayer and, between all four Molloy brothers, they had almost all the building trades covered. Margaret explains that she still lives in the house her brothers built for her, with Thomas running the project from plans right through to completion. 'It was finished, and I moved into the house in September '81. We had a big party to celebrate, and I had to drive the boys home as they could barely stand towards the end of the night! The house is still standing, so I suppose he did a good job. Thomas then went on to build more houses and he was on the cusp of doing great things.' As Margaret and Eileen continue, they describe their brother as a giant of a man who always had a joke or a story. 'Thomas was always a solutions man. There was nothing he couldn't solve. I remember he and his brother-in-law, Martin, found work building a stone wall at St Patrick's Trian in Armagh. Back then, you would say you could do anything just to get the work, and then figure it out when you got there. So, what happened was, they had half of this stone wall put up when the inspectors arrived to check on things. They were supposed to have all these stonemasonry certificates, and Thomas had to figure out how to convince them he knew what he was talking about. So, he lit a cigarette and bamboozled them with facts. He told this big spiel about the process of placing each stone, how the stones came from this particular place, and all of that, and went on and on until the inspectors were happy. Thomas hadn't a clue where the stones he was using came from! But that was the type of him: a solutions man. And that wall is still there and looks the part.'

When he was nineteen, Thomas met Gabrielle, and the pair were soon seeing one another. Before long they were married and had their first child, Angela, in 1982. Thomas and his new family lived initially in Armagh city, where they welcomed two more daughters, Felicity and Mary, into the world, before Thomas built a new house back on the home farm in Tullyroan on the edge of Clonmore. 'He didn't like town life and wanted to get back to the country. They then welcomed their son, Robert, into their family. Many people wondered at him naming his son Robert, but we as his family knew he was named after Robert Emmet. He had everything he wanted living back home and his family around him. He was so looking forward to getting Robert involved in the club. He was a fantastic father, and his kids became his life. All of that was cruelly taken from him and his family that winter night.'

Thomas Molloy was thirty-two years old when he was shot dead on the evening of 11 February 1993 by the UVF. He was sitting in his living room, with one-year-old Robert in his arms, while his wife was making his lunch for the next day and his daughters were by his side watching the TV. He was just handing his son over to Gabrielle when a gunman crept up to the window of the living room and opened fire into their home. Thomas was killed instantly. Robert was struck by a ricocheting bullet. As their home was only built, there was no phone for Gabrielle to make an emergency call and so, having checked that Thomas was dead, Gabrielle had to take her children by the hand and leave their home to walk along the dark lane towards Malachy's house. No one has ever been convicted of Thomas's killing. There had been several UDR checkpoints locally in the days prior to the killing, and Thomas's family suspect collusion to have played a key part in the circumstances of his death.

'The children were all terrified to leave the house and go into the darkness of a quiet country rampart. As they got onto the lane, they could still see the gunmen's car slowly driving away.'

The Molloy family remain deeply connected to the GAA and their beloved Clonmore club. Thomas's siblings have all served their time in the club, either as players or members of committees, and the younger generations of his family all played or continue to play Gaelic games. This remains a fact that Thomas would be proud of today. Amongst a plethora of achievements by the younger generations of the Molloy family mentioned by Eileen and Margaret is that his nephew Alan Molloy played for County Down for several years and Sean's three sons all play for Dungannon Clarkes in Tyrone, with his daughter Rachel playing for the Tyrone ladies. Thomas's godson, Raymond, captained Clonmore to their first Junior Championship title in 2005, and so the net involvement of the Molloy family from County Armagh in the GAA has widened to other counties.

Christopher Harte (Críostóir Ó hÁirt)

AOIS/AGE: 24
CUMANN/CLUB: Gort na Móna CLG/Gort na Móna GAC
CONTAE/COUNTY: Aontroim/Antrim
MARAÍODH/KILLED: 12 Feabhra, le Óglaigh na hÉireann/12 February, IRA

'Chris's life completely revolved around the club.' Anto Harte begins to describe the life of his younger brother. 'He played all three codes, he worked in the club, and his circle of friends were also his teammates. He was fully engrossed in it all.'

Christopher Harte, also known as Chris, was born on 1 May 1968 to Moira and Arthur. He was born in England, which is his mother's home country; his father had moved there in search of work. However, when Chris was just a few weeks old, the family relocated to the newly built Dermot Hill estate in West Belfast, where he grew up with his older brother Anto and younger brother Stephen. 'It was great growing up here. I was sixteen or seventeen before I ever left Dermot Hill and Chris was the same because we had everything up here to keep us happy! We had the Black Mountain out our back as our own playground and spent all day playing hurling either in the street, in the field, or on the side of the mountain. Then, of course, we went to school up here too, and that's also where the club was built. There was no reason for us to leave!'

Chris initially attended Holy Trinity Primary School before going on to Gort na Móna Secondary School, which is where the Harte brothers got their first taste for the GAA. 'We were first properly introduced to the GAA by Brother Maroney, a Galway man, in Gort na Móna school. He would take us out to games and for training, and then he and another priest from the school, Brother Eagan from Clare, formed the Gort na Móna GAA club for the local area, and we all joined. It was all just about playing back then, and in the early underage days you never knew if you were playing for the school or for the club, and it didn't really matter either as you were just happy to be out on the field. I remember when we were first going to matches, we wore jerseys donated by the Galway Senior hurling team. They were like dresses on us, dropped around our ankles, but handy if you were a sub as you could tuck your legs into them if you were cold on the sideline! We eventually got our own kit in maroon and blue to represent the counties of the two Brothers who founded the club.'

Chris played hurling, football and handball for Gort na Móna and showed incredible talent from an early age, which was unsurprising given the sporting pedigree he came from. 'Our da played GAA for Clonard and the Burns' GAA clubs in Belfast as a young man before moving to England, and he also ran cross-country. He was a very fit man and there is a story of him walking from Belfast to Ballymena, where he then competed in a cross-country race that same day! When he moved to England, he took up soccer and was scouted by a number of teams and ended up signing for Watford. And so we all inherited that sporting attitude and drive from him, and were only delighted when we finally got our opportunity to play at school and then with the club.'

In doubles handball, despite Gort na Móna being a new club, Chris won Junior and Intermediate County, Provincial and All-Ireland Championships, and in hurling, he represented his county at Minor level. Indeed, a picture of Chris running with the ball on his stick against Cork in the All-Ireland Minor Hurling Championship semi-final was featured in the *Hogan Stand* magazine.

On route to that game, Chris was part of an Antrim Minor panel that won the Ulster Championship. 'We had sticks in our hands from no age and played all codes right through from underage to Senior, and that would have been the same with most players in our club as well in terms of playing dual. There was no such thing as player burnout back then! You just showed up where you were needed and that was that. When he was hitting Minor level, Chris could have been playing five or six games at any given weekend, between the hurling and football teams at Minor, Senior Reserve and Senior levels. But we all loved it and if you didn't feel up for it, our da would be there with the necessary encouragement to make sure we were getting to our matches.'

Both Anto and Moira explain the difficulty in describing Chris's life outside of the GAA because almost all aspects of his life developed with Gort na Móna in the background. 'He was part of a tight circle of friends who all played for the club, and they were all taken under the wing of a man called Robbie McMahon. He was a teacher at Gort na Móna school and a massive organiser for the GAA club. He acted as a real mentor for Chris, and they became really close friends as Chris got older. Robbie got Chris into the youth training programme when he left school, finding him office admin work, and also got him some work in the GAA club behind the bar. So, the club was always in the background of Chris's life and defined a lot of who he was. When Chris was married, Robbie was his best man!' After getting married, Chris had one son, Michael, who was born in 1991. Chris and his wife separated shortly afterwards. 'Chris was a quiet sort of character and would have done anybody a good turn.'

Christopher Harte was abducted and killed by the IRA on 12 February 1993. He was a member of the IRA and accused of being an informant. The circumstances of his death are currently the subject of consideration by Operation Kenova, which is a major investigation into the British State's role in directing an IRA informant called Freddie Scappaticci, codenamed 'Stakeknife'.

In keeping Chris's love for the GAA alive, his family, particularly his brothers, remain committed and active members of Gort na Móna GAA club. Anto played for his club for over thirty years and has also held the position of club registrar.

Peter Gallagher (Peadar O'Gallchobhair)

AOIS/AGE: 44

CUMANN/CLUB: CLG Clann na hÉireann, An Carraigín/Clann na hÉireann GAC, Cargin

CONTAE/COUNTY: Aontroim/Antrim

MARAÍODH/KILLED: 24 Márta, le forsaí dílseach/ 24 March, loyalist forces

'My mum always laughed about the first year Cargin was crowned County Senior Football Champions in 1974. The scenes in the parish were like a carnival. Plans and savings for a new car were out the window as my dad and his close friend and neighbour, David Strathern, went out celebrating the club's achievement.' Seamus Gallagher recalls how his father, Peter, lived for his club, Cargin. 'We didn't win again until 1995. My brother Declan played that day against St John's, and a talented footballer he was. It was a great day but a sad day too. I remember we stopped off at McKeever's pub in Moneynick, a spot my dad enjoyed, on the bus journey back to Toome. I lifted the cup and said, "To Peter Gallagher", because I know if Daddy had been there, he would have been in the middle of it all.'

Peter Gallagher was born on 27 June 1948 to Willie and Sarah. He was the third of five brothers: Francie, John, Peter, Kevin and Gerry. Peter also had two half-brothers, Patsy and Tommy, and one stepsister, Pat. He grew up in the grounds of the Sacred Heart Chapel in Cargin, where his father, Willie, acted as sexton and caretaker, alongside his job as the community's postman. As a young man, Peter could turn his hand to any work offered to him. 'He done everything: labourer, plasterer, painter. He even worked on a milk lorry and in a breaker's yard. A man of all trades if you like, and also a great cook.' Outside of his work, Peter was a man never to miss the craic, becoming a regular at the dances in the 1960s, where he would eventually meet Bernadette. They were married in 1970 and soon started their family together. Peter and Bernie would bring seven children into this world: Shauna, Seamus, Declan, Patricia, Ruairí, Patrick and Cahal. Peter also had a keen sense of community and social justice, and was ever-reliable when it came to organising. Pickets, rallies, marches and more, you could depend on Peter's support – his children recall often being brought to civil rights marches in the early years of the outbreak of the conflict. Whilst his commitment to civil rights activism brought him routine harassment from the British Army and police, Peter never let those who needed him down.

Being a Toome man through and through, Cargin GAA was an integral part of Peter's life. As in the streets under placards and banners, Peter's support on the sidelines for the boys in green was absolute. 'I remember it so well. A bright and sunny Saturday in the stand of Casement Park. Me, Mammy, the three younger brothers and Daddy. We were playing St Paul's in the '91 semi-final. I have no doubt the roars and shouts of my dad in the stand was what got us through the extra time in that game. He lived for it.' The following year, 1992, Seamus was honoured at the annual club dinner as Player of the Year. 'We had the big dinner and all that, and when I got home, there standing at the door with a tear in his eye, was my dad. He was so proud of me – despite it being the only thing I ever won with football too!' That same year, Peter famously refereed a charity game at the club atop a bicycle. Once framed above the clubhouse bar, the picture of Peter with a whistle in his mouth whilst riding a bike on the pitch captures a memory now eternalised in the folklore of Cargin. 'He wasn't able for keeping up with the play, so he took a lend of a bike! A lot of years later, when Cargin opened their new pitch, I did the same in memory of him. I used the exact same bike Daddy had used as well.'

Peter Gallagher was forty-four years old when he was killed on 24 March 1993 by the UDA/UFF in collusion with RUC Special Branch. He was shot in the back as he was unlocking the gates to a work site in West Belfast, having just arrived for his shift that morning. His children were aged from just seven to nineteen. His family have waged a tireless campaign for the truth about Peter's killing, and his death was touched upon in the 2021 Police Ombudsman's report into the death of teenager Damien Walsh, as both involved the same killer. That report found evidence of collusion.

Gerry Dalrymple (Gearóid Dalrymple)

AOIS/AGE: 58

CUMANN/CLUB: Naomh Mhuire CLG, Ros Earcáin/
St Mary's GAC, Rasharkin

CONTAE/COUNTY: Aontroim/Antrim

MARAÍODH/KILLED: 25 Márta, le forsaí dílseach/
25 March, loyalist forces

'Daddy was a stalwart around the community.' Fiona begins describing her father, Gerry. 'He knew everybody, and everybody knew him. He would have done anything for anyone, and you never knew what he was doing half the time or who he was helping. It wasn't until after he died that we realised how much of an impact he had on people's lives.'

Gerry Dalrymple was born on 5 June 1935 to Bob and Mary-Ellen. He was the youngest of their three children, growing up in Rasharkin, in the glens of County Antrim, with his brother Danny and sister Bridie. Gerry attended his local St Patrick's National School before heading into the working world, where he found himself in the joinery trade. As a hard-working, affable character, Gerry found himself working throughout the townlands of Derry and Antrim, bringing with him his characteristic dry wit, his absolute reliability, and all-around good nature. He married Patricia McAleese in 1957 and the couple built a new family together. They had six kids in all, welcoming Joe, Geraldine, Seamus, Eamon, Celine and, eventually, Fiona into the world. 'There was an eight-year gap between Celine and me, so I was daddy's wee'in. Because of the age gap, we were extremely close. I went wherever he went, whether it be to the football club, bowls or any other thing he was doing; I was always there beside him. He was a private person and devoted his time to work, family and the GAA.'

As is the case for many Gaels, the involvement of the GAA in Gerry's life was inherited from his father, who was a member of St Mary's GAA club in Rasharkin. Gerry soon became a committed servant to St Mary's, playing football for his club and helping it maintain a high standard. Whilst details of his playing career have been lost, to an extent, with the passing of time,

Gerry's Minor football team took home the 1949 Antrim Minor Football Championship. Going into Senior football, Gerry laced up his boots to play in the fields across Antrim and Ulster. 'Back in those days, clubs held carnivals, and his team would have played in carnivals all around Ulster, including as far as Donegal! They were a notoriously good team. Daddy was a small man, but all the lads he played with were big, tall footballers, so he wasn't afraid of getting stuck in!' Gerry played Senior football for many years until the arrival of his first child, Joe, in 1959; he then moved into coaching, passing on his learned wisdom and passion for football to the next generations of his parish. Through those coaching years, Gerry took both Juvenile and Senior teams, before moving into the running of the club's affairs, serving as vice-chairman of St Mary's between 1964 and 1972.

Gerry also enjoyed playing bowls and was big into his dancing. 'He was known in the area as being a driving force behind organising local dances. People would come from all over, but at the start, maybe only a handful of people would come, and I'd say to him to pack it in, but he didn't, and he persevered. It got to a stage where the hall couldn't hold any more people! Those dances carried on long after he died and were always great fundraisers for the club.'

Fiona describes a Gael whose commitment to his club was unwavering, and whose values and ethos are an asset cherished in parishes across the country. 'As soon as he finished his dinner, he was down at the club doing pieces and fixing things. He was the club DIY man, and if there were bigger works to be carried out, he would organise it all and act as supervisor. He was always helping in any way he knew how. He was also a great fundraiser for the club and used to run these bazaars, which involved the spinning of this old, rickety wheel-of-fortune type of thing. It was always at Christmas, and he went out and got all the prizes that people hoped to win when they bought a raffle ticket. Mummy helped too with all the organising, and all of us kids were involved and playing for the club from we were no age! He always had his projects. I remember he got temporary Portakabin changing rooms, then converted them into a dance hall. I remember them coming down the road in three pieces and I thought, "There goes another one of Gerry's projects!" Fast-forward thirty years and that temporary, three-piece changing room is still in use today. I laugh at what his reaction would be to know that they're still in use. I didn't know Daddy until he was gone, in a sense, as I began hearing all the stories of how he helped people and the craic he loved to have on the building sites. He was a hard-working man, true to his word. He was just a quiet, unassuming, humble wee man, but he had such an impact on people's lives.'

Gerry Dalrymple was killed on 25 March 1993 by the UDA. He was killed alongside James McKenna, Noel O'Kane and James Kelly (see page 297) as they all arrived to work together in their van in the village of Castlerock, Derry. A fifth person, Gerry McEldowney, survived the attack. A 2022 Police Ombudsman's report into the killings found significant evidence of collusion between the RUC and loyalists in what have become known as the Castlerock killings.

Sean Fox (Seán Mac An tSionnaigh)

AOIS/AGE: 72

CUMANN/CLUB: Naomh Éanna CLG, Clann Ghormlaithe/ St Enda's GAC, Glengormley

CONTAE/COUNTY: Aontroim/Antrim

MARAÍODH/KILLED: 25 Deireadh Fómhair, le forsaí dílseach/25 October, loyalist forces

'Men like my father risked their lives to promote the GAA.' Diarmaid Fox begins describing the role of his father in fostering Gaelic games in North Belfast. 'He grew up steeped in Irish culture, and he committed his life to promoting our language and games.'

Sean Fox was born on 31 October 1921. Diarmaid explains that whilst the details of Sean's early life have been lost over time, his family know that his father was a merchant seaman during the First World War, who sadly died young as a result of diesel poisoning caused by a shipwreck. 'He was never prone to talking a great deal about his own childhood so that virtually nothing remains, which is a great pity.' Sean's mother eventually remarried and moved to Birmingham, England, leaving him in the care of his aunt, Annie, with whom he had already been living. His siblings went to Birmingham with their mother. 'It was common practice for the eldest son of a large family to live with either the grandparents or, as in this case, an aunt. He [Sean] maintained contact with his own family, calling in each day on his way home from St Mary's Christian Brothers School at Barrack Street, but they eventually left to settle in Birmingham while he remained with his aunt in Belfast.' What Diarmaid is certain of is that from a young age Sean was a fluent Irish speaker, and he was taught the value of living a life connected to his heritage and culture.

In later years, Sean met Anna Gervin. 'His consuming interest in the Irish language and culture led my father to the Árdscoil in Divis Street sometime during 1948 for a Céilí Mór, where he met a girl from the country who earned her living by looking after an old woman at her home on Kashmir Road. They "walked out" together, quite literally, for several months, tramping the roads from Clonard to Hannastown and back down to the Glen Road. They often stopped at the old chapel on Hannastown Hill "for a court", as my dad put it, which undoubtedly was a good deal more innocent than the modern equivalent.' Marrying on Easter Monday 1949 and honeymooning in Dublin, the couple later moved, like so many Catholic families, to the new developments in Glengormley in the north of the city with their four young children: Diarmaid, Cormac, Geri and Maolíosa.

Sean began working for T. Keenan & Sons fish firm, taking up the position of manager in their new premises in Glengormley. With the influx to Glengormley of so many Catholic families and no local club in the area, Sean, along with a few other committed Gaels, founded St Enda's GAA club in 1953. Without Sean, it has been recorded, there would be no St Enda's. He threw himself into promoting the club, ensuring that it established itself as the social hub not only for sport but for cultural activity too. Sean had a particular desire to promote the Irish language within the club, and he ran Irish classes each week for everyone in the community to take part in. Indeed, Diarmaid explains that his father ensured that the club was an open and inclusive space for all.

Over the years, Sean played many roles for his club and his commitment never wavered, even during some of its darkest periods. 'Right from the start, the formation of the club was seen as a threat by the majority of the unionist population in the area. It was constantly attacked. Bombs were left in changing rooms, it survived multiple gun attacks, and it was burnt down on many occasions. Each time, my father and other brave Gaels did what they had to do to rebuild the club and keep teams from folding.' Indeed, as is recorded by Des Fahy in his book *How the GAA Survived the Troubles*, 'The experiences of St Enda's through the early part of the 1970s reads more like a military briefing than a sporting history!'

In the face of such violence, Sean stood defiant. He remained undeterred in his mission to promote Gaelic games amongst the local people, and the club continued to go from strength to strength under his stewardship. To this day, an anecdote is still recalled in the club when Sean's name comes up, giving a great insight into the man he was. Retold in the Fahy book, the story concerns a ceremony at the clubhouse in which the tricolour was raised. As the flag was hoisted, Sean gave the nod for the national anthem to play. After a brief pause, and realising that the PA system was faulty, Sean broke the silence and sang 'Amhrán na bhFiann' himself, for all to hear. As was typical for the time, within half an hour an RUC patrol arrived demanding the flag be removed. In later years, and in recognition of all of his efforts, Sean was made honorary president of the club.

Sean Fox was seventy-two years old when UVF gunmen arrived at his door on 25 October 1993. They entered his home, just 200 yards from the St Enda's club, and proceeded to torture him before killing him. No one has ever been convicted of his killing.

In memory of one of their most cherished and committed members, St Enda's run an annual Sean Fox Memorial Day each May Day. Their pitches are filled with teams from across Belfast competing for the Sean Fox Memorial Shield, and Sean's passion for the GAA and the Irish language is celebrated. Now thriving as one of the largest clubs in Belfast, St Enda's also boasts a Bunscoil, through which local children can receive education through the medium of the Irish language, a fact of which Sean would undoubtedly be proud.

Gerard Cairns (Gearóid Ó Ciaráin)

AOIS/AGE: 22

CUMANN/CLUB: Tulach Lís/Tullylish GAC

CONTAE/COUNTY: An Dún/Down

MARAÍODH/KILLED: 28 Deireadh Fómhair, le forsaí dílseach/28 October, loyalist forces

'Gerard was very conscientious; I never had to ask him to do a job about the house twice.' Eamon and Sheila describe their eldest son. 'He was always very tidy and on top of things in all aspects of his life, including his work and training. The rest of the children came under his command. I remember one Saturday morning, we came home from doing the shopping and there was a nice silence about the place. Apart from the birds, all that could be heard was the sound of spades. We peeped around into the garden, and there was Gerard directing the rest of them. All the kids working away at the weeds, in a blissful silence. Of course, we were not for interrupting them and quietly let ourselves into the house. He had them well drilled, let me tell you.'

Gerard Cairns was born on 14 May 1971. He was the eldest sibling of Rory, Liam, Paula and Róisín, and grew up on the land the Cairns family had farmed for generations before him, just outside of Laurencetown, nestled along the border of Armagh and Down, although Eamon is clear – the Cairnses are a Down family. Gerard went to his local primary school in Laurencetown, where, under the guidance of Master McBreen, he saw early footballing success, winning the seven-a-side Primary School League. A young Gerard saw that same success out of school, when, in 1983, his u12 Tullylish football team won the County A Championship. Lining out in the back line, Gerard played his part on the only team in the history of his club to win a club championship. His teammates recall him as a hard, steady player, who no one liked to mark because of his fitness, which would come as no surprise to his friends and family, as Gerard's passion was running. 'He loved running. He and Paula joined St Peter's running club in Lurgan and would cycle there for training back and forth. Many's a memory we have of the two of them running and training along the road and ourselves following in the car keeping them honest! Come rain, hail or snow, the pair of them were out running. We went to competitions all over Ireland and there was no beating them.' Indeed, Róisín remembers that Gerard was well accustomed to training with his brothers and sisters, spending every weekend rolling around the family garden chasing balls and dodging hurls. 'It would be eldest and youngest versus the lads in the middle. I would stand at the net and Gerard would run the pitch and pass it to me right at the line to pop in the easy score, driving Rory and Liam mad. But they knew they couldn't do anything to exact revenge while Gerard was around! It was great craic.'

Those weekends not spent playing were spent watching. Eamon recalled, 'We were in Croke Park up to ten times in the year watching the championships. I remember one particular summer in '83 heading down for the football final: Dublin and Galway. The Twelve Apostles game with John Gough as referee. We always went straight for the Hill, only this time we'd no tickets. A crowd had gathered and before we knew it we were swept up in the action, busting down the gate and spilling into the terraces. Gerard and Rory had disappeared into the crowd and were nowhere to be seen. With the sway of the crowd, the younger and smaller spectators were passed overhead from the front of the Hill to the back and, sure enough, I spotted the pair of them being lifted by the crowd. It just happened that Gerard was being passed in my direction and as he passed over the top of me, I shouted to him where to meet me after the game. And a great game it was for Dublin.'

When Gerard left school, he went on to train at the technical college in Lisburn, where he struggled daily with sectarian abuse from those in his classes. 'He would never let on to us how bad things got for him, but it was evident he was struggling. And to make matters worse, his teacher in the college didn't want to teach. On the day of his results, Gerard failed everything. I went to the college to speak with the teacher, and after my persistence in asking for answers, the teacher admitted that Gerard was unlike his classmates. That all the rest of those boys' fathers worked in the shipyards, in the Aero industry or in the police, and that they all had jobs to walk into, so he was never used to having to teach because results didn't matter. It was unbelievable, but it also wasn't.

Gerard then struggled for work for a short while, going between engineering works until landing a job as a lorry driver for a local company. He was as good a worker anyone could hope for, always willing to work outside of hours for free just to hold down his job. Even if it did drive me mad!'

Sectarianism was a reality of life for Gerard's family, and indeed a dangerous one, where even cycling to training carried its risks. 'I had to start following Gerard and Paula into Lurgan in the car because of the sectarian abuse they got on the bikes. There was this one fella who would drive alongside them on his motorbike and push them off their bikes. But our spirit never faltered, and Gerard wasn't to be deterred by the bigotry, rarely missing a training!'

Gerard Cairns was killed alongside his brother Rory (see next entry) in the living room of their home on the evening of 28 October 1993 by the UVF. They had just finished celebrating Róisín's eleventh birthday, when gunmen came through the back door and shot Gerard and Rory in front of her. The memory of Gerard and Rory is celebrated at Tullylish GAC in the naming of a Juvenile tournament contested annually between local clubs in their honour.

Rory Cairns (Ruaidhrí Ó Ciaráin)

AOIS/AGE: 18

CUMANN/CLUB: Seán Ó Treasaigh, An Lorgain/
Seán Treacy GAC, Lurgan

CONTAE/COUNTY: Ard Mhaca/Armagh

MARAÍODH/KILLED: 28 Deireadh Fómhair, le forsaí dílseach/28 October, loyalist forces

'Rory was a character.' Eamon and Sheila remember their son Rory. 'He was the opposite of his brother Gerard. Laid-back and always the first to take up an opportunity to lay across the couch. He was the life and soul of the party and always in the thick of the craic.'

Rory Cairns was born on 7 March 1975. Younger sibling to Gerard, and older brother to Liam, Paula and Róisín, Rory grew up just outside of Laurencetown, along the border of Armagh and Down. He went to his local primary school in Laurencetown and Róisín explains that from as early as he could hold a hurl, Rory was playing for Seán Treacy's in Lurgan. 'Hurling was in our family, with Dad and his brothers having a bit of experience back in their day, and there was, therefore, a huge passion for Gaelic sports growing up. Dad had us all involved in some form of sport from an early age and his weekends would be spent bringing us all to our training sessions.' Young Rory showed promise on the field, lining out in goals for the u14 county panel. Indeed, just a few years later he would be on the periphery of his club Senior panel. 'Rory was almost sixteen. He had a good year at the hurling and in no time at all he got the call-up to the Senior panel. However, another local hurling team in Lurgan had folded around the same time, which meant that as Rory was supposed to be making his debut, all these older lads suddenly became available from the other club, forcing Rory out. Suffice to say he did not take that news well! As he grew up though, it was a great pleasure to watch Rory at his hurling. He had a real natural swing.'

Off the pitch, Sheila recalls that Rory was a constant source of entertainment. 'He was always first to joke and have a laugh, even from a young age. I remember when he was only five or six years old, bringing him to his first running competition. The field was waterlogged, and he had only a pair of wellies to wear that must have been at least a few sizes too big on him. He entered the race anyway and with us cheering him on, he finally made the finish line. He came dead last. When we got home, everyone was asking him how he got on and he delightfully told all he came third; of course, he wasn't lying because there were only two other kids in his race! But that didn't need mentioning as far as he was concerned.'

As Rory matured, his parents saw him transition into a man. 'Unlike Gerard', Eamon explains, 'I had a terrible time keeping on top of Rory, making sure he was lifting his weight. Every Saturday, everyone had their job. I had Rory mostly picking and washing spuds or chopping wood, and I was hardly off his back because when he was left alone, nothing would get done. But, slowly, there was a change in him. He used to chop wood for the week, and every time he finished, he'd have to be sent out for some more as he would chop just the bare minimum for the week. Then one time he came in with plenty and we could hardly believe it. Then the next week, he didn't even have to be asked; there he was out the back, working away. It was a real moment, and I knew then he had become a man. He understood why he was doing it and understood his responsibility. Something just clicked in him. Although he never lost his love for the living-room couch and TV!'

Rory Cairns was killed alongside his brother Gerard (see page 250) in the living room of their home on the evening of 28 October 1993 by the UVF. Rory's legacy on the pitch is celebrated each year in the form of the award for the most improved hurler at his local primary school, as well as in the naming of a Juvenile tournament at Tullylish GAC in honour of both Gerard and Rory Cairns.

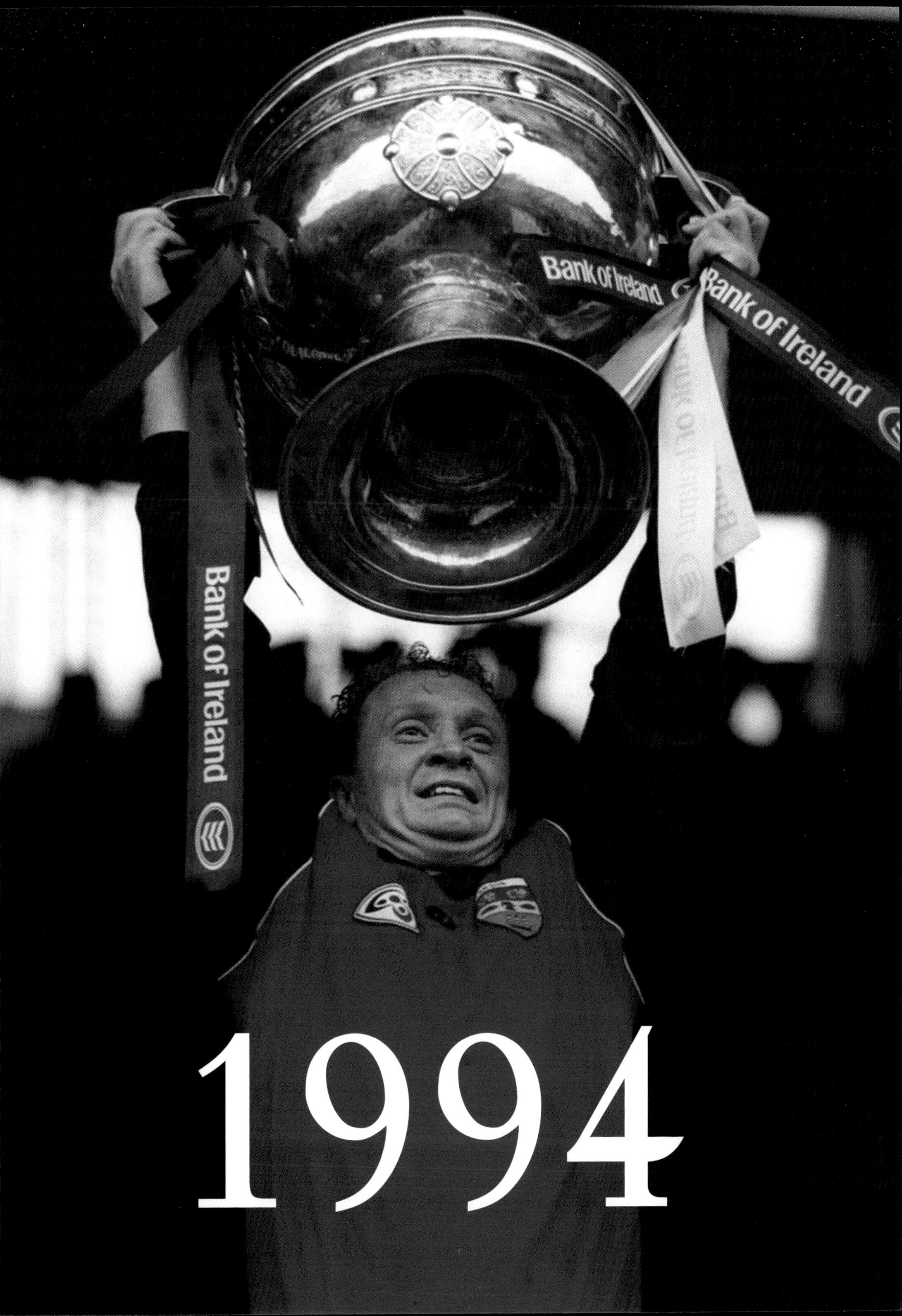

1994

Gavin McShane (Gaibhin Mac Seain)

AOIS/AGE: 17
CUMANN/CLUB: Lámh Dhearg, An Céide/
Lámh Dhearg, Keady
CONTAE/COUNTY: Ard Mhacha/Armagh
MARAÍODH/KILLED: 18 Bealtaine, le forsaí dílseach/
18 May, loyalist forces

'It's hard to remember any particular stand-out performance of Gavin's on the pitch, but only because every time he took to the field, he was the stand-out player.' Alana and Caíonn describe their older brother Gavin's ability as a hurler. 'He was small, but strong as an ox because of all the training he did. No doubt his karate training, for which he usually asked one of us to toughen up his stomach, made him unmovable on the pitch. You knew when he lined out, the bigger fellas would look at this small centre half-back and think they'd walk all over him, only for the first ball to come in and the big lad would be lying on the ground confused and Gavin would have the ball halfway up the field.' Gavin played both hurling and football, but hurling was his first love.

Gavin McShane was the eldest of the three children of Matt and Maria McShane. Gavin, Caíonn and Alana would grow up in Keady, Armagh, with hurls in their hands. This wasn't surprising given that their mother, Maria, was one of the Duffy sisters: a formidable trio of sisters with a fierce and enviable reputation for winning in Ulster camogie circles for both club and county. Also influential in Gavin's hurling career was his PE teacher Paddy Connolly at St Mary's Boys School in the town, who ensured that Gavin and Caíonn, and the rest of the school, became very familiar with the sight and sound of hurls hitting sliotars. Caíonn remembers playing with Gavin, representing club and county together right through the years; Caíonn lining out at full-back, right behind his older brother. Between them, Caíonn recalls proudly, he and his brother represented Armagh in multiple underage All-Ireland finals. 'He always told me I was the better hurler and was always so proud and happy that me and him played on the same team together. Whether or not he believed I was the better hurler is another thing, but he always told me it, I suppose to give me confidence on the pitch. I remember my age group reaching the All-Ireland Féile final, the first team from Armagh to do so, and Gavin couldn't have been prouder. He had tried so hard to get his team over the line, but they couldn't break through the semis, so he was so proud of me and my team that we got through.'

Gavin almost didn't see this world. His mother, Maria, was pregnant with him when she fell victim to a bomb attack on the Step Inn Bar in 1976, which killed Elizabeth McDonald and Gerard McGleenan. Despite only being nineteen at the time, and being blinded in one eye, Maria would display the ultimate symbol of defiance in creating a family full of life and culture, with the GAA at the centre of it all. They always supported one another and Alana remembers travelling the country to spectate from the sidelines in every county. 'We were the family that went everywhere. No matter where it was, we were there shouting on the sidelines. I remember Gavin's last full match, no one was allowed in for the crowds, so the manager told the officials that Mummy was his wife and we managed to get ourselves in to watch. We were sitting in the dugout with the whole team!' Gavin's ability on the pitch was unquestionable and he managed to make his Senior debut the night before he was killed. 'He got a run-out towards the end of the game, which he must've been so happy about as he'd spent months training with the Senior squad. I always think what he would have become on the pitch if he had been allowed to live.'

Gavin McShane was killed alongside his friend Shane McArdle as they played an arcade game in a taxi depot in Armagh city before making their way to school. A member of the mid-Ulster UVF stepped inside the depot and shot them at point-blank range, as well as shooting and injuring the depot's dispatch operator.

Adrian Rogan (Adrian Ó Ruadhagáin)

AOIS/AGE: 34

CUMANN/CLUB: Loch an Oileán CLG/Loughinisland GAC

CONTAE/COUNTY: An Dún/Down

MARAÍODH/KILLED: 18 Meitheamh, le forsaí dílseach/
18 June, loyalist forces

'Loughinisland was in his blood and the club was his passion.' Adrian Rogan's wife, Clare, and daughter, Emma, begin to describe his obsession with the GAA. 'He followed the football everywhere, whether it was the club or the county. It didn't matter if it was in the next parish or down in Cork, we were there!'

Adrian Rogan was born on 29 April 1960 to Mick and May Rogan. He was the youngest of three, growing up in the village of Loughinisland, County Down, with his older sisters Doreen and Sheelagh. He attended Loughinisland Primary School and then went on to St Colmcille's Secondary School in Crossgar. The earliest memories of Adrian's involvement with the GAA are of him as a child walking down to his local club, Loughinisland GAC, with his father, who was involved in helping construct the then new clubhouse and playing field. In later years, Adrian often recalled his fond memories of following his father around the site, lending a hand wherever he could. As for his playing days, details are hard to recall, but he would have begun with Juvenile football. Clare recalls Adrian's father, Mick, saying people often commented on Adrian's ability to play with either foot, and there is little doubting the passion he had for the game.

With his playing days coming to a natural end as he got older, it is Adrian's life as a committed supporter that his family most fondly remembers. 'In later years, when his father wasn't fit to drive, he would have taken him all over the country to games. I don't think they ever missed a match, either for Down or Loughinisland.' Inevitably, when Clare started to go out with Adrian, she too became a dedicated supporter. 'I remember being sat in the pub with him on a Saturday night and him saying we're off to Donegal the next morning. People thought we were mad, heading up to Donegal in the middle of winter for a McKenna Cup game! But the car was always packed, picnic ready, and away we would go on the Sunday. Of course, the '89 Club Championship was a massive occasion, when the club won the County Championship and we got into Ulster. We would travel with the team every game, and he loved the big days out to Monaghan and Cavan.'

As Emma explains, when she and her brother, Tony, came along, the trips to the games were a defining aspect of their childhood. 'Some of my earliest memories are being at the football match. Squeezed into a car and off to this ground or that, and it never mattered where the game was in the country, you could guarantee the car was heading off that Sunday morning. We've been going to Croke Park from we were toddlers.'

As Clare and Emma describe Adrian's passion for football, they struggle to describe the remarkable sense of belonging they felt when they were amongst the crowds of supporters, and when the Down Senior football teams of the 1990s came to the fore, those feelings were only heightened for Adrian and his family. 'When Down came into their good days in the '90s, that meant even more games for us! Hats, scarves, headbands and plenty of Guinness after the game, which, of course, delegated me [Clare] to drive home! It is still hard to describe the atmosphere when we won Sam in '91. I remember the team coming into the village with the trophy. The crowds were everywhere. An indescribable day for our parish, and Adrian was in the middle of it all.'

For Adrian, football brought triumph, heartbreak and all the ups and downs associated with competitive sports. Sitting with family and friends in the pub each weekend, he would perform his own version of *The Sunday Game*, mulling over the action of the week and looking forward to the games to come. 'When you were in the pub in a small, rural village like Loughinisland, people only ever talked about the three Fs: football, farming and funerals. When you got home after a match, it was straight to the pub and every detail of the game was recounted and tactics debated,' Clare laughs. 'And players could be heroes one week and villains the next. I remember the first round of the '94 Championship between Derry and Down. McCabe from Castlewellan was brought on, and Adrian was shouting that he was the wrong sub to bring on. McCabe scored a goal in his first play, and immediately it was all tracked back, and the praise suddenly came. You'd swear McCabe was the best to ever don a Down jersey with the talk of Adrian after that game!'

Whilst the memories of following Down in the early 1990s are overwhelmingly joyful for Adrian's family, Clare also describes memories which kept them ever mindful of the realities of what being a Gael in the North during conflict meant. 'It wasn't easy being a GAA supporter back then. Checkpoints and deliberate road closures on matchdays would put you onto detours that added hours to your journey. You always had to be careful where you stopped off for fuel or a bite to eat, and you were always aware of where you could wear your Down jersey. It's crazy to think now, but back then you wouldn't dream of wearing a GAA jersey in a lot of areas because the reality was that it could get you killed.' In its own right, Adrian's commitment to the support of both his club and county is worthy of recognition, but that recognition must be heightened when considering the aforementioned context under which his support was so passionately given, as it must for all committed Gaels who endured the conflict. In the words of his family, 'football was his life', and so, despite the background, there was still a game to be played and players to be cheered on.

It is nearly an impossible task to describe Adrian's life away from the football, as is evident when Clare describes the details of his life outside of the GAA. 'We met at the football club. I had known of him because he started to work for my brother as a manager of his car-dismantling business. It was All-Ireland final night, and I was with my sister and father, and he [Adrian] happened to be there. And I suppose that's where it all began! He had been previously working for a local steel engineering company before coming to my brother but then stayed at my brother's business until he died. He never missed a day of work in his life and was the backbone of the place. He worked very hard, and it was all to provide for us.' Clare and Adrian married in 1984, and in the same year, they welcomed their son, Tony, who was soon followed by their daughter, Emma, in 1985. 'He was a happy-go-lucky sort of person and a family man through and through. His kids wanted for nothing.' After getting married, Adrian went about building a new home for his young family and began settling into his new life. 'We would travel around Ireland on our holidays and, of course, it would all be scheduled around the footballing calendar! One thing about those trips I can always remember was that before heading off, the car was scrubbed spotless. He loved his cars, and he always had a nice, clean one. I remember his red Audi 80; the wheels were slicked every Sunday! He had a great circle of friends and loved going for a Guinness and having the craic. One thing I'll always remember was how happy he was when my brother's business sponsored the Loughinisland team, and the place he worked had their logo on the jersey.' As Clare and Emma continue, it becomes clear that Adrian's life was fulfilled so long as he had his family and his football, and for all of his life the two were synonymous.

Adrian Rogan was thirty-four years old when he was shot dead on 18 June 1994 by the UVF. Adrian was in The Heights Bar in Loughinisland when he was killed alongside Malcolm Jenkinson, Barney Green, Daniel McCreanor, Patrick O'Hare and Eamon Byrne. Five other patrons were wounded. Adrian was in the bar to pick up tickets for Down's Championship game against Monaghan the following day. Now known as the Loughinisland Massacre, the killing of Adrian and those in The Heights Bar that night caused global shock. The circumstances leading up to the massacre, and the subsequent investigative failings, have led to numerous inquiries and documentaries, with the case being considered as one of the most glaring examples of collusion between loyalist gangs and Crown forces from the entire conflict.

In the aftermath of the massacre, it was the GAA to which Adrian's family turned. 'After the massacre, the GAA became even more important to us as a real sense of identity. It's difficult to explain but we could cling to it in a sense, and say this is ours, this is us; it was a real sense of belonging and solace. All those local rivalries are set aside, and we come together as a big family.' In memory of those killed at The Heights Bar, an annual u12s tournament is held at Loughinisland GAA club, in which teams from all over Ulster come together to compete and celebrate all that is great about the association. As a means of raising funds to support each of the bereaved families of the massacre in the wake of the killings, a charity match was organised between the Down Senior panel and a select team of the local parish clubs of Loughinisland, Drumaness and Teconnaught. The 1994 Down team also signed a jersey and donated it to Adrian's family. It still hangs in the bar.

Adrian's family are still very much involved with Loughinisland GAC and are ardent supporters of the club.

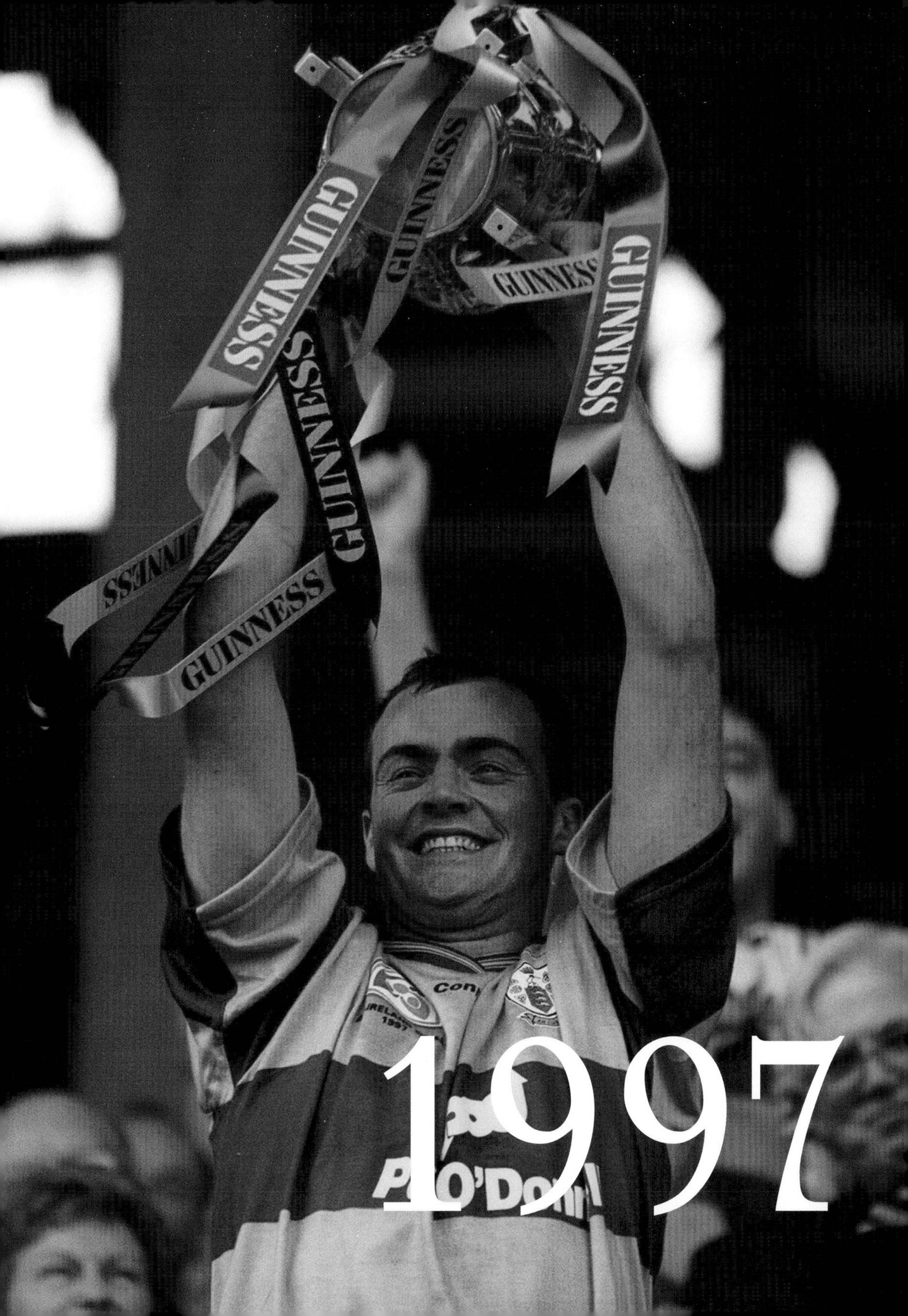

1997

Sean Brown (Seán dé Brún)

AOIS/AGE: 61

CUMANN/CLUB: CLG Bhuilf Tóin, Baile Eachaidh/
Wolfe Tones GAC, Bellaghy

CONTAE/COUNTY: Doire/Derry

MARAÍODH/KILLED: 12 Bealtaine, le forsaí dílseach/
12 May, loyalist forces

'I often think back on it now and wonder how on earth he had the time to do it all,' Clare remembers, in slight awe, with hindsight, of all the roles her father played in his family and community. 'He was chairperson of the club, the patriarchal figure of the extended Brown family on whose advice we all relied, the go-to man for anyone in Bellaghy needing anything fixed, as well as being a full-time teacher! How he did it all, gladly and with a smile I might add, we will never know.'

Sean Brown was born on 20 April 1936 to Jim and Esther. He was the eldest of four boys and grew up in the townland of Ballyscullion, just outside Bellaghy, County Derry, with brothers Seamus, Joe and Chris. 'All of the boys played for Bellaghy Wolfe Tones. There was very little choice in that matter as Granda Jim was a founder member of the club and all of Daddy's uncles would have played in the early days of the club. The Browns are steeped in the history of Bellaghy football in that way and Daddy was no exception. Growing up through the teams, Daddy would have played alongside his brothers, but he would have had no big career with regard to football as he suffered from bad knees.' While his brothers excelled on the pitch for both club and county, Clare, with Sean's grandson Damán, described how Sean's ultimate contribution to Bellaghy Wolfe Tones would come off the pitch. 'He would have been a massive organiser. His initial involvement in the running of the club came when he was appointed assistant treasurer at a young enough age. He then became treasurer himself and held that position in the club for fifteen to twenty years, where he then ultimately became chairperson, right up until the end.'

During his years of service to Bellaghy, Sean pioneered a restructuring of the club. His leadership centred on the foundational use of a committee structure, which enabled the club to draw from the expertise that existed within its wide membership and expanded the pool of decision-makers to the club's benefit. Suddenly, the club could appoint the appropriate people to the tasks in which they had expertise. 'This took Bellaghy from stagnation to great success in its operations. The club was massively in debt and he [Sean] pulled them out of it.' Inevitably, Sean's stewardship translated into positive results on the pitch, where Bellaghy Wolfe Tones saw major county and provincial football success, and indeed reached the All-Ireland football final in 1995. 'Daddy was delighted with all the club's success, of course, but he would have been very conscious of not wanting to be seen as promoting himself. When he was named chairperson, he was so chuffed, but wouldn't have been about pushing his name forward or anything like that. He was very happy to quietly work away in the background while the club took off again.' Over the years, Sean took on whatever task the club asked of him, whether that was organising and fundraising to rebuild the clubhouse after loyalist attackers burnt it down, or washing jerseys and putting flags on the pitch.

To describe Sean's life away from the club would be somewhat oxymoronic because in many respects, as with all committed Gaels, the club was omnipresent throughout all aspects of Sean's life. Clare explains, 'He met my mummy, Bridie, in the early '60s and it wasn't long before Mummy became a central figure at the club alongside him. Mummy was from the neighbouring parish of Lavey and came from a family of Gaels, herself playing camogie and my granda and uncle being big hurlers, so she immediately understood Daddy's devotion to the club and was only too happy to be part of that.' Bridie worked in the local school as a cook when she and Sean were married in 1966. It wasn't long before their first child, James, came along, followed by Siobhan, Damian, Sean, Martin and Clare. Family life for the Browns centred on the GAA and the club. 'Flags would be sewn in our house, kits washed for the club and people would call to buy jerseys. Indeed, the flags Mummy sewed are still in use! And my parents absolutely loved it. They never once complained about it being a burden or anything like that.'

Damán remembers his time with his grandparents. 'I remember the house being the centre of all that was happening with the club, and inevitably, time spent with Granda Brown usually meant time spent at the club. We grandkids would follow him about the club grounds as he did whatever tasks needed doing. A wee line of us following him as he was putting out the flags or lining the pitch.'

'He was great with kids and knew all the young ones about the town. There was a young girl, about six or seven years old, who lived beside us on the street, and she and Daddy would have a small conversation every morning before he left for work. He just loved that,' Clare remembers fondly. Damán adds, 'If anyone was running about the streets acting up, Granda Brown would have been the one to get a hold of them and bring them down to the club. He'd convince them to take all their energy out on the pitch. He gave young people a lot of time and so they all really held him in high regard.' Sean's ability to speak to youth stood well to him in his career as a mechanical engineering teacher at local training colleges. He had initially worked at making aeroplane seats before turning his attention to teaching his engineering skills to young people. 'He was one of those people who could turn his hand to anything. I remember people calling to our house with broken equipment like lawnmowers and such, and he'd fix it for them with no issue. Our outhouse was packed with all his homemade, specialist tools, which were long before their time.' How Sean spent his time, both at work and socially, was illustrative of his nature. 'He really loved to help people and was such a genuinely good person who always tried to see the best in everyone. Daddy was such a gentleman.'

Sean Brown was killed on 12 May 1997 by the LVF. He was abducted as he was locking up the gates to the Bellaghy Wolfe Tones clubhouse following a meeting that night. Sean jnr had left just minutes before his father, who was setting the alarm when loyalists attacked him and took him away in his own car. His body was found ten miles away beside his burnt-out car. He had been shot and his body was burned.

In the absence of any effective investigation from the police, Sean's son and Damán's father, Damian, took on the responsibility of seeking the truth about what happened to his father. 'The work he put in to the case, and all the energy he spent fighting for truth and justice, was monumental. We wouldn't know half of what we know today without him. I can't imagine how tough it would have been for him over those years, having to go into meetings and what he would have heard about his own father's death. And he did it all anyway. He did exactly what Granda would have done in the same situation. He completely took over everything and made sure everybody was taken care of, while also pursuing the case.'

Clare describes her older brother in the wake of their father's death. 'He became a father to me when Daddy died. Everyone always assumed he was the eldest brother because he was just that type of character, but he was actually a middle child. He and Daddy were absolutely cut from the same cloth in that they were two people who had very sensible heads on them!' Damian Brown died in October 2021, in his early fifties, after a short illness. He was known across Ireland for his tireless campaigning to uncover the truth about what happened to his father. As a lifelong Bellaghy Gael, it is only right that Damian is included in his father's entry to this book.

Gerard 'Gerry' Devlin (Gearóid Uí Dhoibhlin)

AOIS/AGE: 36

CUMANN/CLUB: Naomh Éanna CLG, Clann Ghormlaithe/ St Enda's GAC, Glengormley

CONTAE/COUNTY: Aontroim/Antrim

MARAÍODH/KILLED: 5 Nollaig, le forsaí dílseach/ 5 December, loyalist forces

'Gerry used to tell all his team, as a player and then as a coach, "Be Big!" It was his mantra; words to live by both on and off the pitch. It means stand up and be counted, be strong and proud, and make life hard for the opposition.' Kevin Devlin

begins to describe his brother, teammate and closest friend. 'Gerry typified what it means to be a Gael, driven by a clear sense of duty to his club, which was instilled into him by our father.'

James Gerard Devlin, known to everyone as Gerry, was born on 8 August 1961 to Seamus and Margaret. He was the third of their seven children, growing up with brothers Michael, Kevin, Liam and Eamon, and sisters Angela and Oonagh. The family lived initially in Glanworth Drive in North Belfast before moving in 1971 to Glengormley, County Antrim. Kevin explains how sport was omnipresent in the Devlin household and how the family's move to Glengormley would be the beginning of their family's generational and successful service to St Enda's GAC. 'Sport has always been in our family. Our paternal grandfather was a soccer star, playing for various Irish League teams when it was an All-Ireland competition, back before the partitioning of Irish soccer. In fact, he won the Irish Cup in the 1920s with Alton United, beating Shelbourne 1–0 at Dalymount Park in the final! So, we were always aware of that sporting ability and success in the family, and it was certainly a positive influence on Gerry and the rest of us. And while we enjoyed playing soccer, it was a true love for Gaelic football that developed in us lads. As kids, long before moving to Glengormley and joining St Enda's, our father would have regularly taken us to Casement Park to watch different club and county games, and I particularly remember following the famous Antrim u21 footballers of 1969. From Castleblaney to Cork and then, finally, to Croke, our dad took us to each round of that championship campaign, which ended in Antrim lifting the Clarke Cup. Like the rest of us, Gerry's first days getting to play football came when he joined the Christian Brothers at Park Lodge Primary School. His school team were very successful, winning the Raffo Cup twice and the Rice Cup. That success continued when he went on to St Mary's CBS on the Glen Road in West Belfast, with his first-year team winning the league and the Ulster College's Dalton Cup! So, when the move to Glengormley came in '71, joining the ranks of St Enda's was inevitable for us all.

'It was my dad who brought us to the club. There were five boys and two girls in the family, and we would all go over with our dad to the pitch and kick a ball about. At that stage, the club had one Juvenile team and one Senior team, and the clubhouse was just an old *sibín*. As young kids of eight or nine years of age, we would have played with kids of twelve or thirteen, which is a big difference at that age, but all that mattered to us was enjoying the game and getting out onto the field. With Gerry and I only being a year apart, we would have been on the same teams as we went through the age groups, and our dad took all of our teams from u10 right through.' Success seemed to follow Gerry from a young age. In 1973 his team won the u13 South Antrim League, taking home the first underage silverware for St Enda's, which was soon followed by winning the u14 League in 1975 and the Butler Cup in 1976. His ability on the field of play did not go unnoticed and in the following year, 1977, Gerry made his Senior debut aged 16. This period also saw Gerry placed onto the Antrim Minor and u21 football panels, and what became clear to the coaches at St Enda's was that they were sitting on a goldmine of young talent ready to bring the club to new levels, of which Gerry was an integral part.

'When I joined Gerry on the Senior panel, we were in Division 3. Gerard played in the forward line, and I played in the middle of the park. We ended 1984 as Division 3 champions, Gerry being one of the leaders in that team. We then moved up into Division 2 and immediately began chasing Division 1 status, with Gerard leading the charge. Our chance came in 1988 when we reached the playoff final against O'Donnell's, and we took it!' For the first time in the club's history, St Enda's had earned their place in Division 1 Senior Football, with the Devlins playing an integral role. The following season, however, would see Gerard's playing career cut short through injury. Teammates remark on his fearless style of play and how his intense desire to win the ball made him an excellent battler for the high ball and the 50:50, but how it also left him vulnerable. Having suffered an severe injury to the ligaments in his knee and come out the other side during his Senior career, a second knock in the 1989 season proved insurmountable and put an end to Gerard's playing days. 'To Gerard, whilst it was devastating news to a certain extent, a new chapter was just beginning. We had watched our father dedicate his time to coaching and taking teams, and for Gerard, this was now his time to start learning the ropes of management. Our father had instilled in us a view that it was your duty to your club to give what you can because if you didn't step up to look after it, nobody would, and so Gerard then viewed management as the natural next step.'

Coming into the management team, Gerard was immediately given the reins for his newly promoted side and the shock of Division 1 football took some adjusting to. Over the next two seasons, St Enda's bounced between both divisions, before Gerard's management finally saw them cemented as a solid Division 1 team in 1993, during which time he also served as vice-chairman of the club. 'He was meticulous in his planning and record keeping as a manager. We still have numerous A4 diaries containing every date of every training session, including attendance sheets and listed reasons for non-attendance by players. Old players can come and see when and where they went on their holidays! On each Monday in the books, *The Irish News* cut-out is pasted in, detailing the results of the previous week, and on the Tuesday, *The Irish News* cut-out with that week's upcoming fixtures. These books cover every year of his management. He was extremely professional and would fit in so well with today's game and he certainly helped evolve the thinking and mentality around the club about how things are run.'

In 1995 Gerard believed his team would benefit from a fresh perspective and so the club brought in Frank Dawson to take charge for the season, with Gerard as his assistant. That championship campaign saw St Enda's reach the semi-final, but narrowly lose out to eventual winners St Paul's. That was the furthest the club has ever been in the Antrim Senior Football Championship, and Gerard was set to take back full control the following season in the hope of going a step further.

Off the pitch, having finished his O Levels at St Mary's CBS, Gerard joined Rotary International and through the years worked his way up to senior management within the Belfast office, becoming one of their international shipping managers. 'He was quiet enough in his own way. We were best of mates growing up as well as best of brothers, being only eighteen months between us. But the difference between us would have been how he organised himself. Gerry was a bit of a Dapper Dan, with his boots always washed, cleaned and polished and even with his book-keeping, where I was a bit more rough and ready! He then met Hazel when he was in his late teens and the pair became very happy and settled, with them marrying in '81. Gavin then came along, soon followed by Aidan, and with him having two boys and me having two boys, we ended up going on eleven or twelve holidays together as families! He became a real family man and was very comfortable between his family, job and the club.'

Gerard Devlin was killed on 5 December 1997 at the gates of St Enda's clubhouse by the UDA. He was arriving at the club to collect his brother Kevin when the gunmen killed him. The Devlin family and legal counsel have compelling evidence of collusive behaviour between the State and loyalist paramilitaries surrounding Gerard's death. No one has been prosecuted for Gerard's killing.

Gerard's legacy has become foundational to the ethos, identity and spirit of the modern-day St Enda's club. In 2018 the club reached the All-Ireland Intermediate Football Final, becoming County and Provincial champions along the way. Through their incredible footballing campaign, one phrase was repeated again and again, 'Be Big, St Enda's!' In his honour, the Senior Footballer of the Year Award is named after Gerard, and in 2012 Mícheál Ó Muircheartaigh officially opened the new Páirc Ghearóid Uí Doibhlin. In 2006 the Gerry Devlin Tournament was held to commemorate the fiftieth anniversary of the formation of the club, and it hosted Omagh St Enda's, featuring multiple All-Ireland winners; Ulster Club Champions St Gall's; Derry Champions Bellaghy Wolfe Tones; and St Enda's, Belfast. Each year, on Gerard's birthday, St Enda's also organises an annual golf tournament, which continues to be fully subscribed. 'Our Gerry was terrible in the Tee-box and could never get the ball away, so his friends at Rotary bought him a 1-iron and nicknamed it "The Silver Hurl", so now a rule of the annual golf tournament is that everyone must use the 1-iron to tee off on the first hole. If you manage to stay on the fairway, you win the Silver Hurl prize!'

1998

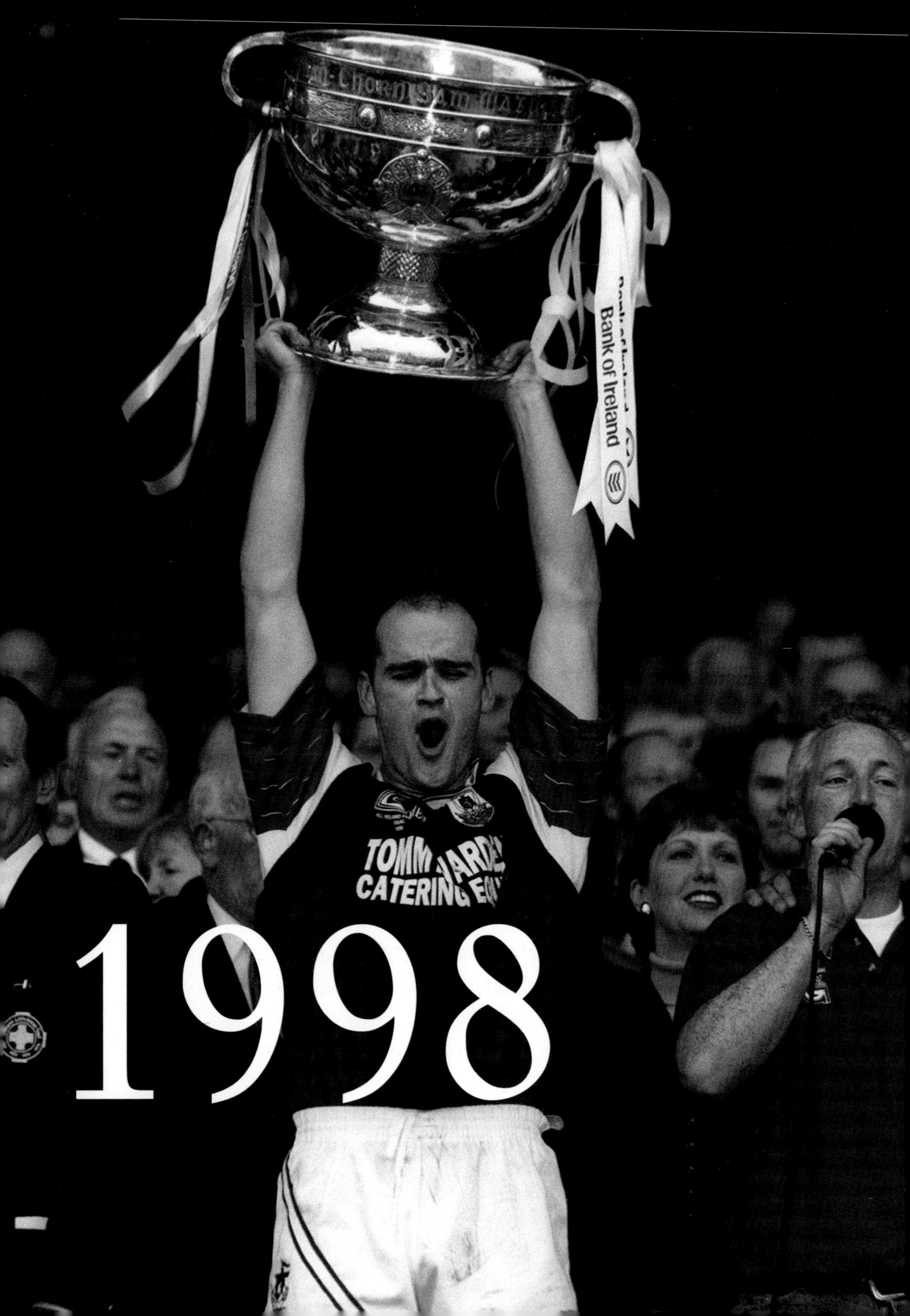

Terry Óg Enright (Tarlach Óg Mac Ionnrachtaigh)

AOIS/AGE: 28
CUMANN/CLUB: Gort na Móna CLG/Gort na Móna GAC
CONTAE/COUNTY: Aontroim/Antrim
MARAÍODH/KILLED: 11 Eanáir, le forsaí dílseach/
11 January, loyalist forces

'Terry was an athlete.' Niall and Feargal Enright describe their older brother. 'He was the type of guy who could pick up a tennis racket and play Wimbledon. He was good at everything. He could ice skate, he was an Irish dancer, he was a very talented boxer, a smashing Gaelic footballer, a great soccer player, he hiked mountains for fun … the list goes on. Physical stuff was his thing, and he had a natural competitiveness, toughness and robustness that made him stand out at it all.'

Terry Óg was born on 11 June 1969 to Terry snr and Mary Enright. He was the couple's first child, and he grew up in Dermott Hill, West Belfast, in the foothills of Black Mountain, with his younger brothers Liam, Niall and Feargal. Terry was the first of the boys to attended St Aidan's Primary School and, as Niall and Feargal explain, that is where they got their first hands-on experience with the GAA. 'The Christian Brothers ran the school, and they would have been very conscious of promoting Gaelic sport. There was a good family connection to the GAA in so far as our uncles were prominent club players in Belfast, but our dad's background was in soccer, so it was really at the school where we got our first introduction. That was the start of what became a lifelong obsession with the GAA for Terry.'

Terry then went on to Gort na Móna Secondary School, which was the natural progression for the Enright boys given its closeness to their home. Indeed, Terry and Liam would walk home together each day for their lunch. Whilst at secondary school, Terry was able to join the new Gort na Móna GAA club, which was established in 1974 by the Christian Brothers in response to the growing number of families moving into the local area. 'My earliest memory of the club is me at five or six years old and Terry taking me up, and it was just this sense of anarchy! There didn't seem to be anybody in charge, with kids running everywhere, kicking footballs and smacking hurls, and even some kids on the roof of the building! I was this shy and timid kid, so what got me through was letting everyone know that Terry was my older brother. Even from that young age, he had a rare respect from people. You see, back then, growing up, the big debates were always: Who's the best fighter? Who's the fastest runner? Who's the best footballer? That's how you measured yourself, and the answer was usually Terry!'

It is unsurprising, therefore, that Terry became a stalwart of the Gort na Móna club, maturing quickly into a reliable and talented hurler and footballer. In 1989, as a young player breaking through to the Senior team, Terry made an important contribution to Gort na Móna's first significant hurling success as the club won their first Intermediate Hurling Championship and the Division 2 league title. The following year, Terry helped his club bring home the 1990 All-County Junior Football Championship. 'When he was playing, Terry would always try to identify the other team's best player, and he'd make it his mission to mark him out of the game. He was always regarded as a very talented player but also a very tough player, so you always wanted him on your team as he'd protect the nippy, smaller players!'

Come 1994 Terry suffered a bad injury to his ankle, requiring surgery, and was told the devastating news that he would never play again. For most, having already brought their club to new heights, the decision to hang up the boots following a serious injury would be a reluctant but necessary one. For Terry, this was another challenge to be overcome. He put himself through recovery and was back playing Senior football the following season, a season in which Gort na Móna found themselves in a Berringer Cup final. 'The final was a derby game against McDermott's, our local rivals, and Terry wasn't starting. There was a perception in the club at that stage that he wasn't committed because his work meant he usually missed training sessions. Half-time came and we were three points down. Terry finally comes on, puts in a major shift, and we end the match as winners. Terry got Man of the Match! We celebrated the win in the club that night, and when the bar closed at 3 a.m., we got a carry-out and went out onto the pitch. A fire was lit, and we continued through to the morning. It was just one of those incredible nights that will live long in the memory of the club.' He also gave a man-of-the-match performance in the 1996 Intermediate hurling championships success, where his robust tackling swung the momentum of a famous club victory.

As a young man off the pitch, Terry's first job was as a glass collector in the GAA club, as was his brother Liam's. 'At that time in Belfast, given the nature of the conflict, local GAA clubs were the social hubs of communities, and provided steady employment for a lot of people. Terry and Liam both worked their way up and began working behind the bar, then Terry eventually became the head doorman when he was twenty-one, which would have been unheard of at his age. Terry struggled in his late teens and early twenties to find his path and figure out what he wanted to do with himself. Then he found youth work.' Niall and Feargal go on to describe the transformation in their brother's life when he found his calling. 'He began a youth training programme for taking outdoor pursuits. He took to it straight away. Terry completed his apprenticeship and started working for Challenge Youth, and he found himself. He very quickly earned a reputation as a youth worker in Belfast, working across the city in all communities. He brought kids who were struggling in their own lives out to the mountains to be amongst nature. He brought them kayaking and exploring and helped them to connect with life and to find their paths in life. He really connected with the kids and youth, probably because he himself was a bit lost at stages in his life. He had a really warm personality and was a very affectionate person. The type of guy that instantly makes an impression on you, with his big smile. Just naturally very good with people and very personable, and that made him a very good youth worker.'

Terry settled instantly into life once he found his calling. He married Deirdre in 1991; they had known one another since childhood. The couple welcomed their first daughter, Ciara, into the world the following year, followed by Aoife in 1996. Their new family moved into a house in Dermot Hill and a new phase of Terry's life began to take shape. Deirdre happened to be a talented camog, and Terry helped coach the Senior camogie team just after it was formed in the early 1990s – a historic development in the club for women's equality.

In 1997 an opportunity arose for Terry, as Niall and Feargal explain. 'He moved to begin working for the Upper Springfield Development Trust, which at the time was the most important community project in West Belfast. Our dad would have played a big part in getting the Trust up and running, and they had just secured a massive amount of funding to help tackle youth unemployment and anti-social behaviour. In the later '90s, West Belfast struggled with problems associated with the exclusion of young people from wider society, and it needed thoughtful solutions. Terry successfully made a bid to develop an outdoor pursuits programme of his own. His whole philosophy was that youth work was the answer to the problems of so-called "hoods". He would say, "When I get them up the Mournes and we're in the middle of nature and building relationships, I can change anybody. I can have them in the palm of my hand. Rather than shooting young people and having them excluded, we need to foster them and show them they have an equal part to play in our community." And so, he began developing his own programme, to work in his own community.'

Terry Óg Enright was killed on 11 January 1998 by the LVF. He was working as a bouncer at a nightclub in Belfast city centre when two gunmen killed him. Whilst his youth work was full-time, Terry was getting some work done to his home and the extra money offered by the odd bouncing shift was very welcome. Despite his having no affiliations with any political organisation, the LVF released a statement claiming Terry's death was in retaliation for the killing of their leader, Billy Wright.

'Terry's murder came on the back of him doing loads of work across different areas of Belfast, and also on the back of our parents doing a lot of work connecting loyalist and republican communities. Terry embodied the new change of that era, and his death was a reaction by those wanting to hold us all back. Instead, in the wake of his death, the spirit of *mól an óige agus tiocfaidh sí* [praise the young and they will flourish] took hold. It had a galvanising effect on the community and on a range of organisations, which each began to look at how they can reach out and help young people. His whole philosophy began to dictate the direction of community work. Over 10,000 people attended his funeral, which was all managed by the club. Gort na Móna named their pitch after him; the Terry Enright Foundation was created by youth workers from across Belfast. His legacy began to have an impact far beyond that which he had before his death because he was only a kid. But his passion, ideas and spirit motivated people. And still do to this day.

'The problem for us as his brothers was that he was just another person. As much as Terry became a symbol for aspiring change, strip it all back and we lost a brother. He was a very loving, very caring and very funny brother. All the normality and ordinariness can sometimes get lost after his death, and it's important we remember back to Terry, our brother; although he was super-hero tough!'

Unquestionably, the Enright family and Gort na Móna have become somewhat synonymous. A mural of Terry adorns the club's changing facilities and there are always Sunday games being played at Páirc Mhic Ionnrachtaigh. His three brothers all became fully invested in Terry's beloved club: Liam became the Senior football manager, with Niall and Feargal playing. 'The club were incredible to us as a family following Terry's death, and we needed to give back. It became far more than sport for us. The club became our second family.'

Fergal McCusker (Fearghal Mac Uisnéir)

AOIS/AGE: 28

CUMANN/CLUB: CLG Watty Graham, Machaire Ratha/ Watty Graham's GAC, Maghera

CONTAE/COUNTY: Doire/Derry

MARAÍODH/KILLED: 18 Eanáir, le forsaí dílseach/ 18 January, loyalist forces

'Fergal was a people person.' Fergal 'Rick' McCusker's family begin describing the type of character he was. 'He got on with everybody and always had people laughing. One sure thing about him was that everyone enjoyed being in Fergal's company.'

Fergal McCusker was born on 3 December 1969 to Jim and Christine. He was the third child of nine and grew up in the town of Maghera, County Derry, with brothers James, Patrick, Michael, Eamon, Christopher and Finbar, and sisters Mary and Róisín. As Finbar explains, the GAA played an immediate role in Fergal's life, as it did for all his siblings. 'We were all involved in the club at different stages of our lives. Although our parents weren't involved in the GAA, growing up in this community, with our neighbours, made it impossible to not want to join and play. Everyone on our estate played for the club.' Fergal was first introduced to the GAA at his local primary school, Glenview, and his family explain that the natural progression for Fergal upon leaving primary school was to join their local Watty Graham's GAC, where he could continue playing football with his friends. 'Those early days growing up were very, very happy days. We all had a great childhood, and Gaelic football was always going on somewhere in the background. Mummy would have struggled to get us in the door because noon to night we were out playing football and running around!'

As he progressed through the age groups at the club, Fergal found himself in an exceptionally talented age group, which was replicated in clubs across Derry, and as a consequence, competition for a place on the first team, when he reached Senior level, was tight. 'Fergal was a very handy footballer but struggled to get into the Senior squad, which had a good few intercounty players. He was more than happy to play up front in the forward line for the Senior Reserves, however. He was always in the middle of the craic with the team, and when a few of the lads he grew up playing with were on the road with the Derry team, Fergal was always first on the supporters' bus behind them.' As Fergal's family describe his love for football and the GAA family, they struggle to describe just how special it was for everyone in the town when Derry was playing in the early 1990s. 'It was the heyday. When Derry won Sam in '93, the team bus came back to Maghera. People would still talk about the bars being open all night long. There was such a crowd in the town that you could hardly get walking from one end to the other. And, of course, Fergal was in the middle of it all.'

Outside of football, other sports formed a large part of Fergal's life. 'He was massively into his sport. Fergal played soccer for the Maghera Strollers, and wasn't a bad soccer player at that, and he also enjoyed playing pool and darts in the local pub leagues.' A lasting memory of Fergal often comes to Christine's mind when she thinks of her son. 'I remember walking home from Mass, up the hill to the house, and I heard the sound of football boots running up the road, and I didn't even have to look. I knew it was Fergal. I turned around and there he was running up to me. He had the whole rig on him: socks, shorts and the top. He loved his sport.'

In terms of work, Fergal left St Patrick's Secondary School in Maghera at sixteen to join a local youth training programme, where he began labouring. 'He did a bit of everything and was happy to have work. He was a very hard worker and certainly would have been a good worker to have on a site, not least because he was always great craic.' As a young man, Fergal began to enjoy socialising and proved himself great company and popular among the local people. 'Fergal was full of life and fun. He was always up for a laugh, playing tricks and telling jokes, and lived to keep people going. He enjoyed the odd beer and if there was no craic in the bar, he would have the craic going inside five minutes.' Christine recalls that Fergal was very similar to her brother, Pat, who, when calling to the house, might have told the odd joke, which Fergal would always remember for when he was next in the bar with his friends. Around the age of twenty-seven, Fergal decided to give life a try in the US and went out to Boston to live and work with his brother Patrick. Experiencing a different culture and giving a different way of life a go, his family explain that Fergal loved life across the water. 'He loved America. He even got to play football while he was out there for the Aidan McAnespie Club. Patrick is still part of the club out there, and he got Fergal involved. He played in nets for them whilst in the States.'

Fergal McCusker was twenty-eight years old when he was shot dead in Maghera by the LVF on 18 January 1998. He had been back in Ireland from Boston for just over two weeks, and was making his way home after a night out with his friends when he was abducted and shot. He was in the middle of planning a more permanent move to the US. No one has ever been convicted of Fergal's killing. A fresh inquest into the circumstances of his death began in early 2023 and has yet to conclude.

In memory of Fergal, and as a tribute to his love for football, an annual underage tournament is held at his beloved Watty Graham's club in which the Aidan McAnespie Shield and Rick McCusker Cup are both competed for by clubs from across Ulster and beyond. An annual memorial game was also established in the early 2000s and is still ongoing, in which a select team of Glen players field against a Derry select panel. Other events have also been held at the club in memory of Fergal, and what is most obvious is that his love for football will always be remembered by his club.

Larry Brennan (Labhrás Ó Braonáin)

AOIS/AGE: **51**

CUMANN/CLUB: **Naomh Maoileachlainn CLG, Béal Feirste/ St Malachy's GAC, Belfast**

CONTAE/COUNTY: **Aontroim/Antrim**

MARAÍODH/KILLED: **19 Eanáir, le forsaí dílseach/ 18 January, loyalist forces**

'He lived for the GAA. Lived and breathed St Malachy's. It gave him life.' Patsy Brennan remembers how important the GAA was to his brother, Larry. 'When he walked out onto the pitch, he really came alive. His name in St Malachy's is still mentioned and he's still very well thought of in the club. He might have played county football if not for a reputation, however undeserved, for his temper!'

Larry Brennan was born on 13 May 1946. He grew up in the Market area of Belfast's inner city with his younger brother, Patsy, a fact which remained a great source of pride throughout Larry's life. 'In the early days of our youth, Sundays were spent on the waste ground. The big thing back then was getting your hands on a Wembley Ball, which cost six shillings and eleven pence. Between the twenty of us, we could scrape enough money to get the ball, and the day would be spent chasing after it. We were decent players too, Larry especially!' Larry attended St Congall's Primary School, as did Patsy, and left aged fourteen to find work, initially in window cleaning and then as a foreman as the years progressed; he eventually ended up as a taxi driver in the later stages of his life. 'He enjoyed a cigar, and often on a Sunday, having had dinner at my house, would leave his Renault 21 here and walk into town to have a drink. I would pick him up and have his cigars waiting on him. You got six of his cigars for a tenner back then. He was an easy-going sort of character, and everyone knew him because he was always so helpful and so kind.' Larry would eventually become a father to Patrick and Claire, kids whom he idolised and of whom, according to Patsy, he would be so proud.

In terms of the GAA, Larry joined St Malachy's GAA club at u16/Minor level. 'Larry played both football and hurling. He loved his hurling but wasn't very good at it! He'd come in for his dinner and out came the two teeth he had knocked out while playing. I remember we were playing up at Sarsfields, and the young lad he was marking was making a so-and-so out of Larry. Hand-passing the ball over his head and running around the back of him, and all that carry on. He had done it twice, and on the third time, Larry left the fist out and his man run into it. Everyone on the pitch started slagging, "Oh, big

Larry lost the head and hit the wee lad." Next thing, Larry chased the man on the sideline who shouted it up the hill! He could lose the head handy all right. On another occasion at the hurling, Larry was doing linesman and a guy hit him on the head with the hurl, so Larry lamped him back with the flagpole! He had us all buckled with laughing as he chased the player across four fields with the flag. He could be a big idiot at times, but an idiot you didn't want to fall out with.'

As Patsy describes his brother, it becomes clear that beyond the stories of an undoubtedly tough and hard man, lies a talented and committed Gael, who proved an invaluable asset to his club. 'Larry was twenty-seven when St Malachy's started to go strong. In 1974 we reached the final of the South Antrim Championship and faced Éire Óg. With a few minutes to go and two points down, we won a free out on the 50. Larry dropped it into the square and the ball was knocked into the back of the onion. The whistle blows for full-time. The last kick of the game and we win.' Indeed, so invaluable to his club was Larry, that Patsy found himself serving the ban that was supposed to be issued to Larry. 'I used to turn up to matches and be told I wasn't playing. When I asked why, I was told that the club gave my name instead of Larry's when a scuffle broke out during a previous game. It happened more times than enough, but the club knew they needed Larry to keep playing. Larry had three lifetime suspensions over the years, all eventually lifted. He was mustard!' As well as playing both codes for his club, Larry also helped with the running of social events and the bar by doing the door, always making sure people were able to enjoy themselves safely. 'When he was on the door, people knew they were safe because when Larry asked someone to leave, they left.'

Alongside the GAA, Larry also played soccer for Immaculata Football Club and tried his hand at boxing, which Patsy confesses Larry had a particular talent for. 'Even though he was right-handed, Henry Cooper's left hook had nothing on Larry's. But whilst my bigger focus was soccer, Larry's first love was the GAA. It took priority over all else.'

Larry Brennan was shot dead by a UFF gunman as he got into his taxi on the Ormeau Road on 19 January 1998. His son, Patrick, witnessed his father's killing. Larry's family believe the circumstances surrounding Larry's killing and the failures of the subsequent investigation into his killing raise significant suspicion as to the level of protection afforded to Larry's killer by the State.

'As my big brother, I worshipped the ground he walked on. I loved him so much it's unbelievable.'

Brenda Logue (Bréannainn Ó Maol Mhaodhóg)

AOIS/AGE: 17

CUMANN/CLUB: Naomh Treasa CLG, Loch Mhic Ruairí/ St Teresa's GAC, Loughmacrory

CONTAE/COUNTY: Tír Eoghain/Tyrone

MARAÍODH/KILLED: 15 Lúnasa, le easaontóirí poblachtacha/15 August, republican dissidents

'Larger than life; that was Brenda.' Brenda Logue's family describe the young girl they know and loved. 'She was a genuinely gifted footballer; she could absolutely play ball. At her funeral, a common remark was that she was that good a footballer she could have played for the men. She only played club football for three years and in that time she breezed onto the Tyrone Minor panel and was called up to the Senior county squad, although she never got the chance to play for the Seniors.'

Brenda Logue was born to Mary on 27 April 1981. Growing up with her older brothers, Cathal and Sean, and younger brother, Karl, in Loughmacrory, County Tyrone, Brenda's evenings and weekends were spent on the field playing football. 'She would have played with the boys and easily held her own. People always commented that she had no fear of the ball coming at her when she played in a game and that would have come from growing up being stuck in nets and having her three brothers rifle shots at her all day. She was also very ahead of her time as a player, with a bravery rarely seen then for a goalkeeper;

she was confident in coming outfield and running the ball up the pitch or helping a defender in trouble.' However, as a young girl, Brenda was unable to properly showcase her talents for her local club, St Teresa's, due to the lack of structures in the women's game. Instead, she had to spend a lot of her time on the sidelines, demoted to watching men play the sport she loved. Despite her age, Brenda was determined to change this and to play, since she knew she was just as good if not better than the boys she grew up playing with. She became a serious driving force in persuading her club to establish a women's football team.

'Around our town, football is like a religion; where people would sooner miss Mass than miss a game. Brenda was very much a part of that and was committed to making sure the young girls growing up in the town could be too. She tortured the men in the club until they agreed to put a ladies team together. Everywhere they turned Brenda was there, "When are you going to do it? When will we have a team?" She was a natural leader.' For her efforts, Brenda is rightly held in high regard in GAA circles. Not only was she a source of inspiration for younger girls, but she was also a pioneer for the club as the first woman to make the county set-up, clearly indifferent to the fact that she was only seventeen and that St Teresa's had only been running women's football for three years. In recognition of her contributions to her club and the women's game, the Division 3 Tyrone Senior Ladies Championship is named after Brenda, as is a tightly contended annual tournament between select Ladies teams from all over Ulster.

Brenda Logue's legacy, however, extends beyond the GAA. Of her own volition, she found herself helping those in need in her community. 'She would go every Sunday after Mass up to old Frank's house, a partially blind man who Brenda took to looking after, to light a fire, just because she wanted to help him. Another time she took to doing the washing for a family up the road whose children had taken meningitis and who almost everyone was afraid to go near except for Brenda. She was also the first to volunteer at the youth club and to take summer schemes in the community. She was well beyond her years.' To all who knew her, Brenda was a steadfast source of comfort, humour and care. Her mum, Mary, recalls how she took care of her while she struggled with physical pain. 'She would have made sure I never had to lift a thing. Always making sure her brothers lifted their weight too, and she never failed to make me laugh. She came up the stairs one day, sat on my bedroom floor and put her feet on the bed. She said, "I have to tell you something, Mummy, I've broken my pledge." I said, "What on earth are you talking about?" Brenda looked at me all serious, "I drunk two hooch. But it's alright! I went up to Father McVeigh's house and renewed my pledge. I sat on the wall outside swinging my feet for two hours trying to pluck the courage to go in and tell him. He told me I made his day when I eventually did." That was Brenda; mad as a box of frogs but the rare type of person that if you fell out with her, she would go out the front door and come straight in the back door. She only lived for seventeen years, but it seemed like she was already here a lifetime; it was like she lived seven lifetimes in one lifetime if that makes sense? Everyone knew her. Truly a once-in-a-generation type of character.'

Brenda Logue was killed on 15 August 1998 in the Omagh bombing, planted by the Real IRA. She was with her mum and grandmother when the explosion killed her, along with twenty-eight others. She was waiting for her GCSE results. No one has ever been convicted for what is the single biggest loss of life of any event during the conflict.

2002

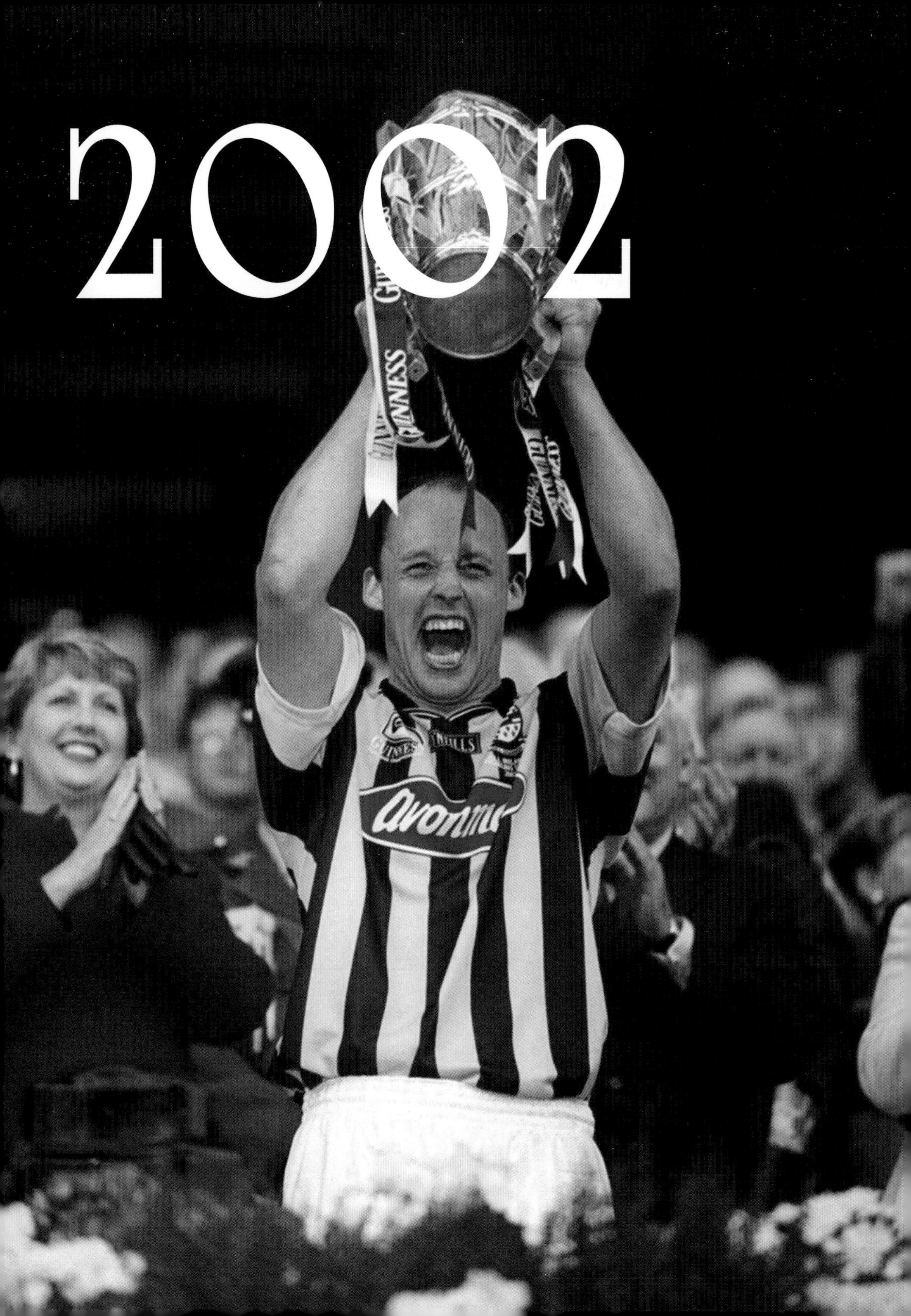

Gerard Lawlor (Gearóid Ó Leathlobhair)

AOIS/AGE: 19

CUMANN/CLUB: Naomh Éanna CLG, Clann Ghormlaithe/ St Enda's GAC, Glengormley

CONTAE/COUNTY: Aontroim/Antrim

MARAÍODH/KILLED: 22 Iúil, le forsaí dílseach/ 22 July, loyalist forces

'Every Sunday after dinner, I used to take the lads to the park with a ball. On this particular day, they said, "Right Da, let's see how high you can jump for this one!" I could see they were whispering with each other, and I knew something was up.' John laughs when recalling his cherished memories of playing football with his sons. 'So anyway, our Conor kicked the ball as high as he could, and when I went up, they all converged on me! I ended up in a heap on the ground and they were all laughing, having come away with the ball. They absolutely nailed me, their own da! Hand up to God, that was the last I kicked a ball with them; the lads were getting big.'

Gerard Lawlor was born on 1 September 1982 to John and Sharon. He was their second child, joining his older brother John jnr to form Irish twins. 'He was a very good baby,' explains Sharon. 'He and John were very close growing up and always had one another; if you saw one, you saw the other. They didn't need outsiders in that sense, even though they always had great friends growing up.' Gerard was from North Belfast in County Antrim, initially growing up in the Rathcoole estate and then in Glengormley, with the move coming once Gerard's younger brother Conor was born. He attended St MacNissi's Primary School, before going on to the Christian Brothers Secondary School in Glengormley. 'He was your typical teenager, always up to harmless mischief and chasing around. There was one day our neighbour called to the door, an elderly woman, and she asked, "John, why are my flowerpots in your garden and all of your flowerpots in mine?" So, we kind of had our suspicions as to who the culprits were, but we waited to see, and sure enough one night we heard the rummaging and looked out to see Gerard and his mates rearranging the flowerpots! He saw us coming and shouted, "Run! My ma's coming." For weeks he was tortured by his mates, with the slagging being that Lawlor's ma would get you.' Laughing, Sharon adds, 'And Lawlor's ma *would* get you!'

Behind all of that harmless fun, John and Sharon explain, was an incredibly kind and selfless young man. 'Our Gerard helped everybody. His friends all knew they could rely on him, and he was always letting them stay at our house if they needed out of their own house for a night or two. Over the years, Gerard's friends would stay with us for sometimes weeks at a time, and it was clear Gerard was always making sure to take care of the people in his life. We only had a three-bed house and it was packed most nights. They were all great kids who were just going through different rough patches, as young lads do, or sometimes they just preferred to be in our house! I can still remember the roaring and laughing of them, with Gerard's signature hearty, warm laugh heard above them all.' When Sharon's mother found herself housebound due to physical illness, sixteen-year-old Gerard didn't hesitate in spending a few nights every week with his grandmother to take care of her, nor did he think twice about acting to help his elderly neighbour from her house during severe flooding.

It is unsurprising, therefore, that Gerard's sense of duty to his friends and family also translated into an impressive work ethic, even if it did develop slightly too early. 'School wasn't really for Gerard. I remember when he was young, I would ask him about his homework and he'd always say it was done. That was the first suspicion. Then each day he'd be out the door and say he's away to see Nanny, who lived down the street, and that was the second. He was only fourteen at this stage, so I followed him one time just to make sure he wasn't getting into trouble, and there he was dressed in a white shirt with a black dickie-bow! Turned out he was working at the local restaurant. Then came a conversation with one of his teachers, who was concerned about Gerard's coursework for his GCSEs. The teacher said they hadn't seen him in over four weeks! He'd been working every day instead of going to school! We sat him down and said he needed to knock all of that on the head, but he said to us, "Look. School's not for me. I need to be hands-on. Let me get out there and work and be active." And sure enough, once he got his GCSEs, he was straight into hard, honest work. And never once had we to ask him for keep; religiously, every Friday, he'd put a few pounds up on top of the hearth and he never asked us for a penny.'

As a young lad Gerard worked at Corr's Corner Hotel and held any number of jobs thereafter, including milk delivery. When his girlfriend, Siobhán, fell pregnant, Gerard's reliable sense of duty shone through once again. 'He stepped up and did what needed to be done. He got himself a great job at the animal feed factory down at the Docks and he worked incredibly hard. Gerard turned eighteen in September and Josh was born in December. He made sure he had everything in place for Josh being born. They loved him everywhere he worked. In fact, Corr's Corner still have his coat hook and nameplate up in the staff area. They told us they just haven't been able to bring themselves to take it down, and the same with the factory down at the Docks. His overalls were left on the hook for almost ten years after he died.'

As for the GAA, Gerard's first involvement came when he joined the Christian Brothers School. 'The boys were very into their soccer, and we as parents had no GAA background, but once they joined the secondary school, all of a sudden everything was about Gaelic football and hurling and then of course St Enda's came into his life. It started when Gerard and a few others would go up to the club and hang about because there wasn't much else to be at for them. Then he gradually would spend more and more time up there, and it sort of evolved into him becoming a full member rather than him ever consciously deciding to join, if that makes sense. The house then was coming down with football boots and hurls and this and that, and I think a big turning point for Gerard and the young lads in the area was when Gerry Devlin (see page 267) was murdered. Gerry would have been the one at the club encouraging Gerard and his friends to join the club and would have helped them with coaching over the years. Once he was killed, Gerard got a real sense of duty to play for St Enda's and he was very proud to say he was a St Enda's man. He went up through the age groups, but when Josh was born the football and hurling went on the back boiler as he was getting things in order. When he eventually went back, he gave it 110 per cent. I think once he realised that he was making inroads onto the Senior panel, that's when he really knuckled down with it. He came in one night after training and said, "My diet isn't good enough and you need to be making me pasta and chicken for all the carbs and protein." I said, listen, there's seven of us in this house and you'll eat whatever's put in front of you!

But he put his head down and committed to it and you could see, physically, the change in him. He wasn't all that tall, but his strength, and the size of his legs! In fact, in the last match he played, he put one over the bar from the 45 and he was told, "You're a Senior footballer now." Strong as an ox he was.'

Just after midnight on 22 July 2002, nineteen-year-old Gerard Lawlor was returning home down the Floral Road in Glengormley, having left the Bellevue Arms on the Antrim Road. A motor scooter with two men on it pulled up and Gerard was shot three times. He was killed where he stood. The killing was claimed first by the Red Hand Defenders, and later by the UDA/UFF. It was a Sunday, and he was due to play a match against Gort na Móna that afternoon, but it was cancelled last-minute, so he and his teammates went for a few pints. In the two hours before Gerard's death, loyalists had carried out four other attempted killings in North Belfast. A community-led expert inquiry into Gerard's killing concluded that collusion between loyalists and the PSNI was a major factor in his death.

'Our last conversation with Gerard was on that Sunday. We were just out of Mass in Newcastle and having a coffee on the water's edge when the phone went. It was Gerard asking, "Mummy, how do I cook a chicken in the oven?" Of course, he was making his chicken and pasta! So, I talked him through it and he asked about using the microwave. I told him to make sure he scrubbed everything as we were due to move house that next week. When we got home, the microwave was scrubbed within an inch of its life, God love him. The next after that was the knock on the door.'

On the twentieth anniversary of his death, St Enda's opened a Garden of Remembrance in Gerard's honour. In a day marked with music, tightly competed games between local clubs and the launching of an updated report into his killing, St Enda's have ensured Gerard's legacy will remain strong in the identity of his beloved club. 'The club have always supported us as a family and have been incredible in keeping his memory alive. It means so much to us to know Gerard is never forgotten.' Planted in the Garden of Remembrance is an oak tree which Gerard himself had begun raising and caring for in his own garden at home.

additional lost gaels

Listed here are the other Gaels we know of lost to the conflict, whose full stories we were not able to include in this book.

Martin Lee (18)
CLG Naomh Trea, Baile Mhich Uiginn
Doire/Derry
18 Nollaig 1971, le pléasc anabaí/18 December 1971, premature explosion

Phelim Grant (32)
CLG Clann na hÉireann, An Carraigín
Aontroim/Antrim
5 Feabhra 1972, le pléasc anabaí/5 February 1972, premature explosion

Charles McCann (28)
CLG Ciceam Ard Eoin
Aontroim/Antrim
5 Feabhra 1972, le pléasc anabaí/5 February 1972, premature explosion

Joseph Cunningham (26)
CLG Naomh Maoileachlainn
Aontroim/Antrim
10 Feabhra 1972, le RUC/
10 February 1972, RUC

Frank Corr (52)
CLG Ciceam Ard Eoin
Aontroim/Antrim
26 Iúil 1972, le forsaí dílseach/
26 July 1972, loyalist forces

Hugh Henry Heron (38)
CLG Naomh Pádraig, Windmill
Tír Eoghain/Tyrone
16 Deireadh Fómhair 1972, Arm na Breataine/16 October 1972, British Army

Joseph McAuley (47)
CLG Naomh Mhuire, Ros Earcáin
Aontroim/Antrim
1 Nollaig 1972, le forsaí dílseach/
1 December 1972, loyalist forces

Patrick Stanley (16)
CLG An Clarach
Uíbh Fháilí/Offaly
28 Nollaig 1972, le forsaí dílseach/28 December 1972, loyalist forces

Edward O'Rawe (27)
CLG Mícheál Ó Duibhir,
Béal Feirste
Aontroim/Antrim
12 Aibreán 1973, Arm na
Breataine/12 April 1973,
British Army

Patrick Carty (28)
CLG Thomáis Uí Chléirigh,
Dún Geanainn
Tír Eoghain/Tyrone
25 Meitheamh 1973, le
pléasc anabaí/25 June 1973,
premature explosion

Seamus Harvey (22)
CLG Naomh Dabhóg, Achadh
Uí Araín
Tír Eoghain/Tyrone
10 Lúnasa 1973, le pléasc anabaí/10
August 1973, premature explosion

Michael McVerry (23)
CLG Naomh Pádraig,
Coilleach Eannach
Ard Mhacha/Armagh
15 Samhain 1973, Arm na
Breataine/15 November 1973,
British Army

Desmond Morgan (19)
CLG Eoghan Rua, Breac an Bhile
Tír Eoghain/Tyrone
26 Samhain 1973, le RUC/
26 November 1973, RUC

Patrick McDonald (21)
CLG Thomáis Uí Chléirigh,
Dún Geanainn
Tír Eoghain/Tyrone
15 Márta 1974, le pléasc anabaí/15
March 1974, premature explosion

Eugene Martin (18)
CLG Roibeard Eiméid,
Cluain Mhór
Ard Mhacha/Armagh
11 Bealtaine 1974, le pléasc
anabaí/11 May 1974,
premature explosion

Colm McCartney (22)
Club unknown
Doire/Derry
24 Lúnasa 1975, le forsaí
dílseach/24 August 1975,
loyalist forces

Sean Campbell (20)
CLG Naomh Pádraig, Dromainn Tí
Ard Mhacha/Armagh
6 Nollaig 1975, le pléasc
anabaí/6 December 1975,
premature explosion

James Lochrie (19)
CLG Naomh Pádraig, Dromainn Tí
Ard Mhacha/Armagh
6 Nollaig 1975, le pléasc anabaí/6 December 1975, premature explosion

Michael Donnelly (14)
CLG An Airgid, Béal Átha
Ard Mhacha/Armagh
19 Nollaig 1975, le forsaí dílseach/19 December 1975, loyalist forces

Ted McQuaid (25)
CLG Ciceam Ard Eoin
Aontroim/Antrim
10 Eanáir 1976, le forsaí dílseach/10 January 1976, loyalist forces

Frank Stagg (34)
Hollymount–Carramore GFC
Maigh Eo/Mayo
12 Feabhra 1976, ar stailc ocrais/12 February 1976, hunger strike

Robert McCullough (41)
O'Neill's GFC, An Port Mór
Ard Mhacha/Armagh
15 Bealtaine 1976, le forsaí dílseach/15 May 1976, loyalist forces

Sean O'Hagan (22)
Club unknown
Ard Mhacha/Armagh
15 Bealtaine 1976, le forsaí dílseach/15 May 1976, loyalist forces

Daniel McGrogan (27)
Naomh Eoin, Béal Feirste
Aontroim/Antrim
29 Iúil 1976, le forsaí dílseach/29 July 1976, loyalist forces

Gerard McGleenan (22)
CLG Lámh Dhearg, An Céide
Ard Mhacha/Armagh
16 Lúnasa 1976, le forsaí dílseach/16 August 1976, loyalist forces

Philomena Greene (16)
Naomh Peadar GAC, An Lorgain
Ard Mhacha/Armagh
28 Samhain 1976, le Óglaigh na hÉireann/28 November 1976, IRA

Paul Duffy (20)
Uí Dhonnabhain Ross, Ard Bó
Tír Eoghain/Tyrone
26 Feabhra 1978, Arm na Breataine/26 February 1978, British Army

John Boyle (16)
CLG Cúchullain, Dun Láthaí
Aontroim/Antrim
11 Iúil 1978, Arm na Breataine/
11 July 1978, British Army

Martin McGuigan (16)
CLG An Ghrainseach Mhór
Ard Mhacha/Armagh
24 Feabhra 1979, le Óglaigh na hÉireann/24 February 1979, IRA

Michael Cassidy (31)
CLG Naomh Colmcille, An Charraig Mhór
Tír Eoghain/Tyrone
16 Aibreán 1979, le Óglaigh na hÉireann/16 April 1979, IRA

William Carson (32)
CLG Pádraig Sáirséil
Aontroim/Antrim
24 Aibreán 1979, le forsaí dílseach/24 April 1979, loyalist forces

Henry Byrne (29)
CLG Coillte Mach
Maigh Eo/Mayo
7 Iúil 1980, le INLA/
7 July 1980, INLA

John Francis Morley (38)
CLG Coillte Mach/CLG Ballach an Doirín
Maigh Eo/Mayo
7 Iúil 1980, le INLA/
7 July 1980, INLA

Raymond McCreesh (24)
CLG Naomh Pádraig, Carraig an Chropáin
Ard Mhacha/Armagh
21 Bealtaine 1981, ar stailc ocrais/21 May 1981, hunger strike

Joe McDonnell (29)
CLG Naomh Treasa, Béal Feirste
Aontroim/Antrim
8 Iúil 1981, ar stailc ocrais/
8 July 1981, hunger strike

Liam Canning (19)
Naomh Éanna, Béal Feirste
Aontroim/Antrim
9 Lúnasa 1981, Arm na Breataine/
9 August 1981, British Army

Peadar Fagan (20)
Clann Éireann GAC, An Lorgain
Ard Mhacha/Armagh
17 Samhain 1981, le forsaí dílseach/17 November 1981, loyalist forces

Michael Tighe (17)
CLG de Bhuilbh Tóin, Doire Mhic Cais
Ard Mhacha/Armagh
24 Samhain 1982, le RUC/
24 November 1982, RUC

Seamus Grew (31)
CLG Naomh Colmcille, An Ghráinseach
Ard Mhacha/Armagh
12 Nollaig 1982, le RUC/
12 December 1982, RUC

Sean McShane (39)
Glenn John Martins GFC
An Dún/Down
10 Deireadh Fómhair 1983, le Óglaigh na hÉireann/10 October 1983, IRA

Gary Sheehan (23)
CLG Eiméid, Carraig Mhachaire Rois
Muineacháin/Monaghan
16 Nollaig 1983, le Óglaigh na hÉireann/16 December 1983, IRA

Daniel McIntyre (28)
Naomh Peadar GAC, An Lorgain
Ard Mhacha/Armagh
27 Eanáir 1984, le forsaí dílseach/
27 January 1984, loyalist forces

Brian Stack (48)
CLG Portlaoise
Laoise/Laois
29 Meán Fómhair 1984, le Óglaigh na hÉireann/29 September 1984, IRA

Colm McCallan (25)
CLG Ciceam Ard Eoin
Aontroim/Antrim
14 Iúil 1986, le forsaí dílseach/
14 July 1986, loyalist forces

Declan Arthurs (21)
CLG Piarsaigh, An Ghallbhaile
Tír Eoghain/Tyrone
8 Bealtaine 1987, Arm na Breataine/8 May 1987, British Army

Seamus Donnelly (19)
CLG Piarsaigh, An Ghallbhaile
Tír Eoghain/Tyrone
8 Bealtaine 1987, Arm na Breataine/8 May 1987, British Army

Tony Gormley (25)
CLG Piarsaigh, An Ghallbhaile
Tír Eoghain/Tyrone
8 Bealtaine 1987, Arm na Breataine/8 May 1987, British Army

Eugene Kelly (25)
CLG Piarsaigh, An Ghallbhaile
Tír Eoghain/Tyrone
8 Bealtaine 1987, Arm na Breataine/8 May 1987, British Army

Paddy Kelly (30)
CLG Thomáis Uí Chléirigh, Dún Geanainn
Tír Eoghain/Tyrone
8 Bealtaine 1987, Arm na Breataine/8 May 1987, British Army

John 'Jack' Kielty (45)
CLG Dún Droma
An Dún/Down
25 Eanáir 1988, le forsaí dílseach/25 January 1988, loyalist forces

Emma Donnelly (13)
Naomh Mhuire, An Port Mór
Ard Mhacha/Armagh
23 Samhain 1988, le Óglaigh na hÉireann/23 November 1988, IRA

John Devine (37)
CLG Uí Dhonaill, Béal Feirste
Aontroim/Antrim
21 Eanáir 1989, le forsaí dílseach/21 January 1989, loyalist forces

Liam McKee (36)
CLG Naomh Pádraig, Lois Na gCearbhach
Aontroim/Antrim
24 Meitheamh 1989, le forsaí dílseach/24 June 1989, loyalist forces

Martin McCaughey (23)
CLG Piarsaigh, An Ghallbhaile
Tír Eoghain/Tyrone
9 Deireadh Fómhair 1990, Arm na Breataine/9 October 1990, British Army

Malachy McIvor (43)
Henry Joy McCracken GAC, Mhúine Mhór
Doire/Derry
8 Samhain 1990, Arm na Breataine/8 November 1990, British Army

Fergal Caraher (20)
CLG Naomh Pádraig, Cuilleach Eannach
Ard Mhacha/Armagh
30 Nollaig 1990, Arm na Breataine/30 December 1990, British Army

Michael Lenaghan (46)
Naomh Gall, Béal Feirste
Aontroim/Antrim
4 Márta 1991, le forsaí dílseach/
4 March 1991, loyalist forces

Thomas Oliver (37)
CLG Ciceim Cúailgne
An Lú/Louth
19 Iúil 1991, le Óglaigh na hÉireann/19 July 1991, IRA

Colin Lundy (16)
Naomh Éanna, Béal Feirste
Aontroim/Antrim
9 Samhain 1991, le forsaí dílseach/
9 November 1991, loyalist forces

Kathleen Lundy (40)
Naomh Éanna, Béal Feirste
Aontroim/Antrim
9 Samhain 1991, le forsaí dílseach/
9 November 1991, loyalist forces

James Gray (39)
CLG Na Cloigthithe, Baile Mhic An Aba
Ard Mhacha/Armagh
4 Márta 1992, le forsaí dílseach/
4 March 1992, loyalist forces

Malachy Carey (36)
CLG Seamróga Loch gCaol
Aontroim/Antrim
12 Nollaig 1992, le forsaí dílseach/12 December 1992, loyalist forces

James Kelly (25)
CLG Eiméid, Sleacht Néill
Doire/Derry
25 Márta 1993, le forsaí dílseach/
25 March 1993, loyalist forces

Edward McHugh (65)
CLG Naomh Dabhóg, Achadh Uí Araín
Tír Eoghain/Tyrone
30 Bealtaine 1993, le forsaí dílseach/30 May 1993, loyalist forces

Michael Edwards (39)
Naomh Pól
Aontroim/Antrim
3 Meán Fómhair 1993, le forsaí dílseach/3 September 1993, loyalist forces

Gary Convie (24)
Sean MacDermott's GAC, Maghery
Ard Mhacha/Armagh
17 Bealtaine 1994, le forsaí dílseach/17 May 1994, loyalist forces

Eamon Fox (44)
CLG Ciceam Ard Eoin
Aontroim/Antrim
17 Bealtaine 1994, le forsaí dílseach/17 May 1994, loyalist forces

Edward O'Brien (21)
Naomh Éanna, Gorey
Loch Garman/Wexford
18 Feabhra 1996, le pléasc anabaí/18 February 1996, premature explosion

Seamus Dillon (46)
CLG Eoghain Ruaidh Uí Néill, Leach Phádraig
Tír Eoghain/Tyrone
27 Nollaig 1997, le forsaí dílseach/27 December 1997, loyalist forces

Ben Hughes (55)
Naomh Gall, Béal Feirste
Aontroim/Antrim
21 Eanáir 1998, le forsaí dílseach/21 January 1998, loyalist forces

Gareth Conway (18)
CLG Naomh Pádraig, An Táilte Riabhach
Tír Eoghain/Tyrone
15 Lúnasa 1998, le easaontóirí poblachtacha/15 August 1998, republican dissidents

Jolene Marlow (17)
CLG Naomh Mhic Artain, An Eochair
Tír Eoghain/Tyrone
15 Lúnasa 1998, le easaontóirí poblachtacha/15 August 1998, republican dissidents

Philomena Skelton (39)
CLG Uilf Tóin, Droim Caoin
Tír Eoghain/Tyrone
15 Lúnasa 1998, le easaontóirí poblachtacha/15 August 1998, republican dissidents

Ed McCoy (28)
Naomh Eoin
Aontroim/Antrim
28 Bealtaine 2000, le easaontóirí poblachtacha/28 May 2000, republican dissidents

Ronan Kerr (25)
An Chraobh Rua, Bearach
Tír Eoghain/Tyrone
2 Aibreán 2011, le easaontóirí poblachtacha/2 April 2011, republican dissidents

Thematically exploring the GAA and the conflict

This section consists of several essays written specifically for this book by expert contributors, as well as the detailed methodology for the project. The essays explore some of the main themes that present themselves when we delve into the history of the GAA during the period of the conflict.

The Importance of Oral History

Anna Bryson, Queen's University Belfast

Up For the Memories: Post-Conflict Oral History in Context

In his essay on 'The Parish and the Universe', Patrick Kavanagh encouraged us to embrace 'the parochial mentality' as: 'Parochialism is universal; it deals with the fundamentals.'[1]

The GAA has, for nearly 140 years, provided local structures for the fundamentals of parish, club and community life. As discussed further in Mark McGovern's essay, the broader political importance of the GAA was heightened for northern nationalists post-partition.[2] The fact that the newly appointed Minister for Home Affairs, Dawson Bates, was inundated with complaints from unionists about the development of the GAA in Ulster in the 1920s underlines its significance.[3] Organisations such as the GAA were 'at the heart of identity formation and allegiance' for northern nationalists, constituting both 'a form of political allegiance by proxy and an important aspect of community expression'.[4] Many of the GAA members I have interviewed over the years have indeed emphasised the importance of broader cultural activities run by local clubs in 'maintaining the nationalist philosophy and culture'.[5] With the intensification of conflict in the late 1960s, the GAA took on the additional task of providing relief from the realities of the streets and, for those families who were directly harmed and bereaved, a lifeline of material and moral support.

There have been significant efforts over the years to capture the GAA's significance in Irish history, not least the oral history project that was commissioned as part of the organisation's 125th anniversary celebrations in 2009.[6] Whilst that project did touch on the ways in which the conflict affected individuals, clubs and the wider organisation, the impact was not systematically explored. With this book, Relatives for Justice has taken on the vitally important task of comprehensively recording family memories of the GAA members who lost their lives as a result of the conflict. In this short piece I have been asked to highlight the wider significance of such oral history initiatives for dealing with the legacy of the past.

Breaking the Silence

For some victims and survivors, 'saying nothing' is a coping mechanism – reflecting an understandable desire to avoid revisiting painful memories. Indeed, in tight-knit communities there is often a tendency towards self-censorship, born of well-grounded fears of placing a loved one at risk or saying something that might upset family, neighbours and friends. However, for those individuals who feel able to put their memories on record, there can be significant benefits.[7]

In the academic field of transitional justice (which explores how societies deal with past violence and human rights abuses), memorialisation processes or memory work is now recognised by the United Nations as a vital 'fifth pillar' – standing alongside truth, justice, reparation and guarantees of non-recurrence. In his 2021 report on memory work, the UN Special Rapporteur for transitional justice suggested that capturing memories of past conflict was essential to the process of building 'a democratic, pluralistic, inclusive and peaceful society' and to 'restoring dignity' to victims whose experiences have previously been ignored.[8] While legal routes to truth, justice and accountability are, of course, crucially important for victims and their families, such processes are inevitably focused on the legal aspects of specific human rights violations rather than complex human consequences.[9] Oral history projects can thus provide a very significant complementary process, opening up the space to engage with a diverse range of individuals and to capture the messiness of 'awkwardly individual lives'.[10]

For many individual victims and their families, the opportunity to reflect on life before, during and after traumatic events is profoundly important. In particular, it can help to counter reductionist labelling by the media. As many victims and survivors have noted, the opportunity to tell their stories and those of their loved ones, with all their intricacies and contradictions, can help to restore the memory of a fully fledged human being with a complex and evolving personal history.[11] The stories captured by this book are a perfect illustration of this point – helping to ensure that individuals are not only defined by the tragic events that took their lives but also by their broad and deep contribution to their families, clubs and communities.[12]

Broadening Out

Another key advantage of an oral history approach is that it is not restricted to what is held in files that have made their way into public archives. Instead, it allows us to actively seek out a diversity of rural and urban perspectives; to engage with young and old; and, perhaps most importantly, to capture the gender dimensions of past conflict. An obvious starting point is to ensure that the stories of those women who lost their lives in the conflict are fully captured, but, as this project exemplifies, oral history can also capture the experiences of the mothers, wives, sisters and daughters of those who died – stories that are too often overlooked or sidelined.[13] Building on the important work that Relatives for Justice has developed in this area, this project is very closely attuned to direct and indirect gender-related harms and their long-term impact on women, their families and wider society.

In gathering these rich and varied testimonies from individual GAA members and their families, this project also informs the broader patterns and themes of the conflict. To date, individual GAA clubs have developed their own memorialisation projects (dedicated shields, cups, tournaments, etc.) to commemorate the lives of deceased members. This project connects the dots, shining a light on the dynamics that underpinned assaults and attacks on GAA members and the manner in which people bonded together in the face of adversity. Whilst suffering is often deeply personal, coping generally demands collective effort. What shines through in these stories is the multitude of ways in which club communities supported one another through dark and challenging times. The GAA has been at the heart of this, providing a vehicle through which a community can come together to show solidarity, assisting with the practicalities of organising wakes and funerals and thus easing the burden on the bereaved.

Independence and Trust

At a time when oral history initiatives are being cynically deployed by the UK government as a smokescreen for impunity (as part of the Northern Ireland Troubles (Legacy and Reconciliation) Bill), it is vitally important that independent and bona fide projects such as this capture memories before it is too late. Collecting and archiving personal testimony in post-conflict societies is challenging and time-consuming work. It simply would not have been possible for this project to collect so many rich and diverse stories in a relatively short space of time had it not been able to draw on the trust and credibility that flows from decades of work by Relatives for Justice on behalf of victims and survivors. This oral history collection has an eye on our troubled past, but it is also a significant gift to posterity – a precious snapshot of the individual and collective suffering of GAA members and of the unique legacy that they and their families have bequeathed to future generations. *Go ndéana Dia trócaire ar a n-anamacha. Mairfidh siad inár gcuimhní go deo.*

Anna Bryson is a Professor in the School of Law at Queen's University Belfast and a Fellow at the Senator George J. Mitchell Institute for Global Peace, Security and Justice. She was appointed Director of Research for QUB Law in 2023.

Endnotes

1 See Mark Storey (ed.), *Poetry and Ireland Since 1800: A Source Book* (Routledge, 1988), pp. 204–6.

2 Sugden and Bairner note that 'of Ireland's many and varied sporting organisations, the GAA has the most obvious political pedigree'. In addition to promoting Gaelic games, the organisation was intent on reversing the anglicisation of language, culture and politics in Ireland. See John Sugden and Alan Bairner, *Sport, Sectarianism and Society in a Divided Ireland* (Leicester University Press, 1993), p. 30 and especially Chapter 2, 'Gaelic Games and Irish Politics'.

3 For example, following a Gaelic match in Lavey, County Derry, in 1925, he was flooded with complaints from local unionists about Gaelic games being allowed in the county. See *Mid-Ulster Observer*, 6 May 1954. See further Dónal McAnallen, 'The GAA, Partition and Unionism' in Gearóid Ó Tuathaigh (ed.), *The GAA & Revolution in Ireland, 1913–1923* (Collins Press, 2015).

4 Thomas P. Burgess (ed.), *The Contested Identities of Ulster Catholics* (Palgrave Macmillan, 2018), pp. 4–5.

5 Interview with Tom Mitchell, Dublin, 6 December 1999.

6 See www.gaa.ie/the-gaa/oral-history/.

7 For a practical guide to the legal, ethical and technical challenges of setting up a post-conflict oral history project see, Anna Bryson, 'Recording Lived Experience: A Toolkit for Victims and Survivors' (2022), https://pureadmin.qub.ac.uk/ws/portalfiles/portal/307916089/VSS_RLE_Toolkit_Online_Version_Final.pdf.

8 United Nations Special Rapporteur, *Memorialization Process in the Context of Serious Violations of Human Rights and International Humanitarian Law: The Fifth Pillar of Transitional Justice* (2020), A/HRC/45/45, p. 4, https://undocs.org/en/A/HRC/45/45.

9 See Kieran McEvoy, 'Beyond Legalism: Towards a Thicker Understanding of Transitional Justice', *Journal of Law and Society*, vol. 34, iss. 4 (2007), pp. 411–40.

10 Many oral historians are particularly attracted to the radical potential for democratising history. As Paul Thompson notes: 'Since the nature of most existing records is to reflect the standpoint of authority, it is not surprising that the judgement of history has more often than not vindicated the wisdom of the powers that be. Oral history by contrast makes a much fairer trial possible: witnesses can now also be called from the under-classes, the unprivileged, and the defeated. It provides a more realistic and fair reconstruction of the past, a challenge to the established account.' Paul Thompson, *The Voice of the Past: Oral History* (4th edn, Oxford University Press, 2017).

11 See further, Anna Bryson, 'Victims, Violence, and Voice: Transitional Justice, Oral History, and Dealing with the Past', *Hastings International and Comparative Law Review*, vol. 39, no. 2 (2016), pp. 299–353.

12 Drawing on extensive research in post-apartheid South Africa, Sean Field suggests that creating space for victims of trauma to place their story in its wider cultural contexts (including childhood and family experiences) is critically important. Sean Field, 'Beyond "Healing": Trauma, Oral History and Regeneration', *Oral History*, vol. 34, no. 1 (2006), pp. 31–42; Sean Field, 'Disappointed Remains: Trauma, Testimony and Reconciliation in Post-Apartheid South Africa', in Donald A. Ritchie (ed.), *The Oxford Handbook of Oral History* (Oxford University Press, 2010), pp. 142–58.

13 See further the 'Gender Principles for Dealing with the Past' compiled by the Legacy Gender Integration Group in 2015, available at www.ulster.ac.uk/__data/assets/pdf_file/0009/66285/Gender-Principle-Report-Sept-2015_Final-Version.pdf. For an incisive analysis of the manner in which truth commissions can succumb to narrow categories of 'acceptable' or 'appropriate' victimhood for women, and in particular the tendency to prioritise public rather than private acts, see Fionnuala Ní Aoláin and Catherine Turner, 'Gender, Truth & Transition', *UCLA Women's Law Journal*, vol. 16 (2007), pp. 265–73.

The GAA and Irish Republicanism in the United States

Paul Darby, Ulster University

The significance of the GAA in the lives of Irish emigrants around the world has been publicly acknowledged at the highest levels of Irish society. Former Uachtarán na hÉireann Mary McAleese has spoken in glowing terms about the contribution of the association to Irish migrant communities. In announcing a partnership between the Irish government and the GAA in 2008 aimed at promoting Gaelic games abroad, then Minister for Foreign Affairs and former Taoiseach Micheál Martin observed: 'The GAA plays a key role in the social and cultural life of Irish communities abroad … it underpins and promotes Irish heritage and identity across the globe.' Similar sentiments were recently echoed by Seán Fleming, Minister of State for International Development and Diaspora, at the launch of the 2023 GAA World Games hosted in Derry.

Beyond Irish shores, there are currently over 500 teams, hailing from every continent bar Antarctica, playing various codes of Gaelic games. Unquestionably, the largest and longest-standing overseas GAA unit can be found in the US, where rudimentary versions of hurling were played decades before the association's formation in Ireland in 1884. While the health of Gaelic games in the US since then has waxed and waned according to fluctuations in Irish emigration, they have long been and remain a focal point in the lives of many of those Irish people who settled in the US, as well as their offspring. But why is this the case and what is it about the GAA that has ensured its survival in the US for more than 125 years?

The association has performed a number of important socio-economic, cultural and political functions for Irish immigrants. In the late nineteenth century joining a Gaelic football or hurling club helped to smooth the transition to what were sprawling and often inhospitable cities. Since then, the GAA has continued to serve as a comforting home away from home for Irish immigrants. It has provided them with opportunities to mix with like-minded individuals, play sport, engage in cultural activities and be in a physical space resonant of home. On a deeper, psychological level, participation in Gaelic games as a player, spectator or volunteer has allowed them to reconnect with the Ireland that they left behind. Involvement with the GAA has also provided entry into social networks that enabled countless newly arrived immigrants to find work and somewhere to live, make friends and experience the excitement of playing or watching competitive sport. As one Boston GAA stalwart told me a number of years ago, 'It helps to take the edge off being 3,000 miles from home.' The other key function of the GAA in the US, and one pointed out to me by Micheál Martin, is that it has allowed Irish immigrants to show pride in and celebrate their Irishness as well as more localised connections to parishes, villages, towns and counties across the island.

Alongside this, Gaelic games have long enabled Irish-Americans to express more politicised versions of nationalism and republicanism. The growth of the GAA in late nineteenth-century America was closely aligned with the nationalist ethos of the association in Ireland. Many of those who established clubs and promoted Gaelic games in the US were leading Irish-American nationalists, and these clubs often adopted names rich in nationalist symbolism, such as Emmets, Redmonds, Davitts and Wolfe Tones. Gaelic games were also supported by nationalist Irish-American organisations such as the Irish National League, Clan na Gael and the Ancient Order of Hibernians. The Irish-American press at the time was correct to describe the efforts to establish the GAA in the US as 'patriotic', imbued with the 'spirit of freedom' and part of the drive for 'Irish emancipation'.

The GAA continued in this vein at the start of the new century when US Gaels got behind the Home Rule campaign. In the lead-up to the Easter Rising, many clubs raised funds for the Irish National Volunteers, and during the War of Independence, fundraising and expressions of support for the IRA were commonplace at matches in New York and Boston. Many Irish republicans who had been defeated by pro-Treaty forces in the Irish Civil War of 1922–23 sought refuge in New York and used the GAA there to help generate finances and build political support for a united Ireland. However, with partition and the assimilation of the Irish into American life, the connection between the GAA and republican politics became much less pronounced.

This changed dramatically with the onset of the Troubles. Anger at the response to the campaign for civil rights, continued domination by the unionist establishment and the increased presence of British soldiers in the North, led to the link between the GAA in America and Irish republicanism resurfacing. This was especially the case in New York, where a close association developed between the GAA and Irish Northern Aid (Noraid). This is hardly surprising because the key figures in setting up Noraid – Michael Flannery, Matthew Higgins, Jack McCarthy and John McGowan – were all influential in the New York GAA. As the Troubles began to unfold in Northern Ireland, these men kept the GAA and its headquarters at Gaelic Park at the forefront of Noraid activities. For example, after the atrocity of Bloody Sunday, the GAA sponsored a series of field days in support of Noraid, which ran throughout 1972. At one fixture at Gaelic Park, 50 per cent of the gate was earmarked for 'Relief of Distress in the North', while a number of US politicians sympathetic to the nationalist cause in Ireland, including Ted Kennedy, were invited to attend.

Following a decline in support, the hunger strikes in Northern Ireland's Maze Prison in 1981 revived Noraid's fortunes, with the GAA once again to the fore in supporting the republican movement politically and financially. For example, three days prior to the death of Bobby Sands, there was a large GAA presence at a protest rally outside the offices of the British Consulate in Manhattan. Following Sands's death on 5 May, the New York GAA cancelled all games scheduled for 10 May and handed over the gate receipts for the following week's fixtures to Noraid's Hunger Strike Defense Fund.

The GAA's support for the republican movement in Ireland and solidarity with those who lost their lives in the conflict extended beyond New York. In Boston, seven years after the killing of Aidan McAnespie by a British soldier in February 1988, the Aidan McAnespie GFC was formed as a fitting and lasting tribute to his memory. Alongside sympathy and remembrance, the founders also saw the club as a platform for highlighting political injustice in Northern Ireland. Further attacks on GAA members in Northern Ireland in the second half of the 1990s strengthened the nationalist character of Gaelic games in Boston. The killing of Fergal McCusker by the LVF in January 1998 was especially significant. McCusker had played Junior football for McAnespies the previous summer and intended to travel back to Boston that spring to look for work and resume his association with the club. In the aftermath of his death, the body responsible for overseeing Gaelic games in the greater Boston area changed its name from the 'New England' to the 'Northeastern' GAA board.

The killings of Aidan McAnespie, Fergal McCusker and other prominent GAA figures in Northern Ireland, such as Sean Brown, chairman of Bellaghy Wolfe Tones GAA club, and Gerry Devlin, manager of St Enda's Senior Gaelic football team, by loyalist paramilitaries hardened the political outlook and attitude of the GAA's northern counties in Ireland. This was reflected in Boston GAA circles in the debate around the motion to remove Rule 21, which barred members of the British Crown forces from participating in Gaelic games. The prominence of clubs with strong membership from the North, and the fact that the McAnespie family spoke out publicly against removing Rule 21, led the Northeastern GAA to vote against the motion.

Around 3,000 miles away, on the Pacific coast, similar support for Irish republicanism could be seen among sections of San Francisco's GAA community. This was most explicit in the Ulster GFC, which had been formed in the city in 1986 by a group of Northern Gaels. They wanted the club to reflect their republican outlook and this was captured in its constitution, which described its aspiration 'to preserve and defend democratic principles enshrined in the Declaration of Independence, and the Proclamation of the Irish Republic, declared on Easter Week 1916'. To this end, the club established a Political Wing Committee and closely aligned itself with the San Francisco chapter of Noraid. Ulster GFC's political orientation was also visible through the remembrance Masses it organised for PIRA volunteers killed in the conflict in Northern Ireland and through its Annual Easter Brunch, organised to commemorate and celebrate those who took part in the 1916 Easter Rising. As one prominent committee member explained to me, the club would often bring members of Sinn Féin, the PIRA and former prisoners to the event to discuss the situation in the North and canvass support. These activities kept Ulster GFC at the forefront of republican politics in the city.

The IRA ceasefires of 1994 and 1997, the signing of the Good Friday Agreement in 1998, IRA decommissioning and its declaration in 2005 that the 'war was over' brought about a commitment to constitutional, non-violent republicanism not only in Ireland but also in the US, where the majority of those with republican sympathies followed Sinn Féin's position and committed themselves to a peaceful, constitutional campaign for a united Ireland. This has been reflected in America's GAA fraternity. The words of a long-standing stalwart of the Ulster GFC capture this perfectly: 'The club would be known for that link [with republicanism] but not as much now because of the ceasefire. With the ceasefire, it has quietened down a lot. The young coming over now, I find, wouldn't have the same interest in these issues compared to when I first came over here [1990]. People were very republican minded. There was a lot of fundraising going on. As a club we wouldn't have been hiding that link. Irish Noraid would be marching in the St Patrick's Day parade and the Ulster Gaelic club would be behind them. Part of that goes back to the days whenever we were commemorating the hunger strike or the border busters campaign that was going on in Ireland then. Now, with the ceasefires, you have the justice, peace and equality campaign and our club would always have been asked to help out with that and would have been glad to.'

US-based Gaels elsewhere in the country have been on a similar journey over the course of the fledgling peace process in Ireland. For example, in May 2006, the Chicago GAA extended an invitation to the Northern Ireland international soccer team to visit Gaelic Park during an end-of-season US tour. The significance of this move lay in the fact that Windsor Park, home of the Northern Ireland team, was viewed as a cold house for Irish Catholics, including players, some of whom were victims of sectarian abuse and death threats. Neil Lennon, the former Celtic player, was the most notable example, and he was forced to retire from the Northern Ireland team in 2002. In these circumstances, the invitation was generous, reflective of a less politicised Irishness, and rooted in the conciliatory spirit of the peace process. It also signified the wider direction of travel for the US GAA in the early decades of the twenty-first century. While it remains intensely proud of its Irishness, the GAA in America has committed itself to a more inclusive and ethnically diverse recruitment strategy as it seeks to preserve and promote Gaelic games on US shores into the future.

Dr Paul Darby is Reader in the sociology of sport at Ulster University and author of Gaelic Games, Nationalism and the Irish Diaspora in the United States *(UCD Press, 2009).*

'The lifeblood of the parish': community, conflict and the GAA

Mark McGovern, Edge Hill University

'The lifeblood of the parish ...'

Let's start, paradoxically, with a game of soccer. On 18 June 1994 two UVF gunmen attacked The Heights Bar (known locally as O'Toole's) in Loughinisland – a small, rural and remote townland in County Down. It would prove to be one of the most deadly of a wave of such attacks launched during a lethal surge in loyalist violence in the latter years of the conflict. That night the tiny bar was packed. Not on this occasion to watch a Gaelic football game, but to cheer the Irish soccer team to one of their most famous victories: defeating Italy in that FIFA World Cup game, taking place some 3,000 miles away in the Giants Stadium in New York.[1] Bursting through the doors, the gunmen opened fire with an assault rifle, killing six local men and badly wounding another five. The loyalist attackers escaped – never to be charged or convicted – leaving behind them a scene of utter carnage and a community in desperate mourning. An Ireland recovering from the wild celebrations of the night before woke up to the horror of what had happened closer to home.

Soccer may have prompted the gathering in O'Toole's that fateful night, but it was towards the GAA, the organisation dedicated to promoting other, specifically Irish, sports that many turned in the days to come. As members of the Loughinisland GAC would later recall (as part of the organisation's own national oral history project), it was the local GAA club – the 'lifeblood of the parish' – that would then provide a vital means for people in the area to come together and collectively cope with the devastation the massacre left in its wake.[2] A massacre which, in no small part, was made possible by collusion between the loyalists who carried it out and members of the RUC; telling another story of communal bonds – and community-state relations – of a very different kind.[3] In microcosm, these events tell us much – and dispel a number of myths – about some often hidden and overlooked dimensions of the conflict, and the place of the GAA within it. But how, we might ask, could the GAA come to occupy such a space and social role for many nationalists within the North and how was that position shaped, over time, by the nature of the northern State itself?

'The most socially valuable organisation in Ireland …'

The GAA, it has recently been noted, is 'the most successful and popular sporting and cultural body across Ireland, and amongst the Irish diaspora'.[4] One eminent commentator describes it as 'the most socially valuable organisation in Ireland'.[5] Another attributes this success and popularity to a feature of the GAA that makes Ireland different, not only in the world of sport, but in terms of culture more broadly: that throughout the twentieth century the organisation 'developed roots that permeated throughout every county and every village … became central to family and community life [and] reached into people's hearts, minds and bodies'.[6] The adoption of a wider, cultural and social (rather than purely sporting) role for the organisation and the valorisation of a collective and voluntary ethos both underpin an emphasis on mass membership and localised and cross-generational activities. It is not by chance that the GAA has more members than any other organisation on the island, with the sole exception of the Catholic Church.

As a result, rootedness in local communities not only constitutes much of what the GAA does, it lies at the core of how it sees itself and presents itself to the world. At times, this may be something of an idealised self-image, masking many inevitable and sometimes deep-seated social and political tensions, both now and in the past. However, as another eminent author noted during the GAA's 125th anniversary celebrations in 2009, all this taken together points to the crucial, and often under-valued, impact the GAA has had on Ireland's collectivist 'associational culture'.[7] As a result, the GAA has also come to serve as 'an important signifier of Irish identity' that marries and entwines localised community ties to a national self-imagination.[8]

In many ways these are the self-same features that have made the GAA the 'lifeblood of the parish', not only in Loughinisland but throughout the North. That is to say, a pivotal, regularly and actively practiced – and so highly visible

– manifestation of a deeply and locally rooted collective identity. Not really so very different to elsewhere on the island and beyond. Here, however, it has also acted as a vivid expression of the integrity and will of a nationalist, Catholic community that has had to struggle for a space to recognise, realise and be itself. To no small degree, this is because those very self-same characteristics that are 'taken for granted' and generally celebrated as positive and benign in other places have sometimes come to be assigned starker, darker and antagonistic social meanings, resonance and significance in the context of a different social and political order. The GAA in the North may share with many other places, in Ireland and elsewhere, its role as a hub and focus for collective social bonds through which the everyday lives of many within the community are lived, but what is different is that in the North that has historically taken place against the backdrop of a divided and at times threatening, hostile and dangerous social terrain.

To say that the GAA has a presence in 'every village' is, of course, also something of an exaggeration, but one which captures a kernel of truth about social life throughout much of the island. Its more pronounced limits to describe the North of Ireland are a reminder of, and reflect, a more difficult and contentious dimension of the social landscape here. In the North, the presence (or absence) of a GAA field and clubhouse in a local town or village is often among the more obvious markers of the many aspects of social, political and cultural life shaped and conditioned by, and evidencing, long-term communal divisions and a history of very different relations between different communities and the State.

From 'underground nation' to a 'state within a state'

Established expressly to promote Irish national identity, the ideas and institutions of both Catholicism and republicanism were interwoven in the GAA from its foundation – indeed it long served as a site of struggle between the two. As part of the broader late-nineteenth-century nationalist movement, it would prove a pivotal institutional means of 'creating and defining Irish popular culture in Gaelic terms'.[9] In turn, an official British State view of the GAA as a subversive organisation during its first decades – an exemplar of the 'underground nation' – accelerated in the revolutionary period. That was to culminate with the British Army targeting of the Croke Park crowd on Bloody Sunday in 1920, in reprisal for the IRA assassination of undercover British agents.[10]

Partition saw the position of the GAA change dramatically south of the border. Not so in the North, where it continued to be an object of official suspicion and exclusion, as this part of the 'underground nation' morphed into the 'state within a state'. As one of the 'few legally functioning national bodies in the North' in the years following partition, the GAA provided northern Catholics with a rare space to express identity and allegiance.[11] It grew and prospered as a result, becoming the most obvious, everyday means to share in the social and cultural life of the rest of the island.[12] While some have talked of the GAA exercising a 'choice of exclusiveness' in forging a mission to foster Irish games, neither its members nor the wider nationalist community chose their exclusion from the levers of power and influence in the new northern State and a world of discrimination in elections, jobs and housing.[13] That was an everyday reality determined for them by others.

That said, throughout the subsequent decades, such social separation and political ostracism buttressed (and was further entrenched by) the GAA's own tendency towards social conservatism and its deep-seated integration with the structures of the Catholic Church. It was a sense of separation exemplified in the rules banning members from playing 'foreign' games (or their being played on GAA grounds) and preventing members of the security forces from joining the organisation. However, that cannot be seen in isolation from the ways in which the GAA had to function within what was, in effect, a one-party, unionist-dominated northern State. Exclusion fosters and valorises an inward gaze in search of self-definition and self-reliance as a collective resource. The GAA would also mirror wider minority community experiences in terms of everyday discrimination and the sometimes mundane consequences of such exclusion. This could include everything from struggles to obtain land for grounds and buildings, or a lack of northern-based media coverage of Gaelic games, through to a Special Powers Act that cast suspicion on GAA clubs as havens of subversive republicanism. Such experiences only reinforced, in the sporting and cultural sphere, that broader sense of estrangement that ultimately fed into the civil rights movement of the late 1960s and the long years of conflict beyond.

'Making people stick together ...'

The GAA in the North was never a monolith, and differences and divisions within the nationalist community – not least in its attitude toward the use of force and armed struggle – were played out in its hierarchy and ranks throughout the conflict, as elsewhere.[14] However, its celebration of Gaelic culture, identification with Catholicism, general anti-partitionist stance and all-Ireland organisation would single it out as an object of ongoing distrust. During the conflict this could lead to intense State surveillance, alongside a 'heightened sense of animosity from the Protestant community generally'.[15] Loyalist paramilitaries denounced the organisation as a front for armed republicanism and identified and targeted GAA clubs and members as supposed 'legitimate targets'.[16]

This would see GAA clubhouses attacked and burned. Many lived for years with bulletproof glass, window grilles and security cages; others with their grounds occupied by the British Army – in the case of Crossmaglen Rangers in south Armagh, for over a quarter of a century.[17] Security force checks or harassment of players and fans on their way to and from games could be routine and carried out with impunity. It was something those who had to pass through a British Army border checkpoint at Aughnacloy, County Tyrone, to get to the nearby Aghaloo O'Neills GAC pitch were long used to. Among them, Aidan McAnespie, who was shot dead near the checkpoint by a British soldier in February 1988, in broad daylight and in sight of the ground.[18] Not until some thirty-five years later, and after a tireless family campaign, was his killer finally brought to some kind of justice – to this point the only British soldier convicted as a result of a post-conflict legacy investigation.[19]

The conflict witnessed many other members of the GAA targeted and killed, both young and old, from the start of the Troubles until its end, right across the North, and most at the hands of loyalists or the security forces. Francis Rowntree was only eleven years old when he was killed by a rubber bullet fired by a British soldier as he walked near the Divis Flats in West Belfast in April

1972. An entirely innocent victim, fired on without warning and with 'excessive force', the death of this young Gael was only officially declared 'not justified' by a coroner's court in 2017.[20] Sixteen-year-old Martin McShane was another early victim, shot dead by British soldiers on the grounds of the GAA club in Coalisland, County Tyrone in 1971.[21] Many more were to follow. Among them Kevin Lynch, who died on hunger strike in the H-Blocks in 1981. A few years earlier he had captained Derry's under-16 hurling team to the All-Ireland title.

Of the over 150 GAA victims of the conflict, roughly a quarter died at the hands of members of the security forces.[22] Almost half of the total were killed by loyalists. In terms of the latter, among the last was thirty-six-year-old Gerry Devlin – a man from a 'GAA family' – who had played for Antrim at both Minor and under-21 levels.[23] As a manager, he led his club, Naomh Éanna GAC of Glengormley, in their first ever Senior Football Championship campaign, later serving as club vice-chairman.[24] He was shot dead by a loyalist gunman as he waited at the entrance of the clubhouse for his brother in 1997.

Evidencing the role of collusion in all too many killings, some perpetrators belonged to both the security forces and loyalist groups. That was the case of the UDR soldier convicted of the 1974 killing of forty-five-year-old Jim Devlin and his wife, Gertrude, shot alongside their daughter, Patricia, near their home in Edendork, County Tyrone.[25] Patricia was injured but survived. A member of the local branch of the SDLP, Jim Devlin was well known in the area. In the 1950s he was a stalwart of the county Senior football team, the most renowned of five brothers who had played for Tyrone. He had been in the side that took on Galway in the 1956 All-Ireland semi-final. Years later, one of his teammates would recall how they had all been stopped and held for an hour by members of the B Specials on their way back from training just before the semi-final match. Another, Jody O'Neill, remembered that when he was Tyrone Senior football manager in the early 1970s he was stopped at a UDR checkpoint driving some of the players home after training. He and the players were hooded, beaten with rifle butts and threatened with being shot.[26] A few months later O'Neill was warned that his name and those of several other high-profile Tyrone GAA men were on a loyalist death list. They all developed their own routines and took precautions, 'checking under their cars, varying their driving routes; the unconscious, automatic oppression caused by living in fear and suspicion'.[27]

Jim and Gertrude were killed shortly afterwards, during a wave of loyalist sectarian killings carried out by the Glenanne Gang in the 'murder triangle' of Tyrone and Armagh; many involving serving and former members of the UDR and the RUC. The notorious loyalist and suspected British agent Robin Jackson was later claimed to have taken part in the shooting.[28] The Glenanne Gang alone was responsible for killing some twenty-eight members of the GAA. Two thousand people attended the Devlins' funeral. 'What was going on … didn't help the football,' recalls Jim McKeever, Derry football great and the inaugural Texaco Footballer of the Year in 1958, 'but had the effect of making people stick together too.'[29]

'He took the load for everyone …'

Almost a quarter of a century after Jim and Gertrude Devlin were killed, GAA people found themselves having to 'stick together' again in the midst of another campaign of intimidation and fear, targeted at communities that loyalists had designated to be part of a supposed 'pan-nationalist front'.[30] That is what happened, for example, in mid-Ulster and McKeever's home county of Derry. One May evening, three years after the Loughinisland massacre and a matter of months before the shooting dead of Gerry Devlin, sixty-one-year-old Sean Brown was locking the gates of the Wolfe Tones Bellaghy GAC in County Derry when he was abducted and killed by loyalists. Brown was the epitome of a GAA man. As we have seen, within GAA circles, communities and families, voluntarism – selflessness – is the most celebrated ethos, conferring status and respect on those seen to personify it. Over years of service, someone can become the sum of values collectively valued – the mark of a dignity quietly admired. That was Sean Brown, someone who 'took the load for everyone'.[31] He was the lifeblood of a parish in an Ulster GAA heartland. That is why he was targeted.

Dehumanising a person means their life is not valued in its own terms but is reduced to becoming a mere means to another end. A person becomes a victim not for who they are or what they have done, but for what they are seen to represent. To attack and kill someone who personifies a hard-earned dignity, dehumanises in just this way, and is designed to disparage, denigrate and seek to debase and render abject what a community values most in itself. It is intended to radically invert the site of blame, shame, stigma and indecency, and reverse the self-image of an 'Other' that sees itself as valid, of value and able to act in its own terms – to sap their collective strength and vitality, their lifeblood. That is what the killers of Sean Brown sought to do. Someone who embodied the GAA was viewed as the means to achieve that end. The rituals of dignified collective mourning and commemoration form a vital, restorative response. Yet, getting to the truth of how such a thing could happen works to truly restore dignity in the present, for Sean Brown, for those killed at Loughinisland, for all those GAA members harmed – whoever they were killed by – and for all victims of the conflict, equally.

Mark McGovern is Professor in Sociology at Edge Hill University, Lancashire. His research is primarily concerned with the study of political violence, conflict and post-conflict transition, particularly in the North of Ireland. He is the author of Counterinsurgency and Collusion in Northern Ireland *(Pluto Press, 2019).*

Endnotes

1 Cobain, 'Northern Ireland loyalist shootings: one night of carnage, 18 years of silence', *The Guardian*, 15 October 2012, www.theguardian.com/uk/2012/oct/15/northern-ireland-loyalist-shootings-loughinisland.

2 GAA, 'Members of Loughinisland GAC', *GAA Oral History Project*, 10 March 2011, www.gaa.ie/the-gaa/oral-history/members-loughlinisland-gac/.

3 M. Maguire, *Report of the Police Ombudsman Relating to a Complaint by the Victims and Survivors of the Murders at the Heights Bar, Loughinisland, 18 June 1994* (Belfast: Office of the Police Ombudsman for Northern Ireland, 2016), www.patfinucanecentre.org/sites/default/files/2017-03/Loughinisland-Report.pdf; M. McGovern, 'See no evil': Collusion in Northern Ireland', *Race and Class*, vol. 58, iss. 3 (2017), pp. 46–63.

4 M. Cronin, M. Duncan and P. Rouse, 'The Gaelic Athletic Association Oral History Project', *The International Journal of the History of Sport*, vol. 36, iss. 13–14 (2019), p. 1312.

5 T.P. Coogan, *The GAA and the War of Independence* (Head of Zeus, 2018), p. 15.

6 K. Liston, 'The GAA and the Sporting Irish', in T. Inglis (ed.), *Are the Irish Different?* (Manchester University Press, 2014), p. 199.

7 Quoted in C. O'Kane, 'Nurturing our communities will keep GAA's lifeblood flowing', *The Irish News*, 7 February 2017, www.irishnews.com/sport/2017/02/07/news/cahair-o-kane-nurturing-our-communities-will-keep-gaa-s-lifeblood-flowing-923258/?param=ds441rif44T.

8 Cronin, Duncan and Rouse, 'The Gaelic Athletic Association Oral History Project', p. 1312.

9 T.J. White, 'Myth-making and the Creation of Irish Nationalism in the 19th Century', *Studi Celtici*, vol. 3 (2004), p. 335.

10 M. de Burca, *The GAA: A History of the Gaelic Athletic Association* (Cumann Lúthchleas Gael, 1980), p. 150.

11 M. Cronin, 'Catholics and Sport in Northern Ireland: Exclusiveness or Inclusiveness?' in T. Chandler and T. Magdalinski (eds), *With God on Their Side: Sport in the Service of Religion* (Routledge, 2002), p. 27.

12 M. Cronin, M. Duncan and P. Rouse, *The GAA: A People's History* (2nd edn, Collins Press, 2014), p. 166.

13 Cronin, 'Catholics and Sport in Northern Ireland', p. 25.

14 M. Reynolds, 'The Gaelic Athletic Association and the 1981 H-Block Hunger Strike', *The International Journal of the History of Sport*, vol. 34, iss. 3–4, (2017), pp. 217–35.

15 Cronin, 'Catholics and Sport in Northern Ireland', p. 29.

16 Reynolds, 'The Gaelic Athletic Association and the 1981 H-Block Hunger Strike', p. 222.

17 Des Fahy, *How the GAA Survived the Troubles* (Wolfhound Press, 2001).

18 Ibid., pp. 40–61.

19 J. Cassidy, 'Aidan McAnespie: Former soldier found guilty of his manslaughter is sentenced', *Belfast Telegraph*, 2 February 2023, www.belfasttelegraph.co.uk/news/courts/aidan-mcanespie-former-soldier-found-guilty-of-his-manslaughter-is-sentenced/1553169740.html.

20 'Francis Rowntree killing "not justified" – coroner', *BBC News*, 17 November 2017, www.bbc.co.uk/news/uk-northern-ireland-42023007.

21 F. McClements, 'GAA and the Troubles: Remembering club members killed in the conflict', *The Irish Times*, 4 September 2021, www.irishtimes.com/culture/heritage/gaa-and-the-troubles-remembering-club-members-killed-in-the-conflict-1.4662170.

22 Ibid.

23 Ibid.

24 C. McParland, 'Glengormley club marks the murder of Gerry Devlin 25 years on', *Belfast Media*, 10 December 2022, https://belfastmedia.com/gerry-devlin-murder-25th-anniversary; Fahy, *How the GAA Survived the Troubles*, pp. 24–39.

25 K. Duggan, 'Tyrone hero Jim Devlin's death still resonates after all these years', *The Irish Times*, 17 May 2014, www.irishtimes.com/sport/gaelic-games/gaelic-football/tyrone-hero-jim-devlin-s-death-still-resonates-after-all-these-years-1.1798905; D. McKittrick, S. Kelters, B. Feeney and C. Thornton, *Lost Lives: The Stories of the Men, Women and Children who Died as a Result of the Northern Ireland Troubles* (Mainstream Publishing, 1999), p. 444.

26 Duggan, 'Tyrone hero Jim Devlin's death still resonates'.

27 Ibid.

28 McKitterick et al., *Lost Lives*, p. 444.

29 Cited in Duggan, 'Tyrone hero Jim Devlin's death still resonates'.

30 M. McGovern, *Counterinsurgency and Collusion in Northern Ireland* (Pluto Press, 2019).

31 G. Brown, 'The murder of Sean Brown: Inherited trauma in Northern Ireland', *The Independent*, 22 September 2022, www.independent.co.uk/independentpremium/long-reads/sean-brown-murder-northern-ireland-troubles-legacy-b2166331.html.

The Hunger Strikes and the GAA

Tommy McKearney

The hunger strike has been used by imprisoned Irish republicans on many occasions throughout the twentieth century.[1] Frequently described as the prisoners' last resort, it was almost always aimed at influencing public opinion in favour of the incarcerated and against the policy of those in power. As such, it was an action that often caused turmoil for the governing authority. On some occasions it even threatened to call into question the legitimacy of the State itself.

By its very nature, a hunger strike entails a battle of wills, but it also becomes a battle for hearts and minds. This results in a struggle for the political high ground – those backing the hunger strike engage the State in a contest to sway public opinion. On one hand hunger-strike sympathisers fight to gain and on the other hand the State fights to deny support emerging from each and every sector of society. This was the context in which the GAA, Ireland's largest sporting body, found itself during the emotionally charged days of the H-Block hunger strikes.

Although the location of the H-Blocks was in the six counties and technically in a different jurisdiction, it was in the Republic of Ireland that the hunger strikes created most tension for and within the GAA.[2] To understand why this was so, it is necessary to first examine the position of the southern-Irish establishment in relation to the North.

For decades after the foundation of the twenty-six-county State, governments in Dublin rhetorically declared support for ending partition and the achievement of Irish reunification. In fact, de Valera's 1937 constitution explicitly stated in Articles 2 and 3 that Leinster House was entitled to govern the entire island. And for decades after the foundation of the southern State, this outlook was broadly endorsed by a majority of the population. Where they differed though, was on how or when this 'ideal situation' was to be achieved.

Throughout the early decades following the 1921 Treaty there remained a small minority of hard-line republicans who believed that partition should be ended immediately. To do so they were prepared to, and occasionally did, resort, albeit unsuccessfully, to the use of arms to effect change. A deep source of frustration for these hard-line republicans was the realisation that a significant majority of the southern-Irish population agreed with their objectives but could not be persuaded to join in with their armed campaigns.

This required a delicate balancing act from the South's ruling class. In public they found it difficult not to endorse the wider consensus opposed to partition, yet privately they entertained a very different outlook. Although for decades after its foundation, the State's economy had been floundering, for some there was a zone of contentment. The business and professional classes had achieved a comfortable standard of living and their good fortune was shared by the political elite. In a nutshell, the Irish bourgeoise was determined not to have its lifestyle disrupted by consideration for suffering northerners.

It was in this light that the South's ruling class viewed matters relating to the six counties. They saw two possible scenarios arising in the North that would threaten their self-interest. Number one was that, in the, admittedly unlikely, event of Northern Ireland voluntarily agreeing to rejoin its southern neighbour, an entirely new and, for them, unwelcome set of circumstances would prevail. The new order would surely disturb the status quo, challenging powerful institutions and rearranging embedded political structures. Moreover, with an influx of northern trade unionists newly released from the shackles of Orangeism, the dreaded spectre of socialism might well rear its head.[3]

Scenario number two was more disturbing still. An insurrectionary uprising by northern nationalists against the oppressive Stormont regime and supported by a majority in the republic was their ultimate nightmare. The resulting conflict would inevitably destroy their cosy existence. This nightmare became a reality in the late 1960s and early 1970s.[4] As a consequence, the southern-Irish ruling class responded by attempting to blame Northern Irish republicans for causing the conflict. Their intention was to demonise the resistance, criminalise the armed campaign and thereby isolate and marginalise it, thus rendering impotent its southern base.

In order to enforce this policy, the southern ruling class actively deployed as many elements of civil society as possible. Some sectors, such as RTÉ and civil servants (especially the gardaí), were obliged by legislation to comply.[5]

Others, such as media outlets owned by wealthy consortia, were only too happy to follow this lead. This meant that pressure was applied on voluntary or sporting bodies to marginalise republicanism, and, obviously, the largest such organisation, the GAA, was a prime target.

How fearful the southern ruling class was that the impact of a hunger strike death could unsettle its designated narrative was evident several years before the H-Block events. In 1976 Mayo native Frank Stagg died on hunger strike in England's Wakefield Prison. Rather than allow his family to receive his body in Dublin and afford him a republican funeral, Garda Special Branch diverted his remains to Shannon airport and had him buried in a government-secured plot.[6] The fact that Stagg had been a member of the GAA was not lost on the authorities, or indeed on the association itself.

Since its foundation in 1884, the GAA has not been a stranger to internal conflict centring on political divisions within the wider spectrum of Irish nationalism.[7] Being an all-Ireland body, the organisation reflects the wide spectrum of political, social and economic opinion held by all but the unionist community in the North. As such, and as it had experienced from its foundation, no single political philosophy can entirely dominate its agenda. Through its early years the association experienced ongoing tension and, on occasion, outright antagonism between Irish Republican Brotherhood supporters and followers of the Irish Parliamentary Party. This scenario returned to torment the body for years following the Treaty, with barely concealed antipathy between Free State and republican supporters.

Yet in spite of what would have created irreconcilable differences leading to a split in almost any other environment, the GAA managed to defy the organisational 'laws of gravity' and remained, if not perfectly united, at least undivided. To identify the reason for this remarkable feat would require the labours of a faculty of sociologists and anthropologists. At a guess, the explanation probably lies in the fact that as a sporting organisation, games fostered by the association retained such wide popular attraction that its appeal was undiminished. Moreover, since its earliest days, the leadership had striven to accommodate differences to such an extent that their efforts bordered on the pusillanimous. As a consequence, it was and is often possible to find significant divergences between counties, clubs or among the four provinces. This fact became very evident as the 1981 hunger strike progressed.

When the hunger strikes began there were approximately 420 republican prisoners participating in the no-wash 'blanket protest'.[8] The overwhelming majority were from across the six counties, with some from the southern border counties. In practice this meant that most nationalist areas in the North knew at least one prisoner and their family. Moreover, since the age profile was broadly speaking that of young men in their twenties, it was axiomatic that many of their friends and acquaintances were also of a similar age. In other words, they were very likely to be participating in sporting activity and be members of sports clubs, and so probably involved with the GAA at some level.

The H-Blocks' republican prisoners and their supporters were acutely aware of the need to win widespread support for their demands. Moreover, they understood only too well that this meant support of a type that would exert political pressure in order to have the issue resolved. How to do so was a matter of ongoing and intense discussion among the prisoners.

It has to be kept in mind that protesting H-Block prisoners had very restricted access to any means of communication. Having lost all 'privileges' due to refusing to conform to prison regulations, they were not allowed access to prison-authorised writing material (although they were adept at circumventing this by other methods). They were, moreover, only afforded one strictly supervised visit per month while being confined to their cells twenty-four hours a day. Deprived of the opportunity to put their case directly before the world, they sought every other avenue available to them.

Many ideas were put forward, some more practical than others. It was hardly surprising, though, given the background of so many prisoners, that seeking to influence the GAA received significant attention. Relatives and friends were prevailed upon to contact their local club and ask for support.[9] For obvious reasons, this strategy was initially more successful in the North. However, Ireland is a small country and the GAA has a permanent and accessible network in which political sympathies are usually known. Before long the impact of the hunger strike was being felt throughout the association, albeit not appreciated in all quarters.

From the outset, the Dublin government and southern establishment were determined to prevent the association offering support to the hunger strikers and by extension to militant republicanism. Therefore, even qualified support was seen as a threat to their interests. In spite of this, during the first hunger strike in 1980, the association was prepared to offer qualified support. After meeting representatives of the H-Block committee, the GAA management committee called on the British government to 'afford normal decent standards and humane treatment to the prisoners'. Between March and the end of May 1981 substantial support, although often ambivalent, emanated from within the association for the striking prisoners. This expression did not, however, have universal approval. One section of the organisation in particular, the gardaí, were frequent and loud critics of what they described as endorsement of 'the men of violence'.

This period of equivocation was severely challenged when it was announced that a number of H-Block prisoners would contest the June 1981 general election in the Republic. Fearing this to be the thin end of a wedge challenging the jealously guarded status quo, the southern establishment pressurised GAA senior management to act. Director General Liam Mulvihill responded on 4 June by issuing a directive to all county boards stating that, in his words, the National H-Block committee had entered the party-political arena and it was no longer possible to be involved with this issue.[10] Consequently, he declared, no unit of the association could issue statements or show support in any way. However, in spite of this clear order to all county boards, it was obvious the directive was neither followed everywhere, nor, maybe more significantly, enforced.

Oddly enough, it wasn't until 28 July 1981 that the general public was made aware of the contents of the Mulvihill directive as a result of newspaper reports in several national publications. When it did become known, many members of the association, particularly in the North, were outraged. Their fury was, however, assuaged by the then GAA President, Paddy McFlynn. A native of County Derry, residing at the time in County Down, he issued a statement that same day apparently contradicting the press reports. Criticising an article in *The Irish Times*, McFlynn said that the impression was being created that the GAA was no longer concerned with the sad situation in the H-Blocks, and he declared that this was not the case.

A few days later McFlynn met with the chairperson of the pressure group Gaels Against The Blocks. Amazingly, the chairperson of the group reported back to his committee that he had been assured by the GAA president that there had never been any directive issued ordering clubs or counties to withdraw support from the protest. Apparently, all members present at the committee meeting (and GAA members elsewhere) were content that the issue had been resolved to their satisfaction and matters rested at that.

Whether there was an arrangement between the director general and the president to send apparently conflicting signals is impossible to know. Quite possibly the two officials had a different understanding of what was required or indeed should be done. In either case it would seem to have been a very typical GAA compromise facilitating a viable *modus operandi*. Two decades later it might well have been described as constructive ambiguity.

Whatever the explanation, an open fracture was avoided. For the remainder of the hunger strike, different units of the GAA continued to back the prison protest, while many others remained indifferent and some downright hostile.

By October 1981 the hunger strikes had ended and for all the anxiety this had caused throughout the organisation, the GAA remained intact.[11] It had never been likely or indeed possible, that the association would, as a body, give wholehearted, unqualified support to a political hunger strike embarked upon by members of the IRA and INLA. That as much support emerged from within the organisation as did was quite remarkable. That the association was able to accommodate such a diversity of opinion was even more remarkable and is testimony to the strength and durability of the GAA.

Today, more than forty years later, the association still reflects, for good or ill, all the complexities of Irish society.

Tommy McKearney was a senior member of the Provisional IRA from the early 1970s until his arrest in 1977. Sentenced to life imprisonment, he served sixteen years, during which time he participated in the 1980 hunger strike in Long Kesh. He is now a freelance journalist and an organiser with the Independent Workers Union and the author of The Provisional IRA *(Pluto, 2011). Tommy's three brothers and uncle are among the Gaels included in this book.*

Endnotes

1 Hunger Strikes, *Prisons Memory Archive*, https://prisonsmemoryarchive.com/pma-for-education/hunger-strikes/.

2 Mark Reynolds, 'The Gaelic Athletic Association and the 1981 H-Block Hunger Strike', *The International Journal of the History of Sport*, vol. 34, iss. 3–4 (2017), pp. 217–35.

3 Peter Berresford Ellis, 'The Northern Revolution', in *A History of the Irish Working Class* (Pluto, 1985), pp. 308–43.

4 Ed Moloney, *A Secret History of the IRA* (Penguin, 2007).

5 '30 Years On: A Short History of Ireland's Section 31 Broadcasting Ban', www.rte.ie/brainstorm/2024/0119/1217560-section-31-broadcasting-ban-censorshop-troubles/.

6 John Gibney, 'Documentary on One: Frank Stagg's Three Funerals', *History Ireland*, vol. 26, iss. 1, www.historyireland.com/documentary-one-frank-staggs-three-funerals/.

7 Joseph E.A. Connell, 'The GAA and the Development of Nationalism', *History Ireland*, vol. 19, iss. 2, www.historyireland.com/the-gaa-and-the-development-of-nationalism/.

8 Reynolds, 'The Gaelic Athletic Association and the 1981 H-Block Hunger Strike', p. 220.

9 Ibid., p. 221.

10 Ibid., p. 224.

11 F. Stuart Ross, *Smashing H-Block: The Rise and Fall of the Popular Campaign Against Criminalization, 1976–1982* (Liverpool University Press, 2011).

methodology

Peadar Thompson

Before setting out on this ambitious project, there needed to be a clear plan developed for each stage of a process that would ultimately produce this book. In this section, I will describe that plan and the overarching rationale behind the decisions to take specific courses of action. At the core of the entire process was a focus on trying to deploy practices which made engagement with this project accessible, transparent, trauma-informed, rewarding and, chiefly, safe for the interviewees.

Preparation Stage

Preparation for this project was guided by best practices adopted by leading oral history projects as set out by Donald Ritchie in *Doing Oral History*.[1] It was important for the project to define its purpose and scope, which would then allow myself and Relatives for Justice to gather the necessary information on who the project should seek to include. In this context, we knew that we wanted to record the life stories of every Gael who lost their lives as a result of conflict-related violence, within a timeframe that incorporated the entire conflict, from August 1969 to the present day. The reason for including events post-Good Friday Agreement is that conflict-related violence did not end with the signing of that peace accord, and it would be a great injustice to the memory of those killed after 1998 not to include their names in this project. The timeline also reflects the one which most processes relating to the recent conflict use, such as the Commission for Victims and Survivors (Northern Ireland).

The question that immediately presented itself to the project was how to define what we meant by the word Gael. Taking into account instructive works that sought to describe the term, or the spirit of the term, we were satisfied with a definition that encompassed any active member of a GAA club.[2] By that we mean to include any member of a registered or previously registered GAA club, who actively contributed to any of the multitude of provisions that a

GAA club offers its community, whether that be as a player, committee member or even as the vital tea and sandwich maker that clubs across the association rely on. We did not stipulate a minimum time of service to the relevant club. Ultimately, the project is of the view that the term Gael is as much a verb as it is a noun, and through our definition, we believe we have best captured the spirit of the association. If a bereaved family was satisfied that their loved one met this definition, then this project was also of that view.

The project then set about gathering a rough estimate as to how many of the total number of victims of the conflict fell within this description. In doing so, we consulted several sources, which can be found in the select bibliography and took note of any victim of the conflict who had any recorded ties to Gaelic games. The project owes a great deal of thanks to Eoin Connolly for conducting much of this preliminary research. With an initial number totalling close to 200 potential Gaels killed during the conflict, we then set about confirming this list's accuracy. Word of mouth was crucial here, and spreading awareness about the project amongst both the victim-support community and the GAA community helped to ensure that the potentially affected families had the opportunity to learn about and contact the project. Mailing lists, both physical and virtual, were created, and information about the project was distributed to the service users of Relatives for Justice, WAVE Trauma Centre, the Pat Finucane Centre and the South-East Fermanagh Foundation. In that way, we ensured that almost all bereaved victims of the conflict currently receiving support from any of the main victim-support organisations were aware of the project. We then also set about ensuring that information was available to the GAA community, and with the great help of the Ulster Council, and Brian McAvoy in particular, details about the project were sent to every GAA club within Ulster and information distributed amongst their membership. Finally, the project ran a number of media campaigns with various newspapers and on social media platforms to increase public awareness and ensure that anyone who potentially fell within its remit was aware of it and had the appropriate opportunity to participate.[3]

With the purpose and scope of the project defined, and an accurate estimation as to the number of potential participants, we then set about developing a process in which people could engage. We not only wanted to record how many Gaels were lost to the conflict but also their individual stories and the role that the GAA played in each of their lives. How that would be best done was influenced by some similar works, including *Children of the Troubles*, where we felt rich and powerful narratives of real human stories had ultimately come to the fore, in spite of great tragedy.[4] Relatives for Justice assisted the author in completing the work and the organisation felt that involvement in that project was of great benefit to its service users. We set about designing an interview process where bereaved relatives and friends of Gaels killed as a result of the conflict could tell their stories.[5] Of particular help in this planning stage was the work of Anna Bryson of Queen's University. Anna ran workshops on best practice and produced a comprehensive manual for conducting an oral history project like this one in the context of the recent conflict in Ireland.[6] Once that was done, my interviews could begin.

Interviewing Stage

This stage can be subdivided into three distinct phases: preparing for interview, conducting an interview and post-interview checks.

Preparation for individual interviews required great care and a particular sensitivity to the trauma that comes with bereavement as a result of conflict-related violence. Relatives for Justice has a breadth of knowledge, skills and experience in working with, and supporting, bereaved and injured victims of the conflict, and this project had the immediate advantage of being able to draw from that pool in designing the interview processes. At the heart of the design was ensuring that each interviewee felt safe and supported if they decided to engage with the process. The word decided is key here: it was paramount that no party felt obliged or pressured into taking part in this project, and that every participant understood exactly what they were consenting to. In making an interviewee's decision to take part an informed one, the project found that speaking with family members directly was the most helpful approach, as any concerns could be addressed, and more information about the project and who Relatives for Justice are could be given. In terms of ensuring interviewee safety and support, the project established clear lines of internal referral within Relatives for Justice. It was important to make interviewees aware that they had access to the range of holistic support services offered by Relatives for Justice, ranging from counselling and therapies through to advocacy support. This proved to be of great help in reassuring interviewees that they were engaging in a professional process, informed by trauma-trained expertise within the organisation. The project was, however, also mindful not to present itself as a regimented process that lacked any outward expressions of empathy or understanding, and so a balance was struck to ensure that engagement was both informal and welcoming, whilst maintaining high standards of professionalism and care.

In conducting the interviews, it was important that the interviewee could choose a location where they felt comfortable. (The exception to this rule was at the beginning of this project, when Covid-19 restrictions had to be adhered to.) I conducted interviews both virtually, via online meeting rooms, over the phone, and physically, at either the offices of Relatives for Justice or at the homes of the interviewees. While face-to-face meetings were preferable, particularly with more elderly interviewees, the space in which the interview was conducted was largely immaterial. I believe a large part of the credit for this must be given to the wonderful interviewees. In every interview, the time and care that went into researching and preparing for the interview, beyond that which was recommended by the project, was clear to see. This undoubtedly ensured that any potential negative impact with regard to the interview venue was rendered negligible.

With a comfortable and private environment established, it was then important to build rapport and trust beyond that developed through initial contact. This generally consisted of small talk, chiefly regarding current GAA fixtures and news, and put both the interviewee and interviewer at ease, allowing for a more natural progression into the recorded interview. In terms of the content of the recorded interview, the project was greatly interested in keeping interviewer input to a minimum and allowing interviewees the space and time to talk about what they wished within the identified subject matter. This generally consisted of me asking open-ended questions about the different stages of the lives of the interviewee's loved one. The project benefited greatly from the fact that it was deliberately focusing on the stories and life events of the person – things the interviewees were more than eager to share – and not, as has been the case with most other similar victim projects, on the circumstances of death. This unique approach meant that little prompting was needed for the vast majority of the interviews, other than comments or questions that encouraged an interviewee to offer greater insights, as the topics of conversation were not typically focused on trauma and pain. Of course, a great deal of empathy was needed to ensure that interviewees knew that I was with them on their journey as they relived their stories, and with such sensitive issues at play, intermittent pauses and breaks were both prompted and naturally incorporated into the interview. It was also important for families to know that they could stop and withdraw at any time during the interview, and that they had absolute control over the contents of anything that was recorded up until that point.

After an interview was completed, it was important to ensure a post-interview process was in place in which I could chat to the interviewees more broadly about the various support services available through Relatives for Justice. This was done to reassure interviewees that should any feelings, such as anxiety, come up in the days or weeks following the interview, they could get in touch with Relatives for Justice and speak privately to the health and well-being staff. An in-house referral system was also established so that interviewees could be contacted by an appropriate member of staff if they indicated that they would like to hear more about the different services available to them. This referral system was vital when interviewees showed signs of distress during interviews – I could, with the permission of the interviewee, ask a member of the health and well-being staff to check in with an interviewee in the days and weeks post-interview. For many participants in this project, this was the very first engagement they had had where they could openly talk about their loss and trauma to someone outside their own circle, and it was vitally important that each participant was supported to the fullest possible extent in order to allow them to safely share their experiences.

Transcription, Analysis and Creating Written Narratives

Interviews were audio recorded, with the intention of using the contents to create a written narrative of the life story of each Gael. This meant that each recording had to be transcribed. Whilst the project sought initially to make use of transcription software, it got a very mixed bag of results, and ultimately transcription was done by me. This not only had the benefit of understanding regional accents but also of understanding the nuances and subject matter of each conversation, ensuring that nothing was missed. This process was greatly informed by *The Oral History Manual* by Barbara W. Sommer and Mary Kay Quinlan. With consent for recordings being given only to serve the end of creating written narratives, once the transcriptions were complete, the audio recordings were deleted.

In analysing the transcriptions, information was pooled to form a timeline of each person's life story and their time in the GAA. Naturally, each interview had varying focuses, and analysing the transcription allowed for both unique and shared themes to be drawn out, which better informed the process of creating written narratives. The project found helpful advice with regard to ordering and analysing themes in a chronological sense within *Oral History for the Qualitative Researcher: Choreographing the Story.*[7]

In terms of the written narratives themselves, the crucial aspect for each story was to convey the story of each Gael, as told directly by their bereaved relatives and friends. The author was conscious that his primary task was only to shepherd the words of the interviewees into uniformity and a chronological structure, with little input beyond illustrating and highlighting the direct quotes from each interview. Beyond that, any further input from the author only seeks to provide contextual information or convey that which was present in the interview, but which perhaps did not find articulation in the form of words which could be quoted. This must not, however, be misconstrued as putting words into the mouths of interviewees, but rather as giving voice to thoughts, feelings and emotions that we all as humans sometimes struggle to express concisely. Additionally, editing of words for clarity and readability was essential.

Final Processes of Consent

Once a written narrative was complete, an initial draft was sent to the interviewee for review. A process of editing would then ensue to ensure that each interviewee had absolute control over the content of their loved one's entry, and a collaborative process ensured a final draft in which each family was satisfied with the content of its particular entry. Of course, proper acknowledgement is given in each entry to the interviewees and any additional source of information used to create the entry.

Personal Reflection on Methodology

I must give proper recognition to every single person who participated in this project. Each and every family made the entire process of writing this book as worthwhile and enjoyable an experience as one could hope. I am still overwhelmed by the generosity, the kindness, the honesty and the strength that I have witnessed. I was invited into the lives and into the homes of the most extraordinary people, and I was trusted with their most vulnerable moments. I have shared laughter, tears and more cups of tea than I could ever hope to keep count of with people I now like to think of as friends. This project will remain singular in the privilege it has given me, and I hope this book helps the families involved in their individual and collective journeys towards healing, recognition and acknowledgement.

Endnotes

1 Donald A. Ritchie, *Doing Oral History* (OUP, 2003).

2 Marcus de Búrca, *The GAA: A History* (Gill & Macmillan, 2000); Mike Cronin, Mark Duncan and Paul Rouse, *The GAA: County by County* (Collins Press, 2011).

3 Connla Young, 'Dublin politicians to hear about GAA members killed in Troubles', *The Irish News*, 7 March 2023; Joe McCann, 'Relatives for Justice bring GAA legacy project to the Oireachtas', *Belfast Media*, 8 March 2023; Freya McClements, 'GAA and the Troubles: Remembering club members killed in the conflict', *The Irish Times*, 4 September 2021.

4 Joe Duffy and Freya McClements, *Children of the Troubles* (Hatchette, 2020).

5 Valerie Raleigh Yow, *Recording Oral History: A Guide for the Humanities and Social Sciences* (AltaMira, 2005).

6 Anna Bryson, 'Recording Lived Experience: A Toolkit for Victims and Survivors' (2022), https://pureadmin.qub.ac.uk/ws/portalfiles/portal/307916089/VSS_RLE_Toolkit_Online_Version_Final.pdf.

7 Valerie Janesick, *Oral History for the Qualitative Researcher: Choreographing the Story* (Guilford Press, 2010).

Closing Remarks

Peadar Thompson

Acknowledgement is one of the most powerful tools we, as individual and collective members of society, possess when we interact with one another. To be seen, to be heard, to be respected – these are the central qualities of human dignity that we each afford to one another that assure each of us of our equal worth as citizens. And it is more often a lack or denial of these qualities to a person or persons that precedes conflict.

It is, therefore, unsurprising to learn that acknowledgement plays a central role in rebuilding relationships broken down by conflict. Indeed, acknowledgement is a fundamental pillar of transitional justice. During violent conflict, the circumstances bringing about victimhood, either physical injury or bereavement, not only have the effect of directly harming the victim, but also have the indirect effect, intentional or not, of silencing the victim. What is crucial, for any new society emerging from conflict, is to reverse that silence. By looking to this class of people emerging from conflict bearing all of its irreparable damage, and listening to their experiences and acknowledging their hurt, we help to restore the conditions necessary for equality of citizenship and ensure that the settings which preceded and perpetuated violent conflict no longer exist.

This book began by quoting the old Irish saying: *ar scáth a chéile a mhaireann na daoine.* The literal translation is *people live in the shadow of one another*, but its meaning is more accurately deciphered as the belief that people rely on one another for shelter in life; that we only truly live when we accept that no one person is an island. That is, fundamentally, what this book is about. As a people, we listen to one another and that is how we grow. I thank you for lending your ear to the stories in this book, and for listening to families and friends of some of the lost Gaels.

select bibliography

Adams, Gerry, *Máire Drumm. A Visionary: A Rebel Heart* (Leargas, 2019)

Ardoyne Commemoration Project, *Ardoyne: The Untold Truth* (Beyond The Pale, 2002)

Cadwallader, Anne, *Lethal Allies: British Collusion in Ireland* (Mercier Press, 2013)

Cronin, Mike, Mark Duncan and Paul Rouse, *The GAA: County by County* (Collins, 2011)

— *The GAA: A People's History* (Collins Press, 2014)

Darby, Paul, *Gaelic Games, Nationalism and the Irish Diaspora in the United States* (University College Dublin, 2009)

De Búrca, M., *The GAA: A History* (Gill & Macmillan, 2000)

Emerson, Robert M., Rachel I. Fretz and Linda L. Shaw, *Writing Ethnographic Fieldnotes* (University of Chicago Press, 1995)

Fahy, Des, *How the GAA Survived the Troubles* (Wolfhound Press, 2001)

Janesick, Valerie, *Oral History for the Qualitative Researcher: Choreographing the Story* (Guilford Press, 2010)

Magee, Gerard, *Tyrone's Struggle* (Tyrone Sinn Féin Commemoration Committee, 2011)

McKittrick, David, Seamus Kelters, Brian Feeney and Chris Thornton, *Lost Lives: The Stories of the Men, Women and Children who Died as a Result of the Northern Ireland Troubles* (Mainstream Publishing, 1999)

Ritchie, Donald A., *Doing Oral History* (Oxford University Press, 2003)

Sommer, Barbara W., and Mary Kay Quinlan, *The Oral History Manual* (AltaMira Press, 2009)

Yow, Valerie Raleigh, *Recording Oral History: A Guide for the Humanities and Social Sciences* (AltaMira Press, 2005)

list of chapter illustrations

1970: Cork captain Paddy Barry lifts the Liam MacCarthy Cup after the county's win in the All-Ireland Senior Hurling final against Wexford. © irishphotoarchive.ie/Lensmen Collection

1971: Offaly captain Willie Bryan lifts the Sam Maguire Cup after his team defeats Galway in the All-Ireland Senior Football final. © Connolly Collection/Sportsfile

1972: Part of the victorious Kilkenny team, taken before their All-Ireland Senior Hurling final against Cork. © irishphotoarchive.ie/Lensmen Collection

1973: Part of the Cork team that would defeat Galway in the All-Ireland Senior Football final. © Connolly Collection/Sportsfile

1974: Dublin captain Sean Doherty lifts the Sam Maguire Cup after Dublin's victory over Galway in the All-Ireland Senior Football final. © Connolly Collection/Sportsfile

1975: Part of the Kilkenny team that would defeat Galway in the All-Ireland Senior Hurling final. © Connolly Collection/Sportsfile

1976: Cork captain Ray Cummins lifts the Liam MacCarthy Cup after his team's victory over Wexford in the All-Ireland Senior Hurling final. © Connolly Collection/Sportsfile

1977: Part of the victorious Dublin team that would defeat Armagh in the All-Ireland GAA Senior Football final. © Connolly Collection/Sportsfile

1980: Part of the Kerry team that would defeat Roscommon in the All-Ireland Senior Football final. © Ray McManus/Sportsfile

1981: Offaly captain Padraig Horan lifts the Liam MacCarthy Cup after the All-Ireland Senior Hurling final with Galway. © Ray McManus/Sportsfile

1983: Dublin captain Tommy Drumm lifts the Sam Maguire Cup after his team defeats Galway in the All-Ireland Football final. © Inpho/Billy Stickland

1984: Cork captain John Fenton is handed the Liam MacCarthy Cup after his team defeats Offaly in the All-Ireland Senior Hurling final. © Inpho/Billy Stickland

1985: Kerry captain Páidi Ó Sé lifts the Sam Maguire Cup after the All-Ireland Senior Football final match with Dublin. Standing beside him is Dr Mick Loftus, President of the GAA. © Ray McManus/Sportsfile

1986: Cork captain Tom Cashman lifts the Liam MacCarthy Cup after his team's victory over Galway in the All-Ireland Senior Hurling final. © Ray McManus/Sportsfile

1987: Meath captain Mick Lyons lifts the Sam Maguire Cup after his team's victory over Cork in the All-Ireland Senior Football final. © Inpho/Billy Stickland

1988: Galway captain Conor Hayes with the Liam MacCarthy Cup after his team defeats Kilkenny in the All-Ireland Senior Hurling final. © Inpho/Billy Stickland

1989: Cork captain Denis Allen lifts the Sam Maguire Cup following the All-Ireland Senior Football final win over Mayo. © Ray McManus/Sportsfile

1990: Cork captain Tomás Mulcahy lifts the Liam MacCarthy Cup after his team's victory over Galway in the All-Ireland Senior Hurling final. © Inpho/ James Meehan

1991: Down captain Paddy O'Rourke lifts the Sam Maguire Cup following victory in the All-Ireland Senior Football final against Meath. © Ray McManus/ Sportsfile

1992: Kilkenny captain Liam Fennelly lifts the Liam MacCarthy Cup following the All-Ireland Senior Hurling final between Kilkenny and Cork. Behind him stands President Mary Robinson. © Ray McManus/Sportsfile

1993: Derry captain Henry Downey lifts the Sam Maguire Cup after defeating Cork in the All-Ireland Senior Football final. © David Maher/Sportsfile

1994: Down captain D.J. Kane lifts the Sam Maguire Cup following victory over Dublin in the All-Ireland Senior Football final. © Inpho

1997: Clare captain Anthony Daly lifts the Liam MacCarthy Cup after victory over Tipperary in the All-Ireland Senior Hurling final. © Inpho/James Meehan

1998: Galway captain Ray Silke lifts the Sam Maguire Cup following victory over Kildare in the All-Ireland Senior Football final. © Inpho/Patrick Bolger

2002: Kilkenny captain Andy Comerford lifts the Liam MacCarthy Cup following victory over Clare in the All-Ireland Senior Hurling final, while President Mary McAleese applauds in the background. © Brendan Moran/ Sportsfile

acknowledgements

First, I would like to thank the families and friends of each Gael included in this book for allowing me the opportunity to tell the stories of their loved ones. The measure of their strength and their kindness, their openness and their humility cannot be overstated. They are every bit as responsible for the writing of this book as I am.

I would also like to thank the incredible staff of Relatives for Justice, and acknowledge the crucial roles played by, in particular, Sue and Siobhán. Their administrative support to both myself and the families involved in this project made the process of creating this book immeasurably smoother. The same must also be said of Jim, Christina and Poilín, who generously made available their time in creating a professional and safe environment, which enabled families to fully engage in this process in the knowledge that their health and well-being would be safeguarded.

Special mention must be given to Eoin Connolly, who spent the better half of a year conducting the initial research for this project. The solid foundations his research built proved a vital transitory phase for this project in going from the conceptual to the tangible. But for Eoin accepting a full-time post within another department at Relatives for Justice, I am sure he would have co-authored this book.

To Mark, Anna, Tommy, Mike and Paul, *míle buíochas* for contributing your time, experience and expertise to this project. The value of your articles to this book is self-evident.

There are also many others to thank for giving their time and local expertise to this project, and for helping the project get in contact with a great many families. From volunteers in GAA clubs across the country to community figures, you helped ensure great accuracy with this project. Thank you.

The project also owes a great debt of gratitude to both the Ulster Council of the GAA, in particular Brian McAvoy, for his support in reaching out to affected families, and to the Oireachtas for allowing us the opportunity to make presentations about the project. We especially want to thank former Senator

Niall Ó Donnghaile and Jim Gibney for their incredible support in Dublin.

I would like to also thank Merrion Press, and extend particular gratitude to Conor and Wendy for their belief in this project, for their expertise and guidance, and for their patience over a great many Zoom calls, emails and edits to ensure that the stories in this book receive the platform they deserve.

And finally, it must be acknowledged that this project and the support required to make it possible is enabled through the resources Relatives for Justice receives from donors and funders. Thank you for your continued generosity and support.

index of names